# Statutes & Conventions on INTERNATIONAL TRADE LAW

Dr Indira Carr & Professor Richard Kidner

Cavendish
Publishing
Limited

First published in Great Britain 1993 by Cavendish Publishing Limited,
23A Countess Road, London NW5 2XH.
Telephone: 071-485 0303 Facsimile: 071-485 0304



**British Library Cataloguing-in-Publication Data**
A catalogue record for this book is available from the British Library

ISBN 1-874241-11-2

Printed and bound in Great Britain

# PREFACE

The study of International Trade Law requires access to a wide range of materials many of which are not easily accessible and the purpose of this book is to provide students with those documents which they are likely to be referred to in courses on this subject. We have provided extracts from statutes and conventions, all of which have been reproduced in their amended and updated form. The collection is necessarily highly selective as the potential range of material is very wide; nevertheless we believe we have selected all the documents which a student is likely to come across in any standard course on international trade law and we hope that this will provide a convenient and relatively inexpensive method of access to materials which might otherwise not be easily available.

The collection is divided into two parts, Statutes and Conventions, and within each section the material is printed in chronological order (and alphabetically within years). The material is printed in its amended form but we have not indicated the source of these amendments and the text is printed as amended even if that amendment is not yet in force. Sections which have been omitted or repealed are noted.

The collection contains material available to us up to February 1st 1993.

Indira Carr
Richard Kidner

# CONTENTS

SECTION I

# STATUTES

# BILLS OF EXCHANGE ACT 1882

CHAPTER 61

PART I

PRELIMINARY

*Negotiation of Bills*



*General Duties of the Holder*



*Liabilities of Parties*



*Discharge of Bill*

*Acceptance and Payments for Honour*



*Lost Instruments*



*Bill in a Set*



*Conflict of Laws*



PART V

SUPPLEMENTARY

## PART I

## PRELIMINARY

**1. [omitted]**

**2. Interpretation of Terms**

In this Act, unless the context otherwise requires—

'Acceptance' means an acceptance completed by delivery or notification.

'Action' includes counter claim and set off.

'Banker' includes a body of persons whether incorporated or not who carry on the business of banking.

'Bankrupt' includes any person whose estate is vested in a trustee or assignee under the law for the time being in force relating to bankruptcy.

'Bearer' means the person in possession of a bill or note which is payable to bearer.

'Bill' means bill of exchange, and 'note' means promissory note.

'Delivery' means transfer of possession, actual or constructive, from one person to another.

'Holder' means the payee or indorsee of a bill or note who is in possession of it, or the bearer thereof.

'Indorsement' means an indorsement completed by delivery.

'Issue' means the first delivery of a bill or note, complete in form to a person who takes it as a holder.

'Person' includes a body of persons whether incorporated or not.

'Value' means valuable consideration.

'Written' includes printed, and 'writing' includes print.

## PART II

## BILLS OF EXCHANGE

### *Form and Interpretation*

**3. Bill of exchange defined**

(1) A bill of exchange is an unconditional order in writing, addressed by one person to another, signed by the person giving it, requiring the person to whom it is addressed to pay on demand or at a fixed or determinable future time a sum certain in money to or to the order of a specified person, or to bearer.

(2) An instrument which does not comply with these conditions, or which orders any act to be done in addition to the payment of money, is not a bill of exchange.

(3) An order to pay out of a particular fund is not unconditional within the meaning of this section; but an unqualified order to pay, coupled with (a) an indication of a particular fund out of which the drawee is to re-imburse himself

or a particular account to be debited with the amount, or (b) a statement of the transaction which gives rise to the bill is unconditional.

(4) A bill is not invalid by reason—
- (a) That it is not dated;
- (b) That it does not specify the value given, or that any value has been given therefor;
- (c) That it does not specify the place where it is drawn or the place where it is payable.

**4. Inland and foreign bills**

(1) An inland bill is a bill which is or on the face of it purports to be
- (a) both drawn and payable within the British Islands, or
- (b) drawn within the British Islands upon some person resident therein. Any other bill is a foreign bill.
  For the purposes of the Act 'British Islands' mean any part of the United Kingdom of Great Britain and Ireland, the islands of Man, Guernsey, Jersey, Alderney, and Sark, and the islands adjacent to any of them being part of the dominions of Her Majesty.

(2) Unless the contrary appear on the face of the bill the holder may treat it as an inland bill.

**5. Effect where different parties to bill are the same person**

(1) A bill may be drawn payable to, or to the order of, the drawer; or it may be drawn payable to, or to the order of, the drawee.

(2) Where in a bill drawer and drawee are the same person, or where the drawee is a fictitious person or a person not having capacity to contract, the holder may treat the instrument, at his option, either as a bill of exchange or as a promissory note.

**6. Address to drawee**

(1) The drawee must be named or otherwise indicated in a bill with reasonable certainty.

(2) A bill may be addressed to two or more drawees whether they are partners or not, but an order addressed to two drawees in the alternative or to two or more drawees in succession is not a bill of exchange.

**7. Certainty required as to payee**

(1) Where a bill is not payable to bearer, the payee must be named or otherwise indicated therein with reasonable certainty.

(2) A bill may be made payable to two or more payees jointly, or it may be made payable in the alternative to one of two, or one or some of several payees. A bill may also be made payable to the holder of an office for the time being.

(3) Where the payee is a fictitious or non-existing person the bill may be treated as payable to bearer.

**8. What bills are negotiable**

(1) When a bill contains words prohibiting transfer, or indicating an intention that it should not be transferable, it is valid as between the parties thereto, but is not negotiable.

(2) A negotiable bill may be payable either to order or to bearer.

(3) A bill is payable to bearer which is expressed to be so payable or on which the only or last indorsement is an indorsement in blank.

(4) A bill is payable to order which is expressed to be so payable, or which is expressed to be payable to a particular person, and does not contain words prohibiting transfer or indicating an intention that it should not be transferable.

(5) Where a bill, either originally or by indorsement, is expressed to be payable to the order of a specified person, and not to him or his order, it is nevertheless payable to him or his order at his option.

**9. Sum payable**

(1) The sum payable by a bill is a sum certain within the meaning of this Act, although it was required to be paid—

- (a) With interest.
- (b) By stated instalments.
- (c) By stated instalments, with a provision that upon default in payment of any instalment the whole shall become due.
- (d) According to an indicated rate of exchange or according to a rate of exchange to be ascertained as directed by the bill.

(2) Where the sum payable is expressed in words and also in figures, and there is a discrepancy between the two, the sum denoted by the words is the amount payable.

(3) Where a bill is expressed to be payable with interest, unless the instrument otherwise provides, interest runs from the date of the bill, and if the bill is undated from the issue thereof.

**10. Bill payable on demand**

(1) A bill is payable on demand—

- (a) Which is expressed to be payable on demand, or at sight, or on presentation; or
- (b) In which no time for payment is expressed.

(2) Where a bill is accepted or indorsed when it is overdue, it shall, as regards the acceptor who so accepts, or any indorser who so indorses it, be deemed a bill payable on demand.

**11. Bill payable at a future time**

A bill is payable at a determinable future time within the meaning of this Act which is expressed to be payable—

(1) At a fixed period after date or sight.

(2) On or at a fixed period after the occurrence of a specified event which is certain to happen, though the time of happening may be uncertain.

An instrument expressed to be payable on a contingency is not a bill, and the happening of the event does not cure the defect.

**12. Omission of date in bill payable after date**

Where a bill expressed to be payable at a fixed period after date is issued undated, or where the acceptance of a bill payable at a fixed period after sight is undated, any holder may insert therein the true date of issue or acceptance, and the bill shall be payable accordingly.

Provided that — (1) where the holder in good faith and by mistake inserts a wrong date, and (2) in every case where a wrong date is inserted, if the bill subsequently comes into the hands of a holder in due course the bill shall not be avoided thereby, but shall operate and be payable as if the date so inserted had been the true date.

**13. Ante-dating and post-dating**

(1) Where a bill or an acceptance or any indorsement on a bill is dated, the date shall, unless the contrary be proved, be deemed to be the true date of the drawing, acceptance, or indorsement, as the case may be.

(2) A bill is not valid by reason only that it is ante-dated or post-dated, or that it bears date on a Sunday.

**14. Computation of time of payment**

Where a bill is not payable on demand the day on which it falls due is determined as follows:

(1) The bill is due and payable in all cases on the last day of the time of payment as fixed by the bill or, if that is a non-business day, on the succeeding business day.

(2) Where a bill is payable at a fixed period after date, after sight, or after the happening of a specified event, the time of payment is determined by excluding the day from which the time is to begin to run and by including the day of payment.

(3) Where a bill is payable at a fixed period after sight, the time begins to run from the date of the acceptance if the bill be accepted, and from the date of noting or protest if the bill be noted or protested for non-acceptance, or for non-delivery.

(4) The term 'month' in a bill means a calendar month.

**15. Case of need**

The drawer of a bill and any indorser may insert therein the name of a person to whom the holder may resort in case of need, that is to say, in case the bill is dishonoured by non-acceptance or non-payment. Such person is called the referee in case of need. It is in the option of the holder to resort to the referee in case of need or not as he may think fit.

**16. Optional stipulations by drawer or indorser**

The drawer of a bill, and any indorser, may insert therein an express stipulation—

(1) Negativing or limiting his own liability to the holder.

(2) Waiving as regards himself some or all of the holder's duties.

**17. Definition and requisites of acceptance**

(1) The acceptance of a bill is the signification by the drawee of his assent to the order of the drawer.

(2) An acceptance is invalid unless it complies with the following conditions, namely:

(a) It must be written on the bill and be signed by the drawee. The mere signature of the drawee without additional words is sufficient.

(b) It must not express that the drawee will perform his promise by any other means than the payment of money.

**18. Time for acceptance**

A bill may be accepted—

(1) Before it has been signed by the drawer, or while otherwise incomplete:

(2) When it is overdue, or after it has been dishonoured by a previous refusal to accept, or by non-payment:

(3) When a bill payable after sight is dishonoured by non-acceptance, and the drawee subsequently accepts it, the holder, in the absence of any different agreement, is entitled to have the bill accepted as of the date of first presentment to the drawee for acceptance.

**19. General and qualified acceptance**

(1) An acceptance is either (a) general or (b) qualified.

(2) A general acceptance assents without qualification to the order of the drawer. A qualified acceptance in expressed terms varies the effect of the bill as drawn. In particular an acceptance is qualified which is—

(a) conditional, that is to say, which makes payment by the acceptor dependent on the fulfilment of a condition therein stated:

(b) partial, that is to say, an acceptance to pay part only of the amount for which the bill is drawn:

(c) local, that is to say, an acceptance to pay only at a particular specified place:

An acceptance to pay at a particular place is a general acceptance, unless it expressly states that the bill is to be paid there only and not elsewhere:

(d) qualified as to time:

(e) the acceptance of some one or more of the drawees, but not of all.

**20. Inchoate instruments**

(1) Where a simple signature on a blank paper is delivered by the signer in order that it may be converted into a bill, it operates as a prima facie authority to fill it up as a complete bill for any amount using the signature for that of the drawer, or the acceptor, or an indorser; and, in like manner, when a bill is wanting in any material particular, the person in possession of it has a prima facie authority to fill up the omission in any way he thinks fit.

(2) In order that any such instrument when completed may be enforceable against any person who became a party thereto prior to its completion, it must be filled up within a reasonable time, and strictly in accordance with the authority given. Reasonable time for this purpose is a question of fact. Provided that if any such instrument after completion is negotiated to a holder in due course it shall be valid and effectual for all purposes in his hands, and he may enforce it as if it had been filled up within a reasonable time and strictly in accordance with the authority given.

**21. Delivery**

(1) Every contract on a bill, whether it be the drawer's, the acceptor's, or an indorser's, is incomplete and revocable, until delivery of the instrument in order to give effect thereto.

Provided that where an acceptance is written on a bill, and the drawee gives notice to or according to the directions of the person entitled to the bill that he has accepted it, the acceptance then becomes complete and irrevocable.

(2) As between immediate parties, and as regards a remote party other than a holder in due course, the delivery—

(a) in order to be effectual must be made either by or under the authority of the party drawing, accepting, or indorsing, as the case may be:

(b) may be shown to have been conditional or for a special purpose only, and not for the purpose of transferring the property in the bill. But if the bill be in the hands of a holder in due course a valid delivery of the bill by all parties prior to him so as to make them liable to him is conclusively presumed.

(3) Where a bill is no longer in the possession of a party who has signed it as drawer, acceptor, or indorser, a valid and unconditional delivery by him is presumed until the contrary is proved.

*Capacity and Authority of Parties*

**22. Capacity of parties**

(1) Capacity to incur liability as a party to a bill is coextensive with capacity to contract.

Provided that nothing in this section shall enable a corporation to make itself liable as drawer, acceptor, or indorser of a bill unless it is competent to it so to do under the law for the time being in force relating to corporations.

(2) Where a bill is drawn or indorsed by an infant, minor, or corporation having no capacity or power to incur liability on a bill, the drawing or indorsement entitles the holder to receive payment of the bill, and to enforce it against any other party thereto.

**23. Signature essential to liability**

No person is liable as drawer, indorser, or acceptor of a bill who has not signed it as such: Provided that

(1) Where a person signs a bill in a trade or assumed name, he is liable thereon as if he had signed it in his own name:

(2) The signature of the name of the firm is equivalent to the signature by the person so signing of the names of all persons liable as partners in that firm.

**24. Forged or unauthorised signature**

Subject to the provisions of this Act, where a signature on a bill is forged or placed thereon without the authority of the person whose signature it purports to be, the forged or unauthorised signature is wholly inoperative, and no right to retain the bill or to give a discharge therefor or to enforce payment thereof against any party thereto can be acquired through or under that signature, unless the party against whom it is sought to retain or enforce payment of the bill is precluded from setting up the forgery or want of authority.

Provided that nothing in this section shall affect the ratification of an unauthorised signature not amounting to a forgery.

**25. Procuration signatures**

A signature by procuration operates as notice that the agent has but a limited authority to sign, and the principal is only bound by such signature if the agent in so signing was acting within the actual limits of his authority.

### 26. Person signing as agent or in representative capacity

(1) Where a person signs a bill as drawer, indorser, or acceptor, and adds words to his signature, indicating that he signs for or on behalf of a principal, or in a representative character, he is not personally liable thereon; but the mere addition to his signature of words describing him as an agent, or as filling a representative character, does not exempt him from personal liability.

(2) In determining whether a signature on a bill is that of the principal or that of the agent by whose hand it is written, the construction most favourable to the validity of the instrument shall be adopted.

*The Consideration for a Bill*

### 27. Value and holder for value

(1) Valuable consideration for a bill may be constituted by—

(a) Any consideration sufficient to support a simple contract;

(b) An antecedent debt or liability. Such a debt or liability is deemed valuable consideration whether the bill is payable on demand or at a future time.

(2) Where value has at any time been given for a bill the holder is deemed to be a holder for value as regards the acceptor and all parties to the bill who became parties prior to such time.

(3) Where the holder of a bill has a lien on it arising either from contract or by implication of law, he is deemed to be a holder for value to the extent of the sum for which he has a lien.

### 28. Accommodation bill or party

(1) An accommodation party to a bill is a person who has signed a bill as drawer, acceptor, or indorser, without receiving value therefor, and for the purpose of lending his name to some other person.

(2) An accommodation party is liable on the bill to a holder for value; and it is immaterial whether, when such holder took the bill, he knew such party to be an accommodation party or not.

### 29. Holder in due course

(1) A holder in due course is a holder who has taken a bill, complete and regular on the face of it, under the following conditions; namely,

(a) That he became the holder of it before it was overdue, and without notice that it had been previously dishonoured, if such was the fact:

(b) That he took the bill in good faith and for value, and that at the time the bill was negotiated to him he had no notice of any defect in the title of the person who negotiated it.

(2) In particular the title of a person who negotiates a bill is defective within the meaning of this Act when he obtained the bill, or the acceptance thereof, by fraud, duress, or force and fear, or other unlawful means, or an illegal consideration, or when he negotiates it in breach of faith, or under such circumstances as amount to a fraud.

(3) A holder (whether for value or not), who derives his title to a bill through a holder in due course, and who is not himself a party to any fraud or illegality affecting it, has all the rights of that holder in due course as regards the acceptor and all parties to the bill prior to that holder.

**30. Presumption of value and good faith**

(1) Every party whose signature appears on a bill is prima facie deemed to have become a party thereto for value.

(2) Every holder of a bill is *prima facie* deemed to be a holder in due course; but if in an action on a bill it is admitted or proved that the acceptance, issue, or subsequent negotiation of the bill is affected with fraud, duress, or force and fear, or illegality, the burden of proof is shifted, unless and until the holder proves that, subsequent to the alleged fraud or illegality, value has in good faith been given for the bill.

*Negotiation of Bills*

**31. Negotiation of bill**

(1) A bill is negotiated when it is transferred from one person to another in such a manner as to constitute the transferee the holder of the bill.

(2) A bill payable to bearer is negotiated by delivery.

(3) A bill payable to order is negotiated by the indorsement of the holder completed by delivery.

(4) Where the holder of a bill payable to his order transfers it for value without indorsing it, the transfer gives the transferee such title as the transferor had in the bill, and the transferee in addition acquires the right to have the indorsement of the transferor.

(5) Where any person is under obligation to indorse a bill in a representative capacity, he may indorse the bill in such terms as to negative personal liability.

**32. Requisites of a valid indorsement**

An indorsement in order to operate as a negotiation must comply with the following conditions, namely—

(1) It must be written on the bill itself and be signed by the indorser. The simple signature of the indorser on the bill without additional words is, sufficient.

An indorsement written on an *allonge*, or on a 'copy' of a bill issued or negotiated in a country where 'copies' are recognised, is deemed to be written on the bill itself.

(2) It must be an indorsement of the entire bill. A partial indorsement, that is to say, an indorsement which purports to transfer to the indorsee a part only of the amount payable, or which purports to transfer the bill to two or more indorsees severally, does not operate as a negotiation of the bill.

(3) Where a bill is payable to the order of two or more payees or indorsees who are not partners all must indorse, unless the one indorsing has authority to indorse for the others.

(4) Where, in a bill payable to order, the payee or indorsee is wrongly designated, or his name is mis-spelt, he may indorse the bill as therein described, adding, if he thinks fit, his proper signature.

(5) Where there are two or more indorsements on a bill, each indorsement is deemed to have been made in the order in which it appears on the bill, until the contrary is proved.

(6) An indorsement may be made in blank or special. It may also contain terms making it restrictive.

**33. Conditional indorsement**

Where a bill purports to be indorsed conditionally the condition may be disregarded by the payer, and payment to the indorsee is valid whether the condition has been fulfilled or not.

**34. Indorsement in blank and special indorsement**

(1) An indorsement in blank specifies no indorsee, and a bill so indorsed becomes payable to bearer.

(2) A special indorsement specifies the person to whom, or to whose order, the bill is to be payable.

(3) The provisions of this Act relating to a payee apply with the necessary modifications to an indorsee under a special indorsement.

(4) When a bill has been indorsed in blank, any holder may convert the blank indorsement into a special indorsement by writing above the indorser's signature a direction to pay the bill to or to the order of himself or some other person.

**35. Restrictive indorsement**

(1) An endorsement is restrictive which prohibits the further negotiation of the bill or which expresses that it is a mere authority to deal with the bill as thereby directed and not a transfer of the ownership thereof, as, for example, if a bill be indorsed 'Pay D. only,' or 'Pay D. for the account of X.,' or 'Pay D. or order for collection.'

(2) A restrictive indorsement gives the indorsee the right to receive payment of the bill and to sue any party thereto that his indorser could have sued, but gives him no power to transfer his rights as indorsee unless it expressly authorise him to do so.

(3) Where a restrictive indorsement authorises further transfer, all subsequent indorsees take the bill with the same rights and subject to the same liabilities as the first indorsee under the restrictive indorsement.

**36. Negotiation of overdue or dishonoured bill**

(1) Where a bill is negotiable in its origin it continues to be negotiable until it has been

(a) restrictively indorsed or

(b) discharged by payment or otherwise.

(2) Where an overdue bill is negotiated, it can only be negotiated subject to any defect of title affecting it at its maturity, and thenceforward no person who takes it can acquire or give a better title than that which the person from whom he took it had.

(3) A bill payable on demand is deemed to be overdue within the meaning and for the purposes of this section, when it appears on the face of it to have been in circulation for an unreasonable length of time. What is an unreasonable length of time for this purpose is a question of fact.

(4) Except where an indorsement bears date after the maturity of the bill, every negotiation is *prima facie* deemed to have been effected before the bill was overdue.

(5) Where a bill which is not overdue has been dishonoured any person who takes it with notice of the dishonour takes it subject to any defect of title attaching thereto at the time of dishonour, but nothing in this sub-section shall affect the rights of a holder in due course.

**37. Negotiation of bill to party already liable thereon**

Where a bill is negotiated back to the drawer, or to a prior indorser or to the acceptor, such party may, subject to the provisions of this Act, re-issue and further negotiate the bill, but he is not entitled to enforce payment of the bill against any intervening party to whom he was previously liable.

**38. Rights of the holder**

The rights and powers of the holder of a bill are as follows:

(1) He may sue on the bill in his own name:

(2) Where he is a holder in due course, he holds the bill free from any defect of title of prior parties, as well as from mere personal defences available to prior

parties among themselves, and may enforce payment against all parties liable on the bill:

(3) Where his title is defective (a) if he negotiates the bill to a holder in due course, that holder obtains a good and complete title to the bill, and (b) if he obtains payment of the bill the person who pays him in due course gets a valid discharge for the bill.

*General Duties of the Holder*

**39. When presentment for acceptance is necessary**

(1) Where a bill is payable after sight, presentment for acceptance is necessary in order to fix the maturity of the instrument.

(2) Where a bill expressly stipulates that it shall be presented for acceptance, or where a bill is drawn payable elsewhere than at the residence or place of business of the drawee, it must be presented for acceptance before it can be presented for payment.

(3) In no other case is presentment for acceptance necessary in order to render liable any party to the bill.

(4) Where the holder of a bill, drawn payable elsewhere than at the place of business or residence of the drawee, has not time, with the exercise of reasonable diligence, to present the bill for acceptance before presenting it for payment on the day that it falls due, the delay caused by presenting the bill for acceptance before presenting it for payment is excused, and does not discharge the drawer and indorsers.

**40. Time for presenting bill payable after sight**

(1) Subject to the provisions of this Act, when a bill payable after sight is negotiated, the holder must either present it for acceptance or negotiate it within a reasonable time.

(2) If he do not do so, the drawer and all indorsers prior to that holder are discharged.

(3) In determining what is a reasonable time within the meaning of this section, regard shall be had to the nature of the bill, the usage of trade with respect to similar bills, and the facts of the particular case.

**41. Rules as to presentment for acceptance, and excuses for non-presentment**

(1) A bill is duly presented for acceptance which is presented in accordance with the following rules:

(a) The presentment must be made by or on behalf of the holder to the drawee or to some person authorised to accept or refuse acceptance on his behalf at a reasonable hour on a business day and before the bill is overdue:

(b) Where a bill is addressed to two or more drawees, who are not partners, presentment must be made to them all, unless one has authority to accept for all, then presentment may be made to him only:
(c) Where the drawee is dead presentment may be made to his personal representative:
(d) Where the drawee is bankrupt, presentment may be made to him or to his trustee:
(e) Where authorised by agreement or usage, a presentment through the post office is sufficient.

(2) Presentment in accordance with these rules is excused, and a bill may be treated as dishonoured by non-acceptance-
(a) Where the drawee is dead or bankrupt, or is a fictitious person or a person not having capacity to contract by bill:
(b) Where, after the exercise of reasonable diligence, such presentment cannot be effected:
(c) Where, although the presentment has been irregular, acceptance has been refused on some other ground.

(3) The fact that the holder has reason to believe that the bill, on presentment, will be dishonoured does not excuse presentment.

**42. Non-acceptance**

When a bill is duly presented for acceptance and is not accepted within the customary time, the person presenting it must treat it as dishonoured by non-acceptance. If he do not, the holder shall lose his right of recourse against the drawer and indorsers.

**43. Dishonour by non-acceptance and its consequences**

(1) A bill is dishonoured by non-acceptance—
(a) when it is duly presented for acceptance, and such an acceptance as is prescribed by this Act is refused or cannot be obtained; or
(b) when presentment for acceptance is excused and the bill is not accepted.

(2) Subject to the provisions of this Act when a bill is dishonoured by non-acceptance, an immediate right of recourse against the drawer and indorsers accrues to the holder, and no presentment for payment is necessary.

**44. Duties as to qualified acceptance**

(1) The holder of a bill may refuse to take a qualified acceptance, and if he does not obtain an unqualified acceptance may treat the bill as dishonoured by non-acceptance.

(2) Where a qualified acceptance is taken, and the drawer or an indorser has not expressly or impliedly authorised the holder to take a qualified acceptance, or does not subsequently assent thereto, such drawer or indorser is discharged from his liability on the bill.

The provisions of this sub-section do not apply to a partial acceptance, whereof due notice has been given. Where a foreign bill has been accepted as to part, it must be protested as to the balance.

(3) When the drawer or indorser of a bill receives notice of a qualified acceptance, and does not within a reasonable time express his dissent to the holder he shall be deemed to have assented thereto.

**45. Rules as to presentment for payment**

Subject to the provisions of this Act a bill must be duly presented for payment. If it be not so presented the drawer and indorsers shall be discharged. A bill is duly presented for payment which is presented in accordance with the following rules—

(1) Where the bill is not payable on demand, presentment must be made on the day it falls due.

(2) Where the bill is payable on demand, then, subject to the provisions of this Act, presentment must be made within a reasonable time after its issue in order to render the drawer liable, and within a reasonable time after its indorsement, in order to render the indorser liable. In determining what is a reasonable time, regard shall be had to the nature of the bill, the usage of trade with regard to similar bills, and the facts of the particular case.

(3) Presentment must be made by the holder or by some person authorised to receive payment on his behalf at a reasonable hour on a business day, at the proper place as herein-after defined, either to the person designated by the bill as payer, or to some person authorised to pay or refuse payment on his behalf if with the exercise of reasonable diligence such person can there be found.

(4) A bill is presented at the proper place—

(a) Where a place of payment is specified in the bill and the bill is there presented.

(b) Where no place of payment is specified, but the address of the drawee or acceptor is given in the bill, and the bill is there presented.

(c) Where no place of payment is specified and no address given, and the bill is presented at the drawee's or acceptor's place of business if known, and if not, at his ordinary residence if known.

(d) In any other case if presented to the drawee or acceptor wherever he can be found, or if presented at his last known place of business or residence.

(5) Where a bill is presented at the proper place, and after the exercise of reasonable diligence no person authorised to pay or refuse payment can be found there, no further presentment to the drawee or acceptor is required.

(6) Where a bill is drawn upon, or accepted by two or more persons who are not partners, and no place of payment is specified, presentment must be made to them all.

(7) Where the drawee or acceptor of a bill is dead, and no place of payment is specified, presentment must be made to a personal representative, if such there be, and with the exercise of reasonable diligence can be found.

(8) Where authorised by agreement or usage a presentment through the post office is sufficient.

**46. Excuses for delay or non-presentment for payment**

(1) Delay in making presentment for payment is excused when the delay is caused by circumstances beyond the control of the holder, and not imputable to his default, misconduct, or negligence. When the cause of delay ceases to operate presentment must be made with reasonable diligence.

(2) Presentment for payment is dispensed with—

(a) Where, after the exercise of reasonable diligence presentment, as required by this Act, cannot be effected. The fact that the holder has reason to believe that the bill will, on presentment, be dishonoured, does not dispense with the necessity for presentment.

(b) Where the drawee is a fictitious person.

(c) As regards the drawer where the drawee or acceptor is not bound as between himself and the drawer, to accept or pay the bill, and the drawer has no reason to believe that the bill would be paid if presented.

(d) As regards an indorser, where the bill was accepted or made for the accommodation of that indorser, and he has no reason to expect that the bill would be paid if presented.

(e) By waiver of presentment, express or implied.

**47. Dishonour by non-payment**

(1) A bill is dishonoured by non-payment (a) when it is duly presented for payment and payment is refused or cannot be obtained, or (b) when presentment is excused and the bill is overdue and unpaid.

(2) Subject to the provisions of this Act, when a bill is dishonoured by non-payment, an immediate right of recourse against the drawer and indorsers accrues to the holder.

**48. Notice of dishonour and effect of non-notice**

Subject to the provisions of this Act, when a bill has been dishonoured by non-acceptance or by non-payment, notice of dishonour must be given to the drawer and each indorser, and any drawer or indorser to whom such notice is not given is discharged: Provided that—

(1) Where a bill is dishonoured by non-acceptance, and notice of dishonour is not given, the rights of a holder in due course, subsequent to the omission, shall not be prejudiced by the omission.

(2) Where a bill is dishonoured by non-acceptance, and due notice of dishonour is given, it shall not be necessary to give notice of a subsequent dishonour by non-payment unless the bill shall in the meantime have been accepted.

**49. Rules as to notice of dishonour**

Notice of dishonour in order to be valid and effectual must be given in accordance with the following rules—

(1) The notice must be given by or on behalf of the holder, or by or on behalf of an indorser who, at the time of giving it, is himself liable on the bill.

(2) Notice of dishonour may be given by an agent either in his own name, or in the name of any party entitled to give notice whether that party be his principal or not.

(3) Where the notice is given by or on behalf of the holder, it enures for the benefit of all subsequent holders and all prior indorsers who have a right of recourse against the party to whom it is given.

(4) Where notice is given by or on behalf of an indorser entitled to give notice as herein-before provided, it enures for the benefit of the holder and all indorsers subsequent to the party to whom notice is given.

(5) The notice may be given in writing or by personal communication, and may be given in any terms which sufficiently identify the bill, and intimate that the bill has been dishonoured by non-acceptance or non-payment.

(6) The return of a dishonoured bill to the drawer or an indorser is, in point of form, deemed a sufficient notice of dishonour.

(7) A written notice need not be signed, and an insufficient written notice may be supplemented and validated by verbal communication. A misdescription of the bill shall not vitiate the notice unless the party to whom the notice is given is in fact misled thereby.

(8) Where notice of dishonour is required to be given to any person, it may be given either to the party himself, or to his agent in that behalf.

(9) Where the drawer or indorser is dead, and the party giving notice knows it, the notice must be given to a personal representative if such there be, and with the exercise of reasonable diligence he can be found.

(10) Where the drawer or indorser is bankrupt, notice may be given either to the party himself or to the trustee.

(11) Where there are two or more drawers or indorsers who are not partners, notice must be given to each of them, unless one of them has authority to receive such notice for the others.

(12) The notice may be given as soon as the bill is dishonoured and must be given within a reasonable time thereafter. In the absence of special circumstances notice is not deemed to have been given within a reasonable time, unless—

(a) where the person giving and the person to receive notice reside in the same place, the notice is given or sent off in time to reach the latter on the day after the dishonour of the bill.

(b) where the person giving and the person to receive notice reside in different places, the notice is sent off on the day after the dishonour of the bill, if there be a post at a convenient hour on that day, and if there be no such post on that day then by the next post thereafter.

(13) Where a bill when dishonoured is in the hands of an agent, he may either himself give notice to the parties liable on the bill or he may give notice to his principal. If he give notice to his principal, he must do so within the same time as if he were the holder, and the principal upon receipt of such notice has himself the same time for giving notice as if the agent had been an independent holder.

(14) Where a party to a bill receives due notice of dishonour, he has after the receipt of such notice the same period of time for giving notice to antecedent parties that the holder has after the dishonour.

(15) Where a notice of dishonour is duly addressed and posted, the sender is deemed to have given due notice of dishonour, notwithstanding any miscarriage by the post office.

**50. Excuses for non-notice and delay**

(1) Delay in giving notice of dishonour is excused where the delay is caused by circumstances beyond the control of the party giving notice, and not imputable to his default, misconduct, or negligence. When the cause of delay ceases to operate the notice must be given with reasonable diligence.

(2) Notice of dishonour is dispensed with—

(a) When, after the exercise of reasonable diligence, notice as required by this Act cannot be given to or does not reach the drawer or indorser sought to be charged:

(b) By waiver express or implied. Notice of dishonour may be waived before the time of giving notice has arrived, or after the omission to give due notice.

(c) As regards the drawer in the following cases, namely, (1) where drawer and drawee are the same person, (2) where the drawee is a fictitious person or a person not having capacity to contract, (3) where the drawer is the person to whom the bill is presented for payment, (4) where the drawee or acceptor is as between himself and the drawer under no obligation to accept or pay the bill, (5) where the drawer has countermanded payment:

(d) As regards the indorser in the following cases, namely, (1) where the drawee is a fictitious person or a person not having capacity to contract, and the indorser was aware of the fact at the time he indorsed the bill, (2) where the indorser is the person to whom the bill is presented for payment, (3) where the bill was accepted or made for his accommodation.

**51. Notice or protest of bill**

(1) Where an inland bill has been dishonoured it may, if the holder think fit, be noted for non-acceptance or non-payment, as the case may be; but it shall not be

necessary to note or protest any such bill in order to preserve the recourse against the drawer or indorser.

(2) Where a foreign bill, appearing on the face of it to be such, has been dishonoured by non-acceptance it must be duly protested for non-acceptance, and where such a bill, which has not been previously dishonoured by non-acceptance, is dishonoured by non-payment it must be duly protested for non-payment. If it be not so protested the drawer and indorsers are discharged. Where a bill does not appear on the face of it to be a foreign bill, protest thereof in case of dishonour in unnecessary.

(3) A bill which has been protested for non-acceptance may be subsequently protested for non-payment.

(4) Subject to the provisions of this Act, when a bill is noted or protested, it may be noted on the day of its dishonour and must be noted not later than the next succeeding business day. When a bill has been duly noted, the protest may be subsequently extended as of the date of the noting.

(5) Where the acceptor of a bill becomes bankrupt or insolvent or suspends payment before it matures, the holder may cause the bill to be protested for better security against the drawer and indorsers.

(6) A bill must be protested at the place where it is dishonoured: Provided that—

(a) When a bill is presented through the post office, and returned by post dishonoured, it may be protested at the place to which it is returned and on the day of its return if received during business hours, and if not received during business hours, then not later than the next business day:

(b) When a bill drawn payable at the place of business or residence of some person other than the drawee has been dishonoured by non-acceptance, it must be protested for non-payment at the place where it is expressed to be payable, and no further presentment for payment to, or demand on, the drawee is necessary.

(7) A protest must contain a copy of the bill, and must be signed by the notary making it, and must specify—

(a) The person at whose request the bill is protested:

(b) The place and date of protest, the cause or reason for protesting the bill, the demand made, and the answer given, if any, or the fact that the drawee or acceptor could not be found.

(8) Where a bill is lost or destroyed, or is wrongly detained from the person entitled to hold it, protest may be made on a copy or written particulars thereof.

(9) Protest is dispensed with by any circumstance which would dispense with notice of dishonour. Delay in noting or protesting is excused when the delay is caused by circumstances beyond the control of the holder, and not imputable to his default, misconduct, or negligence. When the cause of delay ceases to operate the bill must be noted or protested with reasonable diligence.

**52. Duties of holder as regards drawee or acceptor**

(1) When a bill is accepted generally presentment for payment is not necessary in order to render the acceptor liable.

(2) When by the terms of a qualified acceptance presentment for payment is required, the acceptor, in the absence of an express stipulation to that effect, is not discharged by the omission to present the bill for payment on the day that it matures.

(3) In order to render the acceptor of a bill liable it is not necessary to protest it, or that notice dishonour should be given to him.

(4) Where the holder of a bill presents it for payment, he shall exhibit the bill to the person from whom he demands payment, and when a bill is paid the holder shall forthwith deliver it up to the party paying it.

*Liabilities of Parties*

**53. Funds in hands of drawee**

(1) A bill, of itself, does not operate as an assignment of funds in the hands of the drawee available for the payment thereof, and the drawee of a bill who does not accept as required by this Act is not liable on the instrument. This sub-section shall not extend to Scotland.

(2) In Scotland, where the drawee of a bill has in his hands funds available for the payment thereof, the bill operates as an assignment of the sum for which it is drawn in favour of the holder, from the time when the bill is presented to the drawee.

**54. Liability of acceptor**

The acceptor of a bill, by accepting it—

(1) Engages that he will pay it according to the tenor of his acceptance:

(2) Is precluded from denying to a holder in due course:
- (a) The existence of the drawer, the genuineness of his signature, and his capacity and authority to draw the bill;
- (b) In the case of a bill payable to drawer's order, the then capacity of the drawer to indorse, but not the genuineness or validity of his indorsement;
- (c) In the case of a bill payable to the order of a third person, the existence of the payee and his then capacity to indorse, but not the genuineness or validity of his indorsement.

**55. Liability of drawer or indorser**

(1) The drawer of a bill by drawing it—

- (a) Engages that on due presentment it shall be accepted and paid according to its tenor, and that if it be dishonoured he will compensate the holder or any indorser who is compelled to pay it, provided that the requisite proceedings on dishonour be duly taken;

(b) Is precluded from denying to a holder in due course the existence of the payee and his then capacity to indorse.

(2) The indorser of a bill by indorsing it—

(a) Engages that on due presentment it shall be accepted and paid according to its tenor, and that if it be dishonoured he will compensate the holder or a subsequent indorser who is compelled to pay it, provided that the requisite proceedings on dishonour be duly taken.

(b) Is precluded from denying to a holder in due course the genuineness and regularity in all respects of the drawer's signature and all previous endorsements;

(c) Is precluded from denying to his immediate or a subsequent indorsee that the bill was at the time of his indorsement a valid and subsisting bill, and that he had then a good title thereto.

**56. Stranger signing bill liable as indorser**

Where a person signs a bill otherwise than as drawer or acceptor, he thereby incurs the liabilities of an indorser to a holder in due course.

**57. Measure of damages against parties to dishonoured bill**

Where a bill is dishonoured, the measure of damages, which shall be deemed to be liquidated damages, shall be as follows:

(1) The holder may recover from any party liable on the bill, and the drawer who has been compelled to pay the bill may recover from the acceptor, and an indorser who has been compelled to pay the bill may recover from the acceptor or from the drawer, or from a prior indorser—

(a) The amount of the bill:

(b) Interest thereon from the time of presentment for payment if the bill is payable on demand, and from the maturity of the bill in any other case:

(c) The expenses of noting, or, when protest is necessary, and the protest has been extended, the expenses of protest.

(2) [Repealed].

(3) Where by this Act interest may be recovered as damages, such interest may, if justice require it, be withheld wholly or in part, and where a bill is expressed to be payable with interest at a given rate, interest as damages may or may not be given at the same rate as interest proper.

**58. Transferor by delivery and transferee**

(1) Where the holder of a bill payable to bearer negotiates it by delivery without indorsing it he is called a 'transferor by delivery'.

(2) A transferor by delivery is not liable on the instrument.

(3) A transferor by delivery who negotiates a bill thereby warrants to his immediate transferee being a holder for value that the bill is what it purports to be, that he has a right to transfer it, and that at the time of transfer he is not aware of any fact which renders it valueless.

*Discharge of Bill*

**59. Payment in due course**

(1) A bill is discharged by payment in due course by or on behalf of the drawee or acceptor. 'Payment in due course' means payment made at or after the maturity of the bill to the holder thereof in good faith and without notice that his title to the bill is defective.

(2) Subject to the provisions herein-after contained, when a bill is paid by the drawer or an indorser it is not discharged; but

(a) Where a bill payable to, or to the order of, a third party is paid by the drawer, the drawer may enforce payment thereof against the acceptor, but may not re-issue the bill.

(b) Where a bill is paid by an indorser, or where a bill payable to drawer's order is paid by the drawer, the party paying it is remitted to his former rights as regards the acceptor or antecedent parties, and he may, if he thinks fit, strike out his own subsequent indorsements, and again negotiate the bill.

(3) Where an accommodation bill is paid in due course by the party accommodated the bill is discharged.

**60. Banker paying demand draft whereon indorsement is forged**

When a bill payable to order on demand is drawn on a banker, and the banker on whom it is drawn pays the bill in good faith and in the ordinary course of business, it is not incumbent on the banker to show that the indorsement of the payee or any subsequent indorsement was made by or under the authority of the person whose indorsement it purports to be, and the banker is deemed to have paid the bill in due course, although such indorsement has been forged or made without authority.

**61. Acceptor the holder at maturity**

When the acceptor of a bill is or becomes the holder of it at or after its maturity, in his own right, the bill is discharged.

**62. Express waiver**

(1) When the holder of a bill at or after its maturity absolutely and unconditionally renounces his rights against the acceptor the bill is discharged. The renunciation must be in writing, unless the bill is delivered up to the acceptor.

(2) The liabilities of any party to a bill may in like manner be renounced by the holder before, at, or after its maturity: but nothing in this section shall affect the rights of a holder in due course without notice of the renunciation.

**63. Cancellation**

(1) Where a bill is intentionally cancelled by the holder or his agent, and the cancellation is apparent thereon, the bill is discharged.

(2) In like manner any party liable on a bill may be discharged by the intentional cancellation of his signature by the holder or his agent. In such case any indorser who would have had a right of recourse against the party whose signature is cancelled is also discharged.

(3) A cancellation made unintentionally, or under a mistake, or without the authority of the holder is inoperative; but where a bill or any signature thereon appears to have been cancelled the burden of proof lies on the party who alleges that the cancellation was made unintentionally, or under a mistake, or without authority.

**64. Alteration of bill**

(1) Where a bill or acceptance is materially altered without the assent of all parties liable on the bill, the bill is avoided except as against a party who has himself made, authorised, or assented to the alteration, and subsequent indorsers.

Provided that,

Where a bill has been materially altered, but the alteration is not apparent, and the bill is in the hands of a holder in due course, such holder may avail himself of the bill as if it had not been altered, and may enforce payment of it according to its original tenor.

(2) In particular the following alterations are material, namely, any alteration of the date, the sum payable, the time of payment, the place of payment, and, where a bill has been accepted generally, the addition of a place of payment without the acceptor's assent.

*Acceptance and Payment for Honour*

**65. Acceptance for honour supra protest**

(1) Where a bill of exchange has been protested for dishonour by non-acceptance, or protested for better security, and is not overdue, any person, not being a party already liable thereon, may, with the consent of the holder, intervene and accept the bill supra protest, for the honour of any party liable thereon, or for the honour of the person for whose account the bill is drawn.

(2) A bill may be accepted for honour for part only of the sum for which it is drawn.

(3) An acceptance for honour supra protest in order to be valid must- (a) be written on the bill, and indicate that it is an acceptance for honour: (b) be signed by the acceptor for honour.

(4) Where an acceptance for honour does not expressly state for whose honour it is made, it is deemed to be an acceptance for the honour of the drawer.

(5) Where a bill payable after sight is accepted for honour, its maturity is calculated from the date of the noting for non-acceptance, and not from the date of the acceptance for honour.

**66. Liability of acceptor for honour**

(1) The acceptor for honour of a bill by accepting it engages that he will, on due presentment, pay the bill according to the tenor of his acceptance, if it is not paid by the drawee, provided it has been duly presented for payment, and protested for non-payment, and that he receives notice of these facts.

(2) The acceptor for honour is liable to the holder and to all parties to the bill subsequent to the party for whose honour he has accepted.

**67. Presentment to acceptor for honour**

(1) Where a dishonoured bill has been accepted for honour supra protest, or contains a reference in case of need, it must be protested for non-payment before it is presented for payment to the acceptor for honour, or referee in case of need.

(2) Where the address of the acceptor for honour is in the same place where the bill is protested for non-payment, the bill must be presented to him not later than the day following its maturity; and where the address of the acceptor for honour is in some place other than the place where it was protested for non-payment, the bill must be forwarded not later than the day following its maturity for presentment to him.

(3) Delay in presentment or non-presentment is excused by any circumstance which would excuse delay in presentment for payment or non-presentment for payment.

(4) When a bill of exchange is dishonoured by the acceptor for honour it must be protested for non-payment by him.

**68. Payment for honour supra protest**

(1) Where a bill has been protested for non-payment, any person may intervene and pay it supra protest for the honour of any party liable thereon, or for the honour of the person for whose account the bill is drawn.

(2) Where two or more persons offer to pay a bill for the honour of different parties, the person whose payment will discharge most parties to the bill shall have the preference.

(3) Payment for honour supra protest, in order to operate as such and not as a mere voluntary payment, must be attested by a notarial act of honour which may be appended to the protest or form an extension of it.

(4) The notarial act of honour must be founded on a declaration made by the payer for honour, or his agent in that behalf, declaring his intention to pay the bill for honour, and for whose honour he pays.

(5) Where a bill has been paid for honour, all parties subsequent to the party for whose honour it is paid are discharged, but the payer for honour is subrogated for, and succeeds to both the rights and duties of, the holder as regards the party for whose honour he pays, and all parties liable to that party.

(6) The payer for honour on paying to the holder the amount of the bill and the notarial expenses incidental to its dishonour is entitled to receive both the bill itself and the protest. If the holder do not on demand deliver them up he shall be liable to the payer for honour in damages.

(7) Where the holder of a bill refuses to receive payment supra protest he shall lose his right of recourse against any party who would have been discharged by such payment.

*Lost Instruments*

**69. Holder's right to duplicate of lost bill**

Where a bill has been lost before it is overdue the person who was the holder of it may apply to the drawer to give him another bill of the same tenor, giving security to the drawer if required to indemnify him against all persons whatever in case the bill alleged to have been lost shall be found again. If the drawer on request as aforesaid refuses to give such duplicate bill he may be compelled to do so.

**70. Action on lost bill**

In any action or proceeding upon a bill, the court or a judge may order that the loss of the instrument shall not be set up, provided an indemnity be given to the satisfaction of the court or judge against the claims of any other person upon the instrument in question.

*Bill in a Set*

**71. Rules as to sets**

(1) Where a bill is drawn in a set, each part of the set being numbered, and containing a reference to the other parts the whole of the parts constitute one bill.

(2) Where the holder of a set indorses two or more parts to different persons, he is liable on every such part, and every indorser subsequent to him is liable on the part he has himself indorsed as if the said parts were separate bills.

(3) Where two or more parts of a set are negotiated to different holders in due course, the holder whose title first accrues is as between such holders deemed the true owner of the bill; but nothing in this sub-section shall affect the rights of a person who in due course accepts or pays the part first presented to him.

(4) The acceptance may be written on any part, and it must be written on one part only. If the drawee accepts more than one part, and such accepted parts get into the hands of different holders in due course, he is liable on every such part as if it were a separate bill.

(5) When the acceptor of a bill drawn in a set pays it without requiring the part bearing his acceptance to be delivered up to him, and that part at maturity is outstanding in the hands of a holder in due course, he is liable to the holder thereof.

(6) Subject to the preceding rules, where any one part of a bill drawn in a set is discharged by payment or otherwise, the whole bill is discharged.

*Conflict of Laws*

### 72. Rules where laws conflict

Where a bill drawn in one country is negotiated, accepted, or payable in another, the rights, duties, and liabilities of the parties thereto are determined as follows—

(1) The validity of a bill as regards requisites in form is determined by the law of the place of issue, and the validity as regards requisites in form of the supervening contracts, such as acceptance, or indorsement, or acceptance supra protest, is determined by the law of the place where such contract was made.

Provided that—

(a) Where a bill is issued out of the United Kingdom it is not invalid by reason only that it is not stamped in accordance with the law of the place of issue:

(b) Where a bill, issued out of the United Kingdom, conforms, as regards requisites in form, to the law of the United Kingdom, it may, for the purpose of enforcing payment thereof, be treated as valid as between all persons who negotiate, hold, or become parties to it in the United Kingdom.

(2) Subject to the provisions of this Act, the interpretation of the drawing, indorsement, acceptance, or acceptance supra protest of a bill, is determined by the law of the place where such contract is made. Provided that where an inland bill is indorsed in a foreign country the indorsement shall as regards the payer be interpreted according to the law of the United Kingdom.

(3) The duties of the holder with respect to presentment for acceptance or payment and the necessity for or sufficiency of a protest or notice of dishonour, or otherwise, are determined by the law of the place where the act is done or the bill is dishonoured.

(4) [Repealed]

(5) Where a bill is drawn in one country and is payable in another, the due date thereof is determined according to the law of the place where it is payable.

**73.- 89. [omitted]**

## PART V

## SUPPLEMENTARY

### 90. Good faith

A thing is deemed to be done in good faith, within the meaning of this Act, where it is in fact done honestly, whether it is done negligently or not.

### 91. Signature

(1) Where, by this Act, any instrument or writing is required to be signed by any person it is not necessary that he should sign it with his own hand, but it is sufficient if his signature is written thereon by some other person by or under his authority.

(2) In the case of a corporation, where, by this act, any instrument or writing is required to be signed, it is sufficient if the instrument or writing be sealed with the corporate seal. But nothing in this section shall be construed as requiring the bill or note of a corporation to be under seal.

### 92. Computation of time

Where, by this Act, the time limited for doing any act or thing is less than three days, in reckoning time, non-business days are excluded.

'Non-business days' for the purposes of this Act mean—

(a) Saturday Sunday, Good Friday, Christmas Day:

(b) A bank holiday under the Banking and Financial Dealings Act 1971:

(c) A day appointed by Royal proclamation as a public fast or thanksgiving day.

(d) A day declared by an order under section 2 of the Banking and Financial Dealings Act 1971 to be a non-business day.

Any other day is a business day.

### 93. When noting equivalent to protest

For the purposes of this Act, where a bill or note is required to be protested within a specified time or before some further proceeding is taken, it is sufficient that the bill has been noted for protest before the expiration of the specified time or the taking of the proceeding; and the formal protest may be extended at any time thereafter as of the date of the noting.

### 94. Protest when notary not accessible

Where a dishonoured bill or note is authorised or required to be protested, and the services of a notary cannot be obtained at the place where the bill is dishonoured, any householder or substantial resident of the place may, in the presence of two witnesses, give a certificate, signed by them, attesting the dishonour of the bill, and the certificate shall in respects operate as if it were a formal protest of the bill. The form given in Schedule 1 to this Act may be used with necessary modifications, and if used shall be sufficient.
Merchant Shipping Act 1894.

### 95.-100. [omitted]

# MERCHANT SHIPPING ACT 1894

## CHAPTER 60

## PART VII

## DELIVERY OF GOODS

### *Delivery of Goods and Lien for Freight*

### 492. Definitions under Part VII

In this Part of this Act, unless the context otherwise requires—

The expression 'goods' includes every description of wares and merchandise:

The expression 'wharf' includes all wharves, quays, docks, and premises in or upon which any goods, when landed from ships, may be lawfully placed:

The expression 'warehouse' includes all warehouses, buildings, and premises in which goods, when landed from ships, may be lawfully placed:

The expression 'report' means the report required by the customs or excise laws to be made by the master of an importing ship:

The expression 'entry' means the entry required by the customs or excise laws to be made for the landing or discharge of goods from an importing ship:

The expression 'ship owner' includes the master of the ship and every other person authorised to act as agent for the owner or entitled to receive the freight, demurrage, or other charges payable in respect of the ship:

The expression 'owner' used in relation to goods means every person who is for the time entitled, either as owner or agent for the owner, to the possession of the goods, subject in the case of a lien (if any), to that lien:

The expression 'wharfinger' means the occupier of a wharf as herein-before defined: The expression 'warehouseman' means the occupier of a warehouse as herein-before defined.

### 493. Power of shipowner to enter and land goods on default by owner of goods

(1) Where the owner of any goods imported in any ship from foreign parts into the United Kingdom fails to make entry thereof, or, having made entry thereof, to land the same or take delivery thereof, and to proceed therewith with all convenient speed, by the times severally herein-after mentioned, the ship owner may make entry of and land or unship the goods at the following times:-

(a) If a time for the delivery of the goods is expressed in the charter party, bill of lading, or agreement, then at any time after the time so expressed:

(b) If no time for the delivery of the goods is expressed in the charter party, bill of lading, or agreement, then at any time after the expiration of seventy-two hours, exclusive of a Sunday or holiday, from the time of the report of the ship.

(2) Where a ship owner lands goods in pursuance of this section he shall place them, or cause them to be placed-

(a) if any wharf or warehouse is named in the charter party, bill of lading, or agreement, as the wharf or warehouse where the goods are to be placed and if they can be conveniently there received, on that wharf or in that warehouse; and

(b) in any other case on some wharf or in some warehouse on or in which goods of a like nature are usually placed; the wharf or warehouse being, if the goods are dutiable, a wharf or warehouse duly approved by the Commissioners of Customs and Excise for the landing of dutiable goods.

(3) If at any time before the goods are landed or unshipped the owner of the goods is ready and offers to land or take delivery of the same, he shall be allowed to do so, and his entry shall in that case be preferred to any entry which may have been made by the ship owner.

(4) If any goods are, for the purpose of convenience in assorting the same, landed at the wharf where the ship is discharged, and the owner of the goods at the time of that landing has made entry and is ready and offers to take delivery thereof, and to convey the same to some other wharf or warehouse, the goods shall be assorted at landing, and shall, if demanded, be delivered to the owner thereof within twenty-four hours after assortment; and the expense of and consequent on that landing and assortment shall be borne by the ship owner.

(5) If at any time before the goods are landed or unshipped the owner thereof has made entry for the landing and warehousing thereof at any particular wharf or warehouse other than that at which the ship is discharging, and has offered and been ready to take delivery thereof, and the ship owner has failed to make that delivery, and has also failed at the time of that offer to give the owner of the goods correct information of the time at which the goods can be delivered, then the ship owner shall, before landing or unshipping the goods, in pursuance of this section, give to the owner of the goods or of such wharf or warehouse as last aforesaid twenty-four hours notice in writing of his readiness to delivery the goods, and shall, if he lands or unships the same without that notice, do so at his own risk and expense.

**494. Lien for freight on landing goods**

If at the time when any goods are landed from any ship, and placed in the custody of any person as a wharfinger or warehouseman, the ship owner gives to the wharfinger or warehouseman notice in writing that the goods are to remain subject to a lien for freight or other charges payable to the ship owner to an amount mentioned in the notice, the goods so landed shall, in the hands of the wharfinger or warehouseman, continue subject to the same lien, if any, for such charges as they were subject to before the landing thereof; and the wharfinger or warehouseman receiving those goods shall retain them until the lien is discharged as herein-after mentioned, and shall, if he fails so to do, make good to the ship owner any loss thereby occasioned to him.

**495. Discharge of lien**

The said lien for freight and other charges shall be discharged-

(1) upon the production to the wharfinger or warehouseman of a receipt for the amount claimed as due, and delivery to the wharfinger or warehouseman of a copy thereof or of a release of freight from the ship owner, and

(2) upon the deposit by the owner of the goods with the wharfinger or warehouseman of a sum of money equal in amount to the sum claimed as aforesaid by the ship owner; but in the latter case the lien shall be discharged without prejudice to any other remedy which the shipowner may have for the recovery of the freight.

**496. Provisions as to deposits by owners of goods**

(1) When a deposit as aforesaid is made with the wharfinger or warehouseman, the person making the same may, within fifteen days after making it, give to the wharfinger or warehouseman notice in writing to retain it, stating in the notice the sums, if any, which he admits to be payable to the shipowner, or, as the case may be, that he does not admit any sum to be so payable, but if no such notice is given, the wharfinger or warehouseman may, at the expiration of the fifteen days, pay the sum deposited over to the shipowner.

(2) If a notice is given as aforesaid the wharfinger or warehouseman shall immediately apprise the shipowner of it, and shall pay or tender to him out of the sum deposited the sum, if any, admitted by the notice to be payable, and shall retain the balance, or, if no sum is admitted to be payable, the whole of the sum deposited, for thirty days from the date of the notice.

(3) At the expiration of those thirty days unless legal proceedings have in the meantime been instituted by the shipowner against the owner of the goods to recover the said balance or sum, or otherwise for the settlement of any disputes which may have arisen between them concerning the freight or other charges as aforesaid, and notice in writing of those proceedings has been served on the wharfinger or warehouseman, the wharfinger or warehouseman shall pay the balance or sum to the owner of the goods.

(4) A wharfinger or warehouseman shall by any payment under this section be discharged from all liability in respect thereof.

**497. Sale of goods by warehousemen**

(1) If the lien is not discharged, and no deposit is made as aforesaid, the wharfinger or warehouseman may, and, if required by the shipowner, shall, at the expiration of ninety days from the time when the goods were placed in his custody, or, if the goods are of a perishable nature, at such earlier period as in his discretion he thinks fit, sell by public auction, either for home use or for exportation, the goods or so much thereof as may be necessary to satisfy the charges herein-after mentioned.

(2) Before making the sale the wharfinger or warehouseman shall give notice thereof by advertisement in two local newspapers circulating in the neighbourhood, or in one daily newspaper published in London, and in one local newspaper, and also, if the address of the owner of the goods has been stated on the manifest of the cargo, or on any of the documents which have come into the possession of the wharfinger or warehouseman, or is otherwise known to him, send notice of the sale to the owner of the goods by post.

(3) The title of a bona fide purchaser of the goods shall not be invalidated by reason of the omission to send the notice required by this section, nor shall any such purchaser be bound to inquire whether the notice has been sent.

**498. Application of proceeds of sale**

The proceeds of sale shall be applied by the wharfinger or warehouseman as follows, and in the following order:-

- (i) First, if the goods are sold for home use, in payment of any customs or excise duties owing in respect thereof; then
- (ii) In payment of the expenses of the sale; then
- (iii) In payment of the charges of the wharfinger or warehouseman and the shipowner according to such priority as may be determined by the terms of the agreement (if any) in that behalf between them; or, if there is no such agreement-
  - (a) in payment of the rent, rates, and other charges due to the wharfinger or warehouseman in respect of the said goods; and then
  - (b) in payment of the amount claimed by the shipowner as due for freight or other charges in respect of the said goods; and the surplus, if any, shall be paid to the owner of the goods.

**499. Warehouseman's rent and expenses**

Whenever any goods are placed in the custody of a wharfinger or warehouseman, under the authority of this Part of this Act, the wharfinger or warehouseman shall be entitled to rent in respect of the same, and shall also have power, at the expense of the owner of the goods, to do all such reasonable acts as in the judgement of the wharfinger or warehousemen are necessary for the proper custody and preservation of the goods, and shall have a lien on the goods for the rent and expenses.

**500. Warehousemen's protection**

Nothing in this Part of this Act shall compel any wharfinger or warehouseman to take charge of any goods which he would not have been liable to take charge of if this Act had not been passed; nor shall he be bound to see to the validity of any lien claim by any shipowner under this Part of this Act.

# MARINE INSURANCE ACT 1906

CHAPTER 41

## MARINE INSURANCE

1. Marine insurance defined.
2. Mixed sea and land risks.
3. Marine adventure and maritime perils defined.

## INSURABLE INTEREST

4. Avoidance of wagering or gaming contracts.
5. Insurable interest defined.
6. When interest must attach.
7. Defeasible or contingent interest.
8. Partial interest.
9. Re-insurance.
10. Bottomry.
11. Master's and seamen's wages.
12. Advance freight.
13. Charges of insurance.
14. Quantum of interest.
15. Assignment of interest.

## INSURABLE VALUE

16. Measure of insurable value.

## DISCLOSURE AND REPRESENTATIONS

17. Insurance is uberrimae fidei.
18. Disclosure by assured.
19. Disclosure by agent effecting insurance.
20. Representations pending negotiation of contract.
21. When contract is deemed to be concluded.

## THE POLICY

22. Contract must be embodied in policy.
23. What policy must specify.
24. Signature of insurer.
25. Voyage and time policies.
26. Designation of subject-matter.
27. Valued policy.
28. Unvalued policy.
29. Floating policy by ship or ships.

## Partial Losses (Including Salvage, General Average and Particular Charges)



## Measure of Indemnity



## Rights of Insurer on Payment



## Return of Premium



## Mutual Insurance



## Supplemental

## SCHEDULE

Schedule 1 - Form of Policy

## MARINE INSURANCE

### 1. Marine insurance defined

A contract of marine insurance is a contract whereby the insurer undertakes to indemnify the assured, in manner and to the extent thereby agreed, against marine losses, that is to say, the losses incident to marine adventure.

### 2. Mixed sea and land risks

(1) A contract of marine insurance may, by its express terms, or by usage of trade, be extended so as to protect the assured against losses on inland waters or on any land risk which may be incidental to any sea voyage.

(2) Where a ship in course of building, or the launch of a ship, or any adventure analogous to a marine adventure, is covered by a policy in the form of a marine policy, the provisions of this Act, in so far as applicable, shall apply thereto; but, except as by this section provided, nothing in this Act shall alter or affect any rule of law applicable to any contract of insurance other than a contract of marine insurance as by this Act define.

### 3. Marine adventure and maritime perils defined

(1) Subject to the provisions of this Act, every lawful marine adventure may be the subject of a contract of marine insurance.

(2) In particular there is a marine adventure where—

(a) Any ship goods or other moveables are exposed to maritime perils. Such property is in this Act referred to as 'insurable property';

(b)The earning or acquisition of any freight, passage money, commission, profit, or other pecuniary benefit, or the security for any advances, loan, or disbursements, is endangered by the exposure of insurable property to maritime perils;

(c) Any liability to a third party may be incurred by the owner of, or other person interested in or responsible for, insurable property, by reason of maritime perils.

'Maritime perils' means the perils consequent on, or incidental to, the navigation of the sea, that is to say, perils of the seas, fire, war, perils, pirates, rovers, thieves, captures, seizures, restraints, and detainment's of princes and peoples, jettisons, barratry, and any other perils, either of the like kind or which may be designated by the policy.

## INSURABLE INTEREST

### 4. Avoidance of wagering or gaming contracts

(1) Every contract of marine insurance by way of gaming or wagering is void.

(2) A contract of marine insurance is deemed to be a gaming or wagering contract—

(a) Where the assured has not an insurable interest as defined by this Act, and the contract is entered into with no expectation of acquiring such an interest; or

(b) Where the policy is made 'interest or no interest,' or 'without further proof of interest than the policy itself.' or 'without benefit of salvage to the insurer,' or subject to any other like term:

Provided that, where there is no possibility of salvage, a policy may be effected without benefit of salvage to the insurer.

**5. Insurable interest defined**

(1) Subject to the provisions of this Act, every person has an insurable interest who is interested in a marine adventure.

(2) In particular a person is interested in a marine adventure where he stands in any legal or equitable relation to the adventure or to any insurable property at risk therein, in consequence of which he may benefit by the safety or due arrival of insurable property, or may be prejudiced by its loss, or by damage thereto, or by the detention thereof, or may incur liability in respect thereof.

**6. When interest must attach**

(1) The assured must be interested in the subject-matter insured at the time of the loss though he need not be interested when the insurance is effected: Provided that where the subject-matter is insured 'lost or not lost,' the assured may recover although he may not have acquired his interest until after the loss, unless at the time of effecting the contract of insurance the assured was aware of the loss, and the insurer was not.

(2) Where the assured has no interest at the time of the loss, he cannot acquire interest by any act or election after he is aware of the loss.

**7. Defeasible or contingent interest**

(1) A defeasible interest is insurable, as also is a contingent interest.

(2) In particular, where the buyer of goods has insured them, he has an insurable interest, notwithstanding that he might, at his election, have rejected the goods, or have treated them as at the seller's risk, by reason of the latter's delay in making delivery or otherwise.

**8. Partial interest**

A partial interest of any nature is insurable.

### 9. Re-insurance

(1) The insurer under a contract of marine insurance has an insurable interest in his risk, and may re-insure in respect of it.

(2) Unless the policy otherwise provides, the original assured has no right or interest in respect of such re-insurance.

### 10. Bottomry

The lender of money on bottomry or respondentia has an insurable interest in respect of the loan.

### 11. Master's and seamen's wages

The master or any member of the crew of a ship has an insurable interest in respect of his wages.

### 12. Advance freight

In the case of advance freight, the person advancing the freight has an insurable interest, in so far as such freight is not repayable in case of loss.

### 13. Charges of insurance

The assured has an insurable interest in the charges of any insurance which he may effect.

### 14. Quantum of interest

(1) Where the subject-matter insured is mortgaged, the mortgagor has an insurable interest in the full value thereof, and the mortgagee has an insurable interest in respect of any sum due or to become due under the mortgage.

(2) A mortgagee, consignee, or other person having an interest in the subject-matter insured may insure on behalf and for the benefit of other persons interested as well as for his own benefit.

(3) The owner of insurable property has an insurable interest in respect of the full value thereof, notwithstanding that some third person may have agreed, or be liable, to indemnify him in case of loss.

### 15. Assignment of interest

Where the assured assigns or otherwise parts with his interest in the subject-matter insured, he does not thereby transfer to the assignee his rights under the contract of insurance, unless there be an express or implied agreement with the assignee to that effect. But the provisions of this section do not affect a transmission of interest by operation of law.

## INSURABLE VALUE

### 16. Measure of insurable value

Subject to any express provision or valuation in the policy, the insurable value of the subject-matter insured must be ascertained as follows:-

(1) In insurance on ship, the insurable value is the value, at the commencement of the risk, of the ship, including her outfit, provisions and stores for the officers and crew, money advanced for seamen's wages, and other disbursements (if any) incurred to make the ship fit for the voyage or adventure contemplated by the policy, plus the charges of insurance upon the whole: The insurable value, in the case of a steamship, includes also the machinery, boilers, and coals and engine stores if owned by the assured, and, in the case of a ship engaged in a special trade, the ordinary fittings requisite for that trade:

(2) In insurance on freight, whether paid in advance or otherwise, the insurable value is the gross amount of the freight at the risk of the assured, plus the charges of insurance:

(3) In insurance on goods or merchandise, the insurable value is the prime cost of the property insured, plus the expenses of and incidental to shipping and the charges of insurance upon the whole:

(4) In insurance on any other subject-matter, the insurable value is the amount at the risk of the assured when the policy attaches, plus the charges of insurance.

## DISCLOSURE AND REPRESENTATIONS

### 17. Insurance is *uberrimae fidei*

A contract of marine insurance is a contract based upon the utmost good faith, and, if the utmost good faith be not observed by either party, the contract may be avoided by the other party.

### 18. Disclosure by assured

(1) Subject to the provisions of this section, the assured must disclose to the insurer, before the contract is concluded, every material circumstance which is known to the assured, and the assured is deemed to know every circumstance which, in the ordinary course of business, ought to be known by him. If the assured fails to make such disclosure, the insurer may avoid the contract.

(2) Every circumstance is material which would influence the judgment of a prudent insurer in fixing the premium, or determining whether he will take the risk.

(3) In the absence of inquiry the following circumstances need not be disclosed, namely:-

(a) Any circumstance which diminishes the risk:

(b) Any circumstance which is known or presumed to be known to the insurer. The insurer is presumed to know matters of common notoriety or knowledge, and matters which an insurer in the ordinary course of his business, as such, ought to know;

(c) Any circumstances as to which information is waived by the insurer;

(d) Any circumstance which it is superfluous to disclose by reason of any express or implied warranty.

(4) Whether any particular circumstance, which is not disclosed, be material or not is, in each case, a question of fact.

(5) The term 'circumstance' includes any communication made to, or information received by, the assured.

**19. Disclosure by agent effecting insurance**

Subject to the provisions of the preceding section as to circumstances which need not be disclosed, where an insurance is effected for the assured by an agent, the agent must disclose to the insurer—

(a) Every material circumstance which is known to himself, and an agent to insure is deemed to know every circumstance which in the ordinary course of business ought to be known by, or to have been communicated to, him; and

(b) Every material circumstance which the assured is bound to disclose, unless it come to his knowledge too late to communicate it to the agent.

**20. Representations pending negotiation of contract**

(1) Every material representation made by the assured or his agent to the insurer during the negotiations for the contract, and before the contract is concluded, must be true. If it be untrue the insurer may avoid the contract.

(2) A representation is material which would influence the judgment of a prudent insurer in fixing the premium, or determining whether he will take the risk.

(3) A representation may be either a representation as to a matter of fact, or as to a matter of expectation or belief.

(4) A representation as to a matter of fact is true, if it be substantially correct, that is to say, if the difference between what is represented and what is actually correct would not be considered material by a prudent insurer.

(5) A representation as to a matter of expectation or belief is true if it be made in good faith.

(6) A representation may be withdrawn or corrected before the contract is concluded.

(7) Whether a particular representation be material or not is, in each case, a question of fact.

### 21. When contract is deemed to be concluded

A contract of marine insurance is deemed to be concluded when the proposal of the assured is accepted by the insurer, whether the policy be then issued or not; and, for the purpose of showing when the proposal was accepted, reference may be made to the slip or covering note or other customary memorandum of the contract.

## THE POLICY

### 22. Contract must be embodied in policy

Subject to the provisions of any statute, a contract of marine insurance is inadmissible in evidence unless it is embodied in a marine policy in accordance with this Act. The policy may be executed and issued either at the time when the contract is concluded, or afterwards.

### 23. What policy must specify

A marine policy must specify—

(1) The name of the assured, or of some person who effects the insurance on his behalf:

(2)-(5) [Repealed].

### 24. Signature of insurer

(1) A marine policy must be signed by or on behalf of the insurer, provided that in the case of a corporation the corporate seal may be sufficient, but nothing in this section shall be construed as requiring the subscription of a corporation to be under seal.

(2) Where a policy is subscribed by or on behalf of two or more insurers, each subscription, unless the contrary be expressed, constitutes a distinct contract with the assured.

### 25. Voyage and time policies

(1) Where the contract is to insure the subject-matter 'at and from,' or from one place to another or other, the policy is called a 'voyage policy,' and where the contract is to insure the subject-matter for a definite period of time the policy is called a 'time policy.' A contract for both voyage and time may be included in the same policy.

(2) [Repealed].

### 26. Designation of subject-matter

(1) The subject-matter insured must be designated in a marine policy with reasonable certainty.

(2) The nature and extent of the interest of the assured in the subject-matter insured need not be specified in the policy.

(3) Where the policy designates the subject-matter insured in general terms, its shall be construed to apply to the interest intended by the assured to be covered.

(4) In the application of this section regard shall be had to any usage regulating the designation of the subject-matter insured.

**27. Valued policy**

(1) A policy may be either valued or unvalued.

(2) A valued policy is a policy which specifies the agreed value of the subject-matter insured.

(3) Subject to the provisions of this Act, and in the absence of fraud, the value fixed by the policy is, as between the insurer and assured, conclusive of the insurable value of the subject intended to be insured, whether the loss be total or partial.

(4) Unless the policy otherwise provides, the value fixed by the policy is not conclusive for the purpose of determining whether there has been a constructive total loss.

**28. Unvalued policy**

An unvalued policy is a policy which does not specify the value of the subject-matter insured, but subject to the limit of the sum insured, leaves the insurable value to be subsequently ascertained, in the manner herein-before specified.

**29. Floating policy by ship or ships**

(1) A floating policy is a policy which describes the insurance in general terms, and leaves the name of the ship or ships and other particulars to be defined by subsequent declaration.

(2) The subsequent declaration or declarations may be made by indorsement on the policy, or in other customary manner.

(3) Unless the policy otherwise provides, the declarations must be made in the order of dispatch or shipment. They must, in the case of goods, comprise all consignments within the terms of the policy, and the value of the goods or other property must be honestly stated, but an omission or erroneous declaration may be rectified even after loss or arrival, provided the omission or declaration was made in good faith.

(4) Unless the policy otherwise provides, where a declaration of value is not made until after notice of loss or arrival, the policy must be treated as an unvalued policy as regards the subject-matter of that declaration.

### 30. Construction of terms in policy

(1) A policy may be in the form in the First Schedule to this Act.

(2) Subject to the provisions of this Act, and unless the context of the policy otherwise requires, the terms and expressions mentioned in the First Schedule to this Act shall be construed as having the scope and meaning in that schedule assigned to them.

### 31. Premium to be arranged

(1) Where an insurance is effected at a premium to be arranged, and no arrangement is made, a reasonable premium is payable.

(2) Where an insurance is effected on the terms that an additional premium is to be arranged in a given event, and that event happens but no arrangement is made, then a reasonable additional premium is payable.

## DOUBLE INSURANCE

### 32. Double insurance

(1) Where two or more policies are effected by or on behalf of the assured on the same adventure and interest or any part thereof, and the sums insured exceed the indemnity allowed by this Act, the assured is said to be over-insured by double insurance.

(2) Where the assured is over-insured by double insurance—

(a) The assured, unless the policy otherwise provides, may claim payment from the insurers in such order as he may think fit, provided that he is not entitled to receive any sum in excess of the indemnity allowed by this Act;

(b) Where the policy under which the assured claims is a valued policy, the assured must give credit as against the valuation for any sum received by him under any other policy without regard to the actual value of the subject-matter insured;

(c) Where the policy under which the assured claims is an unvalued policy he must give credit, as against the full insurable value, for any sum received by him under any other policy:

(d) Where the assured receives any sum in excess of the indemnity allowed by this Act, he is deemed to hold such sum in trust for the insurers, according to their right of contribution among themselves.

## WARRANTIES, &C.

### 33. Nature of warranty

(1) A warranty, in the following sections relating to warranties, means a promissory warranty, that is to say, a warranty by which the assured undertakes that some particular thing shall or shall not be done, or that some condition shall

be fulfilled, or whereby he affirms or negatives the existence of a particular state of facts.

(2) A warranty may be express or implied.

(3) A warranty, as above defined, is a condition which must be exactly complied with, whether it be material to the risk or not. If it be not so complied with, then, subject to any express provision in the policy, the insurer is discharged from liability as from the date of the breach of warranty, but without prejudice to any liability incurred by him before that date.

**34. When breach of warranty excused**

(1) Non-compliance with a warranty is excused when by reason of a change of circumstances, the warranty ceases to be applicable to the circumstances of the contract, or when compliance with the warranty is rendered unlawful by any subsequent law.

(2) Where a warranty is broken, the assured cannot avail himself of the defence that the breach has been remedied, and the warranty complied with, before loss.

(3) A breach of warranty may be waived by the insurer.

**35. Express warranties**

(1) An express warranty may be in any form of words from which the intention to warrant is to be inferred.

(2) An express warranty must be included in, or written upon, the policy, or must be contained in some document incorporated by reference into the policy.

(3) An express warranty does not exclude an implied warranty, unless it be inconsistent therewith.

**36. Warranty of neutrality**

(1) Where insurable property, whether ship or goods, is expressly warranted neutral, there is an implied condition that the property shall have a neutral character at the commencement of the risk, and that, so far as the assured can control the matter, its neutral character shall be preserved during the risk.

(2) Where a ship is expressly warranted 'neutral' there is also an implied condition that, so far as the assured can control the matter she shall be properly documented, that is to say, that she shall carry the necessary papers to establish her neutrality, and that she shall not falsify or suppress her papers, or use simulated papers. If any loss occurs through breach of this condition, the insurer may avoid the contract.

**37. No implied warranty of nationality**

There is no implied warranty as to the nationality of a ship, or that her nationality shall not be changed during the risk.

**38. Warranty of good safety**

Where the subject-matter insured is warranted 'well' or 'in good safety' on a particular day, it is sufficient if it be safe at any time during that day.

**39. Warranty of seaworthiness of ship**

(1) In a voyage policy there is an implied warranty that at the commencement of the voyage the ship shall be seaworthy for the purpose of the particular adventure insured.

(2) Where the policy attaches while the ship is in port, there is also an implied warranty that she shall, at the commencement of the risk, be reasonably fit to encounter the ordinary perils of the port.

(3) Where the policy relates to a voyage which is performed in different stages, during which the ship requires different kinds of or further preparation or equipment, there is an implied warranty that at the commencement of each stage the ship is seaworthy in respect of such preparation or equipment for the purposes of that stage.

(4) A ship is deemed to be seaworthy when she is reasonably fit in all respects to encounter the ordinary perils of the seas of the adventure insured.

(5) In a time policy there is no implied warranty that the ship shall be seaworthy at any stage of the adventure, but where, with the privity of the assured, the ship is sent to sea in an unseaworthy state, the insurer is not liable for any loss attributable to unseaworthiness.

**40. No implied warranty that goods are seaworthy**

(1) In a policy on goods or other moveables there is no implied warranty that the goods or moveables are seaworthy.

(2) In a voyage policy on goods or other moveables there is an implied warranty that at the commencement of the voyage the ship is not only seaworthy as a ship, but also that she is reasonably fit to carry the goods or other moveables to the destination contemplated by the policy.

**41. Warranty of legality**

There is an implied warranty that the adventure insured is a lawful one, and that, so far as the assured can control the matter, the adventure shall be carried out in a lawful manner.

## The Voyage

### 42. Implied condition as to commencement of risk

(1) Where the subject-matter is insured by a voyage policy 'at and from' or 'from' a particular place, it is not necessary that the ship should be at that place when the contract is concluded, but there is an implied condition that the adventure shall be commenced within a reasonable time, and that if the adventure be not so commenced the insurer may avoid the contract.

(2) The implied condition may be negatived by showing that the delay was caused by circumstances known to the insurer before the contract was concluded, or by showing that he waived the condition.

### 43. Alteration of port of departure

Where the place of departure is specified by the policy, and the ship instead of sailing from that place sails from any other place, the risk does not attach.

### 44. Sailing for different destination

Where the destination is specified in the policy, and the ship, instead of sailing for that destination, sails for any other destination, the risk does not attach.

### 45. Change of voyage

(1) Where, after the commencement of the risk, the destination of the ship is voluntarily changed from the destination contemplated by the policy, there is said to be a change of voyage.

(2) Unless the policy otherwise provides, where there is a change of voyage, the insurer is discharged from liability as from the time of change, that is to say, as from the time when the determination to change it is manifested; and it is immaterial that the ship may not in fact have left the course of voyage contemplated by the policy when the loss occurs.

### 46. Deviation

(1) Where a ship, without lawful excuse, deviates from the voyage contemplated by the policy, the insurer is discharged from liability as from the time of deviation, and it is immaterial that the ship may have regained her route before any loss occurs.

(2) There is a deviation from the voyage contemplated by the policy—
- (a) Where the course of the voyage is specifically designated by the policy, and that course is departed from; or
- (b) Where the course of the voyage is not specifically designated by the policy, but the usual and customary course is departed from.

(3) The intention to deviate is immaterial; there must be a deviation in fact to discharge the insurer from his liability under the contract.

**47. Several ports of discharge**

(1) Where several ports of discharge are specified by the policy, the ship may proceed to all or any of them, but, in the absence of any usage or sufficient cause to the contrary, she must proceed to them, or such of them as she goes to, in the order designated by the policy. If she does not there is a deviation.

(2) Where the policy is to 'ports of discharge,' within a given area, which are not named, the ship must, in the absence of any usage or sufficient cause to the contrary, proceed to them, or such of them as she goes to, in their geographical order. If she does not there is a deviation.

**48.**

In the case of a voyage policy, the adventure insured must be prosecuted throughout its course with reasonable dispatch, and, if without lawful excuse it is not so prosecuted, the insurer is discharged from liability as from the time when the delay became unreasonable.

**49.**

(1) Deviation or delay in prosecuting the voyage contemplated by the policy is excused—

(a) Where authorised by any special term in the policy; or
(b) Where caused by circumstances beyond the control of the master and his employer; or
(c) Where reasonably necessary in order to comply with an express or implied warranty; or
(d) Where reasonably necessary for the safety of the ship or subject-matter insured; or
(e) for the purpose of saving human life, or aiding a ship in distress where human life may be in danger; or
(f) Where reasonably necessary for the purpose of obtaining medical or surgical aid for any person on board the ship; or
(g) Where caused by the barratrous conduct of the master or crew, if barratry be one of the perils insured against.

(2) When the cause excusing the deviation or delay ceases to operate, the ship must resume her course, and prosecute her voyage, with reasonable dispatch.

ASSIGNMENT OF POLICY

**50. When and how policy is assignable**

(1) A marine policy is assignable unless it contains terms expressly prohibiting assignment. It may be assigned either before or after loss.

(2) Where a marine policy has been assigned so as to pass the beneficial interest in such policy, the assignee of the policy is entitled to sue thereon in his own name; and the defendant is entitled to make any defence arising out of the contract which he would have been entitled to make if the action had been brought in the name of the person by or on behalf of whom the policy was effected.

**51. Assured who has no interest cannot assign**

Where the assured has parted with or lost his interest in the subject-matter insured, and has not, before or at the time of so doing, expressly or impliedly agreed to assign the policy, any subsequent assignment of the policy is inoperative: Provided that nothing in this section affects the assignment of a policy after loss.

## THE PREMIUM

**52. When premium payable**

Unless otherwise agreed, the duty of the assured or his agent to pay the premium, and the duty of the insurer to issue the policy to the assured or his agent, are concurrent conditions, and the insurer is not bound to issue the policy until payment or tender of the premium.

**53. Policy effected through broker**

(1) Unless otherwise agreed, where a marine policy is effected on behalf of the assured by a broker, the broker is directly responsible to the insurer for the premium, and the insurer is directly responsible to the assured for the amount which may be payable in respect of losses, or in respect of returnable premium.

(2) Unless otherwise agreed, the broker has, as against the assured, a lien upon the policy for the amount of the premium and his charges in respect of effecting the policy; and, where he has dealt with the person who employs him as a principal, he has also a lien on the policy in respect of any balance on any insurance account which may be due to him from such person, unless when the debt was incurred he had reason to believe that such person was only an agent.

**54. Effect of receipt on policy**

Where a marine policy effected on behalf of the assured by a broker acknowledges the receipt of the premium, such acknowledgement is, in the absence of fraud, conclusive as between the insurer and the assured, but not as between the insurer and broker.

## Loss and Abandonment

### 55. Included and excluded losses

(1) Subject to the provisions of this Act, and unless the policy otherwise provides, the insurer is liable for any loss proximately caused by a peril insured against, but, subject as aforesaid, he is not liable for any loss which is not proximately caused by a peril insured against.

(2) In particular—

(a) The insurer is not liable for any loss attributable to the wilful misconduct of the assured, but, unless the policy otherwise provides, he is liable for any loss proximately caused by a peril insured against, even though the loss would not have happened but for the misconduct or negligence of the master or crew;

(b) Unless the policy otherwise provides, the insurer on ship or goods is not liable for any loss proximately caused by delay, although the delay be caused by a peril insured against;

(c) Unless the policy otherwise provides, the insurer is not liable for ordinary wear and tear, ordinary leakage and breakage, inherent vice or nature of the subject-matter insured, or for any loss proximately caused by rats or vermin, or for any injury to machinery not proximately caused by maritime perils.

### 56. Partial and total loss

(1) A loss may be either total or partial. Any loss other than a total loss, as hereinafter defined, is a partial loss.

(2) A total loss may be either an actual total loss, or a constructive total loss.

(3) Unless a different intention appears from the terms of the policy, an insurance against total loss includes a constructive, as well as an actual, total loss.

(4) Where the assured brings an action for a total loss and the evidence proves only a partial loss, he may, unless the policy otherwise provides, recover for a partial loss.

(5) Where goods reach their destination in specie, but by reason of obliteration of marks, or otherwise, they are incapable of identification, the loss, if any, is partial, and not total.

### 57. Actual total loss

(1) Where the subject-matter insured is destroyed, or so damaged as to cease to be a thing of the kind insured, or where the assured is irretrievably deprived thereof, there is an actual total loss.

(2) In the case of an actual total loss no notice of abandonment need be given.

**58. Missing ship**

Where the ship concerned in the adventure is missing, and after the lapse of a reasonable time no news of her has been received, an actual total loss may be presumed.

**59. Effect of transhipment, &c.**

Where, by a peril insured against, the voyage is interrupted at an intermediate port or place, under such circumstances as, apart from any special stipulation in the contract of affreightment, to justify the master in landing and reshipping the goods or other moveables, or in transhipping them, and sending them on to their destination, the liability of the insurer continues, notwithstanding the landing or transhipment.

**60. Constructive total loss defined**

(1) Subject to any express provision in the policy, there is a constructive total loss where the subject-matter insured is reasonably abandoned on account of its actual total loss appearing to be unavoidable, or because it could not be preserved from actual total loss without an expenditure which would exceed its value when the expenditure had been incurred.

(2) In particular, there is a constructive total loss—

(i) Where the assured is deprived of the possession of his ship or goods by a peril insured against, and (a) it is unlikely that he can recover the ship or goods, as the case may be, or (b) the cost of recovering the ship or goods, as the case may be, would exceed their value when recovered; or

(ii) In the case of damage to a ship, where she is so damaged by a peril insured against that the cost of repairing the damage would exceed the value of the ship when repaired. In estimating the cost of repairs, no deduction is to be made in respect of general average contributions to those repairs payable by other interests, but account is to be taken of the expense of future salvage operations and of any future general average contributions to which the ship would be liable if repaired; or

(iii) In the case of damage to goods, where the cost of repairing the damage and forwarding the goods to their destination would exceed their value on arrival.

**61. Effect of constructive total loss**

Where there is a constructive total loss the assured may either treat the loss as a partial loss, or abandon the subject-matter insured to the insurer and treat the loss as if it were an actual total loss.

**62. Notice of abandonment**

(1) Subject to the provisions of this section, where the assured elects to abandon the subject-matter insured to the insurer, he must give notice of abandonment. If

he fails to do so the loss can only be treated as a partial loss.

(2) Notice of abandonment may be given in writing, or by word of mouth, or partly in writing and partly by word of mouth, and may be given in any terms which indicate the intention of the assured to abandon his insured interest in the subject-matter insured unconditionally to the insurer.

(3) Notice of abandonment must be given with reasonable diligence after the receipt of reliable information of the loss, but where the information is of a doubtful character the assured is entitled to a reasonable time to make inquiry.

(4) Where notice of abandonment is properly given, the rights of the assured are not prejudiced by the fact that the insurer refuses to accept the abandonment.

(5) The acceptance of an abandonment may be either express or implied from the conduct of the insurer. The mere silence of the insurer after notice is not acceptance.

(6) Where notice of abandonment is accepted the abandonment is irrevocable. The acceptance of the notice conclusively admits liability for the loss and the sufficiency of the notice.

(7) Notice of abandonment is unnecessary where, at the time when the assured receives information of the loss, there would be no possibility of benefit to the insurer if notice were given to him.

(8) Notice of abandonment may be waived by the insurer.

(9) Where an insurer has re-insured his risk, no notice of abandonment need by given by him

**63. Effect of abandonment**

(1) Where there is a valid abandonment the insurer is entitled to take over the interest of the assured in whatever may remain of the subject-matter insured, and all proprietary rights incidental thereto.

(2) Upon the abandonment of a ship, the insurer thereof is entitled to any freight in course of being earned, and which is earned by her subsequent to the casualty causing the loss, less the expenses of earning it incurred after the casualty; and, where the ship is carrying the owner's goods, the insurer is entitled to a reasonable remuneration for the carriage of them subsequent to the casualty causing the loss.

## PARTIAL LOSSES (INCLUDING SALVAGE AND GENERAL AVERAGE AND PARTICULAR CHARGES)

**64. Particular average loss**

(1) A particular average loss is a partial loss of the subject-matter insured, caused by a peril insured against, and which is not a general average loss.

(2) Expenses incurred by or on behalf of the assured for the safety or preservation of the subject-matter insured, other than general average and salvage charges, are called particular charges. Particular charges are not included in particular average.

**65. Salvage charges**

(1) Subject to any express provision in the policy, salvage charges incurred in preventing a loss by perils insured against may be recovered as a loss by those perils.

(2) 'Salvage charges' means the charges recoverable under maritime law by a salvor independently of contract. They do not include the expenses of services in the nature of salvage rendered by the assured or his agents, or any person employed for hire by them, for the purpose of averting a peril insured against. Such expenses, where properly incurred, may be recovered as particular charges or as a general average loss, according to the circumstances under which they were incurred.

**66. General average loss**

(1) A general average loss is a loss caused by or directly consequential on a general average act. It includes a general average expenditure as well as a general average sacrifice.

(2) There is a general average act where any extraordinary sacrifice or expenditure is voluntarily and reasonably made or incurred in time of peril for the purpose of preserving the property imperilled in the common adventure.

(3) Where there is a general average loss, the party on whom it falls is entitled, subject to the conditions imposed by maritime law, to a rateable contribution from the other parties interested, and such contribution is called a general average contribution.

(4) Subject to any express provision in the policy, where the assured has incurred a general average expenditure, he may recover from the insurer in respect of the proportion of the loss which falls upon him; and, in the case of a general average sacrifice, he may recover from the insurer in respect of the whole loss without having enforced his right of contribution from the other parties liable to contribute.

(5) Subject to any express provision in the policy, where the assured has paid, or is liable to pay, a general average contribution in respect of the subject insured, he may recover therefor from the insurer.

(6) In the absence of express stipulation, the insurer is not liable for any general average loss or contribution where the loss was not incurred for the purpose of avoiding , or in connection with the avoidance of, a peril insured against.

(7) Where ship, freight, and cargo, or any two of those interests, are owned by the same assured, the liability of the insurer in respect of general average

losses or contributions is to be determined as if those subjects were owned by different persons.

## MEASURE OF INDEMNITY

### 67. Extent of liability of insurer for loss

(1) The sum which the assured can recover in respect of a loss on a policy by which he is insured, in the case of an unvalued policy to the full extent of the insurable value, or, in the case of a valued policy to the full extent of the value fixed by the policy is called the measure of indemnity.

(2) Where there is a loss recoverable under the policy, the insurer, or each insurer if there be more than one, is liable for such proportion of the measure of indemnity as the amount of his subscription bears to the value fixed by the policy in the case of a valued policy, or to the insurable value in the case of an unvalued policy.

### 68. Total loss

Subject to the provisions of this Act and to any express provision in the policy, where there is a total loss of the subject-matter insured,—

(1) If the policy be a valued policy, the measure of indemnity is the sum fixed by the policy:

(2) If the policy be an unvalued policy, the measure of indemnity is the insurable value of the subject-matter insured.

### 69. Partial loss of ship

Where a ship is damaged, but is not totally lost, the measure of indemnity, subject to any express provision in the policy, is as follows:-

(1) Where the ship has been repaired, the assured is entitled to the reasonable cost of the repairs, less the customary deductions, but not exceeding the sum insured in respect of any one casualty:

(2) Where the ship has been only partially repaired, the assured is entitled to the reasonable cost of such repairs, computed as above, and also to be indemnified for the reasonable depreciation, if any, arising from the unrepaired damage, provided that the aggregate amount shall not exceed the cost of repairing the whole damage, computed as above:

(3) Where the ship has not been repaired, and has not been sold in her damaged state during the risk, the assured is entitled to be indemnified for the reasonable depreciation arising from the unrepaired damage, but not exceeding the reasonable cost of repairing such damage, computed as above.

### 70. Partial loss of freight

Subject to any express provision in the policy, where there is a partial loss of freight, the measure of indemnity is such proportion of the sum fixed by the policy in the case of a valued policy, or of the insurable value in the case of an unvalued policy, as the proportion of freight lost by the assured bears to the whole freight at the risk of the assured under the policy.

### 71. Partial loss of goods, merchandise, &c.

Where there is a partial loss of goods, merchandise or other moveables, the measure of indemnity, subject to any express provision in the policy, is as follows:-

(1) Where part of the goods, merchandise or other moveables insured by a valued policy is totally lost, the measure of indemnity is such proportion of the sum fixed by the policy as the insurable value of the part lost bears to the insurable value of the whole, ascertained as in the case of an unvalued policy:

(2) Where part of the goods, merchandise, or other moveables insured by an unvalued policy is totally lost, the measure of indemnity is the insurable value of the part lost, ascertained as in case of total loss:

(3) Where the whole or any part of the goods or merchandise insured has been delivered damaged at its destination, the measure of indemnity is such proportion of the sum fixed by the policy in the case of a valued policy, or of the insurable value in the case of an unvalued policy, as the difference between the gross sound and damaged valued at the place of arrival bears to the gross sound value:

(4) 'Gross value' means the wholesale price, or, if there be no such price, the estimated value, with, in either case, freight, landing charges, and duty paid beforehand; provided that, in the case of goods or merchandise customarily sold in bond, the bonded price is deemed to be the gross value. 'Gross proceeds' means the actual price obtained at a sale where all charges on sale are paid by the sellers.

### 72. Apportionment of valuation

(1) Where different species of property are insured under a single valuation, the valuation must be apportioned over the different species in proportion to their respective insurable values, as in the case of an unvalued policy. The insured value of any part of a species is such proportion of the total insured value of the same as the insurable value of the part bears to the insurable value of the whole, ascertained in both cases as provided by this Act.

(2) Where a valuation has to be apportioned, and particulars of the prime cost of each separate species, quality, or description of goods cannot be ascertained, the division of the valuation may be made over the net arrived sound values of the different species, qualities, or descriptions of goods.

### 73. General average contributions and salvage charges

(1) Subject to any express provision in the policy, where the assured has paid, or is liable for, any general average contribution, the measure of indemnity is the full amount of such contribution, if the subject-matter liable to contribution is insured for its full contributory value, or if only part of it be insured, the indemnity payable by the insurer must be reduced in proportion to the under insurance, and where there has been a particular average loss which constitutes a deduction from the contributory value, and for which the insurer is liable, that amount must be deducted from the insured value in order to ascertain what the insurer is liable to contribute.

(2) Where the insurer is liable for salvage charges the extent of his liability must be determined on the like principle.

### 74. Liabilities to third parties

Where the assured has effected an insurance in express terms against any liability to a third party, the measure of indemnity, subject to any express provision in the policy, is the amount paid or payable by him to such third party in respect of such liability.

### 75. General provisions as to measure of indemnity

(1) Where there has been a loss in respect of any subject-matter not expressly provided for in the foregoing provisions of this Act, the measure of indemnity shall be ascertained, as nearly as may be, in accordance with those provisions, in so far as applicable to the particular case.

(2) Nothing in the provisions of this Act relating to the measure of indemnity shall affect the rules relating to double insurance, or prohibit the insurer from disproving interest wholly or in part, or from showing that at the time of the loss the whole or any part of the subject-matter insured was not at risk under the policy.

### 76. Particular average warranties

(1) Where the subject-matter insured is warranted free from particular average, the assured cannot recover for a loss of part, other than a loss incurred by a general average sacrifice, unless the contract contained in the policy be apportionable; but, if the contract be apportionable, the assured may recover for a total loss of any apportionable part.

(2) Where the subject-matter insured is warranted free from particular average, either wholly or under a certain percentage, the insurer is nevertheless liable for salvage charges, and for particular charges and other expenses properly incurred pursuant to the provisions of the suing and labouring clause in order to avert a loss insured against.

(3) Unless the policy otherwise provides, where the subject-matter insured is warranted free from particular average under a specified percentage, a general

average loss cannot be added to a particular average loss to make up the specified percentage.

(4) For the purpose of ascertaining whether the specified percentage has been reached, regard shall be had only to the actual loss suffered by the subject-matter insured. Particular charges and the expenses of and incidental to ascertaining and proving the loss must be excluded.

**77. Successive losses**

(1) Unless the policy otherwise provides, and subject to the provisions of this Act, the insurer is liable for successive losses, even though the total amount of such losses may exceed the sum insured.

(2) Where, under the same policy, a partial loss, which has not been repaired or otherwise made good, is followed by a total loss, the assured can only recover in respect of the total loss: Provided that nothing in this section shall affect the liability of the insurer under the suing and labouring clause.

**78. Suing and labouring clause**

(1) Where the policy contains a suing and labouring clause, the engagement thereby entered into is deemed to be supplementary to the contract of insurance, and the assured may recover from the insurer any expenses properly incurred pursuant to the clause, notwithstanding that the insurer may have paid for a total loss, or that the subject-matter may have been warranted free from particular average, either wholly or under a certain percentage.

(2) General average losses and contributions and salvage charges, as defined by this Act, are not recoverable under the suing and labouring clause.

(3) Expenses incurred for the purpose of averting or diminishing any loss not covered by the policy are not recoverable under the suing and labouring clause.

(4) It is the duty of the assured and his agents, in all cases, to take such measures as may be reasonable for the purpose of averting or minimising a loss.

RIGHTS OF INSURER ON PAYMENT

**79. Right of subrogation**

(1) Where the insurer pays for a total loss, either of the whole, or in the case of goods of any apportionable part, of the subject-matter insured, he thereupon becomes entitled to take over the interest of the assured in whatever may remain of the subject-matter so paid for, and he is thereby subrogated to all the rights and remedies of the assured in and in respect of that subject-matter as from the time of the casualty causing the loss.

(2) Subject to the foregoing provisions, where the insurer pays for a partial loss, he acquires no title to the subject-matter insured, or such part of it as may remain, but he is thereupon subrogated to all rights and remedies of the assured

in and in respect of the subject-matter insured as from the time of the casualty causing the loss, in so far as the assured has been indemnified, according to this Act, by such payment for the loss.

**80. Right of contribution**

(1) Where the assured is over-insured by double insurance, each insurer is bound, as between himself and the other insurers, to contribute rateably to the loss in proportion to the amount for which he is liable under his contract.

(2) If any insurer pays more than his proportion of the loss, he is entitled to maintain an action for contribution against the other insurers, and is entitled to the like remedies as a surety who has paid more than his proportion of the debt.

**81. Effect of under insurance**

Where the assured is insured for an amount less than the insurable value or, in the case of a valued policy, for an amount less than the policy valuation, he is deemed to be his own insurer in respect of the uninsured balance.

RETURN OF PREMIUM

**82. Enforcement of return**

Where the premium or a proportionate part thereof is, by this Act, declared to be returnable,—

(a) If already paid, it may be recovered by the assured from the insurer; and

(b) If unpaid, it may be retained by the assured or his agent.

**83. Return by agreement**

Where the policy contains a stipulation for the return of the premium, or a proportionate part thereof, on the happening of a certain event, and that event happens, the premium, or, as the case may be, the proportionate part thereof, is thereupon returnable to the assured.

**84. Return for failure of consideration**

(1) Where the consideration for the payment of the premium totally fails, and there has been no fraud or illegality on the part of the assured or his agents, the premium is thereupon returnable to the assured.

(2) Where the consideration for the payment of the premium is apportionable and there is a total failure of any apportionable part of the consideration, a proportionate part of the premium is, under the like conditions, thereupon returnable to the assured.

(3) In particular—

(a) Where the policy is void, or is avoided by the insurer as from the commencement of the risk, the premium is returnable, provided that there has been no fraud or illegality on the part of the assured; but if the risk is not apportionable, and has once attached, the premium is not returnable:

(b) Where the subject-matter insured, or part thereof, has never been imperilled, the premium, or, as the case may be, a proportionate part thereof, is returnable:
Provided that where the subject-matter has been insured 'lost or not lost' and has arrived in safety at the time when the contract is concluded, the premium is returnable unless, at such time, the insurer knew of the safe arrival.

(c) Where the assured has no insurable interest throughout the currency of the risk, the premium is returnable, provided that this rule does not apply to a policy effected by way of gaming or wagering;

(d) Where the assured has a defeasible interest which is terminated during the currency of the risk, the premium is not returnable;

(e) Where the assured has over-insured under an unvalued policy, a proportionate part of the several premiums is returnable;

(f) Subject to the foregoing provisions, where the assured has over-insured by double insurance, a proportionate part of the several premiums is returnable:
Provided that, if the policies are effected at different times, and any earlier policy has at any time borne the entire risk, or if a claim has been paid on the policy in respect of the full sum insured thereby, no premium is returnable in respect of that policy, and when the double insurance is effected knowingly by the assured no premium is returnable.

## MUTUAL INSURANCE

### 85. Modification of Act in case of mutual insurance

(1) Where two or more persons mutually agree to insure each other against marine losses there is said to be a mutual insurance.

(2) The provisions of this Act relating to the premium do not apply to mutual insurance, but a guarantee, or such other arrangement as may be agreed upon, may be substituted for the premium.

(3) The provisions of this Act, in so far as they may be modified by the agreement of the parties, may in the case of mutual insurance be modified by the terms of the policies issued by the association, or by the rules and regulations of the association.

(4) Subject to the exceptions mentioned in this section, the provisions of this Act apply to a mutual insurance.

## SUPPLEMENTAL

### 86. Ratification by assured

Where a contract of marine insurance is in good faith effected by one person on behalf of another, the person on whose behalf it is effected may ratify the contract even after he is aware of a loss.

### 87. Implied obligations varied by agreement or usage

(1) Where any right, duty, or liability would arise under a contract of marine insurance by implication of law, it may be negatived or varied by express agreement, or by usage, if the usage be such as to bind both parties to the contract.

(2) The provisions of this section extend to any right, duty, or liability declared by this Act which may be lawfully modified by agreement.

### 88. Reasonable time, &c. a question of fact

Where by this Act any reference is made to reasonable time, reasonable premium, or reasonable diligence, the question what is reasonable is a question of fact.

### 89. Slip as evidence

Where there is a duly stamped policy, reference may be made, as heretofore, to the slip or covering note, in any legal proceeding.

### 90. Interpretation of terms

In this Act, unless the context or subject-matter otherwise requires,-

'Action' includes counter-claim and set off:

'Freight' includes the profit derivable by a shipowner from the employment of his ship to carry his own goods or moveables, as well as freight payable by a third party, but does not include passage money:

'Moveables' means any moveable tangible property, other than the ship, and includes money, valuable securities, and other documents:

'Policy' means a marine policy.

### 91.-94. [omitted].

# SCHEDULES

## FIRST SCHEDULE

### FORM OF POLICY

Be it known that as well in own name as for and in the name and names of all and every other person or persons to whom the same doth, may, or shall appertain, in part or in all doth make assurance and cause and them, and every of them, to be insured lost or not lost, at and from

Upon any kind of goods and merchandises, and also upon the body, tackle, apparel, ordnance, munition, artillery, boat, and other furniture, of and in the good ship or vessel called the whereof is master under God, for this present voyage, or whosoever else shall go for master in the said ship, or by whatsoever other name or names the said ship, or the master thereof, is or shall be named or called; beginning the adventure upon the said goods and merchandised from the loading thereof aboard the said ship.

upon the said ship, &c.

and so shall continue and endure, during her abode there, upon the said ship, &c. And further, until the said ship, with all her ordnance, tackle, apparel, &c., and goods and merchandises whatsoever shall be arrived at

upon the said ship, &c. until she hath moored at anchor twenty-four hours in good safety; and upon the goods and merchandises, until the same be there discharged and safely landed. And it shall be lawful for the said ship, &c., in this voyage, to proceed and sail to and touch and stay at any ports or places whatsoever

without prejudice to this insurance. The said ship, &c., goods and merchandises, &c., for so much as concerns the assured by agreement between the assured and assurers in this policy, are and shall be valued at

Touching the adventures and perils which we the assurers are contented to bear and do take upon us in this voyage: they are of the seas, men of war, fire, enemies, pirates, rovers, thieves, jettisons, letters of mart and countermart, surprisals, takings at sea, arrests, restraints, and detainments of all kings, princes, and people, of what nation, condition, or quality soever, barratry of the master and mariners, and of all other perils, losses, and misfortunes, that have or shall come to the hurt, detriment, or damage of the said goods and merchandises, and ship, &c., or any part thereof. And in case of any loss or misfortune it shall be lawful to the assured, their factors, servants and assigns, to sue, labour, and travel for, in and about the defence, safeguards, and recovery of the said goods and merchandises, and ship, &c., or any part thereof, without prejudice to this insurance; to the charges whereof we, the assurers, will contribute each one according to the rate and quantity of his sum herein assured. And it is especially declared and agreed that no acts of the insurer or insured in recovering, saving, or preserving the property insured shall be considered as a waiver, or acceptance of abandonment. And it is agreed by us, the insurers, that this writing or policy of assurance shall be of as much force and effect as the surest writing or policy of assurance heretofore made in Lombard Street, or in the Royal Exchange, or elsewhere in London. And so we, the assurers, are contented, and do hereby promise and bind ourselves, each one for his own part, our heirs, executors, and goods to the assured, their executors, administrators, and assigns, for the true performance of the premises, confessing ourselves paid the consideration due unto us for this assurance by the assured, at and after the rate of

In Witness whereof we, the assurers, have subscribed our names and sums assured in London.

N.B.—Corn, fish, salt, fruit, flour, and seed are warranted free from average, unless general, or the ship be stranded-sugar, tobacco, hemp, flax, hides and skins are warranted free from average, under five pounds per cent., and all other goods, also the ship and freight, are warranted free from average, under three pounds per cent. unless general, or the ship be stranded.

## RULES FOR CONSTRUCTION OF POLICY

*The following are the rules referred to by this Act for the construction of a policy in the above or other like form, where the context does not otherwise require:—*

1. Where the subject-matter is insured 'lost or not lost', and the loss has occurred before the contract is concluded, the risk attaches unless, at such time the assured was aware of the loss, and the insurer was not.

2. Where the subject-matter is insured 'from' a particular place, the risk does not attach until the ship starts on the voyage insured.

3.—

(a) Where a ship is insured 'at and from' a particular place, and she is at that place in good safety when the contract is concluded, the risk attaches immediately.

(b) If she be not at that place when the contract is concluded, the risk attaches as soon as she arrives there in good safety, and, unless the policy otherwise provides, it is immaterial that she is covered by another policy for a specified time after arrival.

(c) Where chartered freight is insured 'at and from' a particular place, and the ship is at that place in good safety when the contract is concluded the risk attaches immediately. If she be not there when the contract is concluded, the risk attaches as soon as she arrives there in good safety.

(d) Where freight, other than chartered freight, is payable without special conditions and is insured 'at and from' a particular place, the risk attaches pro rata as the goods or merchandise are shipped; provided that if there be cargo in readiness which belongs to the shipowner, or which some other person has contracted with him to ship, the risk attaches as soon as the ship is ready to receive such cargo.

4. Where goods or other moveables are insured 'from the loading thereof,' the risk does not attach until such goods or moveables are actually on board, and the insurer is not liable for them while in transit from the shore to the ship.

5. Where the risk on goods or other moveables continues until they are 'safely landed,' they must be landed in the customary manner and within a reasonable time after arrival at the port of discharge, and if they are not so landed the risk ceases.

6. In the absence of any further licence or usage, the liberty to touch and stay 'at any port or place whatsoever' does not authorise the ship to depart from the course of her voyage from the port of departure to the port of destination.

7. The term 'perils of the seas' refers only to fortuitous accidents or casualties of the seas. It does not include the ordinary action of the winds and waves.

8. The term 'pirates' includes passengers who mutiny and rioters who attack the ship from the shore.

9. The term 'thieves' does not cover clandestine theft or a theft committed by any one of the ship's company, whether crew or passengers.

10. The term 'arrests, &c., of kings, princes, and people' refers to a political or executive acts, and does not include a loss caused by riot or by ordinary judicial process.

11. The term 'barratry' includes every wrongful act wilfully committed by the master or crew to the prejudice of the owner, or, as the case may be, the charterer.

12. The term 'all other perils' includes only perils similar in kind to the perils specifically mentioned in the policy.

13. The term 'average unless general' means a partial loss of subject-matter insured other than a general average loss, and does not include 'particular charges'.

14. Where the ship has stranded, the insurer is liable for the excepted losses, although the loss is not attributable to the stranding, provided that when the stranding takes place the risk has attached and, if the policy be on goods, that the damaged goods are on board.

15. The term 'ship' includes the hull, materials and outfit, stores and provisions for the officers and crew, and, in the case of vessels engaged in a special trade, the ordinary fittings requisite for the trade, and also, in the case of a steamship, the machinery, boilers, and coals and engine stores, if owned by the assured.

16. The term 'freight' includes the profit derivable by a shipowner from the employment of his ship to carry his own goods or moveables, as well as freight payable by a third party, but does not include passage money.

17. The term 'goods' means goods in the nature of merchandise, and does not include personal effects or provisions and stores for use on board.

In the absence of any usage to the contrary, deck cargo and living animals must be insured specifically, and not under the general denomination of goods.

[Note: by virtue of the Public Order Act 1986 the words 'rioters' in rule 8 and 'riot' in rule 10 shall be construed in accordance with section 1 of that Act.]

# ADMINISTRATION OF JUSTICE ACT 1920

## CHAPTER 81

### PART II

### RECIPROCAL ENFORCEMENT OF JUDGMENTS IN THE UNITED KINGDOM AND IN OTHER PARTS OF HIS MAJESTY'S DOMINIONS

**9. Enforcement in the United Kingdom of judgements obtained in superior courts in other British dominions**

(1) Where a judgment has been obtained in a superior court in any part of His Majesty's dominions outside the United Kingdom to which this Part of this Act extends, the judgment creditor may apply to the High Court in England or Northern Ireland or to the Court of Session in Scotland, at any time within twelve months after the date of the judgment, or such longer period as may be allowed by the court, to have the judgment registered in the court, and on any such application the court may, if in all the circumstances of the case they think it just and convenient that the judgment should be enforced in the United Kingdom, and subject to the provisions of this section, order the judgment to be registered accordingly.

(2) No judgment shall be ordered to be registered under this section if-
- (a) the original court acted without jurisdiction; or
- (b) the judgment debtor, being a person who was neither carrying on business nor ordinarily resident within the jurisdiction of the original court, did not voluntarily appear or otherwise submit or agree to submit to the jurisdiction of that court; or
- (c) the judgment debtor, being the defendant in the proceedings, was not duly served with the process of the original court and did not appear, notwithstanding that he was ordinarily resident or was carrying on business within the jurisdiction of that court or agreed to submit to the jurisdiction of that court; or
- (d) the judgment was obtained by fraud; or
- (e) the judgment debtor satisfies the registering court either that an appeal is pending, or that he is entitled and intends to appeal, against the judgment; or
- (f) the judgment was in respect of a cause of action which for reasons of public policy or for some other similar reason could not have been entertained by the registering court.

(3) Where a judgment is registered under this section-
- (a) the judgment shall, as from the date of registration, be of the same force and effect, and proceedings may be taken thereon, as if it had been a judgment originally obtained or entered up on the date of registration in the registering court;
- (b) the registering court shall have the same control and jurisdiction over the judgment as it has over similar judgments given by itself, but in so far only as relates to execution under this section;

(c) the reasonable costs of and incidental to the registration of the judgment (including the costs of obtaining a certified copy thereof from the original court and of the application for registration) shall be recoverable in like manner as if they were sums payable under the judgment.

(4) and (5) [omitted].

# FOREIGN JUDGMENTS (RECIPROCAL ENFORCEMENT) ACT 1933

## CHAPTER 13

### PART I

*Registration of Foreign Judgments*



### PART II

*Miscellaneous and General*



### PART I

**1. Power to extend Part I of Act to foreign countries giving reciprocal treatment**

(1) If, in the case of any foreign country, Her Majesty is satisfied that, in the event of the benefits conferred by this Part of this Act being extended to, or to any particular class of, judgments given in the courts of that country or in any particular class of those courts, substantial reciprocity of treatment will be assured as regards the enforcement in that country of similar judgments given in similar courts of the United Kingdom, She may order in Council direct-

- (a) that this Part of this Act shall extend to that country;
- (b) that such courts of that country as are specified in the Order shall be recognised courts of that country for the purposes of this Part of this Act; and
- (c) that judgments of any such recognised court, or such judgments of any class so specified, shall, if within subsection (2) of this section, be judgments to which this Part of this Act applies.

(2) Subject to subsection (2A) of this section, a judgment of a recognised court is within this subsection if it satisfies the following conditions, namely-

(a) it is either final and conclusive as between the judgment debtor and the judgment creditor or requires the former to make an interim payment to the latter; and

(b) there is payable under it a sum of money, not being a sum payable in respect of taxes or other charges of a like nature or in respect of a fine or other penalty; and

(c) it is given after the coming into force of the Order in Council which made that court a recognised court.

(2A) The following judgments of a recognised court are not within subsection (2) of this section—

(a) a judgment given by that court on appeal from a court which is not a recognised court;

(b) a judgment or other instrument which is regarded for the purposes of its enforcement as a judgment of that court but which was given or made in another country;

(c) a judgment given by that court in proceedings founded on a judgment of a court in another country and having as their object the enforcement of that judgment.

(3) For the purposes of this section, a judgment shall be deemed to be final and conclusive notwithstanding that an appeal may be pending against it, or that it may still be subject to appeal, in the courts of the country of the original court.

(4) and (5) [omitted].

**2. Application for, and effect of, registration of foreign judgement**

(1) A person, being a judgment creditor under a judgment to which this Part of this Act applies, may apply to the High Court at any time within six years after the date of the judgment, or, where there have been proceedings by way of appeal against the judgment, after the date of the last judgment given in those proceedings, to have the judgment registered in the High Court, and on any such application the court shall, subject to proof of the prescribed matters and to the other provisions of this Act, order the judgment to be registered:

Provided that a judgment shall not be registered if at the date of the application—

(a) it has been wholly satisfied; or

(b) it could not be enforced by execution in the country of the original court.

(2) Subject to the provisions of this Act with respect to the setting aside of registration-

(a) a registered judgment shall, for the purposes of execution, be of the same force and effect; and

(b) proceedings may be taken on a registered judgment; and

(c) the sum for which a judgment is registered shall carry interest; and

(d) the registering court shall have the same control over the execution of a registered judgment;

as if the judgment had been a judgment originally given in the registering court and entered on the date of registration:

Provided that execution shall not issue on the judgment so long as, under this Part of this Act and the Rules of Court made thereunder, it is competent for any party to made an application to have the registration of the judgment set aside, or, where such an application is made, until after the application has been finally determined.

(3) [Repealed].

(4) If at the date of the application for registration the judgment of the original court has been partly satisfied, the judgment shall not be registered in respect of the whole sum payable under the judgment of the original court, but only in respect of the balance remaining payable at that date.

(5) If, on an application for the registration of a judgment, it appears to the registering court that the judgment is in respect of different matters and that some, but not all, of the provisions of the judgment are such that if those provisions had been contained in separate judgments those judgments could properly have been registered, the judgment may be registered in respect of the provisions aforesaid but not in respect of any other provisions contained therein.

(6) [Omitted].

**3. [Omitted].**

**4. Cases in which registered judgments must, or may, be set aside**

(1) On an application in that behalf duly made by any party against whom a registered judgment may be enforced, the registration of the judgment-

(a) shall be set aside if the registering court is satisfied-

(i) that the judgment is not a judgment to which this Part of the Act applied or was registered in contravention of the foregoing provisions of this Act; or

(ii) that the courts of the country of the original court had no jurisdiction in the circumstances of the case; or

(iii) that the judgment debtor, being the defendant in the proceedings in the original court, did not (notwithstanding that process may have been duly served on him in accordance with the law of the country of the original court) receive notice of those proceedings in sufficient time to enable him to defend the proceedings and did not appear; or

(iv) that the judgment was obtained by fraud; or

(v) that the enforcement of the judgment would be contrary to public policy in the country of the registering court; or

(vi) that the rights under the judgment are not vested in the person by whom the application for registration was made;

(b) may be set aside if the registering court is satisfied that the matter in dispute in the proceedings in the original court had previously to the date of the judgment in the original court been the subject of a final and conclusive judgment by a court having jurisdiction in the matter.

(2) For the purposes of this section the courts of the country of the original court shall, subject to the provisions of subsection (3) of this section, be deemed to have had jurisdiction-

(a) in the case of a judgment given in an action in personam-

(i) if the judgment debtor, being a defendant in the original court, submitted to the jurisdiction of that court by voluntarily appearing in the proceedings; or

(ii) if the judgment debtor was plaintiff in, or counter-claimed in, the proceedings in the original court; or

(iii) if the judgment debtor, being a defendant in the original court, had before the commencement of the proceedings agreed, in respect of the subject matter of the proceedings, to submit to the jurisdiction of that court or of the courts of the country of that court; or

(iv) if the judgment debtor, being a defendant in the original court, was at the time when the proceedings were instituted resident in, or being a body corporate had its principal place of business in, the country of that court; or

(v) if the judgment debtor, being a defendant in the original court, had an office or place of business in the country of that court and the proceedings in that court were in respect of a transaction effected through or at that office or place;

(b) in the case of a judgment given in an action of which the subject matter was immovable property or in an action in rem of which the subject matter was movable property, if the property in question was at the time of the proceedings in the original court situate in the country of that court;

(c) in the case of a judgment given in an action other than any such action as is mentioned in paragraph (a) or paragraph (b) of this subsection, if the jurisdiction of the original court is recognised by the law of the registering court.

(3) Notwithstanding anything in subsection (2) of this section, the courts of the country of the original court shall not be deemed to have had jurisdiction—

(a) if the subject matter of the proceedings was immovable property outside the country of the original court; or

(b) [repealed].

(c) if the judgment debtor, being a defendant in the original proceedings, was a person who under the rules of public international law was entitled to immunity from the jurisdiction of the courts of the country of the original court and did not submit to the jurisdiction of that court.

**5. Powers of registering court on application to set aside registration**

(1) If, on an application to set aside the registration of a judgment, the applicant satisfies the registering court either that an appeal is pending, or that he is entitled and intends to appeal, against the judgment, the court, if it thinks fit, may, on such terms as it may think just, either set aside the registration or adjourn the application to set aside the registration until after the expiration of such period as appears to the court to be reasonably sufficient to enable the applicant to take the necessary steps to have the appeal disposed of by the competent tribunal.

(2) Where the registration of a judgment is set aside under the last foregoing subsection, or solely for the reason that the judgment was not at the date of the application for registration enforceable by execution in the country of the original court, the setting aside of the registration shall not prejudice a further application to register the judgment when the appeal has been disposed of or if and when the judgment becomes enforceable by execution in that country, as the case may be.

(3) Where the registration of a judgment is set aside solely for the reason that the judgment, notwithstanding that it had at the date of application for registration been partly satisfied, was registered for the whole sum payable thereunder, the registering court shall, on the application of the judgment creditor, order judgment to be registered for the balance remaining payable at that date.

**6. Foreign judgements which can be registrered not to be enforceable otherwise**

No proceedings for the recovery of a sum payable under a foreign judgment, being a judgment to which the Part of this Act applies, other than proceedings by way of registration of the judgment, shall be entertained by any court in the United Kingdom.

**7. [Omitted].**

PART II

*Miscellaneous and General*

**8. General effect of certain foreign judgements**

(1) Subject to the provisions of this section, a judgment to which Part I of this Act applies or would have applied if a sum of money had been payable thereunder, whether it can be registered or not, and whether, if it can be registered, it is registered or not, shall be recognised in any court in the United Kingdom as conclusive between the parties thereto in all proceedings founded on the same cause of action and may be relied on by way of defence or counter-claim in any such proceedings.

(2) This section shall not apply in the case of any judgment-
- (a) where the judgment has been registered and the registration thereof has been set aside on some ground other than-
  - (i) that a sum of money was not payable under the judgment; or
  - (ii) that the judgment had been wholly or partly satisfied; or
  - (iii) that at the date of the application the judgment could not be enforced by execution in the country of the original court; or
- (b) where the judgment has not been registered, it is shown (whether it could have been registered or not) that if it had been registered the registration thereof would have been set aside on an application for that purpose on some ground other than one of the grounds specified in paragraph (a) of this subsection.

(3) Nothing in this section shall be taken to prevent any court in the United Kingdom recognising any judgment as conclusive of any matter of law or fact decided therein if that judgment would have been so recognised before the passing of this Act.

**9.-14. [Omitted].**

# LAW REFORM (FRUSTRATED CONTRACTS) ACT 1943

## CHAPTER 40

### 1. Adjustment of rights and liabilities of parties to frustrated contracts

(1) Where a contract governed by English law has become impossible of performance or been otherwise frustrated, and the parties thereto have for that reason been discharged from the further performance of the contract, the following provisions of this section shall, subject to the provisions of section two of this Act, have effect in relation thereto.

(2) All sums paid or payable to any party in pursuance of the contract before the time when the parties were so discharged (in this Act referred to as 'the time of discharge') shall, in the case of sums so paid, be recoverable from him as money received by him for the use of the party by whom the sums were paid, and, in the case of sums so payable, cease to be so payable:

Provided that, if the party to whom the sums were so paid or payable incurred expenses before the time of discharge in, or for the purpose of, the performance of the contract, the court may, if it considers it just to do so having regard to all the circumstances of the case, allow him to retain or, as the case may be, recover the whole or any part of the sums so paid or payable, not being an amount in excess of the expenses so incurred.

(3) Where any party to the contract has, by reason of anything done by any other party thereto in, or for the purpose of, the performance of the contract, obtained a valuable benefit (other than a payment of money to which the last foregoing subsection applies) before the time of discharge, there shall be recoverable from him by the said other party such sum (if any), not exceeding the value of the said benefit to the party obtaining it, as the court considers just, having regard to all the circumstances of the case and, in particular,—

(a) the amount of any expenses incurred before the time of discharge by the benefited party in, or for the purpose of, the performance of the contract, including any sums paid or payable by him to any other party in pursuance of the contract and retained or recoverable by that party under the last foregoing subsection, and

(b) the effect, in relation to the said benefit, of the circumstances giving rise to the frustration of the contract.

(4) In estimating, for the purposes of the foregoing provisions of this section, the amount of any expenses incurred by any party to the contract, the court may, without prejudice to the generality of the said provisions, include such sum as appears to be reasonable in respect of overhead expenses and in respect of any work or services performed personally by the said party.

(5) In considering whether any sum ought to be recovered or retained under the foregoing provisions of this section by any party to the contract, the court shall not take into account any sums which have, by reason of the circumstances giving rise to the frustration of the contract, become payable to that party under

any contract of insurance unless there was an obligation to insure imposed by an express term of the frustrated contract or by or under any enactment.

(6) Where any person has assumed obligations under the contract in consideration of the conferring of a benefit by any other party to the contract upon any other person, whether a party to the contract or not, the court may, if in all the circumstances of the case it considers it just to do so, treat for the purposes of subsection (3) of this section any benefit so conferred as a benefit obtained by the person who has assumed the obligations as aforesaid.

**2. Provision as in application of this Act**

(1) This Act shall apply to contracts, whether made before or after the commencement of this Act, as respects which the time of discharge is on or after the first day of July, nineteen hundred and forty-three, but not to contracts as respect which the time of discharge is before the said date.

(2) This Act shall apply to contracts to which the Crown is a party in like manner as to contracts between subject.

(3) Where any contract to which this Act applies contains any provisions which, upon the true construction of the contract, is intended to have effect in the event of circumstances arising which operate, or would but for the said provision operate, to frustrate the contract, or is intended to have effect whether such circumstances arise or not, the court shall give effect to the said provision and shall only give effect to the forgoing section of this Act to such extent, if any, as appears to the court to be consistent with the said provision.

(4) Where it appears to the court that a part of any contract to which this Act applies can properly be severed from the remainder of the contract, being a part wholly performed before the time of discharge, or so performed except for the payment in respect of that part of the contract of sums which are or can be ascertained under the contract, the court shall treat that part of the contract as if it were a separate contract and had not been frustrated and shall treat the foregoing section of this Act as only applicable to the remainder of that contract.

(5) This Act shall not apply-
- (a) to any charterparty, except a time charterparty or a charterparty by way of demise, or to any contract (other than a charterparty) for the carriage of goods by sea; or
- (b) to any contract of insurance, save as is provided by subsection (5) of the foregoing section; or
- (c) to any contract to which section seven of the Sale of Goods Act 1979 (which avoids contracts for the sale of specific goods which perish before the risk has passed to the buyer) applies, or to any other contract for the sale, or for the sale and delivery, of specific goods, where the contract is frustrated by reason of the fact that the goods have perished.

**3. [Omitted].**

# ARBITRATION ACT 1950

## CHAPTER 27

### PART I

### GENERAL PROVISIONS AS TO ARBITRATION

*Effect of Arbitration Agreements, &c.*



*Arbitrators and Umpires*



*Provisions as to Awards*



*Special Cases, Remission and Setting aside of Awards. &c.*



*Enforcement of Award*

## PART I

## GENERAL PROVISIONS AS TO ARBITRATION

### *Effect of Arbitration Agreements, &c.*

**1. Authority of arbitrators and umpires to be irrecovable.**

The authority of an arbitrator or umpire appointed by or by virtue of an arbitration agreement shall, unless a contrary intention is expressed in the agreement, be irrevocable except by leave of the High Court or a judge thereof.

**2. and 3. [Omitted].**

**4. Staying court proceedings where there is submission to arbitration**

(1) If any party to an arbitration agreement, or any person claiming through or under him commences any legal proceedings in any court against any other party to the agreement, or any person claiming through or under him, in respect of any matter agreed to be referred, any party to those legal proceedings may at

any time after appearance, and before delivering any pleadings or taking any other steps in the proceedings, apply to that court to stay the proceedings, and that court or a judge thereof, if satisfied that there is no sufficient reason why the matter should not be referred in accordance with the agreement, and that the applicant was, at the time when the proceedings were commenced, and still remains, ready and willing to do all things necessary to the proper conduct of the arbitration, may make an order staying the proceedings.

(2) [Repealed].

**5. Reference of interpleader issues to arbitration**

Where relief by way of interpleader is granted and it appears to the High Court that the claims in question are matters to which an arbitration agreement, to which the claimants are parties, applies, the High Court may direct the issue between the claimants to be determined in accordance with the agreement.

*Arbitrators and Umpires*

**6. When reference is to a single arbitrator**

Unless a contrary intention is expressed therein, every arbitration agreement shall, if no other mode of reference is provided, be deemed to include a provision that the reference shall be to a single arbitrator.

**7. Power of parties in certain cases to supply vacancy**

Where an arbitration agreement provides that the reference shall be to two arbitrators, one to be appointed by each party, then unless a contrary intention is expressed therein-

(a) if either of the appointed arbitrators refuses to act, or is incapable of acting, or dies, the party who appointed him may appoint a new arbitrator in his place;

(b) if, on such a reference, one party fails to appoint an arbitrator, either originally, or by way of substitution as aforesaid, for seven clear days after the other party, having appointed his arbitrator, has served the party making default with notice to make the appointment, the party who has appointed an arbitrator may appoint that arbitrator to act as sole arbitrator in the reference and his award shall be binding on both parties as if he had been appointed by consent:

Provided that the High Court or a judge thereof may set aside any appointment made in pursuance of this section.

**8. Umpires**

(1) Unless a contrary intention is expressed therein, every arbitration agreement shall, where the reference is to two arbitrators, be deemed to include a provision that the two arbitrators may appoint an umpire at any time after they are themselves appointed and shall do so forthwith is they cannot agree.

(2) Unless a contrary intention is expressed therein, every arbitration agreement shall, where such a provision is applicable to the reference, be deemed to include a provision that if the arbitrators have delivered to any party to the arbitration agreement, or to the umpire, a notice in writing stating that they cannot agree, the umpire may forthwith enter on the reference in lieu of the arbitrators.

(3) At any time after the appointment of an umpire, however appointed, the High Court may, on the application of any party to the reference and notwithstanding anything to the contrary in the arbitration agreement, order that the umpire shall enter upon the reference in lieu of the arbitrators and as if he were a sole arbitrator.

**9. Majority award of three arbitrators**

Unless the contrary intention is expressed in the arbitration agreement, in any case where there is a reference to three arbitrators, the award of any two of the arbitrators shall be binding.

**10. Power of court in certain cases to appoint an arbitrator or umpire**

In any of the following cases-

(a) where an arbitration agreement provides that the reference shall be to a single arbitrator, and all the parties do not, after differences have arisen, concur in the appointment of an arbitrator;

(b) if an appointed arbitrator refuses to act, or is incapable of acting, or dies, and the arbitration agreement does not show that it was intended that the vacancy should not be supplied and the parties do not supply the vacancy;

(c) where the parties or two arbitrators are required or are at liberty to appoint an umpire or third arbitrator and do not appoint him.

(d) where an appointed umpire or third arbitrator refuses to act, or is incapable of acting, or dies, and the arbitration agreement does not show that it was intended that the vacancy should not be supplied, and the parties or arbitrators do not supply the vacancy;

any party may serve the other parties or the arbitrators, as the case may be, with a written notice to appoint or, as the case may be, concur in appointing, an arbitrator, umpire or third arbitrator, and if the appointment is not made within seven clear days after the service of the notice, the High Court or a judge thereof may, on application by the party who gave the notice, appoint an arbitrator, umpire or third arbitrator who shall have the like powers to act in the reference and make an award as if he had been appointed by consent of all parties.

(2) In any case where—

(a) an arbitration agreement provides for the appointment of an arbitrator or umpire by a person who is neither one of the parties nor an existing arbitrator (whether the provision applies directly or in default of agreement by the parties or otherwise), and

(b) that person refuses to make the appointment or does not make it within the time specified in the agreement or, if no time is so specified, within a reasonable time, any party to the agreement may serve the person in question with a written notice to appoint an arbitrator or umpire and, if the appointment is not made within seven clear days after the service of the notice, the High Court or a judge thereof may, on the application of the party who gave the notice, appoint an arbitrator or umpire who shall have the like powers to act in the reference and make an award as if he had been appointed in accordance with the terms of the agreement.

(3) In any case where-

(a) an arbitration agreement provides that the reference shall be to three arbitrators, one to be appointed by each party and the third to be appointed by the two appointed by the parties or in some other manner specified in the agreement; and

(b) one of the parties ('the party in default') refuses to appoint an arbitrator or does not do so within the time specified in the agreement or, if no time is specified, within a reasonable time,

the other party to the agreement, having appointed his arbitrator, may serve the party in default with a written notice to appoint an arbitrator.

(3A) A notice under subsection (3) must indicate whether it is served for the purposes of subsection (3B) or for the purposes of subsection (3C).

(3B) Where a notice is served for the purposes of this subsection, then unless a contrary intention is expressed in the agreement, if the required appointment is not made within seven clear days after the service of the notice-

(a) the party who gave the notice may appoint his arbitrator to act as sole arbitrator in the reference; and

(b) his award shall be binding on both parties as if he had been appointed by consent.

(3C) Where a notice is served for the purposes of this subsection, then, if the required appointment is not made within seven clear days after the service of the notice, the High Court or a judge thereof may, on the application of the party who gave the notice, appoint an arbitrator on behalf of the party in default who shall have the like powers to act in the reference and make an award (and, if the case so required, the like duty in relation to the appointment of a third arbitrator) as if he had been appointed in accordance with the terms of the agreement.

(3D) The High Court or a judge thereof may set aside any appointment made by virtue of subsection (3B)

(4) Except in a case where the arbitration agreement shows that it was intended that the vacancy should not be supplied, paragraph (b) of each of subsections (2) and (3) shall be construed as extending to any such refusal or failure by a person as is there mentioned arising in connection with the replacement of an arbitrator who was appointed by that person (or, in default of being so appointed, was appointed under that subsection) but who refuses to act, or is incapable of acting or has died.

**11. Power of official referee to take arbitrations**

(1) An official referee may, if in all the circumstances he thinks fit, accept appointment as sole arbitrator, or as umpire, by or virtue of an arbitration agreement.

(2) An official referee shall not accept appointment as arbitrator or umpire unless the Lord Chief Justice has informed him that, having regard to the state of official referees' business, he can be made available to do so.

(3) The fees payable for the services of an official referee as arbitrator or umpire shall be taken in the High Court.

(4) Schedule 3 to the Administration of Justice Act 1970 (which modifies this Act in relation to arbitration by judges, in particular by substituting the Court of Appeal for the High Court in provisions whereby arbitrators and umpires, their proceedings and awards are subject to control and review by the court) shall have effect in relation to official referees appointed as arbitrators or umpires as it has effect in relation to judge-arbitrators and judge-umpires (within the meaning of that Schedule).

(5) Any jurisdiction which is exercisable by the High Court in relation to arbitrators and umpires otherwise than under this Act shall, in relation to an official referee appointed as arbitrator or umpire, be exercisable instead by the Court of Appeal.

(6) In this section 'official referee' means any person nominated under section 68(1)(a) of the Supreme Court Act 1981 to deal with official referees' business.

(7) [omitted]

**12. [omitted]**

*Provisions as to Awards*

**13. Time for making award**

(1) Subject to the provisions of subsection (2) of section twenty-two of this Act, and anything to the contrary in the arbitration agreement, an arbitrator or umpire shall have power to make an award at any time.

(2) The time, if any, limited for making an award, whether under this Act or otherwise, may from time to time be enlarged by order of the High Court or a judge thereof, whether that time has expired or not.

(3) The High Court may, on the application of any party to a reference, remove an arbitrator or umpire who fails to use all reasonable dispatch in entering on and proceeding with the reference and making an award, and an arbitrator or umpire who is removed by the High Court under this subsection shall not be entitled to receive any remuneration in respect of his services.

For the purposes of this subsection, the expression 'proceeding with a reference' includes, in a case where two arbitrators are unable to agree, giving notice of that fact to the parties and to the umpire.

**13A Want of prosecution**

(1) Unless a contrary intention is expressed in the arbitration agreement, the arbitrator or umpire shall have power to make an award dismissing any claim in a dispute referred to him if it appears to him that the conditions mentioned in subsection (2) are satisfied.

(2) The conditions are-
- (a) that there has been inordinate and inexcusable delay on the part of the claimant in pursuing the claim; and
- (b) that the delay-
  - (i) will give rise to a substantial risk that it is not possible to have a fair resolution of the issues in that claim; or
  - (ii) has caused, or is likely to cause or to have caused, serious prejudice to the respondent.

(3) - (5) [omitted].

**14. Interim awards**

Unless a contrary intention is expressed therein, every arbitration agreement shall, where such a provision is applicable to the reference, be deemed to contain a provision that the arbitrator or umpire may, if he thinks fit, make an interim award, and any reference in this Part of this Act to an award includes a reference to an interim award.

**15. Specific performance**

Unless a contrary intention is expressed therein, every arbitration agreement shall, where such a provision is applicable to the reference, be deemed to contain a provision that the arbitrator or umpire shall have the same power as the High Court to order specific performance of any contract other than a contract relating to land or any interest in land.

**16. Awards to be final**

Unless a contrary intention is expressed therein, every arbitration agreement shall, where such a provision is applicable to the reference, be deemed to contain a provision that the award to be made by the arbitrator or umpire shall be final and binding on the parties and the persons claiming under them respectively.

**17. Power to correct slips**

Unless a contrary intention is express in the arbitration agreement, the arbitrator or umpire shall have power to correct in an award any clerical mistake or error arising from any accidental slip or omission.

**18.-20. [Omitted] and 21. [Repealed]**

### 22. Power to remit award

(1) In all cases of reference to arbitration the High Court or a judge thereof may from time to time remit the matters referred, or any of them, to the reconsideration of the arbitrator or umpire.

(2) Where an award is remitted, the arbitrator or umpire shall, unless the order otherwise directs, make his award within three months after the date of the order.

### 23. Removal of arbitrator and setting aside of award

(1) Where an arbitrator or umpire has misconducted himself or the proceedings, the High Court may remove him.

(2) Where an arbitrator or umpire has misconducted himself or the proceedings, or an arbitration or award has been improperly procured, the High Court may set the award aside.

(3) Where an application is made to set aside an award, the High Court may order that any money made payable by the award shall be brought into court or otherwise secured pending the determination of the application.

### 24. Power of court to give relief

(1) Where an agreement between any parties provides that disputes which may arise in the future between them shall be referred to an arbitrator named or designated in the agreement, and after a dispute has arisen any party applies, on the ground that the arbitrator so named or designated is not or may not be impartial, for leave to revoke the authority of the arbitrator or for an injunction to restrain any other party or the arbitrator from proceeding with the arbitration, it shall not be a ground for refusing the application that the said party at the time when he made the agreement knew, or ought to have known, that the arbitrator, by reason of his relation towards any other party to the agreement or of his connection with the subject referred, might not be capable of impartiality.

(2) Where an agreement between any parties provides that disputes which may arise in the future between them shall be referred to arbitration, and a dispute which so arises involves the question whether any such party has been guilty of fraud, the High Court shall, so far as may be necessary to enable that question to be determined by the High Court, have power to order that the agreement shall cease to have effect and power to give leave to revoke the authority of any arbitrator or umpire appointed by or by virtue of the agreement.

(3) In any case where by virtue of this section the High Court has power to order that an arbitration agreement shall cease to have effect or to give leave to revoke the authority of an arbitrator or umpire, the High Court may refuse to stay any action brought in breach of the agreement.

**25. Power of court where arbitrator is removed or authority of arbitrator is revoked**

(1) Where an arbitrator (not being a sole arbitrator), or two or more arbitrators (not being all the arbitrators) or an umpire who has not entered on the reference is or are removed by the High Court or the Court of Appeal, the High Court or the Court of Appeal as the case may be may, on the application of any party to the arbitration agreement, appoint a person or persons to act as arbitrator or arbitrators or umpire in place of the person or persons so removed.

(2) Where the authority of an arbitrator or arbitrators or umpire is revoked by leave of the High Court or the Court of Appeal, or a sole arbitrator or all the arbitrators or an umpire who has entered on the reference is or are removed by the High Court or the Court of Appeal, the High Court or the Court of Appeal, as the case may be may, on the application of any party to the arbitration agreement, either—

(a) appoint a person to act as sole arbitrator in place of the person or persons removed; or

(b) order that the arbitration agreement shall cease to have effect with respect to the dispute referred.

(3) A person appointed under this section by the High Court or the Court of Appeal as an arbitrator or umpire shall have the like power to act in the reference and to make an award as if he had been appointed in accordance with the terms of the arbitration agreement.

(4) Where it is provided (whether by means of a provision in the arbitration agreement or otherwise) that an award under an arbitration agreement shall be a condition precedent to the bringing of an action with respect to any matter to which the agreement applies, the High Court or the Court of Appeal, if it orders (whether under this section or under any other enactment) that the agreement shall cease to have effects as regards any particular dispute, may further order that the provision making an award a condition precedent to the bringing of an action shall also cease to have effect as regards that dispute.

*Enforcement of Award*

**26. Enforcement of award**

(1) An award on an arbitration agreement may, by leave of the High Court or a judge thereof, be enforced in the same manner as a judgment or order to the same effect, and where leave is so given, judgment may be entered in terms of the award.

(2) If—

(a) the amount sought to be recovered does not exceed the county court limit, and

(b) a county court so orders.

it shall be recoverable (by execution issued from the county court or otherwise) as if payable under an order of that court and shall not be enforceable under subsection (1) above.

(3) An application to the High Court under this section shall preclude an application to a county court and an application to a county court under this section shall preclude an application to the High Court.

(4) In subsection (2)(a) above 'the county court limit' means the amount which for the time being is the county court limit for the purposes of section 16 of the County Courts Act 1984 (money recoverable by statute).

*Miscellaneous*

**27. Power of court to extend time for commencing arbitration proceedings**

Where the terms of an agreement to refer future disputes to arbitration provide that any claims to which the agreement applies shall be barred unless notice to appoint an arbitrator is given or an arbitrator is appointed or some other step to commence arbitration proceedings is taken within a time fixed by the agreement, and a dispute arises to which the agreement applies, the High Court, if it is of opinion that in the circumstances of the case undue hardship would otherwise be caused, and notwithstanding that the time so fixed has expired, may, on such terms, if any, as the justice of the case may require, but without prejudice to the provisions of any enactment limiting the time for the commencement of arbitration proceedings, extend the time for such period as it thinks proper.

**28.-31. [Omitted].**

**32. Meaning of 'arbitration agreement'**

In this Part of this Act, unless the context otherwise requires, the expression 'arbitration agreement' means a written agreement to submit present or future differences to arbitration, whether an arbitrator is named therein or not.

**33. and 34. [omitted].**

## PART II

## ENFORCEMENT OF CERTAIN FOREIGN AWARDS

**35. Awards to which Part II applies**

(1) This Part of this Act applies to any award made after the twenty-eighth day of July, nineteen hundred and twenty-four-

(a) in pursuance of an agreement for arbitration to which the protocol set out in the First Schedule to this Act applies; and

(b) between persons of whom one is subject to the jurisdiction of some one of such Powers as His Majesty, being satisfied that reciprocal provisions have been made, may by Order in Council declare to be parties to the convention set out in the Second Schedule to this Act, and of whom the other is subject to the jurisdiction of some other of the Powers aforesaid; and

(c) in one such territories as His Majesty, being satisfied that reciprocal provisions have been made; may by Order in Council declare to be territories to which the said convention applies;

and an award to which this Part of this Act applies is in this Part of this Act referred to as 'a foreign award'.

(2) and (3) [omitted].

**36. Effect of foreign awards**

(1) A foreign award shall, subject to the provisions of this Part of this Act, be enforceable in England either by action or in the same manner as the award of an arbitrator is enforceable by virtue of section twenty-six of this Act.

(2) Any foreign award which would be enforceable under this Part of this Act shall be treated as binding for all purposes on the persons as between whom it was made, and may accordingly be relied on by any of those persons by way of defence, set off or otherwise in any legal proceedings in England, and any references in this Part of this Act to enforcing a foreign award shall be construed as including references to relying on an award.

**37. Conditions for enforcement of foreign awards**

(1) In order that a foreign award may be enforceable under this Part of this Act it must have—

(a) been made in pursuance of an agreement for arbitration which was valid under the law by which it was governed;

(b) been made by the tribunal provided for in the agreement or constituted in manner agreed upon by the parties;

(c) been made in conformity with the law governing the arbitration procedure;

(d) become final in the country in which it was made;

(e) been in respect of a matter which may lawfully be referred to arbitration under the law of England;

and the enforcement thereof must not be contrary to the public policy or the law of England.

(2) Subject to the provisions of this subsection, a foreign award shall not be enforceable under this Part of this Act if the court dealing with the case is satisfied that—

(a) the award has been annulled in the country in which it was made; or

(b) the party against whom it is sought to enforce the award was not given notice of the arbitration proceedings in sufficient time to enable him to present his case or was under some legal incapacity and was not properly represented; or

(c) the award does not deal with all the questions referred or contains decisions on matters beyond the scope of the agreement for arbitration:

Provided that, if the award does not deal with all the questions referred, the court may, if it thinks fit, either postpone the enforcement of the award or order its enforcement subject to the giving of such security by the person seeking to enforce it as the court may think fit.

(3) If a party seeking to resist the enforcement of a foreign award proves that there is any ground other than the non-existence of the conditions specified in paragraphs (a), (b) and (c) of subsection (1) of this section, or the existence of the conditions specified in paragraphs (b) and (c) of subsection (2) of this section, entitling him to contest the validity of the award, the court may, if it thinks fit, either refuse to enforce the award or adjourn the hearing until after the expiration of such period as appears to the court to be reasonably sufficient to enable that party to take the necessary steps to have the award annulled by the competent tribunal.

**38. [omitted].**

**39. Meaning of 'final award'**

For the purposes of this Part of this Act, an award shall not be deemed final if any proceedings for the purpose of contesting the validity of the award are pending in the country in which it was made.

**40.-42. [omitted]**

## First Schedule

### Protocol on Arbitration Clauses signed on behalf of His Majesty at a Meeting of the Assembly of the League of Nations held on the twenty-fourth day of September, nineteen hundred and twenty-three

The undersigned, being duly authorised, declare that they accept, on behalf of the countries which they represent, the following provisions:-

1. Each of the Contracting States recognises the validity of an agreement whether relating to existing or future differences between parties, subject respectively to the jurisdiction of different Contracting States by which the parties to a contract agree to submit to arbitration all or any differences that may arise in connection with such contract relating to commercial matters or to any other matter capable of settlement by arbitration, whether or not the arbitration is to take place in a country to whose jurisdiction none of the parties is subject.

Each Contracting State reserves the right to limit the obligation mentioned above to contracts which are considered as commercial under its national law. Any Contracting State which avails itself of this right will notify the secretary-general of the League of Nations, in order that the other Contracting States may be so informed.

2. The arbitral procedure, including the constitution of the arbitral tribunal, shall be governed by the will of the parties and by the law of the country in whose territory the arbitration takes place.

The Contracting States agree to facilitate all steps in the procedure which require to be taken in their own territories, in accordance with the provisions of their law governing arbitral procedure applicable to existing differences.

3. Each Contracting State undertakes to ensure the execution by its authorities and in accordance with the provisions of its national laws of arbitral awards made in its own territory under the preceding Articles.

4. The tribunals of the Contracting Parties, on being seized of a dispute regarding a contract made between persons to whom Article 1 applies and including an arbitration agreement whether referring to present or future differences which is valid in virtue of the said Article and capable of being carried into effect, shall refer the parties on the application of either of them to the decision of the arbitrators.

Such reference shall not prejudice the competence of the judicial tribunals in case the agreement or the arbitration cannot proceed or become inoperative.

Articles 5-8 [omitted]

## SECOND SCHEDULE

### CONVENTION ON THE EXECUTION OF FOREIGN ARBITRAL AWARDS SIGNED AT GENEVA ON BEHALF OF HIS MAJESTY OF THE TWENTY-SIXTH DAY OF SEPTEMBER, NINETEEN HUNDRED AND TWENTY-SEVEN

### ARTICLE I

In the territories of any High Contracting Party to which the present Convention applies, an arbitral award made in pursuance of an agreement, whether relating to existing or future differences (hereinafter called 'a submission to arbitration') covered by the Protocol on Arbitration Clauses, opened at Geneva on September 24, 1923, shall be recognised as binding and shall be enforced in accordance with the rules of the procedure of the territory where the award is relied upon, provided that the said award has been made in a territory of one of the High Contracting Parties to which the present Convention applies and between persons who are subject to the jurisdiction of one of the High Contracting Parties.

To obtain such recognition or enforcement, it shall, further, be necessary—

(a) That the award has been made in pursuance of a submission to arbitration which is valid under the law applicable thereto;

(b) That the subject-matter of the award is capable of settlement by arbitration under the law of the country in which the award is sought to be relied upon;

(c) That the award has been made by the Arbitral Tribunal provided for in the submission to arbitration or constituted in the manner agreed upon by the parties and in conformity with the law governing the arbitration procedure;

(d) That the award has become final in the country in which it has been made, in the sense that it will not be considered as such if it is open to opposition, appel or pourvoi en cassation (in the countries where such forms of procedure exist) or if it is proved that any proceedings for the purpose of contesting the validity of the award are pending;

(e) That the recognition or enforcement of the award is not contrary to the public policy or to the principles of the law of the country in which it is sought to be relied upon.

## ARTICLE 2

Even if the conditions laid down in Article 1 hereof are fulfilled, recognition and enforcement of the award shall be refused if the Court is satisfied:-

(a) That the award has been annulled in the country in which it was made;

(b) That the party against whom it is sought to use the award was not given notice of the arbitration proceedings in sufficient time to enable him to present his case; or that, being under a legal incapacity, he was not properly represented;

(c) That the award does not deal with the differences contemplated by or falling within the terms of the submission to arbitration or that it contains decisions on matters beyond the scope of the submission to arbitration.

If the award has not covered all the questions submitted to the arbitral tribunal, the competent authority of the country where recognition or enforcement of the award is sought can, if it think fit, postpone such recognition or enforcement or grant it subject to such guarantee as that authority may decide.

## ARTICLE 3

If the party against whom the award has been made proves that, under the law governing the arbitration procedure, there is a ground, other than the grounds referred to in Article 1 (a) and (c), and Article 2 (b) and (c), entitling him to contest the validity of the award in a Court of Law, the Court may, if it thinks fit, either refuse recognition or enforcement of the award or adjourn the consideration thereof, giving such party a reasonable time within which to have the award annulled by the competent tribunal.

## ARTICLE 4

The party relying upon an award or claiming its enforcement must supply in particular:-

(1) The original award or a copy thereof duly authenticated, according to the requirements of the law of the country in which it was made;

(2) Documentary or other evidence to prove that the award has become final, in the sense defined in Article 1 (d), in the country in which it was made;

(3) When necessary, documentary or other evidence to prove that the conditions laid down in Article 1, paragraph 1 and paragraph 2 (a) and (c), have been fulfilled.

A translation of the award and of the other documents mentioned in this Article into the official language of the country where the award is sought to be relied upon may be demanded. Such translation must be certified correct by a diplomatic or consular agent of the country to which the party who seeks to rely upon the award belongs or by a sworn translator of the country where the award is sought to be relied upon.

## ARTICLE 5

The provisions of the above Articles shall not deprive any interested party of the right of availing himself of an arbitral award in the manner and to the extent allowed by the law or the treaties of the country where such award is sought to be relied upon.

## ARTICLES 6 - 11 [OMITTED]

# CARRIAGE BY AIR ACT 1961

## CHAPTER 27

### 1. Convention to have force of law

(1) Subject to this section, the provisions of the Convention known as 'the Warsaw Convention as amended at The Hague, 1955' as amended by the provisions of protocols No. 3 and No. 4 signed at Montreal on 25th September 1975 and set out in the First Schedule to this Act shall, so far as they relate to the rights and liabilities of carriers, carriers' servants and agents, passengers, consignors, consignees and other persons, and subject to the provisions of this Act, have the force of law in the United Kingdom in relation to any carriage by air to which the Convention applies, irrespective of the nationality of the aircraft performing that carriage; and the Carriage by Air Act, 1932 (which gives effect to the Warsaw Convention in its original form), shall cease to have effect.

(2) If there is any inconsistency between the text in English in Part I of the First Schedule to this Act and the text in French in Part II of that Schedule, the text in French shall prevail.

(3) and (4) [Omitted].

### 2. and 3. [omitted]

### 4. Limitation of liability

(1) It is hereby declared that the limitations on liability in Article 22 and Article 22A in the First Schedule to this Act apply whatever the nature of the proceedings by which liability may be enforced and that, in particular-

(a) [Repealed].

(b) the limitation for each passenger in paragraph (1) (a) of the said Article 22 applies to the aggregate liability of the carrier in all proceedings which may be brought against him under the law of any part of the United Kingdom, together with any proceedings brought against him outside the United Kingdom.

(2) A court before which proceedings are brought to enforce a liability which is limited by the said Article 22 or Article 22A may at any stage of the proceedings make any such order as appears to the court to be just and equitable in view of the provisions of the said Article 22A, and of any other proceedings which have been, or are likely to be, commenced in the United Kingdom or elsewhere to enforce the liability in whole or in part.

(3) Without prejudice to the last foregoing subsection, a court before which proceedings are brought to enforce a liability which is limited by the said Article 22 or Article 22A shall, where the liability is, or may be, partly enforceable in other proceedings in the United Kingdom or elsewhere, have jurisdiction to award an amount less than the court would have awarded if the

limitation applied solely to the proceedings before the court, or to make any part of its award conditional on the result of any other proceedings.

(4) and (5) [omitted].

**4A. Notice of partial loss**

(1) In Article 26(2) the references to damage shall be construed as including loss of part of the baggage or cargo in question and the reference to the receipt of baggage or cargo shall, in relation to loss of part of it, be construed as receipt of the remainder of it.

(2) It is hereby declared, without prejudice to the operation of any other section of this Act, that the reference to Article 26(2) in the preceding subsection is to Article 26(2) as set out in Part I and Part II of the First Schedule to this Act.

**5. Time for bringing proceedings**

(1) No action against a carrier's servant or agent which arises out of damage to which the Convention relates shall, if he was acting within the scope of his employment, be brought after more than two years, reckoned from the date of arrival at the destination or from the date on which the aircraft ought to have arrived, or from the date on which the carriage stopped.

(2) Article 29 in the First Schedule of this Act shall not be read as applying to any proceedings for contribution between persons liable for any damage to which the Convention relates, but no action shall be brought by a tortfeasor to obtain a contribution from a carrier in respect of a tort to which the said Article 29 applies after the expiration of two years from the time when judgment is obtained against the person seeking to obtain the contribution.

(3) The foregoing provisions of this section and the provisions of the said Article 29 shall have effect as if references in those provisions to an action included references to an arbitration; and subsections (3) and (4) of section thirty four of the Limitation Act 1980, or, in Northern Island, paragraphs (3) and (4) of Article 72 of the Limitation (Northern Ireland) Order 1989 (which determine the time at which an arbitration is deemed to be commenced), shall apply for the purposes of this subsection.

**6. Contributory negligence**

It is hereby declared that for the purposes of Article 21 in the First Schedule to this Act the Law Reform (Contributory Negligence) Act 1945 (including that Act as applied to Scotland), and section two of the Law Reform (Miscellaneous Provisions) Act (Northern Ireland) 1948, are provisions of the law of the United Kingdom under which a court may exonerate the carrier wholly or partly from his liability.

**7.-14. [omitted]**

# SCHEDULE 1

## THE WARSAW CONVENTION AS AMENDED AT THE HAGUE IN 1955 AND BY PROTOCOLS NO. 3 AND NO. 4 SIGNED AT MONTREAL IN 1975

## PART I

## THE ENGLISH TEXT

## CHAPTER I

## SCOPE-DEFINITIONS

### ARTICLE 1

(1) This Convention applies to all international carriage of persons, baggage or cargo performed by aircraft for reward. It applies equally to gratuitous carriage by aircraft performed by an air transport undertaking.

(2) For the 'purposes of this Convention, the expression international carriage means any carriage in which, according to the agreement between the parties, the place of departure and the place of destination, whether or not there be a break in the carriage or a trans-shipment, are situated either within the territories of two High Contracting Parties or within the territory of a single High Contracting Party if there is an agreed stopping place within the territory of another State, even if that State is not a High Contracting Party. Carriage between two points within the territory of a single High Contracting Party without an agreed stopping place within the territory of another State is not international carriage for the purposes of this Convention.

(3) Carriage to be performed by several successive air carriers is deemed, for the purposes of this Convention, to be one undivided carriage if it has been regarded by the parties as a single operation, whether it had been agreed upon under the form of a single contract or a series of contracts, and it does not lose its international character merely because one contract or a series of contracts is to be performed entirely within the territory of the same State.

### ARTICLE 2

(1) This Convention applies to carriage performed by the State or by legally constituted public bodies provided it falls within the conditions laid down in Article 1.

(2) In the carriage of postal items the carrier shall be liable only to the relevant postal administration in accordance with the rules applicable to the relationship between the carriers and the postal administrations.

(3) Except as provided in paragraph (2) of this Article, the provisions of this Convention shall not apply to the carriage of postal items.

# CHAPTER II

## DOCUMENTS OF CARRIAGE

### SECTION 1— PASSENGER TICKET

### ARTICLE 3

(1) In respect of the carriage of passengers an individual or collective document of carriage shall be delivered containing:

(a) an indication of the places of departure and destination;

(b) if the places of departure and destination are within the territory of a single High Contracting Party, one or more agreed stopping places being within the territory of another State, an indication of at least one such stopping place.

(2) Any other means which would preserve a record of the information indicated in (a) and (b) of the foregoing paragraph may be substituted for the delivery of the document referred to in that paragraph.

(3) Non-compliance with the provisions of the foregoing paragraphs shall not affect the existence or the validity of the contract of carriage, which shall, none the less, be subject to the rules of this Convention including those relating to limitation of liability.

### SECTION 2 — BAGGAGE CHECK

### ARTICLE 4

(1) In respect of the carriage of checked baggage, a baggage check shall be delivered, which, unless combined with or incorporated in a document of carriage which complies with the provisions of Article 3, paragraph (1), shall contain:

(a) an indication of the places of departure and destination;

(b) if the places of departure and destination are within the territory of a single High Contracting Party, one or more agreed stopping places being within the territory of another State, an indication of at least one such stopping place.

(2) Any other means which would preserve a record of the information indicated in (a) and (b) of the forgoing paragraph may be substituted for the delivery of the baggage check referred to in that paragraph.

(3) Non-compliance with the provisions of the foregoing paragraphs shall not affect the existence or the validity of the contract of carriage, which shall, none the less, be subject to the rules of this Convention including those relating to limitation of liability.

## SECTION 3 — DOCUMENTATION RELATING TO CARGO

### ARTICLE 5

(1) In respect of the carriage of cargo an air waybill shall be delivered.

(2) Any other means which would preserve a record of the carriage to be performed may, with the consent of the consignor, be substituted for the delivery of an air waybill. If such other means are used, the carrier shall, if so requested by the consignor, deliver to the consignor a receipt for the cargo permitting identification of the consignment and access to the information contained in the record preserved by such other means.

(3) The impossibility of using, at points of transit and destination, the other means which would preserve the record of the carriage referred to in paragraph (2) of this Article does not entitle the carrier to refuse to accept the cargo for carriage.

### ARTICLE 6

(1) The air waybill shall be made out by the consignor in three original parts.

(2) The first part shall be marked 'for the carrier'; it shall be signed by the consignor. The second part shall be marked 'for the consignee'; it shall be signed by the consignor and by the carrier. The third part shall be signed by the carrier and handed by him to the consignor after the cargo has been accepted.

(3) The signature of the carrier and that of the consignor may be printed or stamped.

(4) If, at the request of the consignor, the carrier makes out the air waybill, he shall be deemed, subject to proof to the contrary, to have done so on behalf of the consignor.

### ARTICLE 7

When there is more than one package:

(a) the carrier of cargo has the right to require the consignor to make out separate air waybills;

(b) the consignor has the right to require the carrier to deliver separate receipts when the other means referred to in paragraph (2) of Article 5 are used.

### ARTICLE 8

The air waybill and the receipt for the cargo shall contain:

(a) an indication of the places of departure and destination;

(b) if the places of departure and destination are within the territory of a single High Contracting Party, one or more agreed stopping places being within the territory of another State, an indication of at least one such stopping place; and

(c) an indication of the weight of the consignment.

## ARTICLE 9

Non-compliance with the provisions of Articles 5 to 8 shall not affect the existence or the validity of the contract of carriage, which shall, none the less, be subject to the rules of this Convention including those relating to limitation of liability.

## ARTICLE 10

(1) The consignor is responsible for the correctness of the particulars and statements relating to the cargo inserted by him or on his behalf in the air waybill or furnished by him or on his behalf to the carrier for insertion in the receipt for the cargo or for insertion in the record preserved by the other means referred to in paragraph (2) of Article 5.

(2) The consignor shall indemnify the carrier against all damage suffered by him, or by any other person to whom the carrier is liable, by reason of the irregularity, incorrectness or incompleteness of the particulars and statements furnished by the consignor or on his behalf.

(3) Subject to the provisions of paragraphs (1) and (2) of this Article, the carrier shall indemnify the consignor against all damage suffered by him, or by any other person to whom the consignor is liable, by reason of the irregularity, incorrectness or incompleteness of the particulars and statements inserted by the carrier or on his behalf in the receipt for the cargo or in the record preserved by the other means referred to in paragraph (2) of Article 5.

## ARTICLE 11

(1) The air waybill or the receipt for the cargo is *prima facie* evidence of the conclusion of the contract, of the acceptance of the cargo and of the conditions of carriage mentioned therein.

(2) Any statements in the air waybill or the receipt for the cargo relating to the weight, dimensions and packing of the cargo, as well as those relating to the number of packages, are *prima facie* evidence of the facts stated; those relating to the quantity, volume and condition of the cargo do not constitute evidence against the carrier except so far as they both have been, and are stated in the air waybill to have been, checked by him in the presence of the consignor, or relate to the apparent condition of the cargo.

## ARTICLE 12

(1) Subject to his liability to carry out all his obligations under the contract of carriage, the consignor has the right to dispose of the cargo by withdrawing it at the airport of departure or destination, or by stopping it in the course of the

journey on any landing, or by calling for it to be delivered at the place of destination or in the course of the journey to a person other than the consignee originally designated, or by requiring it to be returned to the airport of departure. He must not exercise this right of disposition in such a way as to prejudice the carrier or other consignors and he must repay any expenses occasioned by the exercise of this right.

(2) If it is impossible to carry out the orders of the consignor the carrier must so inform him forthwith.

(3) If the carrier obeys the orders of the consignor for the disposition of the cargo without requiring the production of the part of the air waybill or the receipt for the cargo delivered to the latter, he will be liable, without prejudice to his right of recovery from the consignor, for any damage which may be caused thereby to any person who is lawfully in possession of that part of the air waybill or the receipt for the cargo.

(4) The right conferred on the consignor ceases at the moment when that of the consignee begins in accordance with Article 13. Nevertheless, if the consignee declines to accept the cargo, or if he cannot be communicated with, the consignor resumes his right of disposition.

## Article 13

(1) Except when the consignor has exercised his right under Article 12, the consignee is entitled, on arrival of the cargo at the place of destination, to require the carrier to deliver the cargo to him, on payment of the charges due and on complying with the conditions of carriage.

(2) Unless it is otherwise agreed, it is the duty of the carrier to give notice to the consignee as soon as the cargo arrives.

(3) If the carrier admits the loss of the cargo, or if the cargo has not arrived at the expiration of seven days after the date on which it ought to have arrived, the consignee is entitled to enforce against the carrier the rights which flow from the contract of carriage.

## Article 14

The consignor and the consignee can respectively enforce all the rights given them by Articles 12 and 13, each in his own name, whether he is acting in his own interest or in the interest of another, provided that he carries out the obligations imposed by the contract of carriage.

## Article 15

(1) Articles 12, 13, and 14 do not affect either the relations of the consignor and the consignee with each other or the mutual relations of third parties whose rights are derived either from the consignor or from the consignee.

(2) The provisions of Articles 12, 13 and 14 can only be varied by express provision in the air waybill or the receipt for the cargo.

## ARTICLE 16

(1) The consignor must furnish such information and such documents as are necessary to meet the formalities of customs, octroi or police before the cargo can be delivered to the consignee. The consignor is liable to the carrier for any damage occasioned by the absence, insufficiency or irregularity of any such information or documents, unless the damage is due to the fault of the carrier, his servants or agents.

(2) The carrier is under no obligation to enquire into the correctness or sufficiency of such information or documents.

## CHAPTER III

## LIABILITY OF THE CARRIER

## ARTICLE 17

(1) The carrier is liable for damage sustained in case of death or personal injury of a passenger upon condition only that the event which caused the death or injury took place on board the aircraft or in the course of any of the operations of embarking or disembarking. However, the carrier is not liable if the death or injury resulted solely from the state of health of the passenger.

(2) The carrier is liable for damage sustained in case of destruction or loss of, or of damage to, baggage upon condition only that the event which caused the destruction, loss or damage took place on board the aircraft or in the course of any of the operations of embarking or disembarking or during any period within which the baggage was in charge of the carrier. However, the carrier is not liable if the damage resulted solely from the inherent defect, quality or vice of the baggage.

(3) Unless otherwise specified, in this Convention the term 'baggage' means both checked baggage and objects carried by the passenger.

## ARTICLE 18

(1) The carrier is liable for damage sustained in the event of the destruction or loss of, or damage to, cargo upon condition only that the occurrence which caused the damage so sustained took place during the carriage by air.

(2) However, the carrier is not liable if he proves that the destruction, loss of, or damage to, the cargo resulted solely from one or more of the following:

(a) inherent defect, quality or vice of that cargo;

(b) defective packing of that cargo performed by a person other than the carrier or his servants or agents;

(c) an act of war or an armed conflict;

(d) an act of public authority carried out in connection with the entry, exit or transit of the cargo.

(3) The carriage by air within the meaning of paragraph (1) of this Article comprises the period during which the cargo is in the charge of the carrier, whether in an airport or on board an aircraft, or, in the case of a landing outside an airport, in any place whatsoever.

(4) The period of the carriage by air does not extend to any carriage by land, by sea or by river performed outside an airport. If, however, such carriage takes place in performance of a contract for carriage by air, for the purpose of loading, delivery or transhipment, any damage is presumed, subject to proof to the contrary, to have been the result of an event which took place during the carriage by air.

## ARTICLE 19

The carrier is liable for damage occasioned by delay in the carriage by air of passengers, baggage or cargo.

## ARTICLE 20

In the carriage of passengers, baggage and cargo, the carrier shall not be liable for damage occasioned by delay if he proves that he and his servants and agents have taken all necessary measures to avoid the damage or that it was impossible for them to take such measures.

## ARTICLE 21

(1) In the carriage of passengers and baggage, if the carrier proves that the damage was caused or contributed to by the negligence or other wrongful act or omission of the person claiming compensation, the carrier shall be wholly or partly exonerated from his liability to such person to the extent that such negligence or wrongful act or omission caused or contributed to the damage. When by reason of the death or injury of a passenger compensation is claimed by a person other than the passenger, the carrier shall likewise be wholly or partly exonerated from his liability to the extent that he proves that the damage was caused or contributed to by the negligence or other wrongful act or omission of that passenger.

(2) In the carriage of cargo, if the carrier proves that the damage was caused by or contributed to by the negligence or other wrongful act or omission of the person claiming compensation, or the person from whom he derives his rights, the carrier shall be wholly or partly exonerated from his liability to the claimant to the extent that such negligence or wrongful act or omission caused or contributed to the damage.

## ARTICLE 22

(1)—

(a) In the carriage of persons the liability of the carrier is limited to the sum of 100,000 special drawing rights for the aggregate of the claims, however founded, in respect of damage suffered as a result of the death or personal injury of each passenger. Where, in accordance with the law of the court seised of the case, damages may be awarded in the form of periodic payments, the equivalent capital value of the said payment shall not exceed 100,000 special drawing rights.

(b) In the case of delay in the carriage of persons the liability of the carrier for each passenger is limited to 4,150 special drawing rights.

(c) In the carriage of baggage the liability of the carrier in the case of destruction, loss, damage or delay is limited to 1,000 special drawing rights for each passenger.

(2)—

(a) The courts of the High Contracting Parties which are not authorised under their law to award the costs of the action, including lawyers' fees, shall, in actions relating to the carriage of passengers and baggage to which this Convention applies, have the power to award, in their discretion, to the claimant the whole or part of the cost of the action, including lawyers' fees which the court considers reasonable.

(b) The costs of the action including lawyers' fees shall be awarded in accordance with the subparagraph (a) only if a claimant gives a written notice to the carrier of the amount claimed including the particulars of the calculation of that amount and the carrier does not make, within a period of six months after his receipt of such notice, a written offer of settlement in an amount at least equal to the compensation awarded within the applicable limit. This period will be extended until the time of commencement of the action if that is later.

(c) The costs of the action including lawyers' fees shall not be taken into account in applying the limits under this Article.

(3) The sums mentioned in terms of special drawing right in this Article shall be deemed to refer to the special drawing right as defined by the International Monetary Fund. Conversion of the sums into national currencies shall, in case of judicial proceedings, be made according to the value of such currencies in terms of the special drawing right at the date of the judgment.

## ARTICLE 22A

(1)—

(a) In the carriage of cargo, the liability of the carrier is limited to a sum of 17 special drawing rights per kilogramme, unless the consignor has made, at the time when the package was handed over to the carrier, a special declaration of interest in delivery at destination and has paid a supplementary sum if the case so requires. In that case the carrier will be liable to pay a sum not exceeding the declared sum, unless he proves that that sum is greater than the consignor's actual interest in delivery at destination.

(b) In the case of loss, damage or delay of part of the cargo, or of any object contained therein, the weight to be taken into consideration in determining the amount to which the carrier's liability is limited shall be only the total weight of the package or packages concerned. Nevertheless, when the loss, damage or delay of a part of the cargo, or of an object contained therein, affects the value of other packages covered by the same air waybill, the total weight of such package or packages shall also be taken into consideration in determining the limit of liability.

(2) The limits prescribed in this Article shall not prevent the court in an action relating to the carriage of cargo from awarding in accordance with its own law, in addition, the whole or part of the court costs and of the other expenses of the litigation incurred by the plaintiff. The foregoing provision shall not apply if the amount of the damages awarded, excluding court costs and other expenses of the litigation, does not exceed the sum which the carrier has offered in writing to the plaintiff within a period of six months from the date of the occurrence causing the damage, or before the commencement of the action, if that is later.

(3) The sums mentioned in terms of special drawing right in this Article shall be deemed to refer to the special drawing right as defined by the International Monetary Fund. Conversion of the sums into national currencies shall, in case of judicial proceedings, be made according to the value of such currencies in terms of the special drawing right at the date of the judgment.

## ARTICLE 23

(1) Any provision tending to relieve the carrier of liability or to fix a lower limit than that which is laid down in this Convention shall be null and void, but the nullity of any such provision does not involve the nullity of the whole contract, which shall remain subject to the provisions of this Convention.

(2) Paragraph (1) of this Article shall not apply to provisions governing loss or damage resulting from the inherent defect, quality or vice of the cargo carried.

## ARTICLE 24

In the carriage of passengers, baggage and cargo, any action for damages, however founded, whether under this Convention or in contract or in tort or otherwise, can only be brought subject to the conditions and limits of liability set out in this Convention without prejudice to the question as to who are the persons who have the right to bring suit and what are their respective rights. Such limits of liability constitute maximum limits and may not be exceeded whatever the circumstances which gave rise to the liability.

## ARTICLE 25A

(1) If an action is brought against a servant or agent of the carrier arising out of damage to which the Convention relates, such servant or agent, if he proves that he acted within the scope of his employment, shall be entitled to avail himself of the limits of liability which that carrier himself is entitled to invoke under this Convention.

(2) The aggregate of the amounts recoverable from the carrier, his servants and agents, in that case, shall not exceed the said limits.

## Article 26

(1) Receipt by the person entitled to delivery of baggage or cargo without complaint is *prima facie* evidence that the same has been delivered in good condition and in accordance with the document of carriage.

(2) In the case of damage, the person entitled to delivery must complain to the carrier forthwith after the discovery of the damage, and at the latest, within seven days from the date of receipt in the case of baggage and fourteen days from the date of receipt in the case of cargo. In the case of delay the complaint must be made at the latest within twenty-one days from the date on which the baggage or cargo have been placed at his disposal.

(3) Every complaint must be made in writing upon the document of carriage or by separate notice in writing despatched within the times aforesaid.

(4) Failing complaint within the times aforesaid, no action shall lie against the carrier, save in the case of fraud on his part.

## Article 27

In the case of the death of the person liable, an action for damages lies in accordance with the terms of this Convention against those legally representing his estate.

## Article 28

(1) An action for damages must be brought, at the option of the plaintiff, in the territory of one of the High Contracting Parties, either before the court having jurisdiction where the carrier is ordinarily resident, or has his principal place of business, or has an establishment by which the contract has been made or before the court having jurisdiction at the place of destination.

(2) In respect of damage resulting from the death, injury or delay of a passenger or the destruction, loss, damage or delay of baggage, the action may be brought before one of the courts mentioned in paragraph (1) of this Article, or in the territory of one of the High Contracting Parties, before the court within the jurisdiction of which the carrier has an establishment if the passenger has his ordinary or permanent residence in the territory of the same High Contracting Party.

(3) Questions of procedure shall be governed by the law of the court seised of the case.

## Article 29

(1) The right to damages shall be extinguished if an action is not brought within two years, reckoned from the date of arrival at the destination, or from the date on which the aircraft ought to have arrived, or from the date on which the carriage stopped.

(2) The method of calculating the period of limitation shall be determined by the law of the court seised of the case.

## Article 30

(1) In the case of carriage to be performed by various successive carriers and falling within the definition set out in the third paragraph of Article 1, each carrier who accepts passengers, baggage or cargo is subjected to the rules set out in this Convention, and is deemed to be one of the contracting parties to the contract of carriage in so far as the contract deals with that part of the carriage which is performed under his supervision.

(2) In the case of carriage of this nature, the passenger or his representative can take action only against the carrier who performed the carriage during which the accident or the delay occurred, save in the case where, by express agreement, the first carrier assumed liability for the whole journey.

(3) As regards baggage or cargo, the passenger or consignor will have a right of action against the first carrier, and the passenger or consignee who is entitled to delivery will have a right of action against the last carrier, and further, each may take action against the carrier who performed the carriage during which the destruction, loss, damage or delay took place. These carriers will be jointly and severally liable to the passenger or to the consignor or consignee.

## Article 30A

Nothing in this Convention shall prejudice the question whether a person liable for damage in accordance with its provisions has a right of recourse against any other person.

# CHAPTER IV

## Provisions Relating to Combined Carriage

## Article 31

(1) In the case of combined carriage performed partly by air and partly by any other mode of carriage, the provisions of this Convention apply only to the carriage by air, provided that the carriage by air falls within the terms of Article 1.

(2) Nothing in this Convention shall prevent the parties in the case of combined carriage from inserting in the documents of air carriage conditions relating to other modes of carriage, provided that the provisions of this Convention are observed as regards the carriage by air.

## CHAPTER V

### General and Final Provisions

### Article 32

Any clause contained in the contract and all special agreements entered into before the damage occurred by which the parties purport to infringe the rules laid down by this convention, whether by deciding the law to be applied, or by altering the rules as to jurisdiction, shall be null and void. Nevertheless for the carriage of cargo arbitration clauses are allowed, subject to this Convention, if the arbitration is to take place within one of the jurisdictions referred to in the first paragraph of Article 28.

### Article 33

Except as provided in paragraph (3) of Article 5, nothing in this Convention shall prevent the carrier either from refusing to enter into any contract of carriage or from making regulations which do not conflict with the provisions of this Convention.

### Article 34

The provisions of Article 3 to 8 inclusive relating to documents of carriage shall not apply in the case of carriage performed in extra-ordinary circumstances outside the normal scope of an air carrier's business.

### Article 35

The expression 'days' when used in this Convention means current days not working days.

### Article 35A

No provision contained in this Convention shall prevent a State from establishing and operating within its territory a system to supplement the compensation payable to claimants under the Convention in respect of death, or personal injury, of passengers. Such a system shall fulfil the following conditions:

(a) it shall not in any circumstances impose upon the carrier, his servants or agents, any liability in addition to that provided under this Convention;

(b) it shall not impose upon the carrier any financial or administrative burden other than collecting in that State contributions from passengers if required so to do;

(c) it shall not give rise to any discrimination between carriers with regard to the passengers concerned and the benefits available to the said passengers under the system shall be extended to them regardless of the carrier whose services they have used;

(d) if a passenger has contributed to the system, any person suffering damage as a consequence of death or personal injury of such passenger shall be entitled to the benefits of the system.

## ARTICLE 40A

(1) [omitted].

(2) For the purposes of the Convention the word territory means not only the metropolitan territory of a State but also all other territories for the foreign relations of which that State is responsible.

## ARTICLES 36-42 [OMITTED]

# CARRIAGE BY AIR (SUPPLEMENTARY PROVISIONS) ACT 1962

## CHAPTER 43

**1. Supplementary Convention to have force of law**

(1) The provisions of the Convention, supplementary to the Warsaw Convention, for the unification of certain rules relating to International carriage by air performed by a person other than the contracting carrier, as set out in the Schedule to this Act, shall, so far as they relate to the rights and liabilities of carriers, carriers' servants and agents, passengers, consignors, consignees, and other persons, and subject to the provisions of this Act, have the force of law in the United Kingdom in relation to any carriage by air to which the Convention applies, irrespective of the nationality of the aircraft performing that carriage.

(2) If there is any inconsistency between the text in English in Part I of the Schedule to this Act and the text in French in Part II of that Schedule, the text in French shall prevail.

**2.-7. [omitted]**

## SCHEDULE

### PART 1

### THE ENGLISH TEXT

### CONVENTION

SUPPLEMENTARY TO THE WARSAW CONVENTION, FOR THE UNIFICATION OF CERTAIN RULES RELATING TO INTERNATIONAL CARRIAGE BY AIR PERFORMED BY A PERSON OTHER THAN THE CONTRACTING CARRIER

### ARTICLE 1

In this Convention:

(a) [omitted]

(b) 'contracting carrier' means a person who as a principal makes an agreement for carriage governed by the Warsaw Convention with a passenger or consignor or with a person acting on behalf of the passenger or consignor;

(c) 'actual carrier' means a person, other than the contracting carrier, who, by virtue of authority from the contracting carrier, performs the whole or part of the carriage contemplated in paragraph (b) but who is not with respect to such part a successive carrier within the meaning of the Warsaw Convention. Such authority is presumed in the absence of proof to the contrary.

## ARTICLE II

If an actual carrier performs the whole or part of carriage which, according to the agreement referred to in Article I, paragraph (b), is governed by the Warsaw Convention, both the contracting carrier and the actual carrier shall, except as otherwise provided in this Convention, be subject to the rules of the Warsaw Convention, the former for the whole of the carriage contemplated in the agreement, the latter solely for the carriage which he performs.

## ARTICLE III

1. The acts and omissions of the actual carrier and of his servants and agents acting within the scope of their employment shall, in relation to the carriage performed by the actual carrier, be deemed to be also those of the contracting carrier.

2. The acts and omissions of the contracting carrier and of his servants and agents acting within the scope of their employment shall, in relation to the carriage performed by the actual carrier, be deemed to be also those of the actual carrier. Nevertheless, no such act or omission shall subject the actual carrier to liability exceeding the limits specified in Article 22 or Article 22A of the Warsaw Convention. Any special agreement under which the contracting carrier assumes obligations not imposed by the Warsaw Convention or any waiver of rights conferred by that Convention or any special declaration of interest in delivery at destination contemplated in Article 22 of the said Convention, shall not affect the actual carrier unless agreed to by him.

## ARTICLE IV

Any complaint to be made or order to be given under the Warsaw Convention to the carrier shall have the same effect whether addressed to the contracting carrier or to the actual carrier. Nevertheless, orders referred to in Article 12 of the Warsaw Convention shall only be effective if addressed to the contracting carrier.

## ARTICLE V

In relation to the carriage performed by the actual carrier, any servant or agent of that carrier or of the contracting carrier shall, if he proves that he acted within the scope of his employment, be entitled to avail himself of the limits of liability which are applicable under this Convention to the carrier whose servant or agent he is unless it is proved that he acted in a manner which, under the Warsaw Convention, prevents the limits of liability from being invoked.

## ARTICLE VI

In relation to the carriage performed by the actual carrier, the aggregate of the amounts recoverable from that carrier and the contracting carrier, and from their servants and agents acting within the scope of their employment, shall not exceed the highest amount which could be awarded against either the contracting carrier or the actual carrier under this Convention, but none of the persons mentioned shall be liable for a sum in excess of the limit applicable to him.

## ARTICLE VII

In relation to the carriage performed by the actual carrier, an action for damages may be brought, at the option of the plaintiff, against that carrier or the contracting carrier, or against both together or separately. If the action is brought against only one of those carriers, that carrier shall have the right to require the other carrier to be joined in the proceedings, the procedure and effects being governed by the law of the court seised of the case.

## ARTICLE VIII

Any action for damages contemplated in Article VII of this Convention must be brought, at the option of the plaintiff, either before a court in which an action may be brought against the contracting carrier, as provided in Article 28 of the Warsaw Convention, or before the court having jurisdiction at the place where the actual carrier is ordinarily resident or has his principal place of business.

## ARTICLE IX

1. Any contractual provision tending to relieve the contracting carrier or the actual carrier of liability under this Convention or to fix a lower limit than that which is applicable according to this Convention shall be null and void, but the nullity of any such provision does not involve the nullity of the whole agreement, which shall remain subject to the provisions of this Convention.

2. In respect of the carriage performed by the actual carrier, the preceding paragraph shall not apply to contractual provisions governing loss or damage resulting from the inherent defect, quality or vice of the cargo carried.

3. Any clause contained in an agreement for carriage and all special agreements entered into before the damage occurred by which the parties purport to infringe the rules laid down by this Convention, whether by deciding the law to be applied, or by altering the rules as to jurisdiction, shall be null and void. Nevertheless, for the carriage of cargo arbitration clauses are allowed, subject to this Convention, if the arbitration is to take place in one of the jurisdictions referred to in Article VIII.

## ARTICLE X

Except as provided in Article VII, nothing in this Convention shall affect the rights and obligations of the two carriers between themselves.

## ARTICLES XI TO XVIII [OMITTED]

# CARRIAGE OF GOODS BY ROAD ACT 1965

## CHAPTER 37

### 1. Convention to have force of law

Subject to the following provisions of this Act, the provisions of the Convention on the Contract for the International Carriage of Goods by Road (in this Act referred to as 'the Convention'), as set out in the Schedule to this Act, shall have the force of law in the United Kingdom so far as they relate to the rights and liabilities of persons concerned in the carriage of goods by road under a contract to which the Convention applies.

### 2.-13. [omitted].

### 14. Short title interpretation and commencement

(1) [omitted].

(2) The persons who, for the purposes of this Act, are persons concerned in the carriage of goods by road under a contract to which the Convention applies are—

- (a) the sender,
- (b) the consignee,
- (c) any carrier who, in accordance with Article 34 in the Schedule to this Act or otherwise, is a party to the contract of carriage,
- (d) any person for whom such a carrier is responsible by virtue of Article 3 in the Schedule to this Act,
- (e) any person to whom the rights and liabilities of any of the persons referred to in paragraphs (a) to (d) of this subsection have passed (whether by assignment or assignation or by operation of law).

(3) and (4) [omitted].

## SCHEDULE

## Convention on the Contract for the International Carriage of Goods by Road

## Chapter I

## Scope of Application

### Article 1

1. This Convention shall apply to every contract for the carriage of goods by road in vehicles for reward, when the place of taking over of the goods and the

place designated for delivery, as specified in the contract, are situated in two different countries, of which at least one is a Contracting country, irrespective of the place of residence and the nationality of the parties.

2. For the purposes of this Convention, 'vehicles' means motor vehicles, articulated vehicles, trailers and semi-trailers as defined in Article 4 of the Convention on Road Traffic dated 19th September 1949.

3. This Convention shall apply also where carriage coming within its scope is carried out by States or by governmental institutions or organisations.

4. This Convention shall not apply:
- (a) to carriage performed under the terms of any international postal convention;
- (b) to funeral consignments;
- (c) to furniture removal.

5. The Contracting Parties agree not to vary any of the provisions of this Convention by special agreements between two or more of them, except to make it inapplicable to their frontier traffic or to authorise the use in transport operations entirely confined to their territory of consignment notes representing a title to the goods.

## ARTICLE 2

1. Where the vehicle containing the goods is carried over part of the journey by sea, rail, inland waterways or air, and, except where the provisions of Article 14 are applicable, the goods are not unloaded from the vehicle, this Convention shall nevertheless apply to the whole of the carriage. Provided that to the extent that it is proved that any loss, damage or delay in delivery of the goods which occurs during the carriage by the other means of transport was not caused by an act or omission of the carrier by road, but by some event which could only have occurred in the course of and by reason of the carriage by that other means of transport, the liability of the carrier by road shall be determined not by this Convention but in the manner in which the liability of the carrier by the other means of transport would have been determined if a contract for the carriage of the goods alone had been made by the sender with the carrier by the other means of transport in accordance with the conditions prescribed by law for the carriage of goods by that means of transport. If, however, there are no such prescribed conditions, the liability of the carrier by road shall be determined by this Convention.

2. If the carrier by road is also himself the carrier by the other means of transport, his liability shall also be determined in accordance with the provisions of paragraph 1 of this Article, but as if, in his capacities as carrier by road and as carrier by the other means of transport, he were two separate persons.

## CHAPTER II

### PERSONS FOR WHOM THE CARRIER IS RESPONSIBLE

### ARTICLE 3

For the purposes of this Convention the carrier shall be responsible for the acts and omissions of his agents and servants and of any other persons of whose services he makes use for the performance of the carriage, when such agents, servants or other persons are acting within the scope of their employment, as if such acts or omissions were his own.

## CHAPTER III

### CONCLUSION AND PERFORMANCE OF THE CONTRACT OF CARRIAGE

### ARTICLE 4

The contract of carriage shall be confirmed by the making out of a consignment note. The absence, irregularity or loss of the consignment note shall not affect the existence or the validity of the contract of carriage which shall remain subject to the provisions of this Convention.

### ARTICLE 5

1. The consignment note shall be made out in three original copies signed by the sender and by the carrier. These signatures may be printed or replaced by the stamps of the sender and the carrier if the law of the country in which the consignment note has been made out so permits. The first copy shall be handed to the sender, the second shall accompany the goods and the third shall be retained by the carrier.

2. When the goods which are to be carried have to be loaded in different vehicles, or are of different kinds or are divided into different lots, the sender or the carrier shall have the right to require a separate consignment note to be made out for each vehicle used, or for each kind or lot of goods.

### ARTICLE 6

1. The consignment note shall contain the following particulars:
   - (a) the date of the consignment note and the place at which it is made out;
   - (b) the name and address of the sender;
   - (c) the name and address of the carrier;
   - (d) the place and the date of taking over the goods and the place designated for delivery;
   - (e) the name and address of the consignee;
   - (f) the description in common use of the nature of the goods and the method of packing, and, in the case of dangerous goods, their generally recognised description;

(g) the number of packages and their special marks and numbers;
(h) the gross weight of the goods or their quantity otherwise expressed;
(i) charges relating to the carriage (carriage charges, supplementary charges, customs duties and other charges incurred from the making of the contract to the time of delivery);
(j) the requisite instructions for Customs and other formalities;
(k) a statement that the carriage is subject, notwithstanding any clause to the contrary, to the provisions of this Convention.

2. Where applicable, the consignment note shall also contain the following particulars:
(a) a statement that transhipment is not allowed;
(b) the charges which the sender undertakes to pay;
(c) the amount of 'cash on delivery' charges;
(d) a declaration of the value of the goods and the amount representing special interest in delivery;
(e) the sender's instructions to the carrier regarding insurance of the goods;
(f) the agreed time-limit within which the carriage is to be carried out;
(g) a list of the documents handed to the carrier.

3. The parties may enter in the consignment note any other particulars which they may deem useful.

## ARTICLE 7

1. The sender shall be responsible for all expenses, loss and damage sustained by the carrier by reason of the inaccuracy or inadequacy of:
(a) the particulars specified in Article 6, paragraph 1, (b), (d), (e), (f), (g), (h) and (j);
(b) the particulars specified in Article 6, paragraph 2;
(c) any other particulars or instructions given by him to enable the consignment note to be made out or for the purpose of their being entered therein.

2. If, at the request of the sender, the carrier enters in the consignment note the particulars referred to in paragraph 1 of this Article, he shall be deemed, unless the contrary is proved, to have done so on behalf of the sender.

3. If the consignment note does not contain the statement specified in Article 6, paragraph 1 (k), the carrier shall be liable for all expenses, loss and damage sustained through such omission by the person entitled to dispose of the goods.

## ARTICLE 8

1. On taking over the goods, the carrier shall check:
(a) the accuracy of the statements in the consignment note as to the number of packages and their marks and numbers, and
(b) the apparent condition of the goods and their packaging.

2. Where the carrier has no reasonable means of checking the accuracy of the statements referred to in paragraph 1 (a) of this Article, he shall enter his

reservations in the consignment note together with the grounds on which they are based. He shall likewise specify the grounds for any reservations which he makes with regard to the apparent condition of the goods and their packaging. Such reservations shall not bind the sender unless he has expressly agreed to be bound by them in the consignment note.

3. The sender shall be entitled to require the carrier to check the gross weight of the goods or their quantity otherwise expressed. He may also require the contents of the packages to be checked. The carrier shall be entitled to claim the cost of such checking. The result of the checks shall be entered in the consignment note.

## ARTICLE 9

1. The consignment note shall be *prima facie* evidence of the making of the contract of carriage, the conditions of the contract and the receipt of the goods by the carrier.

2. If the consignment note contains no specific reservations by the carrier, it shall be presumed, unless the contrary is proved, that the goods and their packaging appeared to be in good condition when the carrier took them over and that the number of packages, their marks and numbers corresponded with the statements in the consignment note.

## ARTICLE 10

The sender shall be liable to the carrier for damage to persons, equipment or other goods, and for any expenses due to defective packing of the goods, unless the defect was apparent or known to the carrier at the time when he took over the goods and he made no reservations concerning it.

## ARTICLE 11

1. For the purposes of the Customs or other formalities which have to be completed before delivery of the goods, the sender shall attach the necessary documents to the consignment note or place them at the disposal of the carrier and shall furnish him with all the information which he requires.

2. The carrier shall not be under any duty to enquire into either the accuracy or the adequacy of such documents and information. The sender shall be liable to the carrier for any damage caused by the absence, inadequacy or irregularity of such documents and information, except in the case of some wrongful act or neglect on the part of the carrier.

3. The liability of the carrier for the consequences arising from the loss or incorrect use of the documents specified in and accompanying the consignment note or deposited with the carrier shall be that of an agent, provided that the compensation payable by the carrier shall not exceed that payable in the event of loss of the goods.

## ARTICLE 12

1. The sender has the right to dispose of the goods, in particular by asking the carrier to stop the goods in transit, to change the place at which delivery is to take place or to deliver the goods to a consignee other than the consignee indicated in the consignment notice.

2. The right shall cease to exist when the second copy of the consignment note is handed to the consignee or when the consignee exercises his right under Article 13, paragraph 1; from that time onwards the carrier shall obey the orders of the consignee.

3. The consignee shall, however, have the right of disposal from the time when the consignment note is drawn up, if the sender makes an entry to that effect in the consignment note.

4. If in exercising his right of disposal the consignee has ordered the delivery of the goods to another person, that other person shall not be entitled to name other consignees.

5. The exercise of the right of disposal shall be subject to the following conditions:

(a) that the sender or, in the case referred to in paragraph 3 of this Article, the consignee who wishes to exercise the right produces the first copy of the consignment note on which the new instructions to the carrier have been entered and indemnifies the carrier against all expenses, loss and damage involved in carrying out such instruction;
(b) that the carrying out of such instructions is possible at the time when the instructions reach the person who is to carry them out and does not either interfere with the normal working of the carrier's undertaking or prejudice the senders or consignees of other consignments;
(c) that the instructions do not result in a division of the consignment.

6. When, by reason of the provisions of paragraph 5(b) of this Article, the carrier cannot carry out the instructions which he receives, he shall immediately notify the person who give him such instructions.

7. A carrier who has not carried out the instructions given under the conditions provided for in this Article, or who has carried them out without requiring the first copy of the consignment note to be produced, shall be liable to the person entitled to make a claim for any loss or damage caused thereby.

## ARTICLE 13

1. After arrival of the goods at the place designated for delivery, the consignee shall be entitled to require the carrier to deliver to him, against a receipt, the second copy of the consignment note and the goods. If the loss of the goods is established or if the goods have not arrived after the expiry of the period provided for in Article 19, the consignee shall be entitled to enforce in his own name against the carrier any rights arising from the contract of carriage.

2. The consignee who avails himself of the rights granted to him under paragraph 1 of this Article shall pay the charges shown to be due on the

consignment note, but in the event of dispute on this matter the carrier shall not be required to deliver the goods unless security has been furnished by the consignee.

## ARTICLE 14

1. If for any reason it is or becomes impossible to carry out the contract in accordance with the terms laid down in the consignment note before the goods reach the place designated for delivery, the carrier shall ask for instructions from the person entitled to dispose of the goods in accordance with the provisions of Article 12.

2. Nevertheless, if circumstances are such as to allow the carriage to be carried out under conditions differing from those laid down in the consignment note and if the carrier has been unable to obtain instructions in reasonable time from the person entitled to dispose of the goods in accordance with the provisions of Article 12, he shall take such steps as seem to him to be in the best interests of the person entitled to dispose of the goods.

## ARTICLE 15

1. Where circumstances prevent delivery of the goods after their arrival at the place designated for delivery, the carrier shall ask the sender for his instructions. If the consignee refuses the goods the sender shall be entitled to dispose of them without being obliged to produce the first copy of the consignment note.

2. Even if he has refused the goods, the consignee may nevertheless require delivery so long as the carrier has not received instruction to the contrary from the sender.

3. When circumstances preventing delivery of the goods arise after the consignee, in exercise of his rights under Article 12, paragraph 3, has given an order for the goods to be delivered to another person, paragraphs 1 and 2 of this Article shall apply as if the consignee were the sender and that other person were the consignee.

## ARTICLE 16

1. The carrier shall be entitled to recover the cost of his request for instructions and any expenses entailed in carrying out such instructions, unless such expenses were caused by the wrongful act or neglect of the carrier.

2. In the cases referred to in Article 14, paragraph 1, and in Article 15, the carrier may immediately unload the goods for account of the person entitled to dispose of them and thereupon the carriage shall be deemed to be at an end. The carrier shall then hold the goods on behalf of the person so entitled. He may however entrust them to a third party, and in that case he shall not be under any liability except for the exercise of reasonable care in the choice of such third party. The charges due under the consignment note and all other expenses shall remain chargeable against the goods.

3. The carrier may sell the goods, without awaiting instructions from the person entitled to dispose of them, if the goods are perishable or their condition warrants such a course, or when the storage expenses would be out of proportion to the value of the goods. He may also proceed to the sale of the goods in other cases if after the expiry of a reasonable period he has not received from the person entitled to dispose of the goods instructions to the contrary which he may reasonably be required to carry out

4. If the goods have been sold pursuant to this Article, the proceeds of sale, after deduction of the expenses chargeable against the goods, shall be placed at the disposal of the person entitled to dispose of the goods. If these charges exceed the proceeds of sale, the carrier shall be entitled to the difference.

5. The procedure in the case of sale shall be determined by the law or custom of the place where the goods are situated.

## CHAPTER IV

## LIABILITY OF THE CARRIER

### ARTICLE 17

1. The carrier shall be liable for the total or partial loss of the goods and for damage thereto occurring between the time when he takes over the goods and time of delivery, as well as for any delay in delivery.

2. The carrier shall however be relieved of liability if the loss, damage or delay was caused by the wrongful act or neglect of the claimant, by the instructions of the claimant given otherwise than as the result of a wrongful act or neglect on the part of the carrier, by inherent vice of the goods or through circumstances which the carrier could not avoid and the consequences of which he was unable to prevent.

3. The carrier shall not be relieved of liability by reason of the defective condition of the vehicle used by him in order to perform the carriage, or by reason of the wrongful act or neglect of the person from whom he may have hired the vehicle or of the agents or servants of the latter.

4. Subject to Article 18, paragraphs 2 to 5, the carrier shall be relieved of liability when the loss or damage arises from the special risks inherent in one or more of the following circumstances:

(a) Use of open unsheeted vehicles, when their use has been expressly agreed and specified in the consignment note;
(b) the lack of, or defective condition of packing in the case of goods which, by their nature, are liable to wastage or to be damaged when not packed or when not properly packed;
(c) handling, loading, stowage or unloading of the goods by sender, the consignee or persons acting on behalf of the sender or the consignee;
(d) the nature of certain kinds of goods which particularly exposes them to total or partial loss or to damage, especially through breakage, rust,

decay, desiccation, leakage, normal wastage, or the action of moth or vermin;
(e) insufficiency or inadequacy of marks or numbers on the packages;
(f) the carriage of livestock.

5. Where under this Article the carrier is not under any liability in respect of some of the factors causing the loss, damage or delay, he shall only be liable to the extent that those factors for which he is liable under this Article have contributed to the loss, damage or delay, he shall only be liable to the extent that those factors for which he is liable under this Article have contributed to the loss, damage or delay.

## ARTICLE 18

1. The burden of proving that loss, damage or delay was due to one of the causes specified in Article 17, paragraph 2, shall rest upon the carrier.

2. When the carrier established that in the circumstances of the case, the loss or damage could be attributed to one or more of the special risks referred to in Article 17, paragraph 4, it shall be presumed that it was so caused. The claimant shall however be entitled to prove that the loss or damage was not, in fact, attributable either wholly or partly to one of these risks.

3. This presumption shall not apply in the circumstances set out in Article 17, paragraph 4 (a), if there has been an abnormal shortage, or a loss of any package.

4. If the carriage is performed in vehicles specially equipped to protect the goods from the effects of heat, cold, variations in temperature or the humidity of the air, the carrier shall not be entitled to claim the benefit of Article 17, paragraph 4 (d), unless he proves that all steps incumbent on him in the circumstances with respect to the choice, maintenance and use of such equipment were taken and that he complied with any special instructions issued to him.

5. The carrier shall not be entitled to claim the benefit of Article 17, paragraph 4 (f), unless he proves that all steps normally incumbent on him in the circumstances were taken and that he complied with any special instructions issued to him.

## ARTICLE 19

Delay in delivery shall be said to occur when the goods have not been delivered within the agreed time-limit or when, failing an agreed time-limit, the actual duration of the carriage having regard to the circumstances of the case, and in particular, in the case of partial loads, the time required for making up a complete load in the normal way, exceeds the time it would be reasonable to allow a diligent carrier.

## ARTICLE 20

1. The fact that goods have not been delivered within thirty days following the expiry of the agreed time-limit, or, if there is no agreed time-limit, within sixty days from the time when the carrier took over the goods, shall be conclusive evidence of the loss of the goods, and the person entitled to make a claim may thereupon treat them as lost.

2. The person so entitled may, on receipt of compensation for the missing goods, request in writing that he shall be notified immediately should the goods be recovered in the course of the year following the payment of compensation. He shall be given a written acknowledgement of such request.

3. Within the thirty days following receipt of such notification, the person entitled as aforesaid may require the goods to be delivered to him against payment of the charges shown to be due on the consignment note and also against refund of the compensation he received less any charges included therein but without prejudice to any claims to compensation for delay in delivery under Article 23 and, where applicable, Article 26.

4. In the absence of the request mentioned in paragraph 2 or of any instructions given within the period of thirty days specified in paragraph 3, or if the goods are not recovered until more than one year after the payment of compensation, the carrier shall be entitled to deal with them in accordance with the law of the place where the goods are situated.

## ARTICLE 21

Should the goods have been delivered to the consignee without collection of the 'cash on delivery' charge which should have been collected by the carrier under the terms of the contract of carriage, the carrier shall be liable to the sender for compensation not exceeding the amount of such charge without prejudice to his right of action against the consignee.

## ARTICLE 22

1. When the sender hands goods of a dangerous nature to the carrier, he shall inform the carrier of the exact nature of the danger and indicate, if necessary, the precautions to be taken. If this information has not been entered in the consignment note, the burden of proving, by some other means, that the carrier knew the exact nature of the danger constituted by the carriage of the said goods shall rest upon the sender or the consignee.

2. Goods of a dangerous nature which, in the circumstances referred to in paragraph 1 of this Article, the carrier did not know were dangerous, may, at any time or place, be unloaded, destroyed or rendered harmless by the carrier without compensation; further, the sender shall be liable for all expenses, loss or damage arising out of their handing over for carriage or of their carriage.

## ARTICLE 23

1. When, under the provisions of this Convention, a carrier is liable for compensation in respect of total or partial loss of goods, such compensation shall be calculated by reference to the value of the goods at the place and time at which they were accepted for carriage.

2. The value of the goods shall be fixed accordingly to the commodity exchange price or, if there is no such price, according to the current market price or, if there is no commodity exchange price or current market price, by reference to the normal value of goods of the same kind and quality.

3. Compensation shall not, however, exceed 8.33 units of account per kilogram of gross weight short.

4. In addition, the carriage charges, Customs duties and other charges incurred in respect of the carriage of the goods shall be refunded in full in case of total loss and in proportion to the loss sustained in case of partial loss, but no further damages shall be payable.

5. In the case of delay, if the claimant proves that damage has resulted therefrom the carrier shall pay compensation for such damage not exceeding the carriage charges.

6. Higher compensation may only be claimed where the value of the goods or a special interest in delivery has been declared in accordance with Articles 24 and 26.

7. The unit of account mentioned in this Convention is the Special Drawing Right as defined by the International Monetary Fund. The amount mentioned in paragraph 3 of this Article shall be converted into the national currency of the State of the Court seised of the case on the basis of the value of that currency on the date of the judgment or the date agreed upon by the Parties.

## ARTICLE 24

The sender may, against payment of a surcharge to be agreed upon, declare in the consignment note a value for the goods exceeding the limit laid down in Article 23, paragraph 3, and in that case the amount of the declared value shall be substituted for that limit.

## ARTICLE 25

1. In case of damage, the carrier shall be liable for the amount by which the goods have diminished in value, calculated by reference to the value of the goods fixed in accordance with Article 23, paragraphs 1, 2 and 4.

2. The compensation may not, however, exceed:
   - (a) if the whole consignment has been damaged the amount payable in the case of total loss;
   - (b) if part only of the consignment has been damaged, the amount payable in the case of loss of the part affected.

## ARTICLE 26

1. The sender may, against payment of a surcharge to be agreed upon, fix the amount of a special interest in delivery in the case of loss or damage or of the agreed time-limit being exceeded, by entering such amount in the consignment note.

2. If a declaration of a special interest in delivery has been made, compensation for the additional loss or damage proved may be claimed, up to the total amount of the interest declared, independently of the compensation provided for in Articles 23, 24 and 25.

## ARTICLES 27

1. The claimant shall be entitled to claim interest on compensation payable. Such interest, calculated at five per centum per annum, shall accrue from the date on which the claim was sent in writing to the carrier or, if no such claim has been made, from the date on which legal proceedings were instituted.

2. When the amounts on which the calculation of the compensation is based are not expressed in the currency of the country in which payment is claimed, conversion shall be at the rate of exchange applicable on the day and at the place of payment of compensation.

## ARTICLE 28

1. In cases where, under the law applicable, loss, damage or delay arising out of carriage under this Convention gives rise to an extra-contractual claim, the carrier may avail himself of the provisions of this Convention which exclude his liability or which fix or limit the compensation due.

2. In cases where the extra-contractual liability for loss, damage or delay of one of the persons for whom the carrier is responsible under the terms of Article 3 is in issue, such person may also avail himself of the provisions of this Convention which exclude the liability of the carrier or which fix or limit the compensation due.

## ARTICLE 29

1. The carrier shall not be entitled to avail himself of the provisions of this chapter which exclude or limit his liability or which shift the burden of proof if the damage was caused by his wilful misconduct or by such default on his part as, in accordance with the law of the court or tribunal seised of the case, is considered as equivalent to wilful misconduct.

2. The same provision shall apply if the wilful misconduct or default is committed by the agents or servants of the carrier or by any other persons of whose services he makes use for the performance of the carriage, when such agents, servants or other persons are acting within the scope of their employment. Furthermore, in such a case such agents, servants or other persons shall not be entitled to avail themselves, with regard to their personal liability, of the provisions of this chapter referred to in paragraph 1.

## CHAPTER V

## CLAIMS AND ACTIONS

### ARTICLE 30

1. If the consignee takes delivery of the goods without duly checking their condition with the carrier or without sending him reservations giving a general indication of the loss or damage, not later than the time of delivery in the case of apparent loss or damage and within seven days of delivery, Sundays and public holidays excepted, in the case of loss or damage which is not apparent, the fact of his taking delivery shall be *prima facie* evidence that he has received the goods in the condition described in the consignment note. In the case of loss or damage which is not apparent the reservations referred to shall be made in writing.

2. When the condition of the goods has been duly checked by the consignee and the carrier, evidence contradicting the result of this checking shall only be admissable in the case of loss or damage which is not apparent and provided that the consignee has duly sent reservations in writing to the carrier within seven days, Sundays and public holidays excepted, from the date of checking.

3. No compensation shall be payable for delay in delivery unless a reservation has been sent in writing to the carrier, within twenty-one days from the time that the goods were placed at the disposal of the consignee.

4. In calculating the time-limits provided for in this Article the date of delivery, or the date of checking, or the date when the goods were placed at the disposal of the consignee, as the case may be, shall not be included.

5. The carrier and the consignee shall give each other every reasonable facility for making the requisite investigations and checks.

### ARTICLE 31

1. In legal proceedings arising out of carriage under this Convention, the plaintiff may bring an action in any court or tribunal of a contracting country designated by agreement between the parties and, in addition, in the courts or tribunals of a country within whose territory

(a) the defendant is ordinarily resident, or has his principal place of business, or the branch or agency through which the contract of carriage was made, or

(b) the place where the goods were taken over by the carrier or the place designated for delivery is situated, and in no other courts or tribunals.

2. Where in respect of a claim referred to in paragraph 1 of this Article an action is pending before a court or tribunal competent under that paragraph, or where in respect of such a claim a judgment has been entered by such a court or tribunal no new action shall be started between the same parties on the same grounds unless the judgment of the court or tribunal before which the first action was brought is not enforceable in the country in which the fresh proceedings are brought.

3. When a judgment entered by a court or tribunal of a contracting country in any such action as is referred to in paragraph 1 of this Article has become enforceable in that country, it shall also become enforceable in each of the other contracting States, as soon as the formalities required in the country concerned have been complied with. The formalities shall not permit the merits of the case to be re-opened.

4. The provisions of paragraph 3 of this Article shall apply to judgments after trial, judgments by default and settlements confirmed by an order of the court, but shall not apply to interim judgments or to awards of damages, in addition to costs against a plaintiff who wholly or partly fails in his action.

5. Security for costs shall not be required in proceedings arising out of carriage under the Convention from nationals of contracting countries resident or having their place of business in one of those countries.

## ARTICLE 32

1. The period of limitation for an action arising out of carriage under this Convention shall be one year. Nevertheless, in the case of wilful misconduct, or such default as in accordance with the law of the court or tribunal seised of the case, is considered as equivalent to wilful misconduct, the period of limitation shall be three years. The period of limitation shall begin to run:

(a) in the case of partial loss, damage or delay in delivery, from the date of delivery;

(b) in the case of total loss, from the thirtieth day after the expiry of the agreed time-limit or where there is no agreed time-limit from the sixtieth day from the date on which the goods were taken over by the carrier;

(c) in all other cases, on the expiry of a period of three months after the making of the contract of carriage.

The day on which the period of limitation begins to run shall not be included in the period.

2. A written claim shall suspend the period of limitation until such date as the carrier rejects the claim by notification in writing and returns the documents attached thereto. If a part of the claim is admitted the period of limitation shall start to run again only in respect of that part of the claim still in dispute. The burden of proof of the receipt of the claim, or of the reply and of the return of the documents, shall rest with the party relying upon these facts. The running of the period of limitation shall not be suspended by further claims having the same object.

3. Subject to the provisions of paragraph 2 above, the extension of the period of limitation shall be governed by the law of the court or tribunal seised of the case. That law shall also govern the fresh accrual of rights of action.

4. A right of action which has become barred by lapse of time may not be exercised by way of counter-claim or set-off.

### ARTICLE 33

The contract of carriage may contain a clause conferring competence on an arbitration tribunal if the clause conferring competence on the tribunal provides that the tribunal shall apply this Convention.

## CHAPTER VI

## PROVISIONS RELATING TO CARRIAGE PERFORMED BY SUCCESSIVE CARRIERS

### ARTICLE 34

If carriage governed by a single contract is performed by successive road carriers, each of them shall be responsible for the performance of the whole operation, the second carrier and each succeeding carrier becoming a party to the contract of carriage, under the terms of the consignment note, by reason of his acceptance of the goods and the consignment note.

### ARTICLE 35

1. A carrier accepting the goods from a previous carrier shall give the latter a dated and signed receipt. He shall enter his name and address on the second copy of the consignment note. Where applicable, he shall enter on the second copy of the consignment note and on the receipt reservations of the kind provided for in Article 8, paragraph 2.

2. The provisions of Article 9 shall apply to the relations between successive carriers.

### ARTICLE 36

Except in the case of a counter-claim or a set-off raised in an action concerning a claim based on the same contract of carriage, legal proceedings in respect of liability for loss, damage or delay may only be brought against the first carrier, the last carrier or the carrier who was performing that portion of the carriage during which the event causing the loss, damage or delay occurred; an action may be brought at the same time against several of these carriers.

### ARTICLE 37

A carrier who has paid compensation in compliance with the provisions of this Convention, shall be entitled to recover such compensation, together with interest thereon and all costs and expenses incurred by reason of the claim, from the other carriers who have taken part in the carriage, subject to the following provisions:

(a) the carrier responsible for the loss or damage shall be solely liable for the compensation whether paid by himself or by another carrier;

(b) when the loss or damage has been caused by the action of two or more carriers, each of them shall pay an amount proportionate to his share of liability; should it be impossible to apportion the liability, each carrier shall be liable in proportion to the share of the payment for the carriage which is due to him;

(c) if it cannot be ascertained to which carriers liability is attributable for the loss or damage, the amount of the compensation shall be apportioned between all the carriers as laid down in (b) above.

## ARTICLE 38

If one of the carriers is insolvent, the share of the compensation due from him and unpaid by him shall be divided among the other carriers in proportion to the share of the payment for the carriage due to them.

## ARTICLE 39

1. No carrier against whom a claim is made under Articles 37 and 38 shall be entitled to dispute the validity of the payment made by the carrier making the claim if the amount of the compensation was determined by judicial authority after the first mentioned carrier had been given due notice of the proceedings and afforded an opportunity of entering an appearance.

2. A carrier wishing to take proceedings to enforce his right of recovery may make his claim before the competent court or tribunal of the country in which one of the carriers concerned is ordinarily resident, or has his principal place of business or the branch or agency through which the contract of carriage was made. All the carriers concerned may be made defendants in the same action.

3. The provisions of Article 31, paragraphs 3 and 4, shall apply to judgments entered in the proceedings referred to in Articles 37 and 38.

4. The provisions of Article 32 shall apply to claims between carriers. The period of limitation shall, however, begin to run either on the date of the final judicial decision fixing the amount of compensation payable under the provisions of this Convention, or, if there is no such judicial decision, from the actual date of payment.

## ARTICLE 40

Carriers shall be free to agree among themselves on provisions other than those laid down in Articles 37 and 38.

## Chapter VII

## Nullity of Stipulations Contrary to the Convention

### Article 41

1. Subject to the provisions of Article 40, any stipulation which would directly or indirectly derogate from the provisions of this Convention shall be null and void. The nullity of such a stipulation shall not involve the nullity of the other provisions of the contract.

2. In particular, a benefit of insurance in favour of the carrier or any other similar clause, or any clause shifting the burden of proof shall be null and void.

## Protocol of Signature

1. This Convention shall not apply to traffic between the United Kingdom of Great Britain and Northern Ireland and the Republic of Ireland.

# UNIFORM LAWS ON INTERNATIONAL SALES ACT 1967

## CHAPTER 45

### 1. Application of Uniform Law on the International Sale of Goods

(1) In this Act 'the Uniform Law on Sales' means the Uniform Law on the International Sale of Goods forming the Annex to the First Convention and set out, with the modification provided for by Article III of that Convention, in Schedule 1 to this Act; and 'the First Convention' means the Convention relating to a Uniform Law on the International Sale of Goods done at The Hague on 1st July 1964.

(2) The Uniform Law on Sales shall, subject to the following provisions of this section, have the force of the law in the United Kingdom.

(3) While an Order of Her Majesty in Council is in force declaring that a declaration by the United Kingdom under Article V of the First Convention (application only by choice of parties) has been made and not withdrawn the Uniform Law on Sales shall apply to a contract of sale only if it has been chosen by the parties to the contract as the law of the contract.

(4) In determining the extent of the application of the Uniform Law on Sales by virtue of Article 4 thereof (choice of parties)-
  (a) and (b) [omitted]
  (c) in relation to a contract made on or after 1 February 1978, no provision of that law shall be so regarded except sections 12 to 15 of the Sale of Goods Act 1979.`

(5) to (8) [omitted]

### 2. Application of Uniform Law on the Formation of Contracts for the International Sale of Goods

(1) In this Act 'the Uniform Law on Formation' means the Law forming Annex I to the Second Convention as set out, with the modifications provided for by paragraph 3 of Article I of that Convention, in Schedule 2 to this Act; and 'the Second Convention' means the Convention relating to a Uniform Law on the Formation of Contracts for the International Sale of Goods done at The Hague on 1st July 1964.

(2) Subject to subsection (3) of this section the Uniform Law on Formation shall have the force of law in the United Kingdom.

(3) The Uniform Law on Formation shall not apply to offers, replies and acceptances made before such date as Her Majesty may by Order in Council declare to be the date on which the Second Convention comes into force in respect of the United Kingdom.

(4) [omitted]

**3. to 5. [omitted]**

# SCHEDULES

## SCHEDULE 1

## THE UNIFORM LAW ON THE INTERNATIONAL SALE OF GOODS

### CHAPTER I — SPHERE OF APPLICATION OF THE LAW

### ARTICLE 1

1. The present Law shall apply to contracts of sale of goods entered into by parties whose places of business are in the territories of different Contracting States, in each of the following cases:

   (a) where the contract involves the sale of goods which are at the time of the conclusion of the contract in the course of carriage or will be carried from the territory of one State to the territory of another;

   (b) where the acts constituting the offer and the acceptance have been effected in the territories of different States;

   (c) where delivery of the goods is to be made in the territory of a State other than that within whose territory the acts constituting the offer and the acceptance have been effected.

2. Where a party to the contract does not have a place of business, reference shall be made to his habitual residence.

3. The application of the present Law shall not depend on the nationality of the parties.

4. In the case of contracts by correspondence, offer and acceptance shall be considered to have been effected in the territory of the same State only if the letters, telegrams or other documentary communications which contain them have been sent and received in the territory of that State.

5. For the purpose of determining whether the parties have their places of business or habitual residences in 'different States', any two or more States shall not be considered to be 'different State' if a valid declaration to that effect made under Article 11 of the Convention dated the 1st day of July 1964 relating to a Uniform Law on the International Sale of Goods is in force in respect of them.

### ARTICLE 2

Rules of private international law shall be excluded for the purposes of the application of the present Law, subject to any provision to the contrary in the said Law.

## Article 3

The parties to a contract of sale shall be free to exclude the application thereto of the present Law either entirely or partially. Such exclusion may be express or implied.

## Article 4

The present Law shall also apply where it has been chosen as the law of the contract by the parties, whether or not their places of business or their habitual residences are in different States and whether or not such States are Parties to the Convention dated the 1st day of July 1964 relating to the Uniform Law on the International Sale of Goods, to the extent that it does not affect the application of any mandatory provisions of law which would have been applicable if the parties had not chosen the Uniform Law.

## Article 5

1. The present Law shall not apply to sales:
   (a) of stocks, shares, investment securities, negotiable instruments or money;
   (b) of any ship, vessel or aircraft, which is or will be subject to registration;
   (c) of electricity;
   (d) by authority of law or on execution or distress.

2. The present Law shall not affect the application of any mandatory provision of national law for the protection of a party to a contract which contemplates the purchase of goods by that party by payment of the price by instalments.

## Article 6

Contracts for the supply of goods to be manufactured or produced shall be considered to be sales within the meaning of the present Law, unless the party who orders the goods undertakes to supply an essential and substantial part of the materials necessary for such manufacture or production.

## Article 7

The present Law shall apply to sales regardless of the commercial or civil character of the parties or of the contracts.

## Article 8

The present Law shall govern only the obligations of the seller and the buyer arising from a contract of sale. In particular, the present Law shall not, except as otherwise expressly provided there, be concerned with the formation of the contract, nor with the effect which the contract may have on the property in the goods sold, nor with the validity of the contract or of any of its provisions or of any usage.

## CHAPTER II — GENERAL PROVISIONS

### ARTICLE 9

1. The parties shall be bound by any usage which they have expressly or impliedly made applicable to their contract and by any practices which they have established between themselves.

2. They shall also be bound by usages which reasonable persons in the same situation as the parties usually consider to be applicable to their contract. In the event of conflict with the present Law, the usages shall prevail unless otherwise agreed by the parties.

3. Where expressions, provisions or forms of contract commonly used in commercial practice are employed, they shall be interpreted according to the meaning usually given to them in the trade concerned.

### ARTICLE 10

For the purposes of the present Law, a breach of contract shall be regarded as fundamental wherever the party in breach knew, or ought to have known, at the time of the conclusion of the contract, that a reasonable person in the same situation as the other party would not have entered into the contract if he had foreseen the breach and its effects.

### ARTICLE 11

Where under the present Law an act is required to be performed 'promptly', it shall be performed within as short a period as possible, in the circumstances, from the moment when the act could reasonably be performed.

### ARTICLE 12

For the purposes of the present Law, the expression 'current price' means a price based upon an official market quotation, or, in the absence of such a quotation, upon those factors which, according to the usage of the market, serve to determine the price.

### ARTICLE 13

For the purposes of the present Law, the expression 'a party knew or ought to have known', or any similar expression, refers to what should have been known to a reasonable person in the same situation.

### ARTICLE 14

Communications provided for by the present Law shall be made by the means usual in the circumstances.

## ARTICLE 15

A contract of sale need not be evidenced by writing and shall not be subject to any other requirements as to form. In particular, it may be proved by means of witnesses.

## ARTICLE 16

Where under the provisions of the present Law one party to a contract of sale is entitled to require performance of any obligation by the other party, a court shall not be bound to enter or enforce a judgment providing for specific performance except in accordance with the provisions of Article VII of the Convention dated the 1st day of July 1964 relating to a Uniform Law on the International Sale of Goods.

## ARTICLE 17

Questions concerning matters governed by the present Law which are not expressly settled therein shall be settled in conformity with the general principals on which the present Law is based.

# CHAPTER III — OBLIGATIONS OF THE SELLER

## ARTICLE 18

The seller shall effect delivery of the goods, hand over any documents relating thereto and transfer the property in the goods, as required by the contract and the present Law.

## SECTION I. -DELIVERY OF THE GOODS

## ARTICLE 19

1. Delivery consists in the handing over of goods which conform with the contract.

2. Where the contract of sale involves carriage of the goods and no other place for delivery has been agreed upon, delivery shall be effected by handing over the goods to the carrier for transmission to the buyer.

3. Where the goods handed over to the carrier are not clearly appropriated to performance of the contract by being marked with an address or by some other means, the seller shall, in addition to handing over the goods, sent to the buyer notice of the consignment and, if necessary, some document specifying the goods.

*Sub-section 1.-Obligations of the seller as regards the date and place of delivery*

### A—Date of Delivery

### Article 20

Where the parties have agreed upon a date for delivery or where such date is fixed by usage, the seller shall, without the need for any other formality, be bound to deliver the goods at that date, provided that the date thus fixed is determined or determinable by the calendar or is fixed in relation to a definite event, the date of which can be ascertained by the parties.

### Article 21

Where by agreement of the parties or by usage delivery shall be effected within a certain period (such as a particular month or season), the seller may fix the precise date of delivery, unless the circumstances indicate that the fixing of the date was reserved to the buyer.

### Article 22

Where the date of delivery has not been determined in accordance with the provisions of Articles 20 or 21, the seller shall be bound to deliver the goods within a reasonable time after the conclusion of the contract, regard being had to the nature of the goods and to the circumstances.

### B—Place of Delivery

### Article 23

1. Where the contract of sale does not involve carriage of the goods, the seller shall deliver the goods at the place where he carried on business at the time of the conclusion of the contract, or, in the absence of a place of business, at his habitual residence.

2. If the sale relates to specific goods and the parties knew that the goods were at a certain place at the time of the conclusion of the contract, the seller shall deliver the goods at that place. The same rule shall apply if the goods sold are unascertained goods to be taken from a specified stock or if they are to be manufactured or produced at a place known to the parties at the time of the conclusion of the contract.

### C—Remedies for the seller's failure to perform his obligations as regards the date and place of delivery

1. Where the seller fails to perform his obligations as regards the date or the place of delivery, the buyer may, as provided in Articles 25 to 32:
   (a) require performance of the contract by the seller;
   (b) declare the contract avoided.

2. The buyer may also claim damages as provided in Article 82 or in Articles 84 to 87.

3. In no case shall the seller be entitled to apply to a court or arbitral tribunal to grant him a period of grace.

## ARTICLE 25

The buyer shall not be entitled to require performance of the contract by the seller, if it is in conformity with usage and reasonably possible for the buyer to purchase goods to replace those to which the contract relates. In this case the contract shall be ipso facto avoided as from the time when such purchases should be effected.

### *(a) Remedies as regards the date of delivery*

## ARTICLE 26

1. Where the failure to deliver the goods at the date fixed amounts to a fundamental breach of the contract, the buyer may either require performance by the seller or declare the contract avoided. He shall inform the seller of his decision within a reasonable time; otherwise the contract shall be ipso facto avoided.

2. If the seller requests the buyer to make known his decision under paragraph 1 of this Article and the buyer does not comply promptly, the contract shall be ipso facto avoided.

3. If the seller has effected delivery before the buyer has made known his decision under paragraph 1 of this Article and the buyer does not exercise promptly his right to declare the contract avoided, the contract cannot be avoided.

4. Where the buyer has chosen performance of the contract and does not obtain it within a reasonable time, he may declare the contract avoided.

## ARTICLE 27

1. Where failure to deliver the goods at the date fixed does not amount to a fundamental breach of the contract, the seller shall retain the right to effect delivery and the buyer shall retain the right to require performance of the contract by the seller.

2. The buyer may however grant the seller an additional period of time of reasonable length. Failure to deliver the goods at the date fixed shall amount to a fundamental breach of the contract whenever a price for such goods is quoted on a market where the buyer can obtain them.

## Article 28

Failure to deliver the goods at the date fixed shall amount to a fundamental breach of the contract whenever a price for such goods is quoted on a market where the buyer can obtain them.

## Article 29

Where the seller tenders delivery of the goods before the date fixed, the buyer may accept or reject delivery; if he accepts, he may reserve the right to claim damages in accordance with Article 82.

### *(b) Remedies as regards the place of delivery*

## Article 30

1. Where failure to deliver the goods at the place fixed amounts to a fundamental breach of the contract, and failure to deliver the goods at the date fixed would also amount to a fundamental breach, the buyer may either require performance of the contract by the seller or declare the contract avoided. The buyer shall inform the seller of his decision within a reasonable time; otherwise the contract shall be ipso facto avoided.

2. If the seller requests the buyer to make known his decision under paragraph 1 of this Article and the buyer does not comply promptly, the contract shall be ipso facto avoided.

3. If the seller has transported the goods to the place fixed before the buyer has made known his decision under paragraph 1 of this Article and the buyer does not exercise promptly his right to declare the contract avoided, the contract cannot be avoided.

## Article 31

1. In cases not provided for in Article 30, the seller shall retain the right to effect delivery at the place fixed and the buyer shall retain the right to require performance of the contract by the seller.

2. The buyer may however grant the seller an additional period of time of reasonable length. Failure to deliver within this period at the place fixed shall amount to a fundamental breach of the contract.

## Article 32

1. If delivery is to be effected by handing over the goods to a carrier and the goods have been handed over at a place other than that fixed, the buyer may declare the contract avoided, whenever the failure to deliver the goods at the place fixed amounts to a fundamental breach of the contract. He shall lose this right if he has not promptly declared the contract avoided.

2. The buyer shall have the same right, in the circumstances and on the conditions provided in paragraph 1 of this Article, if the goods have been despatched to some place other than that fixed.

3. If despatch from a place or to a place other than that fixed does not amount to a fundamental breach of the contract, the buyer may only claim damages in accordance with Article 82.

*Sub-section 2.-Obligations of the seller as regards the conformity of the goods*

*A.-Lack of conformity*

## ARTICLE 33

1. The seller shall not have fulfilled his obligation to deliver the goods, where has has handed over:

(a) part only of the goods sold or a larger or a smaller quantity of the goods than he contracted to sell;

(b) goods which are not those to which the contract relates or goods of a different kind;

(c) goods which lack the qualities of a sample or model which the seller has handed over or sent to the buyer, unless the seller has submitted it without any express or implied undertaking that the goods would conform therewith;

(d) goods which do not possess the qualities necessary for their ordinary or commercial use;

(e) goods which do not possess the qualities for some particular purpose expressly or impliedly contemplated by the contract;

(f) in general, goods which do not possess the qualities and characteristics expressly or impliedly contemplated by the contract.

2. No difference in quantity, lack of part of the goods or absence of any quality or characteristic shall be taken into consideration where it is not material.

## ARTICLE 34

In the cases to which Article 33 relates, the rights conferred on the buyer by the present Law exclude all other remedies based on lack of conformity of the goods.

## ARTICLE 35

1. Whether the goods are in conformity with the contract shall be determined by their condition at the time when risk passes. However, if risk does not pass because of a declaration of avoidance of the contract or of a demand for other goods in replacement, the conformity of the goods with the contract shall be determined by their condition at the time when risk would have passed had they been in conformity with the contract.

2. The seller shall be liable for the consequences of any lack of conformity occurring after the time fixed in paragraph 1 of this Article if it was due to an act of the seller or of a person for whose conduct he is responsible.

## Article 36

The seller shall not be liable for the consequences of any lack of conformity of the kind referred to in sub-paragraphs (d), (e) or (f) of paragraph 1 of Article 33, if at the time of the conclusion of the contract the buyer knew, or could not have been unaware of, such lack of conformity.

## Article 37

If the seller has handed over goods before the date fixed for delivery he may, up to that date, deliver other goods which are in conformity with the contract or remedy any defects in the goods handed over, provided that the exercise of this right does not cause the buyer either unreasonable inconvenience or unreasonable expense.

### *B.—Ascertainment and notification of lack of conformity*

## Article 38

1. The buyer shall examine the goods, or cause them to be examined, promptly.

2. In case of carriage of the goods the buyer shall examine them at the place of destination.

3. If the goods are redespatched by the buyer without transhipment and the seller knew or ought to have known, at the time when the contract was concluded, of the possibility of such redespatch, examination of the goods may be deferred until they arrive at the new destination.

4. The methods of examination shall be governed by the agreement of the parties or, in the absence of such agreement, by the law or usage of the place where the examination is to be effected.

## Article 39

1. The buyer shall lose the right to rely on a lack of conformity of the goods if he has not given the seller notice thereof promptly after he has discovered the lack of conformity or ought to have discovered it. If a defect which could not have been revealed by the examination of the goods provided for in Article 38 is found later, the buyer may nonetheless rely on that defect, provided that he gives the seller notice thereof promptly after its discovery. In any event, the buyer shall lose the right to rely on a lack of conformity of the goods if he has not given notice thereof to the seller within a period of two years from the date

on which the goods were handed over, unless the lack of conformity constituted a breach of a guarantee covering a longer period.

2. In giving notice to the seller of any lack of conformity, the buyer shall specify its nature and invite the seller to examine the goods or to cause them to be examined by his agent.

3. Where any notice referred to in paragraph 1 of this Article has been sent by letter, telegram or other appropriate means, the fact that such notice is delayed or fails to arrive at its destination shall not deprive the buyer of the right to rely thereon.

## ARTICLE 40

The seller shall not be entitled to rely on the provisions of Articles 38 and 39 if the lack of conformity relates to facts of which he knew, or of which he could not have been unaware, and which he did not disclose.

### *C.-Remedies for lack of conformity*

## ARTICLE 41

1. Where the buyer has given due notice to the seller of the failure of the goods to confirm with the contract, the buyer may, as provided in Articles 42 to 46:
(a) require performance of the contract by the seller;
(b) declare the contract avoided;
(c) reduce the price.

2. The buyer may also claim damages as provided in Article 82 or in Articles 84 to 87.

## ARTICLE 42

1. The buyer may require the seller to perform the contract:
(a) if the sale relates to goods to be produced or manufactured by the seller, by remedying defects in the goods, provided the seller is in a position to remedy the defects;
(b) if the sales relates to specific goods, by delivering the goods to which the contract refers or the missing part thereof;
(c) if the sale relates to unascertained goods, by delivering other goods which are in conformity with the contract or by delivering the missing part or quantity, except where the purchase of goods in replacement is in conformity with usage and reasonably possible.

2. If the buyer does not obtain performance of the contract by the seller within a reasonable time, he shall retain the rights provided in Articles 43 to 46.

## ARTICLE 43

The buyer may declare the contract avoided if the failure of the goods to conform to the contract and also the failure to deliver on the date fixed amount to fundamental breaches of the contract. The buyer shall lose his right to declare the contract avoided if he does not exercise it promptly after giving the seller notice of the lack of conformity or, in the case to which paragraph 2 of Article 42 applies, after the expiration of the period referred to in that paragraph.

## ARTICLE 44

1. In cases not provided for in Article 43, the seller shall retain, after the date fixed for the delivery of the goods, the right to deliver any missing part or quantity of the goods or to deliver other goods which are in conformity with the contract or to remedy any defect in the goods handed over, provided that the exercise of this right does not cause the buyer either unreasonable inconvenience or unreasonable expense.

2. The buyer may however fix an additional period of time of reasonable length for the further delivery or for the remedying of the defect. If at the expiration of the additional period the seller has not delivered to goods or remedied the defect, the buyer may choose between requiring the performance of the contract or reducing the price in accordance with Article 46 or, provided that he does so promptly, declare the contract avoided.

## ARTICLE 45

1. Where the seller has handed over part only of the goods or an insufficient quantity or where part only of the goods handed over is in conformity with the contract, the provisions of Articles 43 and 44 shall apply in respect of the part or quantity which is missing or which does not conform with the contract.

2. The buyer may declare the contract avoided in its entirety only if the failure to effect delivery completely and in conformity with the contract amounts to a fundamental breach of the contract.

## ARTICLE 46

Where the buyer has neither obtained performance of the contract by the seller nor declared the contract avoided, the buyer may reduce the price in the same proportion as the value of the goods at the time of the conclusion of the contract has been diminished because of their lack of conformity with the contract.

## ARTICLE 47

Where the seller has proffered to the buyer a quantity of unascertained goods greater than that provided for in the contract, the buyer may reject or accept the excess quantity. If the buyer rejects the excess quantity, the seller shall be liable only for damages in accordance with Article 82. If the buyer accepts the whole or part of the excess quantity, he shall pay for it at the contract rate.

## ARTICLE 48

The buyer may exercise the rights provided in Articles 43 to 46, even before the time fixed for delivery, if it is clear that goods which would be handed over would not be in conformity with the contract.

## ARTICLE 49

1. The buyer shall lose his right to reply on lack of conformity with the contract at the expiration of a period of one year after he has given notice as provided in Article 39, unless he has been prevented from exercising his right because of fraud on the part of the seller.

2. After the expiration of this period, the buyer shall not be entilted to rely on the lack of conformity, even by way of defence to an action. Nevertheless, if the buyer has not paid for the goods and provided that he has given due notice of the lack of conformity promptly, as provided in Article 39, he may advance as a defence to a claim for payment of the price a claim for a reduction in the price or for damages.

*Section II Handing over documents*

## ARTICLE 50

Where the seller is bound to hand over to the buyer any documents relating to the goods, he shall do so at the time and place fixed by the contract or by usage.

## ARTICLE 51

If the seller fails to hand over the documents as provided in Article 50 at the time and place fixed or if he hands over documents which are not in conformity with those which he was bound to hand over, the buyer shall have the same rights as those provided under Articles 24 to 32 or under Articles 41 to 49, as the case may be.

*Section III - Transfer of Property*

## ARTICLE 52

1. Where the goods are subject to a right or claim of a third person, the buyer, unless he agreed to take the goods subject to such right or claim, shall notify the seller of such right or claim, unless the seller already knows thereof, and request that the goods should be freed therefrom within reasonable time or that other goods free from all rights and claims of third persons to be delivered to him by the seller.

2. If the seller complies with a request made under paragraph 1 of this Article and the buyer nevertheless suffers a loss, the buyer may claim damages in accordance with Article 82.

3. If the seller fails to comply with a request made under paragraph 1 of the Article and a fundamental breach of the contract results thereby, the buyer may declare the contract avoided and claim damages in accordance with Articles 84 to 87. If the buyer does not declare the contract avoided or if there is no fundamental breach of the contract, the buyer shall have the right to claim damages in accordance with Article 82.

4. The buyer shall lose his right to declare the contract avoided if he fails to act in accordance with paragraph 1 of this Article within a reasonable time from the moment when he became aware or ought to have become aware of the right or claim of the third person in respect of the goods.

### Article 53

The rights conferred on the buyer by Article 52 exclude all other remedies based on the fact that the seller has failed to perform his obligation to transfer the property in the goods or that the goods are subject to a right or claim of a third person.

*Section IV - Other Obligations of the Seller*

### Article 54

1. If the seller is bound to despatch the goods to the buyer, he shall make, in the usual way and on the usual terms, such contracts as are necessary for the carriage of the goods to the place fixed.

2. If the seller is not bound by the contract to effect insurance in respect of the carriage of the goods, he shall provide the buyer, at his request, with all information necessary to enable him to effect such insurance.

### Article 55

1. If the seller fails to perform any obligation other than those referred to in Articles 20 to 53, the buyer may:

(a) where such failure amounts to a fundamental breach of the contract, declare the contract avoided, provided that he does so promptly, and claim damages in accordance with Articles 84 to 87, or

(b) in any other case, claim damages in accordance with Article 82.

2. The buyer may also require performance by the seller of his obligation unless the contract is avoided.

## Chapter IV — Obligations of the Buyer

### Article 56

The buyer shall pay the price for the goods and take delivery of them, as required by the contract and the present law.

*Section I - Payment of the Price*

*A— Fixing the Price*

## ARTICLE 57

Where a contract has been concluded but does not state a price or make provision for the determination of the price, the buyer shall be bound to pay the price generally charged by the seller at the time of the conclusion of the contract.

## ARTICLE 58

Where the price is fixed according to the weight of the goods, it shall , in case of doubt, be determined by the net weight.

*B—Place and date of payment*

## ARTICLE 59

1. The buyer shall pay the price to the seller at the seller's place of business or, if he does not have a place of business, at his habitual residence, or where the payment is to be made against the handing over of the goods or of documents, at the place where such handing over takes place.

2. Where in consequence of a change in the place of business or habitual residence of the seller subsequent to the conclusion of the contract, the expenses incidental to payment are increased, such increase shall be borne by the seller.

## ARTICLE 60

Where the parties have agreed upon a date for the payment of the price or where such a date is fixed by usage, the buyer shall, without the need for any other formality, pay the price at that date.

*C—Remedies for non -payment*

## ARTICLE 61

1. If the buyer fails to pay the price in accordance with the contract and with the present law, the seller may require the buyer to perform his obligation.

2. The seller shall not be entitled to require payment of the price by the buyer if it is in conformity with usage and reasonably possible for the seller to resell the goods. In that case the contract shall be ipso facto avoided as from the time when such resale should be effected.

## ARTICLE 62

1. Where failure to pay the price at the date fixed amounts to a fundamental breach of the contract, the seller may either require the buyer to pay the price or declare the contract avoided. He shall inform the buyer of his decision within a reasonable time; otherwise the contract shall be ipso facto avoided.

2. Where the failure to pay the price at the date fixed does not amount to a fundamental breach of the contract, the seller may grant to the buyer an additional period of time of reasonable length. If the buyer has not paid the price at the expiration of the additional period, the seller may either require the payment of the price by the buyer or provided that he does so promptly, declare the contract avoided.

## ARTICLE 63

1. Where the contract is avoided because of failure to pay the price, the seller shall have the right to claim damages in accordance with Articles 84 to 87.

2. Where the contract is not avoided , the seller shall have the right to claim damages in accordance with Articles 82 and 83.

## ARTICLE 64

In no case shall the buyer be entitled to apply to a court or arbitral tribunal to grant him a period of grace for the payment of the price.

### *Section II - Taking delivery*

## ARTICLE 65

Taking delivery consists in the buyer's doing all such acts as are necessary in order to enable the seller to hand over the goods and actually taking them over.

## ARTICLE 66

1. Where the buyer's failure to take delivery of the goods in accordance with the contract amounts to a fundamental breach of the contract or gives the seller good grounds for fearing that the buyer will not pay the price, the seller may declare the contract avoided.

2. Where the failure to take delivery of the goods does not amount to a fundamental breach of contract, the seller may grant to the buyer an additional period, the seller may declare the contract avoided, provided that he does so promptly.

## ARTICLE 67

1. If the contract reserves to the buyer the right subsequently to determine the form, measurement or other features of the goods (sale by specification) and he fails to make such specification either on the date expressly or impliedly agreed upon or within a reasonable time after receipt of a request from the seller, the seller may declare the contract avoided, provided that he does so promptly, or to make the specification himself in accordance with the requirements of the buyer in so far as these are known to him.

2. If the seller makes the specification himself, he shall inform the buyer of the details thereof and shall fix a reasonable period of time within which the buyer may submit a different specification. If the buyer fails to do so the specification made by the seller shall be binding.

## ARTICLE 68

1. Where the contract is avoided because of the failure of the buyer to accept delivery of the goods or to make a specification, the seller shall have the right to claim damages in accordance with Articles 84 to 87.

2. Where the contract is not avoided, the seller shall have the right to claim damages in accordance with Article 82.

### *Section III - Other obligations of the buyer*

## ARTICLE 69

The buyer shall take the steps provided for in the contract, by usage or by laws and regulations in force, for the purpose of making provision for or guaranteeing payment of the price, such as the acceptance of a bill of exchange, the opening of a documentary credit or the giving of a banker's guarantee.

## ARTICLE 70

1. If the buyer fails to perform any obligation other than those referred to in Sections I and II of this Chapter, the seller may:

(a) where such failure amounts to a fundamental breach of the contract, declare the contract avoided, provided that he does so promptly, and claim damages in accordance with Articles 84 to 87; or

(b) in any other case, claim damages in accordance with Articles 82.

2. The seller may also require performance by the buyer of his obligation, unless the contract is avoided.

## CHAPTER V — PROVISIONS COMMON TO THE OBLIGATIONS OF THE SELLER AND OF THE BUYER

### *Section I - Concurrence between delivery of the goods and payment of the price*

### ARTICLE 71

Except as otherwise provided in Article 72, delivery of the goods and payment of the price shall be concurrent conditions. Nevertheless, the buyer shall not be obliged to pay the price until he has had an opportunity to examine the goods.

### ARTICLE 72

1. Where the contract involves carriage of the goods and where delivery is by virtue of paragraph 2 of Article 19, effected by handing over the goods to the carrier, the seller may either postpone despatch of the goods until he receives payment or proceed to despatch them on terms that reserve to himself the right of disposal of the goods during transit. In the latter case, he may require that the goods shall not be handed over to the buyer at the place of destination except against payment of the price and the buyer shall not be bound to pay the price until he has had an opportunity to examine the goods.

2. Nevertheless, when the contract requires payment against documents, the buyer shall not be entitled to refuse payment of the price on the ground that he has not had the opportunity to examine the goods.

### ARTICLE 73

1. Each party may suspend the performance of his obligations whenever, after the conclusion of the contract, the economic situation of the other party appears to have become so difficult that there is good reason to fear that he will not perform a material part of his obligations.

2. If the seller has already despatched the goods before the economic situation of the buyer described in paragragh 1 of this Article becomes evident, he may prevent the handing over of the goods to the buyer even if the latter holds a document which entitles him to obtain them.

3. Nevertheless, the seller shall not be entitled to prevent the handing over of the goods if they are claimed by a third person who is a lawful holder of a document which entitles him to obtain the goods unless the document contains a reservation concerning the effects of its transfer or unless the seller can prove that the holder of the document when he acquired it, knowingly acted to the detriment of the seller.

*Section II - Exemptions*

## ARTICLE 74

1. Where one of the parties has not performed one of his obligations, he shall not be liable for such non-performance if he can prove that it was due to circumstances which according to the intention of the parties at the time of the conclusion of the contract, he was not bound to take into account or to avoid or to overcome; in the absence of any expression of the intention of the parties, regard shall be had to what reasonable persons in the same situation would have intended.

2. Where the circumstances which gave rise to the non-performance of the obligation constituted only a temporary impediment to performance, the party in default shall nevertheless be permanently relieved of his obligation if, by reason of the delay, performance would be so radically changed as to amount to the performance of an obligation quite different from that contemplated by the contract.

3. The relief provided by this Article for one of the parties shall not include the avoidance of the contract under some other provision of the present Law or deprive the other party of any right which he has under the present Law to reduce the price, unless the circumstances which entitled the first party to relief were caused by the act of the other party or of some person for whose conduct he was responsible.

*Section III - Supplementary rules concerning the avoidance of the contract*

*A—Supplementary grounds for avoidance*

## ARTICLE 75

1. Where, in the case of contracts for delivery of goods by instalments, by reason of any failure by one party of his obligations under the contract in respect of any instalment, the other party has good reason to fear failure of performance in respect of future instalments, he may declare the contract avoided for the future, provided that he does so promptly.

2. The buyer may also, provided that he does so promptly, declare the contract avoided in respect of future deliveries or in respect of deliveries already made or both, if by reason of their interdependence such deliveries would be worthless to him.

## ARTICLE 76

Where prior to the date fixed for performance of the contract it is clear that one of the parties will commit a fundamental breach of the contract, the other party shall have the right to declare the contract avoided.

## ARTICLE 77

Where the contract has been avoided under Article 75 or Article 76, the party declaring the contract avoided may claim damges in accordance with Articles 84 to 87.

### *B—Effects of avoidance*

## ARTICLE 78

1. Avoidance of the contract releases both parties from their obligations thereunder, subject to any damages which may be due.

2. If one party has performed the contract either wholly or in part, he may claim the return of whatever he has supplied or paid under the contract. If both parties are required to make restitution, they shall do so concurrently.

## ARTICLE 79

1. The buyer shall lose his right to declare the contract avoided where it is impossible for him to return the goods in the condition in which he received them.

2. Nevertheless, the buyer may declare the contract avoided:
- (a) if the goods or part of the goods have perished or deteriorated as a result of the defect which justifies the avoidance;
- (b) if the goods or part of the goods have perished or deteriorated as a result of the examination prescribed in Article 38;
- (c) if part of the goods have been consumed or transformed by the buyer in the course of normal use before the lack of conformity with the contract was discovered;
- (d) if the impossibility of returning the goods or of returning them in the condition in whch they were received is not due to the act of the buyer, or of some other person for whose conduct he is responsible;
- (e) if the deterioration of transformation of the goods is unimportant.

## ARTICLE 80

The buyer who has lost the right to declare the contract avoided by virtue of Article 79 shall retain all the other rights conferred on him by the present Law.

## ARTICLE 81

1. Where the seller is under an obligation to refund the price, he shall also be liable for the interest thereon at the rate fixed by Article 83, as from the date of payment.

2. The buyer shall be liable to account to the seller for all benefits which he has derived from the goods or part of them, as the case may be:

(a) where he is under an obligation to return the goods or part of them;
(b) where it is impossible for him to return the goods or part of them, but the contract is nevertheless avoided.

*Section IV - Supplementary rules concerning damages*

*A—Damages where the contract is not avoided.*

## ARTICLE 82

Where the contract is not avoided, damages for a breach of contract by one party shall consist of a sum equal to the loss of profit, suffered by the other party. Such damages shall not exceed the loss which the party in breach ought to have foreseen at the time of the conclusion of the contract, in the light of the facts and matters which then were known or ought to have been known to him, as a possible consequence of the breach of the contract.

## ARTICLE 83

Where the breach of contract consists of delay in the payment of the price , the seller shall in any event be entitled to interest on such sum as in arrear at a rate equal to the official discount rate in the country where he has his place of business, or if he has no place of business, his habitual residence, plus 1%.

*B—Damages where the contract is avoided.*

## ARTICLE 84

1. In the case of avoidance of the contract, where there is a current price for the goods, damages shall be equal to the difference between the price fixed by the contract and the current price on the date on which the contract is avoided.

2. In calculating the amount of damages under paragraph 1 of this Article , the current price to be taken into account shall be that prevailing in the market in which the transaction took place, if there is no such current price or if its application is inappropriate, the price in a market which serves as a reasonable substitute, making due allowance for differences in the cost of transporting goods.

## ARTICLE 85

If the buyer has bought goods in replacement or the seller has resold goods in a reasonable manner, he may recover the difference between the contract price and the price paid for the goods bought in replacement or that obtained by the resale.

## ARTICLE 86

The damages referred to in Articles 84 and 85 may be increased by the amount of any reasonable expenses incurred as a result of the breach or up to the amount of any loss, including loss of profit, which should have been foreseen by the party in breach, at the time of the conclusion of the contract, in the light of the facts and matters which were known or ought to have been known to him, as a possible consequence of the breach of the contract.

## ARTICLE 87

If there is no current price for the goods, damages shall be calculated on the same basis as that provided in Article 82.

### *C—General provisions concerning damages*

## ARTICLE 88

The party who relies on a breach of the contract shall adopt all reasonable measures to mitigate the loss resulting from the breach. If he fails to adopt such measures, the party in breach may claim reduction in the damages.

## ARTICLE 89

In case of fraud, damages shall be determined by the rules applicable in respect of contracts of sale not governed by the present law.

### *Section V -Expenses*

## ARTICLE 90

The expenses of delivery shall be borne by the seller; all expenses after delivery shall be borne by the buyer.

### *Section VI-Preservation of the Goods*

## ARTICLE 91

Where the buyer is in delay in taking delivery of the goods or in paying the price, the seller shall take reasonable steps to preserve the goods; he shall have the right to retain them until he has been reimbursed his reasonable expenses by the buyer.

## ARTICLE 92

1. Where the goods have been received by the buyer, he shall take reasonable steps to preserve them if he intends to reject them: he shall have the right to retain them until he has been reimbursed his reasonable expenses by the seller.

2. Where the goods despatched to the buyer have been put at his disposal at their place of destination and he exercises the right to reject them he shall be bound to take possession of them on behalf of the seller, provided that this may be done without payment of the price and without reasonable inconvenience or unreasonable expense. This provision shall not apply where the seller or a person authorised to take charge of the goods on his behalf is present at such destination.

## ARTICLE 93

The party who is under an obligation to take steps to preserve the goods may deposit them in the warehouse of a third person at the expense of the other party provided that the expense incurred is not unreasonable.

## ARTICLE 94

1. The party who, in the cases to which Articles 91 and 92 apply, is under an obligation to take steps to preserve the goods may sell them by any appropriate means, provided that there has been unreasonable delay by the other party in accepting them or taking them back or in paying the costs of preservation and provided that due notice has been given to the other party of the intention to sell.

2. The party selling the goods shall have the right to retain out of the proceeds of sale an amount equal to the reasonable costs of preserving the goods and of selling them and shall transmit the balance to the other party.

## ARTICLE 95

Where, in the cases to which Articles 91 and 92 apply, the goods are subject to loss or rapid deterioration or their preservation would involve unreasonable expense, the party under the duty to preserve them is bound to sell them in accordance with Article 94.

# CHAPTER VI — PASSING OF THE RISK

## ARTICLE 96

Where the risk has passed to the buyer, he shall pay the price notwithstanding the loss or deterioration of the goods, unless this is due to the act of the seller or of some other person for whose conduct the seller is responsible.

## ARTICLE 97

1. The risk shall pass to the buyer when delivery of the goods is effected in accordance with the provision of the contract and the present Law.

2. In the case of the handing over of goods which are not in conformity with the contract, the risk shall pass to the buyer from the moment when the handing over has, apart from the lack of conformity, been effected in accordance with the provisions of the contract and of the present Law, where the buyer has neither declared the contract avoided nor required goods in replacement.

## ARTICLE 98

1. Where the handing over of the goods is delayed owing to the breach of an obligation of the buyer, the risk shall pass to the buyer as from the last date when, apart from such breach, the handing over could have been made in accordance with the contract.

2. Where the contract relates to a sale of unascertained goods, delay on the part of the buyer shall cause the risk to pass only when the seller has set aside goods manifestly appropriated to the contract and has notified the buyer that this has been done.

3. Where unascertained goods are of such a kind that the seller cannot set aside a part of them until the buyer takes delivery, it shall be sufficient for the seller to do all acts necessary to enable the buyer to take delivery.

## ARTICLE 99

1. Where the sale is of goods in transit by sea, the risk shall be borne by the buyer as from the time at which the goods were handed over to the carrier.

2 Where the seller, at the time of the conclusion of the contract, knew or ought to have known that the goods had been lost or had deteriorated, the risk shall remain with him until the time of the conclusion of the contract.

## ARTICLE 100

If, in the case to which paragraph 3 of Article 19 applies, the seller, at the time of sending the notice or other document referred to in that paragraph knew or ought to have known that the goods had been lost or had deteriorated after they were handed over to the carrier , the risk shall remain with the seller until the time of sending such notice or document.

## ARTICLE 101

The passing of the risk shall not necessarily be determined by the provisions of the contract concerning expenses.

## SCHEDULE 2

## THE UNIFORM LAW ON THE FORMATION OF CONTRACTS FOR THE INTERNATIONAL SALES OF GOODS

### ARTICLE 1

The present law shall apply to the formation of contracts of sale of goods which, if they were concluded, would be governed by the Uniform Law on the International Sale of Goods.

### ARTICLE 2

1. The provision of the following Articles shall apply except to the extent that it appears from the preliminary negotiations, the offer, the reply, the practices which the parties have established between themselves or usage, that other rules apply.

2. However, a term of the offer stipulating that silence shall amount to acceptance is invalid.

### ARTICLE 3

An offer or an acceptance need not be evidenced by writing and shall not be subject to any other requirement as to form. In particular, they may be proved by means of witnesses.

### ARTICLE 4

1. The communication which one person addresses to one or more specific persons with the object of concluding a contract of sale shall not constitute an offer unless it is sufficiently definite to permit the conclusion of the contract by acceptance and indicates the intention of the offeror to be bound.

2. This communication may be interpreted by reference to and supplemented by the preliminary negotiations, any practices which the parties have established between themselves, usage and the provisions of the Uniform Law on the International Sale of Goods.

### ARTICLE 5

1. The offer shall not bind the offeror until it has been communicated to the offeree; it shall lapse if its withdrawal is communicated to the offeree before or at the same time as the offer.

2. After an offer has been communicated to the offeree it can be revoked unless the revocation is not made in good faith or in conformity with fair dealing or unless the offer states a fixed time for acceptance or otherwise indicates that it is firm or irrevocable.

3. An indication that the offer is firm or irrevocable may be express or implied from the circumstances, the preliminary negotiations, any practices which the parties have established between themselves or usage.

4. A revocation of an offer shall only have effect if it has been communicated to the offeree before he has despatched his acceptance or has done any act treated as acceptance under paragraph 2 of Article 6.

## ARTICLE 6

1. Acceptance of an offer consists of a declaration communicated by any means whatsoever to the offeror.

2. Acceptance may also consist of the despatch of the goods or of the price or of any other act which my be considered to be equivalent to the declaration referred to in paragraph 1 of this Article either by virtue of the offer or as a result of practices which the parties have established between themselves or usage.

## ARTICLE 7

1. An acceptance containing additions, limitations or other modifications shall be a rejection of the offer and shall constitute a counter-offer.

2. However, a reply to an offer which purports to be an acceptance but which contains additional or different terms which do not materially alter the terms of the offer shall constitute an acceptance unless the offeror promptly objects to the discrepancy; if he does not so object the terms of the contract shall be the terms of the offer with the modifications contained in the acceptance.

## ARTICLE 8

1. A declaration of acceptance of an offer shall have effect only if it is communicated to the offeror within the time he has fixed or, if no such time is fixed, within a reasonable time, due account being taken of the circumstances of the transaction, including the rapidity of the means of communication employed by the offeror, and usage. In the case of an oral offer, the acceptance shall be immediate, if the circumstances do not show that the offeree shall have time for reflection.

2. If a time for acceptance is fixed by an offeror in a letter or in a telegram, it shall be presumed to begin to run from the day the letter was dated or the hour of the day the telegram was handed in for despatch.

3. If an acceptance consists of an act referred to in paragraph 2 of Article 6, the act shall have effect only if it is done within the period laid down in paragraph 1 of the present Article.

## ARTICLE 9

1. If the acceptance is late, the offeror may nevertheless consider it to have arrived in due time on condition that he promptly so informs the acceptor orally or by despatch of a notice.

2. If however the acceptance is communicated late, it shall be considered to have been communicated in due time, if the letter or document which contains the acceptance shows that it has been sent in such circumstances that if its transmission had been normal it would have been communicated in due time; this provision shall not however apply if the offeror has promptly informed the acceptor orally or by despatch of a notice that he considers his offer as having lapsed.

## ARTICLE 10

An acceptance cannot be revoked except by a revocation which is communicated to the offeror before or at the same time as the acceptance.

## ARTICLE 11

The formation of the contract is not affected by the death of the parties or by his becoming incapable of contracting before acceptance unless the contrary results from the intention of the parties, usage or the nature of the transaction.

## ARTICLE 12

1. For the purpose of the present law, the expression "to be communicated " means to be delivered at the address of the person to whom the communication is directed.

2. Communications provided for by the present Law shall be made by the means usual in the circumstances.

## ARTICLE 13

1. "Usage" means any practice or method of dealing which reasonable persons in the same situation as the parties usually consider to be applicable to the formation of their contract.

2. Where expressions, provisions or forms of contract commonly used in commercial practice are employed, they shall be interpreted according to the meaning usually given to them in the trade concerned.

# CARRIAGE OF GOODS BY SEA ACT 1971

## CHAPTER 19

**1. Application of Hague Rules as amended**

(1) In this Act, "the Rules" means the International Convention for the unification of certain rules of law relating to bills of lading signed at Brussels on 25th August 1924, as amended by the Protocol signed at Brussels on 23rd February 1968 and by the Protocol signed at Brussels on 21st December 1979.

(2). The provisions of the Rules as set out in the Schedule to this Act shall have the force of law.

(3) Without prejudice to subsection (2) above, the said provisions shall have effect (and have the force of law) in relation to and in connection with the carriage of goods by sea in ships where the port of shipment is a port in the United Kingdom, whether or not the carriage is between ports in two different states within the meaning of Article X of the Rules.

(4) Subject to subsection (6) below, nothing in this section shall be taken as applying anything in the Rules to any contract for the carriage of goods by sea, unless the contract expressly or by implication provides for the issue of a bill of lading or any similar document of title.

(5) [Repealed].

(6) Without prejudice to Article X(c) of the Rules, the Rules shall have the force of law in relation to-

(a) any bill of lading if the contract contained in or evidenced by it expressly provides that the Rules shall govern the contract, and

(b) any receipt which is a non-negotiable document marked as such if the contract contained in or evidenced by it is a contract for the carriage of goods by sea which expressly provides that the Rules are to govern the contract as if the receipt were a bill of lading,

but subject, where paragraph (b) applies, to any necessary modifications and in particular with the omission in Article III of the Rules of the second sentence of paragraph 4 and of paragraph 7.

(7) If and so far as the contract contained in or evidenced by a bill of lading or receipt within paragraph (a) or (b) of subsection (6) above applies to deck cargo or live animals, the Rules as given the force of law by that subsection shall have effect as it Article 1(c) did not exclude deck cargo and live animals.

In this subjection "deck cargo" means cargo which by the contract of carriage is stated as being carried on deck and is so carried.

**2. [Omitted].**

### 3. Absolute warranty of seaworthiness not to be implied in contracts to which Rules apply

There shall not be implied in any contract for the carriage of goods by sea to which Rules apply by virtue of this Act any absolute undertaking by the carrier of the goods to provide a seaworthy ship.

### 4.-5. [Omitted].

### 6. Supplemental

(1)-(3) [Omitted].

(4) It is hereby declared that for the purposes of Article VIII of the Rules section 502 of the Merchant Shipping act 1894 (which , as amended by the Merchant Shipping (Liability of Shipowners and Others) Act 1958, section 18 of the Merchant Shipping Act 1979 (which entirely exempts shipowners and others in certain circumstances from liability for loss of, or damage to, goods) is a provision relating to limitation of liability.

## SCHEDULE

## THE HAGUE RULES AS AMENDED BY THE BRUSSELS PROTOCOL 1968

### ARTICLE 1

In these Rules the following words are employed with the meaning set out below:-

(a) "Carrier" includes the owner or the charterer who enters into a contract of carriage with a shipper.

(b) "Contract of carriage" applies only to contracts of carriage covered by a bill of lading or any similar document of title, in so far as such document relates to the carriage of goods by sea, including any bill of lading or any similar document as aforesaid issued under or pursuant to a charter party from the moment at which such bill of lading or similar document of title regulates the relations between a carrier and a holder of the same.

(c) "Goods" includes goods, wares, merchandise and articles of every kind whatsoever except live animals and cargo which by the contract of carriage is stated as being carried on deck and is so carried.

(d) "ship" means any vessel used for the carriage of goods by sea.

(e) "carriage of goods" covers the period from the time when the goods are loaded on to the time they are discharged from the ship.

### ARTICLE II

Subject to the provisions of Article VI, under every contract of carriage of goods by sea the carrier, in relation to the loading, handling, stowage, carriage, custody, care and discharge of such goods, shall be subject to the responsibilities and liabilities, and entitled to the rights and immunities hereinafter set forth.

## ARTICLE III

1. The carrier shall be bound and at the beginning of the voyage to exercise due diligence to-

(a) Make the ship seaworthy.
(b) Properly man, equip and supply the ship.
(c) Make the holds, refrigerating and cool chambers, and all other parts of the ship in which goods are carried, fit and safe for their reception, carriage and preservation.

2. Subject to the provisions of Article IV, the carrier shall properly and carefully load, handle, stow, carry, keep, care for, and discharge the goods carried.

3. After receiving the goods into his charge the carrier or the master or agent of the carrier shall, on demand of the shipper, issue to the shipper a bill of lading showing among other things-

(a) The leading marks necessary for identification of the goods as the same are furnished in writing by the shipper before the loading of such goods starts, provided such marks are stamped or otherwise shown clearly upon the goods if uncovered, or on the cases or coverings in which such goods are contained, in such a manner as should ordinarily remain legible until the end of the voyage.
(b) Either the number of packages or pieces, or the quantity, or weight, as the case may be, as furnished in writing by the shipper .
(c) The apparent order and conditions of the goods.

Provided that no carrier, master or agent of the carrier shall be bound to state or show in the bill of lading any marks, number, quantity, or weight which he has reasonable ground for suspecting not accurately to represent the goods actually received or which he has had no reasonable means of checking.

4. Such a bill of lading shall be prima facie evidence of the receipt by the carrier of the goods as therein described in accordance with paragraph 3(a), (b) and (c). However, proof to the contrary shall not be admissible when the bill of lading has been transferred to a third party acting in good faith.

5. The shipper shall be deemed to have guaranteed to the carrier the accuracy at the time of shipment of the marks, number, quantity and weight, as furnished by him, and the shipper shall indemnify the carrier against all loss, damages and expenses arising or resulting from inaccuracies in such particulars. The right of the carrier to such indemnity shall in no way limit his responsibility and liability under the contract of carriage to any person other than the shipper.

6. Unless notice of loss or damage and the general nature of such loss or damage be given in writing to the carrier or his agent at the port of discharge before or at the time of the removal of the goods into the custody of the person entitled to delivery thereof under the contract of carriage, or, if the loss or damage be not apparent, within three days, such removal shall be *prima facie* evidence of the delivery by the carrier of the goods as described in the bill of lading.

The notice in writing need not be given if the state of the goods has, at the time of their receipt been the subject of joint survey or inspection.

Subject to paragraph 6*bis* the carrier and the ship shall in any event be discharged from all liability whatsoever in respect of the goods, unless suit is brought within one year of their delivery or of the date when they should have been delivered. This period may, however, be extended if the parties so agree after the cause of action has arisen.

In the case of any actual or apprehended loss or damage the carrier and the receiver shall give all reasonable facilities to each other for inspecting and tallying the goods.

6 *bis*. An action for indemnity against a third person may be brought even after the expiration of the year provided for in the preceding paragraph if brought within the time allowed by the law of the Court seized of the case. However, the time allowed shall be not less than three months, commencing from the day when the person bringing such action for indemnity has settled the claim or has been served with process in the action against himself.

7. After the goods are loaded the bill of lading to be issued by the carrier, master, or agent of the carrier to the shipper shall, if the shipper so demands, be a "shipped" bill of lading, provided that if the shipper shall have previously taken up any document of title to such goods, he shall surrender the same as against the issue of the "shipped" bill of lading , but at the option of the carrier such document of title may be noted at the port of shipment by the carrier, master, or agent with the name or names of the ship or ships upon which the goods have been shipped and the date or dates of shipment, and when so noted, if it shows the particulars mentioned in paragraph 3 of Article III, shall for the purpose of this Article be deemed to constitute a "shipped" bill of lading.

8. Any clause, covenant, or agreement in a contract of carriage relieving the carrier or the ship from liability for loss or damage to, or in connection with goods, arising from negligence, fault, or failure in the duties and obligations provided in this Article or lessening such liability otherwise than as provided in these Rules shall be null and void and of no effect. A benefit of insurance in favour of the carrier or similar clause shall be deemed to be clause relieving the carrier from liability.

## Article IV

1. Neither the carrier nor the ship shall be liable for loss or damage arising or resulting from-

(a) Act, neglect, or default of the master, mariner, pilot, or the servants of the carrier in the navigation or in the management of the ship.
(b) Fire, unless caused by the actual fault or privity of the carrier.
(c) Perils, dangers and accidents of the sea or other navigable waters.
(d) Act of God.
(e) Act of public enemies.
(g) Arrest or restraint of princes, rulers or people, or seizure under legal process.
(h) Quarantine restrictions.
(i) Act or omission of the shipper or owner of the goods, his agent or representative.
(j) Strikes or lockouts or stoppage or restraint of labour from whatever cause, whether partial or general.
(k) Riots and civil commotions.

(l) Saving or attempting to save life or property at sea.
(m) Wastage in bulk or weight or any other loss or damage arising from inherent defect, quality or vice of the goods.
(n) Insufficiency of packing
(o) Insufficiency or inadequacy of marks.
(p) Latent defects not discoverable by due diligence
(q) Any other cause arising without the actual fault or privity of the carrier, or without the fault or neglect of the agents or servants of the carrier, but the burden of proof shall be on the person claiming the benefit of this exception to show that neither the actual fault or privity of the carrier nor the fault or neglect of the agents or servants of the carrier contributed to the loss or damage.

3. The shipper shall not be responsible for loss or damage sustained by the carrier or the ship arising or resulting from any cause without the act, fault or neglect of the shipper, his agents or his servants.

4. Any deviation in saving or attempting to save life or property at sea or any reasonable deviation shall not be deemed to be an infringement or breach of these Rules or of the contract of carriage, and the carrier shall not be liable for any loss or damage resulting therefrom.

5.—

(a) Unless the nature and value of such goods have been declared by the shipper before shipment and inserted in the bill of lading, neither the carrier nor the ship shall in any event be or become liable for any loss or damage to or in connection with the goods in an amount exceeding 666.67 units of account per package or unit or 2 units of account per kilogram of gross weight of the goods lost or damaged, whichever is the higher.
(b) The total amount recoverable shall be calculated by reference to the value of such goods at the place and time at which the goods are discharged from the ship in accordance with the contract or should have been so discharged.
The value of the goods shall be fixed according to the commodity exchange price, or, if there be no such price, according to the current market price, or if there be no commodity exchange price or current market price, by reference to the normal value of goods of the same kind and quality.
(c) Where a container, pallet or similar article of transport is used to consolidate goods, the number of packages or units enumerated in the bill of lading as packed in such article of transport shall be deemed the number of packages or units for the purpose of this paragraph as far as these packages or units are concerned. Except as aforesaid such article of transport shall be considered the package or unit.
(d) The unit of account mentioned in this Article is the special drawing right as defined by the International Monetary Fund. The amounts mentioned in sub-paragraph (a) of this paragraph shall be converted into national currency on the basis of the value of that currency on a date to be determined by the law of the Court seized of the case.
(e) Neither the carrier nor the ship shall be entitled to the benefit of the limitation of liability provided for in this paragraph if it is proved that the damage resulted from an act or omission of the carrier done with intent to cause damage, or recklessly and with knowledge that damage would probably result .

(f) The declaration mentioned in sub-paragraph (a) of this paragraph if embodied in the bill of lading shall be *prima facie* evidence, but shall not be binding or conclusive on the carrier.

(g) By agreement between the carrier, master or agent of the carrier and the shipper other maximum amounts than those mentioned in sub-paragraph (a) of this paragraph may be fixed, provided that no maximum amount so fixed shall be less than the appropriate maximum mentioned in that sub-paragraph .

(h) Neither the carrier nor the ship shall be responsible in any event for loss or damage to, or in connection with goods, if the nature or value thereof has been knowingly mis-stated by the shipper in the bill of lading.

6. Goods of an inflammable, explosive or dangerous nature to the shipment whereof the carrier, master or agent of the carrier has not consented with knowledge of their nature and character, may at any time before discharge be landed at any place, or destroyed or rendered innocuous by the carrier without compensation and the shipper of such goods shall be liable for all damages and expenses directly or indirectly arising out of or resulting from such shipment. If any such goods shipped with such knowledge and consent shall become a danger to the ship or cargo, they may in like manner be landed at any place, or destroyed or rendered innocuous by the carrier without liability on the part of the carrier except to general average, if any.

## ARTICLE IV *BIS*

1. The defences and limits of liability provided for in these Rules shall apply in any action against the carrier in respect of loss or damage to goods covered by a contract of carriage whether the action be founded in contract or in tort.

2. If such an action is bought against a servant or agent of the carrier (such servant or agent not being an independent contractor), such servant or agent shall be entitled to avail himself of the defences and limits of liability which the carrier is entitled to invoke under these Rules.

3. The aggregate of the amounts recoverable from the carrier, and such servants and agents, shall in no case exceed the limit provided for in these Rules.

4. Nevertheless, a servant or agent of the carrier shall not be entitled to avail himself of the provisions of this Article, if it is proved that the damage resulted from an act or omission of the servant or agent done with intent to cause damage or recklessly and with knowledge that damage would probably result.

## ARTICLE V

A carrier shall be at liberty to surrender in whole or in part all or any of his rights and immunities or to increase any of his responsibilities and obligations under these Rules, provided such surrender or increase shall be embodied in the bill of lading issued to the shipper. The provisions of these Rules shall not be applicable to charter parties, but if bills of lading are issued in the case of a ship under a charter party they shall comply with the terms of these Rules.

Nothing in these Rules shall be held to prevent the insertion in a bill of lading of any lawful provision regarding general average.

## ARTICLE VI

Notwithstanding the provisions of the preceding Articles, a carrier, master or agent of the carrier and a shipper shall in regard to any particular goods be at liberty to enter into any agreement in any terms as to the responsibility and liability of the carrier for such goods, and as to the rights and immunities of the carrier in respect of such goods, or his obligation as to seaworthiness, so far as this stipulation is not contrary to public policy, or the care or diligence of his servant or agents in regard to the loading, handling, stowage, carriage, custody, care and discharge of the goods carried by sea, provided that in this case no bill of lading has been or shall be issued and that the terms agreed shall be embodied in a receipt which shall be a non-negotiable document and shall be marked as such.

Any agreement so entered into shall have legal effect.

Provided that this Article shall not apply to ordinary commercial shipments made in the ordinary course of trade, but only to other shipments where the character or condition of the property to be carried or the circumstances, terms and conditions under which the carriage is to be performed are such as reasonably to justify a special agreement.

## ARTICLE VII

Nothing herein contained shall prevent a carrier or a shipper from entering into any agreement, stipulation, condition, reservation or exemption as to the responsibility and liability of the carrier or the ship for the loss or damage to , or in connection with, the custody and care and handling of goods prior to the loading on, and subsequent to the discharge from, the ship on which the goods are carried by sea.

## ARTICLE VIII

The provisions of these Rules shall not affect the rights and obligations or the carrier under any statute for the time being in force relating to the limitation of the liability of owners of sea-going vessels.

## ARTICLE IX

These rules shall not affect the provisions of any international Convention or national law governing liability for nuclear damage.

## ARTICLE X

The provisions of these Rules shall apply to every bill of lading relating to the carriage of goods between ports in two different States if:

(a) the bill of lading is issued in a contracting State, or
(b) the carriage is from a port in a contacting State, or
(c) the contract contained in or evidenced by the bill of lading provides that these Rules or legislation of any State giving effect to them are to govern the contract.

whatever may be the nationality of the ship, the carrier, the shipper, the consignee, or any other interested person.

## ARTICLES 11-16 [OMITTED].

# ARBITRATION ACT 1975

## CHAPTER 3



*Effect of arbitration agreement on court proceedings*

### 1. Staying court proceedings where party proves arbitration agreement

(1) If any party to an arbitration agreement to which this section applies, or any person claiming through or under him, commences any legal proceedings in any court against any other party to the agreement, or any person claiming through or under him , in respect of any matter agreed to be referred, any party to the proceedings may at any time after appearance, and before delivering any pleadings or taking any other steps in the proceedings, apply to the court to stay the proceedings; and the court, unless satisfied that the arbitration agreement is null and void, inoperative or incapable of being performed or that there is not in fact any dispute between the parties with regard to the matter agreed to be referred, shall make an order staying the proceedings.

(2) This section applies to any arbitration agreement which is not a domestic arbitration agreement; and neither section 4(1) of the Arbitration Act 1950 nor section 4 of the Arbitration Act (Northern Ireland) 1937 shall apply to an arbitration agreement to which this section applies.

(3) In the application of this section to Scotland, for the references to staying proceedings there shall be substituted references to sisting proceedings.

(4) In this section "domestic arbitration agreement" means an arbitration agreement which does not provide, expressly or by implication, for arbitration in a State other than the United Kingdom and to which neither—

(a) an individual who is a national of, or habitually resident in, any State other than the United Kingdom; nor

(b) a body corporate which is incorporated in, or whose central management and control is exercised in, any State other than the United Kingdom;

is a party at the time the proceedings are commenced.

*Enforcement of Convention Awards*

**2. Replacement of former provisions.**

Sections 3 to 6 of this Act shall have effect with respect to the enforcement of Convention awards; and where a Convention award would, but for this section, be also a foreign award within the meaning of Part II of the Arbitration Act 1950, that part shall not apply to it.

**3. Effect of Convention awards.**

(1) A convention award shall, subject to the following provisions of this Act, be enforceable-

(a) in England and Wales, either by action or in the same manner as the award of an arbitrator is enforceable by virtue of section 26 of the Arbitration Act 1950.

(b) in Scotland either by action or in a case where the arbitration agreement contains consent to the registration of the award in the Books of Council and Session for execution and the award is to registered , by summary diligence;

(c) in Northern Ireland , either by action or in the same manner as the award of an arbitrator is enforceable by virtue of section 16 of the Arbitration Act (Northern Ireland) 1937.

(2) Any Convention award which would be enforceable under this Act shall be treated as binding for all purposes on the persons as between whom it was made, and may accordingly be relied on by any of those persons by way of defence, set off or otherwise in any legal proceedings in the United Kingdom; and any reference to this Act to enforcing a Convention award shall be construed as including references to relying on such an award.

**4. [Omitted].**

**5. Refusal of enforcement**

(1) Enforcement of a Convention award shall not be refused except in the cases mentioned in this section.

(2) Enforcement of a Convention award may be refused if the person against whom it is invoked proves-

(a) that a party to the arbitration agreement was (under the law applicable to him) under some incapacity; or

(b) that the arbitration agreement was not valid under the law to which the parties subjected it or, failing any indication thereon, under the law of the country where the award was made; or

(c) that he was not given proper notice of the appointment of the arbitrator or of the arbitration proceedings or was otherwise unable to present his case; or

(d) (subject to subsection (4) of this section) that the award deals with a difference not contemplated by or not falling within the terms of the submission to arbitration or contains decisions on matters beyond the scope of the submission to arbitration; or

(e) that the composition of the arbitral authority or the arbitral procedure was not in accordance with the agreement of the parties or, failing such agreement, with the law of the country where the arbitration took place; or

(f) that the award has not yet become binding on the parties, or has been set aside or suspended by a competent authority of the country in which, or under the law of which, it was made.

(3) Enforcement of a Convention award may also be refused if the award is in respect of a matter which is not capable of settlement by arbitration, or it would be contrary to public policy to enforce the award.

(4) A Convention award which contains decisions on matters not submitted to arbitration may be enforced to the extent that it contains decisions on matters submitted to arbitration which can be separated from those on matters not so submitted.

(5) Where an application for the setting aside or suspension of a Convention award has been made to such a competent authority as is mentioned in subsection (2) (f) of this section, the court before which enforcement of the award is sought may, if it thinks fit, adjourn the proceedings and may, on the application of the party seeking to enforce the award, order the other party to give security.

**6. —**

Nothing in this Act shall prejudice any right to enforce or rely on an award otherwise than under this Act or Part II of the Arbitration Act 1950

*General*

**7. Interpretation**

(1) In this Act-

'arbitration agreement' means an agreement in writing (including an agreement contained in an exchange of letters or telegrams) to submit to arbitration present or future differences capable of settlement by arbitration;

'Convention award' means an award made in pursuance of an arbitration agreement in the territory of a State, other than the United Kingdom, which is a party to the New York Convention; and

'the New York Convention' means the Convention on the Recognition and Enforcement of Foreign Arbitral Awards adopted by the United Nations Conference on International Commercial Arbitration on 10th June 1958.

(2) and (3) [Omitted].

**8. [Omitted].**

# UNFAIR CONTRACT TERMS ACT 1977

CHAPTER 50

**1.-25. [Omitted].**

*Miscellaneous*

**26. International supply contracts**

(1) The limits imposed by this Act on the extent to which a person may exclude or restrict liability by reference to a contract term do not apply to liability arising under such a contract as is described in subsection (3) below.

(2) The terms of such a contract are not subject to any requirement of reasonableness under Section 3 or 4; and nothing in Part II of this Act shall require the incorporation of the terms of such a contract to be fair and reasonable for them to have effect.

(3) Subject to subsection (4), that description of contract is one whose characteristics are the following-

(a) either it is a contract of sale or goods or it is one under or in pursuance of which the possession or ownership of goods passes; and
(b) it is made by parties whose places of business (or, if they have none, habitual residences) are in the territories of different States (the Channel Islands and the Isle of Man being treated for this purpose as different States from the United Kingdom).

(4) A contract falls within subsection (3) above only if either-

(a) the goods in question are, at the time of the conclusion of the contract, in the course of carriage, or will be carried, from the territory of one State to the territory of another; or
(b) the acts constituting the offer and acceptance have been done in territories of different states; or
(c) the contract provides for the goods to be delivered to the territory of a State other than that within those territory those acts were done.

**27. Choice of law clauses**

(1) Where the law applicable to a contract is the law of any part of the United Kingdom only by choice of the parties (and apart from that choice would be the law of some country outside the United Kingdom) sections 2 to 7 and 16 to 21 of this Act operate as part of the law applicable to the contract.

2) This Act has effect notwithstanding any contract term which applies or purports to apply the law of some country outside the United Kingdom, where (either or both)-

(a) the term appears to the court, or arbitrator or arbiter to have been imposed wholly or mainly for the purpose of enabling the party imposing it to evade the operation of this Act; or

(b) in the making of the contract one of the parties dealt as consumer, and he was than habitually resident in the United Kingdom, and the essential steps necessary for the making of the contract were taken there, whether by him or by others on his behalf.

(3) In the application of subsection (2) above to Scotland, for paragraph (b) there shall be substituted—

'(b) the contract is a consumer contract as defined in Part II of this Act, and the consumer at the date when the contract was made was habitually resident in the United Kingdom, and the essential steps necessary for the making of the contract were taken there, whether by him or by others on his behalf.'

**28.-32. and Schedules [Omitted].**

# STATE IMMUNITY ACT 1978

## CHAPTER 33

## PART 1

## PROCEEDINGS IN UNITED KINGDOM BY OR AGAINST OTHER STATES



## PART I

## PROCEEDINGS IN UNITED KINGDOM BY OR AGAINST OTHER STATES

*Immunity from Jurisdiction*

### 1. General Immunity from jurisdiction

(1) A State is immune from the jurisdiction of the courts of the United Kingdom except as provided in the following provisions of this part of the Act.

(2) A court shall give effect to the immunity conferred by this section even though the State does not appear in the proceedings in question.

*Exceptions from immunity*

**2. Submission to jurisdiction**

(1) A state is not immune as respects proceedings in respect of which it has submitted to the jurisdiction of the courts of the United Kingdom.

(2) A state may submit after the dispute giving rise to the proceedings has arisen or by a prior written agreement: but a provision in any agreement that it is to be governed by the law of the United Kingdom is not be regarded as a submission.

(3) A state is deemed to have submitted—
(a) if it has instituted the proceedings; or
(b) subject to subsections (4) and (5) below, if it has intervened or taken any step in the proceedings.

(4) Subsection (3) (b) above does not apply to intervention or any step taken for the purpose only of-
(a) claiming immunity; or
(b) asserting an interest in property in circumstances such that the State would have been entitled to immunity if the proceedings had been brought against it

(5) Subsection (3)(b) above does not apply to any step taken by the State in ignorance of facts entitling it to immunity if those facts could not reasonably have been ascertained and immunity is claimed as soon as reasonably practicable.

(6) A submission in respect of any proceedings extends to any appeal but not to any counter-claim unless it arises out of the same legal relationship or facts as the claim.

(7) The head of a State's diplomatic mission in the United Kingdom, or the person for the time being performing his functions, shall be deemed to have authority to submit on behalf of the State in respect of any proceedings; and any person who has entered into a contract on behalf of and with the authority of a State shall be deemed to have authority to submit on its behalf in respect of proceedings arising out of the contract.

**3. Commercial transactions and contracts to be performed in United Kingdom**

(1) A state is not immune as respects proceedings relating to—
(a) a commercial transaction entered into by the State; or
(b) an obligation of the State which by virtue of a contract (whether a commercial transaction or not) falls to be performed wholly or partly in the United Kingdom.

(2) This section does not apply if the parties to the dispute are States or have otherwise agreed in writing ; and subsection (1)(b) above does not apply if the contract (not being a commercial transaction) was made in the territory of the State concerned and the obligation in question is governed by its administrative law.

(3) In this section 'commercial transaction' means—

(a) any contract for the supply of goods or services;

(b) any loan or other transaction for the provision of finance and any guarantee or indemnity in respect of any such transaction or of any other financial obligation; and

(c) any other transaction or activity (whether of a commercial industrial, financial, professional or other similar character) into which a state enters or in which it engages otherwise than in the exercise of sovereign authority;

but neither paragraph of subsection (1) above applies to a contract of employment between a State and an individual.

**4.-8. [Omitted].**

**9. Arbitrations**

(1) Where a State has agreed in writing to submit a dispute which has arisen, or may arise, to arbitration, the State is not immune as respects proceedings in the courts of the United Kingdom which relate to the arbitration.

(2) This section has effect subject to any contrary provision in the arbitration agreement and does not apply to any arbitration agreement between states.

**10. Ships used for commercial purposes**

(1) This section applies to—

(a) Admiralty proceedings; and

(b) proceedings on any claim which could be made the subject of Admiralty proceedings.

(2) A State is not immune as respects-

(a) an action in rem against a ship belonging to that State; or

(b) an action in personam for enforcing a claim in connection with such a ship,

if, at the time when the cause of action arose, the ship was in use or intended for use for commercial purposes.

(3) Where an action in rem is brought against a ship belonging to a State for enforcing a claim in connection with another ship belonging to that State, subsection (2) (a) above does not apply as respects the first-mentioned ship unless at the time when the cause of action relating to the other ship arose, both ships were in use or intended for use for commercial purposes.

(4) A State is not immune as respects-

(a) an action in rem against a cargo belonging to that State if both the cargo and the ship carrying it were, at the time when the cause of action arose, in use or intended for use for commercial purposes; or

(b) an action in personam for enforcing a claim in connection with such a cargo if the ship carrying it was then in use or intended for use as aforesaid.

(5) In the foregoing provisions references to a ship or cargo belonging to a State include references to a ship or cargo in its possession or control or in which it claims an interest; and, subject to subsection (4) above, subsection (2) above applies to property other than a ship as it applies to a ship.

(6) Sections 3 to 5 above do not apply to proceedings of the kind described in subsection (1) above if the State in question is a party to the Brussels Convention and the claim relates to the operation of a ship owned or operated by that State, the carriage of cargo or passengers on any such ship or the carriage of cargo owned by that State on any other ship.

**11.-13. [Omitted].**

*Supplementary Provisions*

**14. States entitled to immunities and privileges**

(1) The immunities and privileges conferred by this Part of this Act apply to any foreign or commonwealth State other than the United Kingdom; and references to a State include references to—

(a) the sovereign or other head of that State in his public capacity;
(b) the government of that State; and
(c) any department of that government,

but not to any entity (hereafter referred to as a "separate entity") which is distinct from the executive organs of the government of the State and capable of suing or being sued.

(2) A separate entity is immune from the jurisdiction of the courts of the United Kingdom if, and only if-

(a) the proceedings relate to anything done by it in the exercise of sovereign authority; and
(b) the circumstances are such that a State (or, in the case of proceedings to which Section 10 above applies, a State which is not a party to the Brussels Convention) would have been so immune.

(3) If a separate entity (not being a State's central bank or other monetary authority) submits to the jurisdiction in respect of proceedings in the case of which it is entitled to immunity by virtue of subsection (2) above, subsections (1) to (4) of section 13 above shall apply to it in respect of those proceedings as if references to a State were references to that entity.

(4) Property of a State's central bank or other monetary authority shall not be regarded for the purposes of subsection (4) of section 13 above as in use or intended for use for commercial purposes; and where any such bank or authority is a separate entity subsections (1) to (3) of that section shall apply to it as if references to a State were references to the bank or authority.

(5) Section 12 above applies to proceedings against the constituent territories of a federal State; and her Majesty may by Order in Council provide for the other provisions of this Part of this Act to apply to any such constituent territory specified in the Order as they apply to a State.

(6) Where the provisions of this Part of this Act do not apply to a constituent territory by virtue of any such Order subsections (2) and (3) above shall apply to it as if it were a separate entity.

**15.-16. [Omitted].**

**17. Interpretation of Part I**

(1) In this Part of the Act "the Brussels Convention" means the International Convention for the Unification of Certain Rules Concerning the Immunity of State-owned Ships signed in Brussels on 10th April 1926.

'commercial purposes' means purposes of such transactions or activities as are mentioned in section 3(3) above;

'ship' includes hovercraft.

(2) In sections 2(2) and 13(3) above references to an agreement include references to a treaty, convention or other international agreement.

(3) For the purposes of sections 3 to 8 above the territory of the United Kingdom shall be deemed to include any dependent territory in respect of which the United Kingdom is a party to the European Convention on State Immunity.

(4) In sections 3(1), 4(1), 5 and 16(2) above references to the United Kingdom include references to its territorial waters and any area designated under section 1(7) of the Continental Shelf Act 1964.

(5) In relation to Scotland in this Part of this Act "action in rem" means such an action only in relation to Admiralty proceedings.

**18.- 23. [Omitted].**

# ARBITRATION ACT 1979

## CHAPTER 42



### 1. Judicial review of arbitration awards

(1) In the Arbitration Act 1950 (in this Act referred to as "the principal Act" section 21 (statement of case for a decision of the of High Court) shall cease to have effect and without prejudice to the right of appeal conferred by subsection (2) below, the High Court shall not have jurisdiction to set aside or remit an award on an arbitration agreement on the ground of errors of fact or law on the face of the award.

(2) Subject to subsection (3) below , an appeal shall lie to the High Court on any question of law arising out of an award made on an arbitration agreement; and on the determination of such an appeal the High Court may by order-

(a) confirm, vary or set aside the award; or

(b) remit the award to the reconsideration of the arbitrator or umpire together with the court's opinion on the question of law which was the subject of the appeal;

and where the award is remitted under paragraph (b) above the arbitrator or umpire shall, unless the order otherwise directs, make his award within three months after the date of order.

(3) An appeal under this section may be brought by any of the parties to the reference-

(a) with the consent of all the other parties to the reference; or

(b) subject to section 3 below, with the leave of the court.

(4) The High Court shall not grant leave under subsection (3)(b) above unless it considers that, having regard to all the circumstances , the determination of the question of law concerned could substantially affect the rights of one or more of the parties to the arbitration agreement; and the court may make any leave which it gives conditional upon the applicant complying with such conditions as it considers appropriate.

(5) Subject to subsection (6) below, if an award is made and, on an application made by any of the parties to the reference,-

(a) with the consent of all the other parties to the reference, or

(b) subject to section 3 below, with the leave of the court,

it appears to the High Court that the award does not or does not sufficiently set out the reasons for the award, the court may order the arbitrator or umpire concerned to state the reasons for his award in sufficient detail to enable the court, should an appeal be brought under this section, to consider any question of law arising out of the award.

(6) In any case where an award is made without any reason being given, the High Court shall not make an order under subsection (5) above unless it is satisfied—

(a) that before the award was made one of the parties to the reference gave notice to the arbitrator or umpire concerned that a reasoned award would be required; or

(b) that there is some special reason why such a notice was not given.

(6A) Unless the High Court gives leave, no appeal shall lie to the Court of Appeal from a decision of the High Court—

(a) to grant or refuse leave under subsection (3)(b) or (5)(b) above; or

(b) to make or not to make an order under subsection (5) above.

(7) No appeal shall lie to the Court of Appeal from a decision of the High Court on an appeal under this section unless-

(a) the High Court or the Court of Appeal gives leave; and

(b) it is certified by the High Court that the question of law to which its decision relates either is one of general public importance or is one which for some other special reason should be considered by the Court of Appeal.

(8) Where the award of an arbitrator or umpire is varied on appeal, the award as varied shall have effect (except for the purposes of this section) as if it were the award of the arbitrator or umpire.

**2. Determination of preliminary point of law by court**

(1) Subject to subsection (2) and section 3 below, on an application to the High Court made by any of the parties to a reference—

(a) with the consent of an arbitrator who has entered on the reference or, if an umpire has entered on the reference, with his consent, or

(b) with the consent of all the other parties.

the High Court shall have jurisdiction to determine any question of law arising in the course of the reference.

(2) The High Court shall not entertain an application under subsection (1)(a) above with respect to any question of law unless it is satisfied that -

(a) the determination of the application might produce substantial savings in costs to the parties; and

(b) the question of law is one in respect of which leave to appeal would be likely to be given under section 1(3)(b) above.

(2A) Unless the High Court gives leave, no appeal shall lie to the Court of Appeal from a decision of the High Court to entertain or not to entertain an application under subsection (1)(a) above.

(3) A decision of the High Court under subsection (1) above shall be deemed to be a judgement of the court within the meaning of section 16 of the Supreme Court Act 1981 (appeals to the Court of Appeal), but no appeal shall lie from such a decision unless-

(a) the High Court or the Court of Appeal gives leave; and
(b) it is certified by the High Court that the question of law to which its decision relates either is one of general public importance or is one which for some other special reason should be considered by the Court of Appeal.

**3. Exclusion agreements affecting rights under sections 1 and 2**

(1) Subject to the following provisions of this section and section 4 below—
(a) the High Court shall not, under section 1(3)(b) above, grant leave to appeal with respect to a question of law arising out of an award , and
(b) the High Court shall not, under section 1(5)(b) above, grant leave to make application with respect to an award, and
(c) no application may be made under section 2(1)(a) above with respect to a question of law,

if the parties to the reference in question have entered into an agreement in writing (in this section referred to as an "exclusion agreement") which excludes the right of appeal under section 1 above in relation to that award or, in a case falling within paragraph (c) above, in relation to an award to which the determination of the question of law is material.

(2) An exclusion agreement may be expressed so as to relate to a particular award, to awards under a particular reference or to any other description of awards, whether arising out of the same reference or not; and an agreement may be an exclusion agreement for the purposes of this section whether it is entered into before or after the passing of this Act and whether or not it forms part of an arbitration agreement.

(3) In any case where -
(a) an arbitration agreement, other than a domestic arbitration agreement provides for disputes between the parties to be referred to arbitration , and
(b) a dispute to which the agreement relates involves the question whether a party has been guilty of fraud, and
(c) the parties have entered into an exclusion agreement which is applicable to any award made on the reference of that dispute.

then except in so far as the exclusion agreement otherwise provides, the High Court shall not exercise its powers under section 24(2) of the principal Act (to take steps necessary to enable the question to be determined by the High Court) in relation to that dispute.

(4) Except as provided by subsection (1) above, sections 1 and 2 above shall have effect notwithstanding anything in any agreement purporting-
(a) to prohibit or restrict access to the High Court; or
(b) to restrict the jurisdiction of that court; or
(c) to prohibit or restrict the making of a reasoned award.

(5) An exclusion agreement shall be of no effect in relation to an award made on, or a question of law arising in the course of a reference under, a statutory arbitration, that is to say, such an arbitration as is referred to in subsection (1) of section 31 of the principal Act.

(6) An exclusion agreement shall be of no effect in relation to an award made on, or a question of law arising in the course of a reference under, an

arbitration agreement which is a domestic arbitration agreement unless the exclusion agreement is entered into after the commencement of the arbitration in which the award is made or, as the case may be, in which the question of law arises.

(7) In this section 'domestic arbitration agreement' means an arbitration agreement which does not provide, expressly or by implication, for arbitration in a State other than the United Kingdom and to which neither-

(a) an individual who is a national of, or habitually resident in any State other than the United Kingdom, nor

(b) a body corporate which is incorporated in, or whose central management and control is exercised in, any State other than the United Kingdom.

is a party at the time the arbitration agreement is entered into.

**4. Exclusion agreements not to apply in certain cases**

(1) Subject to subsection (3) below, if an arbitration award or a question of law arising in the course of a reference relates, in whole or in part to—

(a) a question or claim falling within the Admiralty jurisdiction of the High Court or

(b) a dispute arising out of a contract of insurance, or

(c) a dispute arising out of a commodity contract,

an exclusion agreement shall have no effect in relation to the award or question unless either —

(i) the exclusion agreement is entered into after the commencement of the arbitration in which the award is made or, as the case may be, in which the question of law arises, or

(ii) the award or question relates to a contract which is expressed to be governed by a law other than the law of England and Wales.

(2) In subsection (1)(c) above "commodity contract" means a contract-

(a) for the sale of goods regularly dealt with on a commodity market or exchange in England or Wales which is specified for the purposes of this section by an order made by the Secretary of State; and

(b) of a description so specified.

(3) The Secretary of State may by order provide that subsection (1) above-

(a) shall cease to have effect; or

(b) subject to such conditions as may be specified in the order, shall not apply to any exclusion agreement made in relation to an arbitration award of a description so specified;

and an order under this subsection may contain such supplementary, incidental and transitional provisions as appear to the Secretary of State to be necessary or expedient.

(4) The power to make an order under subsection 92) or subsection (3) above shall be exercisable by statutory instrument which shall be subject to annulment in persuance of a resolution of either House of Parliament.

(5) In this section "exclusion agreement" has the same meaning as in section 3 above.

**5. Interlocutory orders**

(1) If any party to a reference under an arbitration agreement fails within the time specified in the order or, if no time is so specified, within a reasonable time to comply with an order made by the arbitrator or umpire in the course of the reference, then, on the application of the arbitrator or umpire or of any party to the reference, the High Court may make an order extending the powers of the arbitrator or umpire as mentioned in subsection (2) below.

(2) If an order is made by the High Court under this section, the arbitrator or umpire shall have power, to the extent and subject to any conditions specified in that order, to continue with the reference in default of appearance or of any other act by one of the parties in like manner as a judge of the High Court might continue with proceedings in that court where a party fails to comply with an order of that court or a requirement of rules of court.

(3) Section 4(5) of the Administration of Justice Act 1970 (jurisdiction of the High Court to be exercisable by the Court of Appeal in relation to judge-arbitrators and judge-umpires) shall not apply in relation to the power of the High Court to make an order under this section, but in the case of a reference to a judge-arbitrator or judge-umpire that power shall be exercisable as in the case of any order reference to arbitration and also by the judge-arbitrator or judge umpire himself.

(4) Anything done by a judge-arbitrator or judge-umpire in the exercise of the power conferred by subsection (3) above shall be done by him in his capacity as judge of the High Court and have effect as if done by that court.

(5) The preceding provisions of this section have effect notwithstanding anything in any agreement but do not derogate from any powers conferred on an arbitrator or umpire, whether by an arbitration agreement or otherwise.

(6) In this section "Judge-arbitrator" and "Judge-Umpire" have the same meaning as in Schedule 3 to the Administration of Justice Act 1970.

**6. [Omitted].**

**7. Application and interpretation of certain provisions of Part I of principal Act**

(1) References in the following provisions of Part I of the principal Act to that Part of that Act shall have effect as if the preceding provisions of this Act were included in that Part, namely,—

(a) section 14 (interim awards);
(b) section 28 (terms as to cost of orders);
(c) section 30 (Crown to be bound);
(d) section 31 (application to statutory arbitrations;) and
(e) section 32 (meaning of "arbitration agreement")

(2) Subsections (2) and (3) of section 29 of the Principal Act shall apply to determine when an arbitration is deemed to be commenced for the purposes of this Act.

**8. [Omitted].**

# MERCHANT SHIPPING ACT 1979

## CHAPTER 39

*Liability of shipowners and salvors*

### 17. Limitation of liability

(1) The provisions of the Convention on Limitation of Liability for Maritime Claims 1976 as set out in Part I of Schedule 4 to this Act (hereafter in this section and in part II of that Schedule referred to as 'the Convention') shall have the force of law in the United Kingdom.

(2) The provisions of Part II of that Schedule shall have effect in connection with the Convention and the preceding subsection shall have effect subject to the provisions of that Part.

### 18. Exclusion of liability

(1) Subject to subsection (3) of this section, the owner of a British ship shall not be liable for any loss or damage in the following cases, namely—

(a) where any property on board the ship is lost or damaged by reason of fire on board the ship; or

(b) where any gold , silver, watches, jewels or precious stones on board the ship are lost or damaged by reason of theft, robbery or other dishonest conduct and their nature and value were not at the time of shipment declared by their owner or shipper to the owner or master of the ship in the bill of lading or otherwise in writing.

(2) Subject to subsection (3) of this section, where the loss or damage arises from anything done or omitted by any person in his capacity as master or member of the crew or (otherwise than in that capacity) in the course of his employment as a servant of the owner of the ship, the preceding subsection shall also exclude the liability of—

(a) the master, member of the crew or servant; and

(b) in a case where the master or member of the crew is the servant of a person whose liability would not be excluded by that subsection apart from this paragraph, the person whose servant he is.

(3) This section does not exclude the liability of any person for any loss or damage resulting from any such personal act or omission of his as is mentioned in Article 4 of the Convention in Part I of Schedule 4 to this Act.

(4) In this section "owner" in relation to a ship, includes any part owner and any charterer, manager or operator of the ship.

# SCHEDULE 4

## CONVENTION ON LIMITATION OF LIABILITY FOR MARITIME CLAIMS 1976

## PART I

## TEXT OF CONVENTION

## CHAPTER I. THE RIGHT OF LIMITATION

### ARTICLE 1

*Persons entitled to limit liability*

1. Shipowners and salvors, as hereinafter defined, may limit their liability in accordance with the rules of this Convention for claims set out in Article 2.

2. The term 'shipowner' shall mean the owner, charterer, manager or operator of a seagoing ship.

3. Salvor shall mean any person rendering services in direct connection with salvage operations. Salvage operations shall also include operations referred to in Article 2, paragraph 1(d), (e) and (f)

4. If any claims set out in Article 2 are made against any person for whose act, neglect or default the shipowner or salvor is responsible , such person shall be entitled to avail himself of the limitation of liability provided for in this Convention.

5. In this Convention the liability of a shipowner shall include liability in an action brought against the vessel herself.

6. An insurer of liability for claims subject to limitation in accordance with the rules of this Convention shall be entitled to the benefits of this Convention to the same extent as the assured himself.

7. The act of invoking limitation of liability shall not constitute an admission of liability.

### ARTICLE 2

*Claims subject to limitation*

1. Subject to Articles 3 and 4 the following claims, whatever the basis of liability may be, shall be subject to limitation of liability;

(a) claims in respect of loss of life or personal injury or loss of or damage to property (including damage to harbour works, basins and waterways and aids to navigation) occurring on board or in direct connection with the operation of the ship or with salvage operations and consequential loss resulting therefrom;

(b) claims in respect of loss resulting from delay in the carriage by sea of cargo, passengers or their luggage;

(c) claims in respect of other loss resulting from infringement of rights other than contractual rights, occurring in direct connection with the operation of the ship or salvage operations;

(d) claims in respect of the raising, removal, destruction or the rendering harmless of a ship which is sunk, wrecked, stranded or abandoned, including anything that is or has been on board such ship;

(e) claims in respect of the removal, destruction or the rendering harmless of the cargo of the ship;

(f) claims of a person other than the person liable in respect of measures taken in order to avert or minimise loss for which the person liable may limit his liability in accordance with this Convention, and further loss caused by such measures.

2. Claims set out in paragraph 1 shall be subject to limitation of liability even if brought by way of recourse or for indemnity under a contract or otherwise. However, claims set out under paragraph (d), (e) and (f) shall not be subject to limitation of liability to the extent that they relate to remuneration under a contract with the person liable.

## ARTICLE 3

*Claims excepted from limitation*

The rules of this Convention shall not apply to:

(a) claims for salvage or contribution in general average;

(b) claims for oil pollution damage within the meaning of the international Convention on Civil Liability for Oil Pollution Damage dated 29th November 1969 or of any amendment or Protocol thereto which is in force:

(c) claims subject to any international convention or national legislation governing or prohibiting limitation of liability for nuclear damage;

(d) claims against the shipowner of a nuclear ship for nuclear damage;

(e) claims by servant of the shipowner or salvor whose duties are connected with the ship or the salvage operations, including claims of their heirs, dependants or other persons entitled to make such claims, if under the law governing the contract of service between the shipowner or salvor and such servant the shipowner or salvor is not entitled to limit his liability in respect of such claims, or if he is by such law only permitted to limit his liability to an amount greater than that provided for in Article 6.

## ARTICLE 4

*Conduct barring limitation*

A person liable shall not be entitled to limit his liability if it is proved that the loss resulted from his personal act or omission, committed with the intent to cause such loss, or recklessly and with knowledge that such loss would probably result.

## ARTICLE 5

*Counterclaims*

Where a person entitled to limitation of liability under the rule of this Convention has a claim against the claimant arising out of the same occurrence, their respective claims shall be set off against each other and the provisions of this Convention shall only apply to the balance, if any.

## CHAPTER II. LIMITS OF LIABILITY

## ARTICLE 6

*The general limits*

1. The limits of liability for claims other than those mentioned in Article 7, arising on any distinct occasion, shall be calculated as follows:

(a) in respect of claims for loss of life or personal injury,

(i) 333,000 Units of Account for a ship with a tonnage not exceeding 500 tons,

(ii) for a ship with a tonnage in excess thereof, the following amount in addition to that mentioned in (i):
for each ton from 501 to 3,000 tons, 500 Units of Account;
for each ton from 3,001 to 30,000 tons, 333 Units of Account;
for each ton from 30,001 to 70,000 tons, 250 Units of Account; and
for each ton in excess of 70,000 tons, 167 Units of Account.

(b) in respect of any other claims,

(i) 167,000 Units of Account for a ship with a tonnage not exceeding 500 tons,

(ii) for a ship with a tonnage in excess thereof the following amount in addition to that mentioned in (i):
for each ton from 501 to 30,000 tons, 167 Units of Account;
for each ton from 30,0001 to 70,000 tons, 125 Units of Account; and
for each ton in excess of 70,000 tons, 83 Units of Account.

2. Where the amount calculated in accordance with paragraph 1(a) is insufficient to pay the claims mentioned therein in full, the amount calculated in accordance with paragraph 1(b) shall be available for payment of the unpaid balance of claims under paragraph 1(a) and such unpaid balance shall rank rateably with claims mentioned under paragraph 1(b).

3. The limits of liability for any salvor not operating from any ship or for any salvor operating solely on the ship to, or in respect of which he is rendering salvage services, shall be calculated according to a tonnage of 1,500 tons.

## ARTICLE 7

*The limit for passenger claims*

1. In respect of claims arising on any distinct occasion for loss of life or personal injury to passengers of a ship, the limit of liability of the shipowner thereof shall be an amount of 46,666 Units of Account multiplied by the number of passengers which the ship is authorised to carry according to the ship's certificate, but not exceeding 25 million Units of Account.

2. For the purpose of this Article 'claims for loss of life or personal injury to passengers of a ship' shall mean any such claims brought by or on behalf of any person carried in that ship:

(a) under a contract of passenger carriage, or

(b) who, with the consent of the carrier, is accompanying a vehicle or live animals which are covered by a contract for the carriage of goods.

## ARTICLE 8

*Unit of Account*

1. The Unit of Account referred to in Articles 6 and 7 is the Special Drawing Right as defined by the International Monetary Fund. The amounts mentioned in Articles 6 and 7 shall be converted into the national currency of the State in which limitation is sought, according to the value of that currency at the date the limitation fund shall have been constituted, payment is made, or security is given which under the law of that State is equivalent to such payment.

## ARTICLE 9

*Aggregation of claims*

1. The limits of liability determined in accordance with Article 6 shall apply to the aggregate of all claims which arise on any distinct occasion:

(a) against the person or persons mentioned in paragraph 2 of Article 1 and any person for whose act, neglect or default he or they are responsible; or

(b) against the shipowner of a ship rendering salvage services from that ship and the salvor or salvors operating from such ship and any person for whose act, neglect or default he or they are responsible; or

(c) against the salvor or salvors who are not operating from a ship or who are operating solely on the ship to, or in respect of which, the salvage services are rendered and any person for whose act, neglect or default he or they are responsible.

2. The limits of liability determined in accordance with Article 7 shall apply to the aggregate of all claims subject thereto which may arise on any distinct occasion against the person or persons mentioned in paragraph 2 of Article 1 in respect of the ship referred to in Article 7 and any person for whose act, neglect or default he or they are responsible.

## ARTICLE 10

*Limitation of liability without constitution of a limitation fund*

1. Limitation of liability may be invoked notwithstanding that a limitation fund as mentioned in Article 11 has not been constituted.

2. If limitation of liability is invoked without the constitution of a limitation fund, the provisions of Article 12 shall apply correspondingly.

3. Questions of procedure arising under the rules of this Article shall be decided in accordance with the national law of the State Party in which action is brought.

# CHAPTER III. THE LIMITATION FUND

## ARTICLE 11

*Constitution of the fund*

1. Any person alleged to be liable may constitute a fund with the Court or other competent authority in any State Party in which legal proceedings are instituted in respect of claims subject to limitation. The fund shall be constituted in the sum of such of the amounts set out in Articles 6 and 7 as are applicable to claims for which that person may be liable, together with interest thereon from the date of the occurrence giving rise to the liability until the date of the constitution of the fund. Any fund thus constituted shall be available only for the payment of claims in respect of which limitation of liability can be invoked.

2. A fund may be constituted, either by depositing the sum, or by producing a guarantee acceptable under the the legislation of the State Party where the fund is constituted and considered to be adequate by the court or other competent authority.

3. A fund constituted by one of the persons mentioned in paragraph 1(a) (b) or (c) or paragraph 2 of Article 9 or his insurer shall be deemed constituted by all persons mentioned in paragraph 1(a), (b) or (c) or paragraph 2, respectively.

## ARTICLE 12

*Distribution of the Fund*

1. Subject to the provisions of paragraphs 1 and 2 of Article 6 and of Article 7, the fund shall be distributed among the claimants in proportion to their established claims against the fund.

2. If, before the fund is distributed, the person liable, or his insurer, has settled a claim against the fund such person shall up to the amount he has paid , acquire by subrogation the rights which the person so compensated would have enjoyed under this Convention.

3. The right of subrogation provided for in paragraph 2 may also be exercised by persons other than those therein mentioned in respect of any amount of compensation which they may have paid, but only to the extent that such subrogation is permitted under the applicable national law.

4. Where the person liable or any other person establishes that he may be compelled to pay, at a later day, in whole or in part any such amount of compensation with regard to which such person would have enjoyed a right of subrogation pursuant to paragraphs 2 and 3 had the compensation been paid before the fund was distributed, the Court or other competent authority of the State where the fund has been constituted may order that a sufficient sum shall be provisionally set aside to enable such person at such later date to enforce his claim against the fund.

## ARTICLE 13

*Bar to other actions*

1. Where a limitation fund has been constituted in accordance with Article 11, any person having made a claim against the fund shall be barred from exercising any right in respect of such a claim against any other assets of a person by or on behalf of whom the fund has been constituted.

2. After a limitation fund has been constituted in accordance with Article 11, any ship or other property, belonging to a person on behalf of whom the fund has been constituted, which has been arrested or attached within the jurisdiction of a State Party for a claim which may be raised against the fund , or any security given, may be released by order of the Court or other competent authority of such State. However, such release shall always be ordered if the limitation fund has been constituted:

(a) at the port where the occurrence took place, or, if it took place out of port, at the first port of call thereafter; or
(b) at the port of disembarkation in respect of claims for loss of life or personal injury; or
(c) at the port of discharge in respect of damage to cargo; or
(d) in the State where the arrest is made.

3. The rules of paragraphs 1 and 2 shall apply only if the claimant may bring a claim against the limitation fund before the Court administering that fund and the fund is actually available and freely transferable in respect of that claim.

## ARTICLE 14

*Governing Law*

Subject to the provisions of this Chapter the rules relating to the constitution and distribution of a limitation fund, and all rules of procedure in connection therewith, shall be governed by the law of the State Party in which the fund is constituted.

## CHAPTER IV. SCOPE OF APPLICATION

### ARTICLE 15

This Convention shall apply whenever any person referred to in Article 1 seeks to limit his liability before the Court of a State Party or seeks to procure the release of a ship or other property or the discharge of any security given within the jurisdiction of any such State.

## PART II

## PROVISIONS HAVING EFFECT IN CONNECTION WITH CONVENTION

*Interpretation*

1. In this part of this Schedule any reference to a numbered Article is a reference to the Article of the Convention which is so numbered.

*Right to limit liability*

2. The right to limit liability under the convention shall apply in relation to any ship whether seagoing or not, and the definition of "shipowner" in paragraph 2 of Article 1 shall be construed accordingly.

*Claims subject to limitation*

3. (1) Paragraph 1(d) of Article 2 shall not apply unless provision has been made by an order of the Secretary of State for the setting up and management of a fund to be used for the making to harbour or conservancy authorities of payments needed to compensate them for the reduction, in consequence of the said paragraph 1(d), of amounts recoverable by them in claims of the kind there mentioned, and to be maintained by contributions from such authorities raised and collected by them in respect of vessels in like manner as other sums so raised by them.

(2) Any order under sub-paragraph (1) above may contain such incidental and supplemental provisions as appear to the Secretary of State to be necessary or expedient

(3) If immediately before the coming into force of section 17 of this Act an order is in force under section 2(6) of the Merchant Shipping (Liability of Shipowners and Others) Act 1958 (which contains provisions corresponding to those of this paragraph) that order shall have effect as if made under this paragraph.

*Claims excluded from limitation*

4. (1) The claims excluded from the Convention by paragraph (b) of Article 3 are claims in respect of any liability incurred under section 1 of the Merchant Shipping (Oil Pollution) Act 1971.

(2) The claims excluded from the Convention by paragraph (c) of Article 3 are claims made by virtue of any of sections 7 to 11 of the Nuclear Installations Act 1965.

*The general limits*

5. (1) In the application of Article 6 to a ship with a tonnage less than 300 tons that Article shall have effect as if-

(a) paragraph (a)(i) referred to 166,667 Units of Account; and

(b) paragraph (b)(i) referred to 83,333 Units of Account

(2) For the purposes of Article 6 and this paragraph a ship's tonnage shall be its gross tonnage calculated in such manner as may be prescribed by an order made by the Secretary of State.

(3) Any order under this paragraph shall, so far as appears to the Secretary of State to be practicable, give effect to the regulations in Annex 1 of the International Convention on Tonnage Measurement of Ships 1969.

*Limit for passenger claims*

6. (1) In the case of a passenger steamer within the meaning of part III of the Merchant Shipping Act 1894 the ship's certificate mentioned in paragraph 1 of Article 7 shall be the passenger steamer's certificate issued under section 274 of that Act.

(2) In paragraph 2 of Article 7 the reference to claims brought on behalf of a person includes a reference to any claim in respect of the death of a person under the Fatal Accidents Act 1976, the Fatal Accidents (Northern Ireland) Order 1977 or the Damages (Scotland) Act 1976.

*Units of Account*

7. (1) For the purpose of converting the amounts mentioned in Articles 6 and 7 from special drawing rights into sterling one special drawing right shall be treated as equal to such a sum in sterling as the International Monetary Fund have fixed as being the equivalent of one special drawing right for -

(a) the relevant date under paragraph 1 of Article 8; or

(b) if no sum has been so fixed for that date, the last proceeding date for which a sum has been so fixed.

(2) A certificate given by or on behalf of the Treasury stating-

(a) that a particular sum in sterling has been fixed as mentioned in the preceding sub-paragraph for a particular date; or

(b) that no sum has been so fixed for that date and that a particular sum in sterling has been so fixed for a date which is the last preceding date for which a sum has been so fixed,

Shall be conclusive evidence of those matters for the purposes of those Articles; and a document purporting to be such a certificate shall, in any proceedings, be received in evidence and unless the contrary is proved be deemed to be such a certificate.

*Constitution of fund*

8. (1) The Secretary of State may from time to time with the concurrence of the Treasury, by order prescribe the rate of interest to be applied for the purposes of paragraph 1 of Article 11.

(2) Where a fund is constituted with the court in accordance with Article 11 for the payment of claims arising out of any occurrence, the court may stay any proceedings relating to any claim arising out of that occurrence which are pending against the person by whom the fund has been constituted.

*Distribution of land*

9. No lien or other right in respect of any ship or property shall affect the proportions in which under Article 12 the fund is distributed among several claimants.

*Bar to other actions*

10. Where the release of a ship or other property is ordered under paragraph 2 of Article 13 the person on whose application it is ordered to be release shall be deemed to have submitted to (or, in Scotland, prorogated) the jurisdiction of the court to adjudicate on the claim for which the ship or property was arrested or attached.

*Meaning of 'court'*

11. References in the Convention and the preceding provisions of this Part of this Schedule to the court are-

(a) in relation to England and Wales, references to the High Court;
(b) in relation to Scotland, references to the Court of Session
(c) in relation to Northern Ireland, references to the High Court of Justice in Northern Ireland

*Meaning of "ship"*

12. References in the Convention and in the preceding provisions of this Part of this Schedule to a ship include references to any structure (whether completed or in course of completion) launched and intended for use in navigation as a ship or part of a ship.

*Meaning of "State Party"*

13. An Order in Council made for the purposes of this paragraph and declaring that any State specified in the Order is a party to the Convention shall, subject to the provisions of any subsequent Order made for those purposes be conclusive evidence that the State is a party to the Convention.

# SALE OF GOODS ACT 1979

## CHAPTER 54

## PART II

## FORMATION OF THE CONTRACT

*Contract of sale*



*Formalities of contract*



*Subject matter of contract*



*The Price*



*Conditions and Warranties*



*Sale by Sample*

## PART III

### EFFECTS OF THE CONTRACT

*Transfer of property as between seller and buyer*

16. Goods must be ascertained
17. Property passes when intended to pass
18. Rules for ascertaining intention.
19. Reservation of right of disposal
20. Risk *prima facie* passes with property.

*Transfer of title*

21. Sale by person not the owner
23. Sale under voidable title
24. Seller in possession after sale
25. Buyer in possession after sale.
26. Supplementary to sections 24 and 25

## PART IV

*Performance of the Contract*

27. Duties of seller and buyer
28. Payment and delivery are concurrent conditions
29. Rules about delivery
30. Delivery of wrong quantity.
31. Instalment deliveries
32. Delivery to carrier
33. Risk where goods are delivered at distant place.
34. Buyer's right of examining the goods.
35. Acceptance
36. Buyer not bound to return rejected goods.
37. Buyer's liability for not taking delivery of goods

## PART V

### RIGHTS OF UNPAID SELLER AGAINST THE GOODS

*Preliminary*

38. Unpaid seller defined.
39. Unpaid seller's rights

*Unpaid Seller's lien*



*Stoppage in transit*



*Re-sale etc. by buyer*



*Rescission and re-sale by seller*



## PART VI

## ACTIONS FOR BREACH OF THE CONTRACT

*Seller's remedies*



*Buyer's remedies*



*Interest etc.*



## PART VII

*Supplementary*

## PART II

## FORMATION OF THE CONTRACT

*Contract of Sale*

### 2. Contract of sale

(1) A contract of sale of goods is a contract by which the seller transfers or agrees to transfer the property in goods to the buyer for a money consideration, called the price.

(2) There may be a contract of sale between one part owner and another.

(3) A contract of sale may be absolute or conditional.

(4) Where under a contract of sale the property in the goods is transferred from the seller to the buyer the contract is called a sale.

(5) Where under a contract of sale the transfer of the property in the goods is to take place at a future time or subject to some condition later to be fulfilled the contract is called an agreement to sell.

(6) An agreement to sell becomes a sale when the time elapses or the conditions are fulfilled subject to which the property in the goods is to be transferred.

### 3. Capacity to buy and sell

(1) Capacity to buy and sell is regulated by the general law concerning capacity to contract and to transfer and acquire property.

(2) Where necessaries are sold and delivered to a minor or a person who by reason of mental incapacity or drunkenness is incompetent to contract, he must pay a reasonable price for them.

(3) In subsection (2) above 'necessaries' means goods suitable to the condition in life of the minor or other person concerned and to his actual requirements at the time of the sale and delivery.

*Formalities of Contract*

### 4. How contract of sale is made

(1) Subject to this and any other Act, a contract of sale may be made in writing (either with or without seal), or by world of mouth, or partly in writing and partly by word of mouth, or may be implied from the conduct of the parties.

(2) Nothing in this section affects the law relating to corporations

*Subject matter of contract*

**5. Existing or future goods**

(1) The goods which form the subject of a contract of sale may be either existing goods, owned or possessed by the seller, or goods to be manufactured or acquired by him after the making of the contract of sale, in this Act called future goods.

(2) There may be a contract for the sale of goods the acquisition of which by the seller depends on a contingency which may or may not happen.

(3) Where by a contract of sale the seller purports to effect a present sale of future goods, the contract operates as an agreement to sell the goods.

**6. Goods which have perished**

Where there is a contract for the sale of specific goods, and the goods without the knowledge of the seller have perished at the time when the contract is made, the contract is void.

**7. Goods perishing before sale but after agreement to sell**

Where there is an agreement to sell specific goods and subsequently the goods , without any fault on the part of the seller or buyer perish before the risk passes to the buyer, the agreement is avoided.

*The Price*

**8. Ascertainment of price**

(1) The price in a contract of sale may be fixed by the contract, or may be left to be fixed in a manner agreed by the contract, or may be determined by the course of dealing between the parties.

(2) Where the price is not determined as mentioned in sub-section (1) above the buyer must pay a reasonable price.

(3) What is a reasonable price is a question of fact dependent on the circumstances of each particular case.

**9. Agreement to sell at valuation**

(1) Where there is an agreement to sell goods on the terms that the price is to be fixed by the valuation of a third party, and he cannot or does not make the valuation, the agreement is avoided; but if the goods or any part of them have been delivered to and appropriated by the buyer he must pay a reasonable price for them.

(2) Where the third party is prevented from making the valuation by the fault of the seller or buyer, the party not at fault may maintain an action for damages against the party at fault.

*Conditions and warranties*

**10. Stipulations about time**

(1) Unless a different intention appears from the terms of the contract, stipulations as to time of payment are not of the essence of a contract of sale.

(2) Whether any other stipulation as to time is or is not of the essence of the contract depends on the terms of the contract.

(3) In a contract of sale "month" *prima facie* means calendar month

**11. When condition to be treated as warranty**

(1) Subsections (2) to (4) and (7) below do not apply to Scotland and subsection (5) below applies only to Scotland .

(2) Where a contract of sale is subject to a condition to be fulfilled by the seller the buyer may waive the condition, or may elect to treat the breach of the condition as a breach of warranty and not as a ground for treating the contract as repudiated.

(3) Whether a stipulation in a contract of sale is a condition, the breach of which may give rise to a right to treat the contract as repudiated, or a warranty, the breach of which may give rise to a claim for damages but not a right to reject the goods and treat the contract as repudiated, depends in each case on the construction of the contract; and a stipulation may be a condition, although called a warranty in the contract.

(4) Where a contract of sale is not severable and the buyer has accepted the goods or part of them, the breach of a condition to be fulfilled by the seller can only be treated as a breach of warranty, and not as a ground for rejecting the goods and treating the contract as repudiated, unless there is an express or implied term of the contract to that effect.

(5) In Scotland, failure by the seller to perform any material part of a contract of sale is a breach of contract, which entitles the buyer either within a reasonable time after delivery to reject the goods and treat the contract as repudiated, or to retain the goods and treat the failure to perform such material part as a breach which may give rise to a claim for compensation or damages.

(6) Nothing in this section affects a condition or warranty whose fulfilment is excused by law by reason of impossibility or otherwise.

(7) [Omitted].

**12. Implied terms about title, etc.**

(1) In a contract of sale, other than one to which subsection (3) below applies, there is an implied condition on the part of the seller that in the case of a sale he has the right to sell the goods, and in the case of an agreement to sell he will have such a right at the time when the property is to pass.

(2) In a contract of sale, other than one to which subsection (3) below applies, there is also an implied warranty that—

(a) the goods are free, and will remain free until the time when the property is to pass, from any charge or encumbrance not disclosed or known to the buyer before the contract is made, and

(b) the buyer will enjoy quiet possession of the goods except so far as it may be disturbed by the owner or other person entitled to the benefit of any charge or encumbrance so disclosed or known.

(3) This subsection applies to a contract of sale in the case of which there appears from the contract or is to be inferred from its circumstances an intention that the seller should transfer only such title as he or a third person may have.

(4) In a contract to which subsection (3) above applies there is an implied warranty that all charges or encumbrances known to the seller and not known to the buyer have been disclosed to the buyer before the contract is made.

(5) In a contract to which subsection (3) above applies there is also an implied warranty that none of the following will disturb the buyer's quiet possession of the goods, namely—

(a) the seller

(b) in a case where the parties to the contract intend that the seller should transfer only such title as a third person may have, that person;

(c) anyone claiming through or under the seller or that third person otherwise than under a charge or encumbrance disclosed or known to the buyer before the contract is made.

(6) [Omitted].

**13. Sale by description**

(1) Where there is a contract for the sale of goods by description, there is an implied condition that the goods will correspond with the description.

(2) If the sale is by sample as well as by description it is not sufficient that the bulk of the goods corresponds with the sample if the goods do not also correspond with the description.

(3) A sale of goods is not prevented from being a sale by description by reason only that, being exposed for sale or hire, they are selected by the buyer.

(4) [Omitted].

**14. Implied terms about quality or fitness**

(1) Except as provided by this section and section 15 below and subject to any other enactment, there is no implied condition or warranty about the quality or fitness for any particular purpose of goods supplied under a contract of sale.

(2) Where the seller sells goods in the course of a business, there is an implied condition that the goods supplied under the contract are of merchantable quality, except that there is no such condition—

(a) as regards defects specifically drawn to the buyer's attention before the contract is made; or

(b) if the buyer examines the goods before the contract is made, as regards defects which that examination ought to reveal.

(3) Where the seller sells goods in the course of a business and the buyer, expressly or by implication, makes known—

(a) to the seller, or

(b) where the purchase price or part of it is payable by instalments and the goods were previously sold by a credit-broker to the seller, to that credit-broker

any particular purpose for which the goods are being bought, there is an implied condition that the goods supplied under the contract are reasonable fit for that purpose, whether or not that is a purpose for which such goods are commonly supplied, except where the circumstances show that the buyer does not rely, or that it is unreasonable for him to rely, on the skill or judgement of the seller or credit-broker.

(4) An implied condition or warranty about quality or fitness for a particular purpose may be annexed to a contract of sale by usage.

(5) The preceding provisions of this section apply to a sale by a person who in the course of a business is acting as agent for another as they apply to a sale by a principal in the course of a business, except where that other is not selling in the course of a business and either the buyer knows that fact or reasonable steps are taken to bring it to the notice of the buyer before the contract is made

(6) Goods of any kind are of merchantable quality within the meaning of subsection (2) above if they are as fit for the purpose or purposes for which goods of that kind are commonly bought as it is reasonable to expect having regard to any description applied to them, the price (if relevant) and all the other relevant circumstances.

(7) and (8) [Omitted].

*Sale by sample*

**15. Sale by sample**

(1) A contract of sale is a contract for sale by sample where there is an express or implied term to that effect in the contract.

(2) In the case of a contract for sale by sample there is an implied condition—

(a) that the bulk will correspond with the sample in quality;
(b) that the buyer will have a reasonable opportunity of comparing the bulk with the sample;
(c) that the goods will be free from any defect, rendering them unmerchantable, which would not be apparent on reasonable examination of the sample.

(3) In subsection (2)(c) above 'unmerchantable' is to be construed in accordance with section 14(6) above.

(4) [Omitted].

## PART III

## EFFECTS OF THE CONTRACT

*Transfer of Property as between seller and buyer*

### 16. Goods must be ascertained

Where there is a contract for the sale of unascertained goods no property in the goods is transferred to the buyer unless and until the goods are ascertained.

### 17. Property passes when intended to pass

(1) Where there is a contract for the sale of specific or ascertained goods the property in them is transferred to the buyer at such time as the parties to the contract intend it to be transferred.

(2) For the purpose of ascertaining the intention of the parties regard shall be had to the terms of the contract, the conduct of the parties and the circumstances of the case.

### 18. Rules for ascertaining intention

Unless a different intention appears, the following are rules for ascertaining the intention of the parties as to the time at which the property in the goods is to pass to the buyer.

*Rule 1*—Where there is an unconditional contract for the sale of specific goods in a deliverable state the property in the goods passes to the buyer when the contract is made, and it is immaterial whether the time of payment or the time of delivery, or both, be postponed.

*Rule 2*—Where there is a contract for the sale of specific goods and the seller is bound to do something to the goods for the purpose of putting them into a deliverable state, the property does not pass until the thing is done and the buyer has notice that it has been done.

*Rule 3*—Where there is a contract for the sale of specific goods in a deliverable state but the seller is bound to weigh, measure, test or do some other act or thing with reference to the goods for the purpose of ascertaining the price, the property does not pass until the act or thing is done and the buyer has notice that it has been done.

*Rule 4*—When goods are delivered to the buyer on approval or on sale or return or other similar terms the property in the goods passes to the buyer:-

(a) when he signifies his approval or acceptance to the seller or does any other act adopting the transaction;

(b) if he does not signify his approval or acceptance to the seller but retains the goods without giving notice of rejection, then, if a time has been fixed for the return of the goods on the expiration of that time, and if no time has been fixed, on the expiration of a reasonable time.

*Rule 5*—

(1) Where there is a contract for the sale of unascertained or future goods by description, and goods of that description and in a deliverable state are unconditionally appropriated to the contract, either by the seller with the assent of the buyer or by the buyer with the assent of the seller, the property in the goods then passes to the buyer; and the assent may be express or implied, and may be given either before or after the appropriation is made.

(2) Where, in pursuance of the contract, the seller delivers the goods to the buyer or to a carrier or other bailee or custodier (whether named by the buyer or not) for the purpose of transmission to the buyer, and does not reserve the right of disposal, he is to be taken to have unconditionally appropriated the goods to the contract.

## 19. Reservation of right of disposal

(1) Where there is a contract for the sale of specific goods or where goods are subsequently appropriated to the contract, the seller may, by the terms of the contract or appropriation, reserve the right of disposal of the goods until certain conditions are fulfilled; and in such a case, notwithstanding the delivery of the goods to the buyer, or to the carrier or other bailee or custodier for the purpose of transmission to the buyer, the property in the goods does not pass to the buyer until the conditions imposed by the seller are fulfilled.

(2) Where goods are shipped and by the bill of lading the goods are deliverable to the order of the seller or his agent, the seller is *prima facie* to be taken to reserve the right of disposal.

(3) Where the seller of goods draws on the buyer for the price and transmits the bill of exchange and bill of lading to the buyer together to secure acceptance or payment of the bill of exchange, the buyer is bound to return the bill of lading if he does not honour the bill of exchange, and if he wrongfully retains the bill of lading the property in the goods does not pass to him.

## 20. Risk *prima facie* passes with property

(1) Unless otherwise agreed, the goods remain at the seller's risk until the property in them is transferred to the buyer, but when the property in them is

transferred to the buyer the goods are at the buyer's risk whether delivery has been made or not.

(2) But where delivery has been delayed through the fault of either buyer or seller the goods are at the risk of the party at fault as regards any loss which might not have occurred but for such fault.

(3) Nothing in this section affects the duties or liabilities of either seller or buyer as a bailee or custodier of the goods of the other party.

*Transfer of title*

**21. Sale by person not the owner**

(1) Subject to this Act, where goods are sold by a person who is not their owner and who does not sell them under the authority or with the consent of the owner, the buyer acquires no better title to the goods than the seller had, unless the owner of the goods is by his conduct precluded from denying the seller's authority to sell.

(2) Nothing in this Act affects-
- (a) the provisions of the Factors Acts or any enactment enabling the apparent owner of goods to dispose of them as if he were their true owner;
- (b) the validity of any contract of sale under any special common law or statutory power of sale or under the order of a court of competent jurisdiction.

**22. [Omitted].**

**23. Sale under voidable title**

When the seller of goods has a voidable title to them, but his title has not been avoided at the time of the sale, the buyer acquires a good title to the goods, provided he buys them in good faith and without notice of the seller's defect of title.

**24. Seller in possession after sale**

Where a person having sold goods continues or is in possession of the goods, or of the documents of title to the goods, the delivery or transfer by that person, or by a mercantile agent acting for him, of the goods or documents of title under any sale, pledge, or other disposition thereof, to any person receiving the same in good faith and without notice of the previous sale, has the same effect as if the person making the delivery or transfer were expressly authorised by the owner of the goods to make the same.

**25. Buyer in possession after sale**

(1) Where a person having bought or agreed to buy goods obtains, with the consent of the seller, possession of the goods or the documents of title to the goods or documents of title, under any sale, pledge, or other disposition thereof, to any person receiving the same in good faith and without notice of any lien or other right of the original seller in respect of the goods, has the same effect as if the person making the delivery or transfer were a mercantile agent in possession of the goods or documents of title with the consent of the owner.

(2) For the purposes of subsection (1) above:
- (a) the buyer under a conditional sale agreement is to be taken not to be a person who has bought or agreed to buy goods, and
- (b) 'conditional sale agreement' means an agreement for the sale of goods which is a consumer credit agreement within the meaning of the Consumer Credit Act 1974 under which the purchase price or part of it is payable by instalments, and the property in the goods is to remain in the seller (notwithstanding that the buyer is to be in possession of the goods) until such conditions as to the payment of instalments or otherwise as may be specified in the agreement are fulfilled.

(3) and (4) [Omitted].

**26. Supplementary to sections 24 and 25**

In sections 24 and 25 above 'mercantile agent' means a mercantile agent having in the customary course of his business as such agent authority either:
- (a) to sell goods, or
- (b) to consign goods for the purpose of sale, or
- (c) to buy goods, or
- (d) to raise money on the security of goods.

## PART IV

## PERFORMANCE OF THE CONTRACT

**27. Duties of seller and buyer**

It is the duty of the seller to deliver the goods, and of the buyer to accept and pay for them, in accordance with the terms of the contract of sale.

**28. Payment and delivery are concurrent conditions**

Unless otherwise agreed, delivery of the goods and payment of the price are concurrent conditions, that is to say, the seller must be ready and willing to give possession of the goods to the buyer in exchange for the price and the buyer must be ready and willing to pay the price in exchange for possession of the goods.

**29. Rules about delivery**

(1) Whether it is for the buyer to take possession of the goods or for the seller to send them to the buyer is a question depending in each case on the contract, express or implied, between the parties.

(2) Apart from any such contract, express or implied, the place of delivery is the seller's place of business if he has one, and if not, his residence; except that, if the contract is for the sale of specific goods, which to the knowledge of the parties when the contract is made are in some other place, then that place is the place of delivery.

(3) Where under the contract of sale the seller is bound to send the goods to the buyer, but no time for sending them is fixed, the seller is bound to send them within a reasonable time.

(4) Where the goods at the time of sale are in the possession of a third person, there is no delivery by seller to buyer unless and until the third person acknowledges to the buyer that he holds the goods on his behalf; but nothing in this section affects the operation of the issue or transfer of any document of title to goods.

(5) Demand or tender of delivery may be treated as ineffectual unless made at a reasonable hour; and what is a reasonable hour is a question of fact.

(6) Unless otherwise agreed, the expenses of and incidental to putting the goods into a deliverable state must be borne by the seller.

**30. Delivery of wrong quantity**

(1) Where the seller delivers to the buyer a quantity of goods less than he contracted to sell, the buyer may reject them, but if the buyer accepts the goods so delivered he must pay for them at the contract rate.

(2) Where the seller delivers to the buyer a quantity of goods larger than he contracted to sell, the buyer may accept the goods included in the contract and reject the rest, or he may reject the whole.

(3) Where the seller delivers to the buyer a quantity of goods larger than he contracted to sell and the buyer accepts the whole of the goods so delivered he must pay for them at the contract rate.

(4) Where the seller delivers to the buyer the goods he contracted to sell mixed with goods of a different description not included in the contract, the buyer may accept the goods which are in accordance with the contract and reject the rest, or he may reject the whole.

(5) This section is subject to any usage of trade, special agreement, or of course of dealing between the parties.

### 31. Instalment deliveries

(1) Unless otherwise agreed, the buyer of goods is not bound to accept delivery of them by instalments.

(2) Where there is a contract for the sale of goods to be delivered by stated instalments, which are to be separately paid for, and the seller makes defective deliveries in respect of one or more instalments or the buyer neglects or refuses to take delivery of or pay for one or more instalments, it is a question in each case depending on the terms of the contract and the circumstances of the case whether the breach of contract is a repudiation of the whole contract or whether it is a severable breach giving rise to a claim for compensation but not to a right to treat the whole contract as repudiated.

### 32. Delivery to carrier

(1) Where, in pursuance of a contract of sale, the seller is authorised or required to send the goods to the buyer, delivery of the goods to a carrier (whether named by the buyer or not) for the purpose of transmission to the buyer is *prima facie* deemed to be a delivery of the goods to the buyer.

(2) Unless otherwise authorised by the buyer, the seller must make such contract with the carrier on behalf of the buyer as may be reasonable having regard to the nature of the goods and the other circumstances of the case; and if the seller omits to do so, and the goods are lost or damaged in course of transit, the buyer may decline to treat the delivery to the carrier as a delivery to himself or may hold the seller responsible in damages.

(3) Unless otherwise agreed, where goods are setnt by the seller to the buyer by a route involving sea transit, under circumstances in which it is usual to insure, the seller must give such notice to the buyer as may enable him to insure them during their sea transit; and if the seller fails to do so, the goods are at his risk during such sea transit.

### 33. Risk where goods are delivered at distant place

Where the seller of goods agrees to deliver them at his own risk at a place other than that where they are when sold, the buyer must nevertheless (unless otherwise agreed) take any risk of deterioration in the goods necessarily incident to the course of transit.

### 34. Buyer's right of examining the goods

(1) Where goods are delivered to the buyer, and he has not previously examined them, he is not deemed to have accepted them until he has had a reasonable opportunity of examining them for the purpose of ascertaining whether they are in conformity with the contract.

(2) Unless otherwise agreed, when the seller tenders delivery of goods to the buyer, he is bound on request to afford the buyer a reasonable opportunity of examining the goods for the purpose of ascertaining whether they are in conformity with the contract.

**35. Acceptance**

(1) The buyer is deemed to have accepted the goods when he intimates to the seller that he has accepted them, or (except where section 34 above otherwise provides) when the goods have been delivered to him and he does any act in relation to them which is inconsistent with the ownership of the seller, or when after the lapse of a reasonable time he retains the goods without intimating to the seller that he has rejected them.

(2) [Omitted].

**36. Buyer not bound to return rejected goods.**

Unless otherwise agreed, where goods are delivered to the buyer, and he refuses to accept them, having the right to do so, he is not bound to return them to the seller, but it is sufficient if he intimates to the seller that he refuses to accept them.

**37. Buyer's liability for not taking delivery of goods**

(1) When the seller is ready and willing to deliver the goods, and requests the buyer to take delivery, and the buyer does not within a reasonable time after such request take delivery of the goods, he is liable to the seller for any loss occasioned by his neglect or refusal to take delivery, and also for a reasonable charge for the care and custody of the goods.

(2) Nothing in this section affects the rights of the seller where the neglect or refusal of the buyer to take delivery amounts to a repudiation of the contract.

## Part V

## Rights of Unpaid Seller Against the Goods

*Preliminary*

**38. Unpaid seller defined**

(1) The seller of goods is an unpaid seller within the meaning of this Act:

(a) when the whole of the price has not been paid or tendered;

(b) when a bill of exchange or other negotiable instrument has been received as conditional payment, and the condition on which it was received has not been fulfilled by reason of the dishonour of the instrument or otherwise

(2) In this Part of this Act 'seller' includes any person who is in the position of a seller, as, for instance, an agent of the seller to whom the bill of lading has been indorsed, or a consignor or agent who has himself paid (or is directly responsible for) the price.

**39. Unpaid seller's rights**

(1) Subject to this and any other Act, notwithstanding that the property in the goods may have passed to the buyer, the unpaid seller of goods, as such, has by implication of law:
(a) a lien on the goods or right to retain them for the price while he is in possession of them;
(b) in case of the insolvency of the buyer, a right of stopping the goods in transit after he has parted with the possession of them;
(c) a right of re-sale as limited by this Act.

(2) Where the property in goods has not passed to the buyer, the unpaid seller has (in addition to his other remedies) a right of withholding delivery similar to and co-extensive with his rights of lien or retention and stoppage in transit where the property has passed to the buyer.

**40. [Repealed].**

*Unpaid seller's lien*

**41. Seller's lien**

(1) Subject to this Act, the unpaid seller of goods who is in possession of them is entitled to retain possession of them until payment or tender of the price in the following cases:—
(a) where the goods have been sold without any stipulation as to credit;
(b) where the goods have been sold on credit but the term of credit has expired;
(c) where the buyer becomes insolvent.

(2) The seller may exercise his lien or right of retention notwithstanding that he is in possession of the goods as agent or bailee or custodier for the buyer.

**42. Part delivery**

Where an unpaid seller has made part delivery of the goods, he may exercise his lien or right of retention on the remainder, unless such part delivery has been made under such circumstances as to show an agreement to waive the lien or right of retention.

**43. Termination of lien**

(1) The unpaid seller of goods loses his lien or right of retention in respect of them—
(a) when he delivers the goods to a carrier or other bailee or custodier for the purpose of transmission to the buyer without reserving the right of disposal of the goods;
(b) when the buyer or his agent lawfully obtains possession of the goods;
(c) by waiver of the lien or right of retention.

(2) An unpaid seller of goods who has a lien or right of retention in respect of them does not lose his lien or right of retention by reason only that he has obtained judgment or decree for the price of the goods.

*Stoppage in transit*

**44. Right of stoppage in transit**

Subject to this Act, when the buyer of goods becomes insolvent the unpaid seller who has parted with the possession of the goods has the right of stopping them in transit, that is to say, he may resume possession of the goods as long as they are in course of transit, and may retain them until payment or tender the price.

**45. Duration of transit**

(1) Goods are deemed to be in course of transit from the time when they are delivered to a carrier or other bailee or custodier for the purpose of transmission to the buyer, until the buyer or his agent in that behalf takes delivery of them from the carrier or other bailee or custodier.

(2) If the buyer or his agent in that behalf obtains delivery of the goods before their arrival at the appointed destination, the transit is at an end.

(3) If, after the arrival of the goods at the appointed destination, the carrier or other bailee or custodier acknowledges to the buyer or his agent that he holds the goods on his behalf and continues in possession of them as bailee or custodier for the buyer or his agent, the transit is at an end, and it is immaterial that a further destination for the goods may have been indicated by the buyer.

(4) If the goods are rejected by the buyer, and the carrier or other bailee or custodier continues in possession of them, the transit is not deemed to be at an end, even if the seller has refused to receive them back.

(5) When goods are delivered to a ship chartered by the buyer it is a question depending on the circumstances of the particular case whether they are in the possession of the master as a carrier or as agent to the buyer.

(6) Where the carrier or other bailee or custodier wrongfully refuses to deliver the goods to the buyer or his agent in that behalf, the transit is deemed to be at an end.

(7) Where part delivery of the goods has been made to the buyer or his agent in that behalf, the remainder of the goods may be stopped in transit, unless such part delivery has been made under such circumstances as to show an agreement to give up possession of the whole of the goods.

**46. How stoppage in transit is effected**

(1) The unpaid seller may exercise his right of stoppage in transit either by taking actual possession of the goods or by giving notice of his claim to the carrier or other bailee or custodier in whose possession the goods are.

(2) The notice may be given either to the person in actual possession of the goods or to his principal.

(3) If given to the principal, the notice is ineffective unless given at such time and under such circumstances that the principal, by the exercise of reasonable diligence, may communicate it to his servant or agent in time to prevent a delivery to the buyer.

(4) When notice of stoppage in transit is given by the seller to the carrier or other bailee or custodier in possession of the goods, he must re-deliver the goods to, or according to the directions of, the seller; and the expenses of the re-delivery must be borne by the seller.

*Re-sale etc., by buyer*

**47. Effect of sub-sale etc., by buyer**

(1) Subject to this Act, the unpaid seller's right of lien or retention or stoppage in transit is not affected by any sale or other disposition of the goods which the buyer may have made, unless the seller has assented to it.

(2) Where a document of title to goods has been lawfully transferred to any person as buyer or owner of the goods, and that person transfers the document to a person who takes it in good faith and for valuable consideration, then;

(a) if the last-mentioned transfer was by way of sale the unpaid seller's right of lien or retention or stoppage in transit is defeated; and

(b) if the last-mentioned transfer was made by way of pledge or other disposition for value, the unpaid seller's right of lien or retention or stoppage in transit can only be exercised subject to the rights of the transferee.

*Rescission: and re-sale by seller*

**48. Rescission and re-sale by seller**

(1) Subject to this section, a contract of sale is not rescinded by the mere exercise by an unpaid seller of his right of lien or retention or stoppage in transit.

(2) Where an unpaid seller who has exercised his right of lien or retention or stoppage in transit re-sells the goods, the buyer acquires a good title to them as against the original buyer.

(3) Where the goods are of a perishable nature, or where the unpaid seller gives notice to the buyer of his intention to re-sell, and the buyer does not within a reasonable time pay or tender the price, the unpaid seller may re-sell the goods and recover from the original buyer damages for any loss occasioned by his breach of contract.

(4) Where the seller expressly reserves the right of re-sale in case the buyer should make default, and on the buyer making default re-sells the goods, the original contract of sale is rescinded but without prejudice to any claim the seller may have for damages.

## PART VI

## ACTIONS FOR BREACH OF THE CONTRACT

*Seller's remedies*

### 49. Action for price

(1) Where, under a contract of sale, the property in the goods has passed to the buyer and he wrongfully neglects or refuses to pay for the goods according to the terms of the contract, the seller may maintain an action against him for the price of the goods.

(2) Where, under a contract of sale, the price is payable on a day certain irrespective of delivery and the buyer wrongfully neglects or refuses to pay such price, the seller may maintain an action for the price, although the property in the goods has not passed and the goods have not been appropriated to the contract.

(3) Nothing in this section prejudices the right of the seller in Scotland to recover interest on the price from the date of tender of the goods, or from the date on which the price was payable, as the case may be.

### 50. Damages for non-acceptance

(1) Where the buyer wrongfully neglects or refuses to accept and pay for the goods, the seller may maintain an action against him for damages for non-acceptance.

(2) The measure of damages is the estimated loss directly and naturally resulting, in the ordinary course of events, from the buyer's breach of contract.

(3) Where there is an available market for the goods in question the measure of damages is *prima facie* to be ascertained by the difference between the contract price and the market or current price at the time or times when the goods ought to have been accepted or (if no time was fixed for acceptance) at the time of the refusal to accept.

*Buyer's remedies*

### 51. Damages for non-delivery

(1) Where the seller wrongfully neglects or refuses to deliver the goods to the buyer, the buyer may maintain an action against the seller for damages for non-delivery.

(2) The measure of damages is the estimated loss directly and naturally resulting, in the ordinary course of events, from the seller's breach of contract.

(3) Where there is an available market for the goods in question the measure of damages is *prima facie* to be ascertained by the difference between the contract price and the market or current price of the goods at the time or times when they ought to have been delivered or (if no time was fixed) at the time of the refusal to deliver.

**52. Specific performance**

(1) In any action for breach of contract to deliver specific or ascertained goods the court may, if it thinks fit, on the plaintiff's application, by its judgement or decree direct that the contract shall be performed specifically, without giving the defendant the option of retaining the goods on payment of damages.

(2) The plaintiff's application may be made at any time before judgement or decree.

(3) The judgement or decree may be unconditional, or on such terms and conditions as to damages, payment of the price and otherwise as seem just to the court.

(4) The provisions of this section shall be deemed to be supplementary to, and not in derogation of, the right of specific implement in Scotland.

**53. Remedy for breach of warranty**

(1) Where there is a breach of warranty by the seller, or where the buyer elects (or is compelled) to treat any breach of a condition on the part of the seller as a breach of warranty, the buyer is not by reason only of such breach of warranty entitled to reject the goods; but he may:

- (a) set up against the seller the breach of warranty in diminution or extinction of the price, or
- (b) maintain an action against the seller for damages for the breach of warranty.

(2) The measure of damages for breach of warranty is the estimated loss directly and naturally resulting, in the ordinary course of events, from the breach of warranty.

(3) In the case of breach of warranty of quality such loss is *prima facie* the difference between the value of the goods at the time of delivery to the buyer and the value they would have had if they had fulfilled the warranty.

(4) The fact that the buyer has set up the breach of warranty in diminution or extinction of the price does not prevent him from maintaining an action for the same breach of warranty if he has suffered further damage.

(5) Nothing in this section prejudices or affects the buyer's right of rejection in Scotland as declared by this Act.

*Interest, etc.,*

**54. Interest etc.**

Nothing in this Act affects the right of the buyer or the seller to recover interest or special damages in any case where by law interest or special damages may be recoverable, or to recover money paid where the consideration for the payment of it has failed.

## PART VII

## SUPPLEMENTARY

**55. Exclusion of implied terms**

(1) Where a right, duty or liability would arise under a contract of sale of goods by implication of law, it may (subject to the Unfair Contract Terms Act 1977) be negatived or varied by express agreement, or by the course of dealing between the parties, or by such usage as binds both parties to the contract.

(2) An express condition or warranty does not negative a condition or warranty implied by this Act unless inconsistent with it.

(3) [Omitted].

**56. [Omitted].**

**57. Auction sales**

(1) Where goods are put up for sale by auction in lots, each lot is *prima facie* deemed to be the subject of a separate contract of sale

(2) A sale by auction is complete when the auctioneer announces its completion by the fall of the hammer, or in other customary manner; and until the announcement is made any bidder may retract his bid.

(3) A sale by auction may be notified to be subject to a reserve or upset price, and a right to bid may also be reserved expressly by or on behalf of the seller.

(4) Where a sale by auction is not notified to be subject to a right to bid by or on behalf of the seller, it is not lawful for the seller to bid himself or to employ any person to bid at the sale, or for the auctioneer knowingly to take any bid from the seller or any such person.

(5) A sale contravening subsection (4) above may be treated as fraudulent by the buyer.

(6) Where, in respect of a sale by auction, a right to bid is expressly reserved (but not otherwise) the seller or any one person on his behalf may bid at the auction.

**58. [Omitted].**

**59. Reasonable time a question of fact**

Where a reference is made in this Act to a reasonable time the question what is a reasonable time is a question of fact.

**60. Rights etc. enforceable by action**

Where a right, duty or liability is declared by this Act, it may (unless otherwise provided by this Act) be enforced by action

**61. Interpretation**

(1) In this Act, unless the context or subject matter otherwise requires,—

'action' includes counterclaim and set-off, and in Scotland condescendence and claim and compensation;
'business' includes a profession and the activities of any Government department (including a Northern Ireland department) or local or public authority;
'buyer' means a person who buys or agrees to buy goods;
'contract of sale' includes an agreement to sell as well as a sale;
'credit-broker' means a person acting in the course of a business of credit brokerage carried on by him, that is a business of effecting introduction of individuals desiring to obtain credit:
(a) to persons carrying on any business so far as it relates to the provision of credit, or
(b) to other persons engaged in credit brokerage;
'defendant' includes in Scotland defender, respondent, and claimant in a multiplepoinding;
'delivery' means voluntary transfer of possession from one person to another;
'document of title to goods' has the same meaning as it has in the Factors Acts;
'Factors Acts' means the Factors Act 1889, the Factors (Scotland) 1890, and any enactment amending or substituted for the same;
'fault' means wrongful act or default;
'future goods' means goods to be manufactured or acquired by the seller after the making of the contract of sale;
'goods' includes all personal chattels other than things in action and money, and in Scotland all corporeal moveables except money; and in particular "goods" includes emblements, industrial growing crops, and things attached to or forming part of the land which are agreed to be severed before sale or under the contract of sale;
'plaintiff' includes pursuer, complainer, claimant in a multiple poinding and defendant or defender counter-claiming;
'property' means the general property in goods, and not merely a special property;
'quality', in relation to goods, includes their state or condition;
'sale' includes a bargain and sale as well as a sale and delivery;

'seller' means a person who sells or agrees to sell goods;
'specific goods' means goods identified and agreed on at the time a contract of sale is made;
'warranty' (as regards England and Wales and Northern Ireland) means an agreement with reference to goods which are the subject of a contract of sale, but collateral to the main purpose of such contract, the breach of which gives rise to a claim for damages, but not to a right to reject the goods and treat the contract as repudiated.

(2) As regards Scotland a breach of warranty shall be deemed to be a failure to perform a material part of the contract.

(3) A thing is deemed to be done in good faith within the meaning of this Act when it is in fact done honestly, whether it is done negligently or not..

(4) A person is deemed to be insolvent within the meaning of this Act if he has either ceased to pay his debts in the ordinary course of business or he cannot pay his debts as they become due.

(5) Goods are in a deliverable state within the meaning of this Act when they are in such a state that the buyer would under the contract be bound to take delivery of them.

(6) [Omitted].

**62.-64. and Schedules 1-4 [Omitted].**

# LIMITATION ACT 1980

## CHAPTER 58

### PART I

### ORDINARY TIME LIMITS FOR DIFFERENT CLASSES OF ACTION

*Time limits under Part I subject to extension or exclusion under Part II*

*Actions founded on tort*

2. Time limit for actions founded on tort.
3. Time limit in case of successive conversions and extinction of title of owner of converted goods.

*Actions founded on simple contract*

5. Time limit for actions founded on simple contract.
6. Special time limit for actions in respects of certain loans.
7. Time limit for actions to enforce certain awards.

*General rule for actions on a specialty*

8. Time limit for actions on a specialty.

*Actions for sums recoverable by statute*

9. Time limit for actions for sums recoverable by statute.
10. Special time limit for claiming contribution.

*Actions in respect of latent damage not involving personal injuries*

14A. Special time limit for negligence actions where facts relevant to cause of action are not known at date of accrual,

14B. Overriding time limit for negligence actions not involving personal injuries.

### PART III

### MISCELLANEOUS AND GENERAL

34. Application of Act and other limitation enactments to arbitrations.

## PART I

## ORDINARY TIME LIMITS FOR DIFFERENT CLASSES OF ACTION

**1. [Omitted].**

*Actions founded on tort*

**2. Time limit for actions founded on tort.**

An action founded on tort shall not be brought after the expiration of six years from the date on which the cause of action accrued.

**3. Time limit in case of successive conversions and extinction of title of owner of converted goods.**

(1) Where any cause of action in respect of the conversion of a chattel has accrued to any person and, before he recovers possession of the chattel, a further conversion take place, no action shall be brought in respect of the further conversion after the expiration of six years from the accrual of the cause of action in respect of the original conversion.

(2) Where any such cause of action has accrued to any person and the period prescribed for bringing that action has expired and he has not during that period recovered possession of the chattel, the title of that person to the chattel shall be extinguished.

**4. and 4A. [Omitted].**

*Actions founded on simple contract*

**5. Time limit for actions founded on simple contract.**

An action founded on simple contract shall not be brought after the expiration of six years from the date on which the cause of action accrued.

**6. Special time limit for actions in respect of certain loans.**

(1) Subject to subsection (3) below, section 5 of this Act shall not bar the right of action on a contract of loan to which this section applies.

(2) This section applies to any contract of loan which—

(a) does not provide for repayment of the debt on or before a fixed or determinable date; and

(b) does not effectively (whether or not it purports to do so) make the obligation to repay the debt conditional on a demand for repayment made by or on behalf of the creditor or on any other matter;

except where in connection with taking the loan the debtor enters into any collateral obligation to pay the amount of the debt or any part of it (as, for example, by delivering a promissory note as security for the debt) on terms which would exclude the application of this section to the contract of loan if they applied directly to repayment of the debt.

(3) Where a demand in writing for repayment of the debt under a contract of loan to which this section applies is made by or on behalf of the creditor (or, where there are joint creditors, by or on behalf of any one of them) section 5 of this Act shall thereupon apply as if the cause of action to recover the debt had accrued on the date on which the demand was made.

(4) In this section 'promissory note' has the same meaning as in the Bills of Exchange Act 1882.

**7. Time limit for actions to enforce certain awards.**

An action to enforce an award, where the submission is not by an instrument under seal, shall not be brought after the expiration of six years from the date on which the cause of action accrued.

*General rule for actions on a specialty*

**8. Time limit for actions on a specialty.**

(1) An action upon a specialty shall not be brought after the expiration of twelve years from the date on which the cause of action accrued.

(2) Subsection (1) above shall not affect any action for which a shorter period of limitation is prescribed by any other provision of this Act.

*Actions for sums recoverable by statute*

**9. Time limit for actions for sums recoverable by statute.**

(1) An action to recover any sum recoverable by virtue of any enactment shall not be brought after the expiration of six years from the date on which the cause of action accrued.

(2) Subsection (1) above shall not affect any action to which section 10 of this Act applies.

**10. Special time limit for claiming contribution.**

(1) Where under section 1 of the Civil Liability (Contribution) Act 1978 any person becomes entitled to a right to recover contribution in respect of any other person, no action to recover contribution by virtue of that right shall be brought after the expiration of two years from the date on which that right accrued.

(2) For the purposes of this section the date on which a right to recover contribution in respect of any damage accrues to any person (referred to below in this section as "the relevant date") shall be ascertained as provided in subsection (3) and (4) below.

(3) If the person in question is held liable in respect of that damage—
(a) by a judgement given in any civil proceedings; or
(b) by an award made on any arbitration;
the relevant date shall be the date on which the judgement is given, or the date of the award (as the case may be).

For the purposes of this subsection no account shall be taken of any judgement or award given or made on appeal in so far as it varies the amount of damages awarded against the person in question.

(4) If, in any case not within subsection (3) above, the person in question makes or agrees to make any payment to one or more persons in compensation for that damage (whether he admits any liability in respect of the damage or not), the relevant date shall be the earliest date on which the amount to be paid by him is agreed between him (or his representative) and the person (or each of the persons, as the case may be) to whom the payment is to be made.

(5) An action to recover contribution shall be one to which sections 28, 32, and 35 of this Act apply, but otherwise Parts II and III of this Act (except sections 34, 27 and 38) shall not apply for the purposes of this section.

**11.-14. [Omitted].**

*Actions in respect of latent damage not involving personal injuries*

**14A. Special time limit for negligence actions where facts relevant to cause of action are not known at date of accrual.**

(1) This section applies to any action for damages for negligence, other than one to which section 11 of this Act applies, where the starting date for reckoning the period of limitation under subsection (4)(b) below falls after the date on which the cause of action accrued.

(2) Section 2 of this Act shall not apply to an action to which this section applies.

(3) An action to which this section applies shall not be brought after the expiration of the period applicable in accordance with subsection (4) below.

(4) That period is either;
(a) six years from the date on which the cause of action accrued; or
(b) three years from the starting date as defined by subsection (5) below, if that period expires later than the period mentioned in paragraph (a) above.

(5) For the purposes of this section, the starting date for reckoning the period of limitation under subsection (4)(b) above is the earliest date on which the plaintiff or any person in whom the cause of action was vested before him first

had both the knowledge required for bringing an action for damages in respect of the relevant damage and a right to bring such an action.

(6) In subsection (5) above "the knowledge required for bringing an action for damages in respect of the relevant damage" means knowledge both;

(a) of the material facts about the damage in respect of which damages are claimed; and

(b) of the other facts relevant to the current action mentioned in subsection (8) below.

(7) For the purposes of subsection (6)(a) above, the material facts about the damage are such facts about the damage as would lead a reasonable person who had suffered such damage to consider it sufficiently serious to justify his instituting proceedings for damages against a defendant who did not dispute liability and was able to satisfy a judgement.

(8) The other facts referred to in subsection (6)(b) above are;

(a) that the damage was attributable in whole or in part to the act or omission which is alleged to constitute negligence; and

(b) the identity of the defendant; and

(c) if it is alleged that the act or omission was that of a person other than the defendant, the identity of that person and the additional facts supporting the bringing of an action against the defendant.

(9) Knowledge that any acts or omissions did or did not , as a matter of law, involve negligence is irrelevant for the purposes of subsection (5) above.

(10) For the purposes of this section a person's knowledge includes knowledge which he might reasonably have been expected to acquire

(a) from facts observable or ascertainable by him; or

(b) from facts ascertainable by him with the help of appropriate expert advice which it is reasonable for him to seek;

but a person shall not be taken by virtue of this subsection to have knowledge of a fact ascertainable only with the help of expert advice so long as he has taken all reasonable steps to obtain (and, where appropriate, to act on) that advice.

**14B. Overriding time limit for negligence actions not involving personal injuries.**

(1) An action for damages for negligence, other than one to which section 11 of this Act applies, shall not be brought after the expiration of fifteen years from the date (or, if more than one, from the last of the dates) on which there occurred any act or omission:

(a) which is alleged to constitute negligence; and

(b) to which the damage in respect of which damages are claimed is alleged to be attributable (in whole or in part).

(2) This section bars the right of action in a case to which subsection (1) above applies notwithstanding that:

(a) the cause of action has not yet accrued; or

(b) where section 14A of this Act applies to the action, the date which is for the purposes of that section the starting date for reckoning the period mentioned in subsection (4)(b) of that section has not yet occurred;

before the end of the period of limitation prescribed by this section.

[Note: Section 11 applies for actions in relation to personal injuries or death.]

**15.-33. [Omitted].**

## PART III

## MISCELLANEOUS AND GENERAL

**34. Application of Act and other limitation enactments to arbitrations.**

(1) This Act and any other limitation enactment shall apply to arbitrations as they apply to actions in the High Court.

(2) Notwithstanding any term in an arbitration agreement to the effect that no cause of action shall accrue in respect of any matter required by the agreement to be referred until an award is made under the agreement, the cause of action shall, for the purposes of this Act and any other limitation enactment whether in their application to arbitrations or to other proceedings), be deemed to have accrued in respect of any such matter at the time when it would have accrued but for that term in the agreement.

(3) For the purposes of this Act and of any other limitation enactment an arbitration shall be treated as being commenced;

(a) when one party to the arbitration serves on the other party or parties a notice requiring him or them to appoint an arbitrator or to agree to the appointment of an arbitrator; or

(b) where the arbitration agreement provides that the reference shall be to a person named or designated in the agreement, when one party to the arbitration serves on the other party or parties a notice requiring him or them to submit the dispute to the person so named or designated.

(4) Any such notice may be served either—

(a) by delivering it to the person on whom it is to be served; or

(b) by leaving it at the usual or last-known place of abode in England and Wales of that person; or

(c) by sending it by post in a registered letter addressed to that person at his usual or last-known place of abode in England and Wales;

as well as in any other manner provided in the arbitration agreement.

(5) Where the High Court;

(a) orders that an award be set aside; or

(b) orders, after the commencement of an arbitration, that the arbitration agreement shall cease to have effect with respect to the dispute referred:

the court may further order that the period between the commencement of the arbitration and the date of the order of the court shall be excluded in computing the time prescribed by this Act or by any other limitation enactment for the commencement of proceedings (including arbitration) with respect to the dispute referred).

(6) This section shall apply to an arbitration under an Act of Parliament as well as to an arbitration pursuant to an arbitration agreement.

Subsections (3) and (4) above shall have effect, in relation to an arbitration under an Act, as if for the references to the arbitration agreement there were substituted references to such of the provisions of the Act or of any order, scheme, rules, regulations or bylaws made under the Act as relate to the arbitration.

(7) In this section—
- (a) 'arbitration', 'arbitration agreement' and 'award' have the same meanings as in Part I of the Arbitration Act 1950; and
- (b) references to any other limitation enactment are references to any other enactment relating to the limitation of actions, whether passed before or after the passing of this Act.

**35.-41. [Omitted].**

# CIVIL JURISDICTION AND JUDGMENTS ACT 1982

## CHAPTER 27

## PART I

## IMPLEMENTATION OF THE CONVENTIONS

*Main implementing provisions*

1. Interpretation of references to the Conventions and Contracting States.
2. The Conventions to have the force of law.
3. Interpretations of the Conventions.
3A. The Lugano Convention to have the force of law.
3B. Interpretation of the Lugano Convention.

*Provisions relating to recognition and enforcement of judgements*

31. Overseas judgements given against states etc.,
32. Overseas judgements given in proceedings brought in breach of agreements for settlement of disputes.
33. Certain steps not to amount to submission to jurisdiction of overseas court.

## PART V

## SUPPLEMENTARY AND GENERAL PROVISIONS

*Domicile*

41. Domicile of individuals
42. Domicile and seat of corporation or association.
43. Seat of corporation or association for purposes of Article 16(2) and related provisions.
44. Persons deemed to be domiciled in the United Kingdom for certain purposes.
45. Domicile of trusts.
46. Domicile and seat of the Crown.

## SCHEDULES

Schedule 1. Text of 1968 convention, as amended
Schedule 3C. Text of the Lugano Convention

## PART I

## IMPLEMENTATION OF THE CONVENTIONS

*Main implementing provisions*

**1. Interpretation of references to the Conventions and Contracting States.**

(1) In this Act—

'the 1968 Convention' means the Convention on jurisdiction and the enforcement of judgements in civil and commercial matters (including the Protocol annexed to that Convention), signed at Brussels on 27th September 1968;

'the 1971 Protocol' means the Protocol on the interpretation of the 1968 Convention by the European Court, signed at Luxembourg on 3rd June 1971;

'the Accession convention' means the Convention on the accession to the 1968 convention and the 1971 Protocol of Denmark, the Republic of Ireland and the United Kingdom, signed at Luxembourg on 9th October 1978;

'the 1982 Accession Convention' means the Convention on the accession of the Hellenic republic to the 1968 Convention and the 1971 Protocol, with the adjustments made to them by the Accession Convention, signed at Luxembourg on 25th October 1982;

'the 1989 Accession Convention' means the Convention on the accession of the Kingdom of Spain and the Portuguese Republic to the 1968 convention and the 1971 Protocol, with the adjustments made to them by the Accession convention and the 1982 Accession Convention, signed at Donostia-San Sebastian on 26th May 1989,

'the Brussels Conventions' means the 1968 Convention, the 1971 Protocol, the Accession Convention, the 1982 Accession Convention and the 1989 Accession Convention.

'the Lugano Convention' means the Convention on jurisdiction and the enforcement of judgements in civil and commercial matters (including the Protocols annexed to that Convention) opened for signature at Lugano on 16th September 1988 and signed by the United Kingdom on 18th September 1989.

(2) [Omitted].

(3) In this Act—

'Contracting State', without more, in any provision means—

(a) in the application of the provision in relation to the Brussels Conventions, a Brussels Contracting State; and

(b) in the application of the provision in relation to the Lugano Convention, a Lugano Contracting State:

'Brussels Contracting State' means—

(a) one of the original parties to the 1968 Convention (Belgium, the Federal Republic of Germany, France, Italy, Luxembourg and The Netherlands); or

(b) one of the parties acceding to that Convention under the Accession Convention (Denmark, the Republic of Ireland and the United Kingdom), or under the 1982 Accession convention (the Hellenic Republic), or under the 1989 Accession convention (Spain and Portugal),

being a state in respect of which the Accession convention has entered into force in accordance with Article 39 of that Convention, or being a state in respect of which the 1982 Accession Convention has entered into force in accordance with Article 15 of that Convention, or being a state in accordance with Article 32 of that Convention, as the case might be.

'Lugano Contracting State' means one of the original parties to the Lugano Convention, that is to say—

Austria, Belgium, Denmark, Finland, France, the Federal Republic of Germany, the Hellenic Republic, Iceland, the Republic of Ireland, Italy, Luxembourg, the Netherlands, Norway, Portugal, Spain, Sweden, Switzerland and the United Kingdom,

being a State in relation to which that convention has taken effect in accordance with paragraph 3 or 4 of Article 61.

**2. The Conventions to have the force of law.**

(1) The Brussels Conventions shall have the force of law in the United Kingdom, and judicial notice shall be taken of them.

(2) [Omitted].

**3. Interpretation of the Conventions.**

(1) Any question as to the meaning or effect of any provision of the Brussels Conventions shall, if not referred to the European Court in accordance with the 1971 Protocol, be determined in accordance with the principles laid down by any relevant decision of the European Court.

(2) Judicial notice shall be taken of any decision of, or expression of opinion by, the European Court on any such question.

(3) Without prejudice to the generality of subsection (1), the following reports (which are reproduced in the Official Journal of the Communities), namely—

(a) the reports by Mr. P. Jenard on the 1968 Convention and the 1971 Protocol;

(b) the report by Professor Peter Schlosser on the Accession Convention,

(c) the report by Professor Demetrios I Evvigenis and Professor K D Kerameus on the 1982 Accession Convention; and

(d) the report by Mr Martinho de Almeida Cruz, Mr Manuel Desantes Real and Mr P Jenard on the 1989 Accession Convention.

may be considered in ascertaining the meaning or effect of any provision of the Brussels Conventions and shall be given such weight as is appropriate in the circumstances.

**3A. The Lugano Convention to have the force of law**

(1) The Lugano Convention shall have the force of law in the United Kingdom, and judicial notice shall be taken of it.

(2) [Omitted].

**3B. Interpretation of the Lugano Convention**

(1) In determining any question as to the meaning or effect of a provision of the Lugano Convention, a court in the United Kingdom shall, in accordance with Protocol No.2 to that Convention, take account of any principles laid down in any relevant decision delivered by a court of any other Lugano Contracting State concerning provisions of the Convention.

(2) Without prejudice to any practice of the courts as to the matters which may be considered apart from this section, the report on the Lugano Convention by Mr P Jenard and Mr G Moller (which is reproduced in the official Journal of the communities of 28th July 1990) may be considered in ascertaining the meaning or effect of any provision of the Convention and shall be given such weight as is appropriate in the circumstances.

**4.-30. [Omitted].**

## PART IV

## MISCELLANEOUS PROVISIONS

*Provisions relating to recognition and enforcement of judgements*

**31. Overseas judgments given against states, etc.**

(1) A judgement given by a court of an overseas country against a state to which that court belongs shall be recognised and enforced in the United Kingdom if, and only if—

(a) it would be so recognised and enforced if it had not been given against a state; and

(b) that court would have had jurisdiction in the matter if it had applied rules corresponding to those applicable to such matters in the United Kingdom in accordance with sections 2 to 11 of the State Immunity Act 1978.

(2) References in subsection (1) to a judgement given against a state include references to judgements of any of the following descriptions given in relation to a state:

(a) judgements against the government, or a department of the government, of the state but not (except as mentioned in paragraph (c)) judgements against an entity which is distinct from the executive organs of Government;

(b) judgements against the sovereign or head of state in his public capacity;

(c) judgements against any such separate entity as is mentioned in paragraph (a) given in proceedings relating to anything done by it in the exercise of the sovereign authority of the state.

(3) Nothing in subsection (1) shall affect the recognition or enforcement in the United Kingdom of a judgement to which Part I of the Foreign Judgements (Reciprocal Enforcement) Act 1933 applies by virtue of section 4 of the Carriage of Goods by Road Act 1965, section 17(4) of the Nuclear Installations Act 1965, section 13(3) of the Merchant Shipping (Oil Pollution) Act 1971, section 5 of the International Transport Conventions Act 1983 or section 5 of the Carriage of Passengers by Road Act 1974.

(4) Sections 12, 13 and 14(3) and (4) of the State Immunity Act 1978 (service of process and procedural privileges) shall apply to proceedings for the recognition or enforcement in the United Kingdom of a judgement given by a court of an overseas country (whether or not that judgement is within subsection (1) of this section) as they apply to other proceedings.

(5) In this section "state", in the case of a federal state, includes any of its constituent territories.

**32. Overseas judgments given in proceedings brought in breach of agreement for settlement of disputes.**

(1) Subject to the following provisions of this section, a judgement given by a court of an overseas country in any proceedings shall not be recognised or enforced in the United Kingdom if—

(a) the bringing of those proceedings in that court was contrary to an agreement under which the dispute in question was to be settled otherwise than by proceedings in the courts of that country; and

(b) those proceedings were not brought in that court by, or with the agreement of, the person against whom the judgement was given; and

(c) that person did not counterclaim in the proceedings or otherwise submit to the jurisdiction of that court.

(2) Subsection (1) does not apply where the agreement referred to in paragraph (a) of that subsection was illegal, void or unenforceable or was incapable of being performed for reasons not attributable to the fault of the party bringing the proceedings in which the judgement was given.

(3) In determining whether a judgement given by a court of an overseas country should be recognised or enforced in the United Kingdom, a court in the United Kingdom shall not be bound by any decision of the overseas court relating to any of the matters mentioned in subsection (1) or (2).

(4) Nothing in subsection (1) shall affect the recognition or enforcement in the United Kingdom of—

(a) a judgement which is required to be recognised or enforced there under the 1968 Convention or the or the Lugano Convention.

(b) a judgement to which Part I of the Foreign Judgements (Reciprocal Enforcement) Act 1933 applies by virtue of section 4 of the Carriage of Goods by Road Act 1965, section 17(4) of the Nuclear Installations Act 1965, section 13(3) of the Merchant Shipping (Oil Pollution) Act 1971, section 6 of the International Transport Conventions, section 5 of the Carriage of Passengers by Road Act 1974 or section 6(4) of the Merchant Shipping Act 1974).

**33. Certain steps not to amount to submission to jurisdiction of overseas court.**

(1) For the purposes of determining whether a judgement given by a court of an overseas country should be recognised or enforced in England and Wales or Northern Ireland, the person against whom the judgement was given shall not be regarded as having submitted to the jurisdiction of the court by reason only of the fact that he appeared (conditionally or otherwise) in the proceedings for all or any one or more of the following purposes, namely—

(a) to contest the jurisdiction of the court;

(b) to ask the court to dismiss or start the proceedings on the ground that the dispute in question should be submitted to arbitration or to the determination of the courts of another country;

(c) to protect, or obtain the release of, property seized or threatened with seizure in the proceedings.

(2) Nothing in this section shall affect the recognition or enforcement in England and Wales or Northern Ireland of a judgement which is required to be recognised or enforced there under the 1968 Convention or the Lugano Convention.

**34. Certain judgments a bar to further proceedings on the same cause of action.**

No proceedings may be brought by a person in England and Wales or Northern Ireland on a cause of action in respect of which a judgement has been given in his favour in proceedings between the same parties, or their privies, in a court in another part of the United Kingdom or in a court of an overseas country, unless that judgement is not enforceable or entitled to recognition in England and Wales or, as the case may be, in Northern Ireland.

**35.-40 [Omitted].**

## PART V

## SUPPLEMENTARY AND GENERAL PROVISIONS

### *Domicile*

**41. Domicile of individuals.**

(1) Subject to Article 52 (which contains provisions for determining whether a party is domiciled in a Contracting State), the following provisions of this

section determine, for the purposes of the 1968 Convention, the Lugano Convention and this Act, whether an individual is domiciled in the United Kingdom or in a particular part of, or place in, the United Kingdom or in a state other than a Contracting State.

(2) An individual is domiciled in the United Kingdom if and only if—
(a) he is resident in the United Kingdom; and
(b) the nature and circumstances of his residence indicate that he has a substantial connection with the United Kingdom.

(3) Subject to subsection (5), an individual is domiciled in a particular part of the United Kingdom if and only if—
(a) he is resident in that part; and
(b) the nature and circumstances of his residence indicate that he has a substantial connection with that part.

(4) An individual is domiciled in a particular place in the United Kingdom if and only if he—
(a) is domiciled in the part of the United Kingdom in which that place is situated; and
(b) is resident in that place.

(5) An individual who is domiciled in the United Kingdom but in whose case the requirements of subsection (3)(b) are not satisfied in relation to any particular part of the United Kingdom shall be treated as domiciled in the part of the United Kingdom in which he is resident.

(6) In the case of an individual who—
(a) is resident in the United Kingdom, or in a particular part of the United Kingdom; and
(b) has been so resident for the last three months or more, the requirements of subsection (2)(b) or, as the case may be, subsection (3)(b) shall be presumed to be fulfilled unless the contrary is proved.

(7) An individual is domiciled in a state other than a Contracting State if and only if—
(a) he is resident in that state; and
(b) the nature and circumstances of his residence indicate that he has a substantial connection with that state.

**42. Domicile and seat of corporation or association.**

(1) For the purposes of this Act the seat of a corporation or association (as determined by this section) shall be treated as its domicile.

(2) The following provisions of this section determine where a corporation or association has its seat—
(a) for the purpose of Article 53 (which for the purposes of the 1968 convention or, as the case may be, the Lugano Convention equates the domicile of such a body with its seat); and
(b) for the purposes of this Act other than the provisions mentioned in section 43(1)(b) and (c).

(3) A corporation or association has its seat in the United Kingdom if and only if—

(a) it was incorporated or formed under the law of a part of the United Kingdom and has its registered office or some other official address in the United Kingdom; or

(b) its central management and control is exercised in the United Kingdom.

(4) A corporation or association has its seat in a particular part of the United Kingdom if and only if it has its seat in the United Kingdom and-

(a) it has its registered office or some other official address in that part; or

(b) its central management and control is exercised in that part; or

(c) it has a place of business in that part.

(5) A corporation or association has its seat in a particular place in the United Kingdom if and only if it has its seat in the part of the United Kingdom in which that place is situated and—

(a) it has its registered office or some other official address in that place; or

(b) its central management and control is exercised in that place; or

(c) it has a place of business in that place.

(6) Subject to subsection (7), a corporation or association has its seat in a state other than the United Kingdom if and only if—

(a) it was incorporated or formed under the law of that state and has its registered office or some other official address there; or

(b) its central management and control is exercised in that state.

(7) A corporation or association shall not be regarded as having its seat in a Contracting State other than the United Kingdom if it is shown that the courts of that state would not regard it as having its seat there.

(8) In this section—

'business' includes any activity carried on by a corporation or association and 'place of business' shall be construed accordingly;

'official address', in relation to a corporation or association, means an address which it is required by law to register, notify or maintain for the purposes of receiving notices or other communications.

**43. Seat of corporation or association for purposes of Article 16(2) and related provisions.**

(1) The following provisions of this section determine where a corporation or association has its seat for the purposes of—

(a) Article 16(2) of the 1968 Convention or of the Lugano Convention (which confers exclusive jurisdiction over proceedings relating to the formation or dissolution of such bodies, or to the decisions of their organs);

(b) Articles 5A and 16(2) in Schedule 4; and

(c) Rules 2(12) and 4(1)(b) in Schedule 8.

(2) A corporation or association has its seat in the United Kingdom if and only if-

(a) it was incorporated or formed under the law of a part of the United Kingdom; or
(b) its central management and control is exercised in the United Kingdom.

(3) A corporation or association has its seat in a particular part of the United Kingdom if and only if it has its seat in the United Kingdom and—
(a) subject to subsection (5), it was incorporated or formed under the law of that part; or
(b) being incorporated or formed under the law of a state other than the United Kingdom, its central management and control is exercised in that part.

(4) A corporation or association has its seat in a particular place in Scotland if and only if it has its seat in Scotland and-
(a) it has its registered office or some other official address in that place; or
(b) it has no registered office or other official address in Scotland, but its central management and control is exercised in that place.

(5) A corporation or association incorporated and formed under-
(a) an enactment forming part of the law of more than one part of the United Kingdom; or
(b) an instrument having effect in the domestic law of more than one part of the United Kingdom,

shall, if it has a registered office, be taken to have its seat in the part of the United Kingdom in which that office is situated, and not in any other part of the United Kingdom.

(6) Subject to subsection (7), a corporation or association has its seat in a Contracting State other than the United Kingdom if and only if—
(a) it was incorporated or formed under the law of that state; or
(b) its central management and control is exercised in that state.

(7) A corporation or association shall not be regarded as having its seat in a Contracting State other than the United Kingdom if—
(a) it has its seat in the United Kingdom by virtue of subsection (2)(a); or
(b) it has shown that the courts of that other state would not regard it for the purposes of Article 16(2) as having its seat there.

(8) In this section "official address" has the same meaning as in section 42.

**44. Persons deemed to be domiciled in the United Kingdom for certain purposes.**

(1) This section applies to—
(a) proceedings within Section 3 of Title II of the 1968 Convention or Section 3 of Title II of the Lugano Convention (insurance contracts), and
(b) proceedings within Section 4 of Title II of either of those Conventions (consumer contacts).

(2) A person who, for the purposes of proceedings to which this section applies arising out of the operations of a branch, agency of other establishment

in the United Kingdom, is deemed for the purposes of the 1968 Convention or, as the case may be, of the Lugano Convention to be domiciled in the United Kingdom by virtue of—

(a) Article 8, second paragraph (insurers); or

(b) Article 13, second paragraph (suppliers of goods, services or credit to consumers),

shall for the purposes of those proceedings, be treated for the purposes of this Act as so domiciled and as domiciled in the part of the United kingdom in which the branch, agency or establishment in question is situated.

**45. Domicile of trusts.**

(1) The following provisions of this section determine, for the purposes of the 1968 Convention, the Lugano Convention and this Act, where a trust is domiciled.

(2) A trust is domiciled in the United Kingdom if and only if it is by virtue of subsection (3) domiciled in a part of the United Kingdom.

(3) A trust is domiciled in a part of the United Kingdom if and only if the system of law of that part is the system of law with which the trust has its closest and most real connection.

**46. Domicile and seat of the Crown.**

(1) For the purposes of this Act the seat of the Crown (as determined by this section) shall be treated as its domicile.

(2) The following provisions of this section determine where the Crown has its seat—

(a) for the purposes of the 1968 Convention and the Lugano Convention, (in each of which Article 53 equates the domicile of a legal person with its seat); and

(b) for the purposes of this Act.

(3) Subject to the provisions of any Order in Council for the time being in force under subsection (4)—

(a) the Crown in right of Her Majesty's government in the United Kingdom has its seat in every part of, and every place in, the United Kingdom; and

(b) the Crown in right of Her Majesty's government in Northern Ireland has its seat in, and in every place in, Northern Ireland.

(4) Her Majesty may by Order in Council provide that, in the case of proceedings of any specified description against the Crown in right of Her Majesty's government in the United Kingdom, the Crown shall be treated for the purposes of the 1968 Convention, the Lugano Convention and this Act as having its seat in, and in every place in, a specified part of the United Kingdom and not in any other part of the United Kingdom.

(5) An Order in council under subsection (4) may frame a description of proceedings in any way, and in particular may do so by reference to the

government department or officer of the Crown against which or against whom they fall to be instituted.

(6) [Omitted].

(7) Nothing in this section applies to the Crown otherwise than in right of her Majesty's government in the United Kingdom or Her Majesty's government in Northern Ireland.

**47.-55. [Omitted].**

## SCHEDULE I

## TEXT OF THE 1968 CONVENTION, AS AMENDED

### TITLE I

### ARTICLE 1

This Convention shall apply in civil and commercial matters whatever the nature of the court or tribunal. It shall not extend, in particular, to revenue, customs or administrative matters.

The Convention shall not apply to—

(1) The status or legal capacity of natural persons, rights in property arising out of a matrimonial relationship, wills and succession.

(2) Bankruptcy, proceedings related to the winding up of insolvent companies or other legal persons, judicial arrangements, compositions and analogous proceedings.

(3) Social security.

(4) Arbitration.

### TITLE II

### SECTION 1

*General Provisions*

### ARTICLE 2

Subject to the provisions of this Convention, persons domiciled in a Contracting State shall, whatever their nationality, be sued in the courts of that State.

Persons who are not nationals of the State in which they are domiciled shall be governed by the rules of jurisdiction applicable to nationals of that State.

### ARTICLE 3

Persons domiciled in a Contracting State may be sued in the courts of another Contracting State only by virtue of the rules set out in Sections 2 to 6 of this Title.

In particular the following provisions shall not be applicable as against them:

—[part omitted]

—in the United Kingdom: the rules which enable jurisdiction to be founded on:

(a) the document instituting the proceedings having been served on the defendant during his temporary presence in the United Kingdom; or

(b) the presence within the United Kingdom of property belonging to the defendant; or

(c) the seizure by the plaintiff of property situated in the United Kingdom.

### ARTICLE 4

If the defendant is not domiciled in a Contracting State, the jurisdiction of the courts of each Contracting state shall, subject to the provisions of Article 16, be determined by the law of that State.

As against such a defendant, any person domiciled in a Contracting State may, whatever his nationality, avail himself in that State of the rules of jurisdiction there in force, and in particular those specified in the second paragraph of Article 3, in the same way as the nationals of that State.

## SECTION 2

*Special jurisdiction*

### ARTICLE 5

A person domiciled in a Contracting State may, in another Contracting state, be sued—

(1) In matters relating to a contract, in the courts for the place of performance of the obligation in question; in matters relating to individual contracts of employment, this place is that where the employee habitually carries out his work, or if the employee does not habitually carry out his work in any one country, the employer may also be sued in the courts for the place where the business which engaged the employee was or is now situated.

(2) In matters relating to maintenance, in the courts for the place where the maintenance creditor is domiciled or habitually resident or, if the matter is ancillary to proceedings concerning the status of a person, in the court which, according to its own law, has jurisdiction to entertain those proceedings, unless that jurisdiction is based solely on the nationality of one of the parties.

(3) In matters relating to tort, delict or quasi-delict, in the courts for the place where the harmful event occurred.

(4) As regards a civil claim for damages or restitution which is based on an act giving rise to criminal proceedings, in the court seised of those proceedings, to the extent that that court has jurisdiction under its own law to entertain civil proceedings.

(5) As regards a dispute arising out of the operations of a branch, agency or other establishment, in the courts for the place in which the branch, agency or other establishment is situated.

(6) As settlor, trustee or beneficiary of a trust created by the operation of a statute, or by a written instrument, or created orally and evidenced in writing, in the courts of the Contracting State in which the trust is domiciled.

(7) As regards a dispute concerning the payment of remuneration claimed in respect of the salvage of cargo or freight, in the court under the authority of which the cargo and freight in question-

(a) has been arrested to secure such payment, or

(b) could have been so arrested, but bail or other security has been given;

provided that this provision shall apply only if it is claimed that the defendant has an interest in the cargo or freight or had such an interest at the time of salvage.

## ARTICLE 6

A person domiciled in a Contracting State may also be sued—

(1) Where he is one of a number of defendants, in the courts for the place where any one of them is domiciled.

(2) As a third party in an action on a warranty or guarantee or in any other third party proceedings, in the court seised of the original proceedings, unless these were instituted solely with the objective of removing him from the jurisdiction of the court which would be competent in his case.

(3) On the counter-claim arising from the same contract or facts on which the original claim was based, in the court in which the original claim is pending.

(4) In matters relating to a contract, if the action may be combined with an action against the defendant in matters relating to rights in rem in immovable property, in the court of the Contracting State in which the property is situated.

## ARTICLE 6A

Where by virtue of this Convention a court of a Contracting State has jurisdiction in actions relating to liability from the use or operation of a ship, that court, or any other court substituted for this purpose by the internal law of that State, shall also have jurisdiction over claims for limitation of such liability.

## SECTION 3

*Jurisdiction in matters relating to insurance*

### ARTICLE 7

In matters relating to insurance, jurisdiction shall be determined by this section, without prejudice to the provisions of Articles 4 and 5(5).

### ARTICLE 8

An insurer domiciled in a Contracting State may be sued—

(1) in the courts of the state where he is domiciled, or

(2) in another Contracting State, in the courts for the place where the policy-holder is domiciled, or

(3) if he is a co-insurer, in the courts of a Contracting State in which proceedings are brought against the leading insurer.

An insurer who is not domiciled in a Contracting State but has a branch, agency or other establishment in one of the Contracting States shall, in disputes arising out of the operations of the branch, agency or establishment, be deemed to be domiciled in that State.

### ARTICLE 9

In respect of liability insurance or insurance of immovable property, the insurer may in addition be sued in the courts for the place where the harmful event occurred. The same applies if moveable and immovable property are covered by the same insurance policy and both are adversely affected by the same contingency.

### ARTICLE 10

In respect of liability insurance, the insurer may also, if the law of the court permits it, be joined in proceedings which the injured party had brought against the insured.

The provisions of Article 7, 8 and 9 shall apply to actions brought by the insured party directly against the insurer, where such direct actions are permitted.

If the law governing such direct actions provides that the policy-holder or the insured may be joined as a party to the action, the same court shall have jurisdiction over them.

### ARTICLE 11

Without prejudice to the provisions of the third paragraph of Article 10, an insurer may bring proceedings only in the courts of the Contracting State in which the defendant is domiciled, irrespective of whether he is the policy-holder, the insured or a beneficiary.

The provisions of this section should not effect the right to bring a counterclaim in the court in which, in accordance with this Section, the original claim is pending.

## ARTICLE 12

The provisions of this Section may be departed from only with an agreement on jurisdiction—

1. which is entered into after the dispute has arisen, or

2. which allows the policy-holder, the insured or a beneficiary to bring proceedings in courts other than those indicated in this Section, or

3. which is concluded between a policy-holder and an insurer, both of whom are domiciled in the same Contracting State, and which has the effect of conferring jurisdiction on the courts of that State even if the harmful event were to occur abroad, provided that such an agreement is not contrary to the law of that State, or

4. which is concluded with a policy-holder who is not domiciled in a Contracting State, except in so far as the insurance is compulsory or relates to immovable property in a Contracting State, or

5. which relates to a contract of insurance in so far as it covers one or more of the risks set out in Article 12A.

## ARTICLE 12A

The following are the risks referred to in Article 12(5)—

1. Any loss or damage to—
   - (a) sea-going ships, installations situated offshore or on the high seas, or aircraft, arising from perils which relate to their use for commercial purposes;
   - (b) goods in transit other than passengers' baggage where the transit consists of or includes carriage by such ships or aircraft.

2. Any liability, other than for bodily injury to passengers or loss of or damage to their baggage-
   - (a) arising out of the use or operation of ships, installations or aircraft as referred to in 1(a) above in so far as the law of the Contracting State in which such aircraft are registered does not prohibit agreements on jurisdiction regarding insurance of such risks;
   - (b) for loss or damage caused by goods in transit as described in 1(b) above.

3. Any financial loss connected with the use or operation of ships, installations or aircraft as referred to in 1(a) above, in particular loss of freight or charter-hire.

4. Any risk or interest connected with any of those referred to in 1 to 3 above.

## SECTION 4

*Jurisdiction over consumer contracts*

### ARTICLE 13

In proceedings concerning a contract concluded by a person for a purpose which can be regarded as being outside his trade or profession, hereinafter called "the consumer", jurisdiction shall be determined by this Section, without prejudice to the provisions of Article 4 and Article 5(5), if it is—

1. A contract for the sale of goods on instalment credit terms, or

2. A contract for a loan repayable by instalments, or for any other form of credit, made to finance the sale of goods, or

3. Any other contract for the supply of goods or a contract for the supply of services, and
   (a) in the State of the consumer's domicile the conclusion of the contract was preceded by a specific invitation addressed to him, or by advertising; and
   (b) the consumer took in that State the steps necessary for the conclusion of that contract.

Where a consumer enters into a contract with a party who is not domiciled in a Contracting State but has a branch, agency or establishment in one of the Contracting States, that party shall, in disputes arising out of the operations of the branch, agency or establishment, be deemed to be domiciled in that State.

This section shall not apply to contracts of transport.

### ARTICLE 14

A consumer may bring proceedings against the other party to a contract either in the courts of the Contracting State in which that party is domiciled or in the courts of the Contracting State in which he is himself domiciled.

Proceedings may be brought against a consumer by the other party to the contract only in the courts of the Contracting State in which the consumer is domiciled.

These provisions shall not affect the right to bring a counter-claim in the court in which, in accordance with this section, the original claim is pending.

### ARTICLE 15

The provisions of this section may be departed from only by an agreement—

1. which is entered into after the dispute has arisen, or

2. which allows the consumer to bring proceedings in courts other than those indicated in this Section, or

3. which is entered into by the consumer and the other party to the contract, both of whom are at the time of conclusion of the contract domiciled or habitually resident in the same Contracting State, and which confers jurisdiction on the courts of that State, provided that such an agreement is not contrary to the law of that State.

## SECTION 5

### *Exclusive Jurisdiction*

### ARTICLE 16

The following courts shall have exclusive jurisdiction, regardless of domicile:

1. (a) in proceedings which have as their object rights in rem in immovable property or tenancies of immovable property, the courts of the Contracting State in which the property is situated;
   (b) however, in proceedings which have as their object tenancies of immovable property concluded for temporary private use for a maximum period of six consecutive months, the courts of the Contracting State in which the defendant is domiciled shall also have jurisdiction, provided that the landlord and the tenant are natural persons and are domiciled in the same Contracting State.

2. In proceedings which have as their object the validity of the constitution, the nullity or the dissolution of companies or other legal persons or associations of natural or legal persons, or the decisions of their organs, the courts of the Contracting State in which the company, legal person or association has its seat.

3. In proceedings which have as their object the validity of entries in public registers, the courts of the Contracting State in which the register is kept.

4. In proceedings concerned with the registration or validity of patents, trademarks, designs, or other similar rights required to be deposited or registered, the courts of the Contracting State in which the deposit or registration has been applied for, has taken place or is under the terms of an international convention deemed to have taken place.

5. In proceedings concerned with the enforcement of judgements, the courts of the Contracting State in which the judgement has been or is to be enforced.

## SECTION 6

*Prorogation of jurisdiction*

### ARTICLE 17

If the parties, one or more of whom is domiciled in a Contracting State, have agreed that a court or the courts of a Contracting State are to have jurisdiction to settle any disputes which have arisen or which may arise in connection with a particular legal relationship, that court or those courts shall have exclusive jurisdiction. Such an agreement conferring jurisdiction shall be either—

(a) in writing or evidenced in writing, or

(b) in a form which accords with practices which the parties have established between themselves, or

(c) in international trade or commerce, in a form which accords with a usage of which the parties are or ought to have been aware and which in such trade or commerce is widely known to, and regularly observed by, parties to contracts of the type involved in the particular trade or commerce concerned.

Where such an agreement is concluded by parties, none of whom is domiciled in a Contracting State, the courts of other Contracting States shall have no jurisdiction over their disputes unless the court or courts chosen have declined jurisdiction.

The court or courts of a Contracting State on which a trust instrument has conferred jurisdiction shall have exclusive jurisdiction in any proceedings brought against a settlor, trustee or beneficiary, if relations between these persons or their rights or obligations under the trust are involved.

Agreements or provisions of a trust instrument conferring jurisdiction shall have no legal force if they are contrary to the provisions of Articles 12 or 15, or if the courts whose jurisdiction they purport to exclude have exclusive jurisdiction by virtue of Article 16.

If an agreement conferring jurisdiction was concluded for the benefit of only one of the parties, that party shall retain the right to bring proceedings in any other court which has jurisdiction by virtue of this Convention.

In matters relating to individual contracts of employment an agreement conferring jurisdiction shall have legal force only if it is entered into after the dispute has arisen or if the employee invokes it to seise courts other than those for the defendant's domicile or those specified in Article 5 (1).

### ARTICLE 18

Apart from jurisdiction derived from other provisions of this Convention, a court of a Contracting State before whom a defendant enters an appearance shall have jurisdiction. This rule shall not apply where appearance was entered solely to contest the jurisdiction, or where another court has exclusive jurisdiction by virtue of Article 16.

## SECTION 7

*Examination as to jurisdiction and admissibility*

### ARTICLE 19

Where a court of a Contracting State is seised of a claim which is principally concerned with a matter over which the courts of another Contracting State have exclusive jurisdiction by virtue of Article 16, it shall declare of its own motion that it has no jurisdiction.

### ARTICLE 20

Where a defendant domiciled in one Contracting State is sued in a court of another Contracting State and does not enter an appearance, the court shall declare of its own motion that it has no jurisdiction unless its jurisdiction is derived from the provisions of the Convention.

The court shall stay the proceedings so long as it is not shown that the defendant has been able to receive the document instituting the proceedings or an equivalent document in sufficient time to enable him to arrange for his defence, or that all necessary steps have been taken to this end.

The provisions of the foregoing paragraph shall be replaced by those of Article 15 of the Hague Convention of 15th November 1965 on the service abroad of judicial and extra judicial documents in civil or commercial matters, if the document instituting the proceedings or notice thereof had to be transmitted abroad in accordance with that Convention.

## SECTION 8

*Lis pendens-related actions*

### ARTICLE 21

Where proceedings involving the same cause of action and between the same parties are brought in the courts of different Contracting States, any court other than the court first seised shall of its own motion stay its proceedings until such time as the jurisdiction of the court first seised is established.

Where the jurisdiction of the court first seised is established, any court other than the court first seised shall decline jurisdiction in favour of that court.

### ARTICLE 22

Where related actions are brought in the courts of different Contracting States, any court other than the court first seised may, while the actions are pending at first instance, stay its proceedings.

A court other than the court first seised may also, on the application of one of the parties, decline jurisdiction if the law of that court permits the consolidation of related actions and the court first seised has jurisdiction over both actions.

For the purposes of this Article, actions are deemed to be related where they are so closely connected that it is expedient to hear and determine them together to avoid the risk of irreconcilable judgements resulting from separate proceedings.

## Article 23

Where actions come within the exclusive jurisdiction of several courts, any court other than the court first seised shall decline jurisdiction in favour of that court.

## Section 9

*Provisional, including protective, measures*

## Article 24

Application may be made to the courts of a Contracting State for such provisional, including protective, measures as may be available under the law of that State, even if, under this Convention, the courts of another Contracting State have jurisdiction as to the substance of the matter.

## Title III

## Article 25

For the purposes of this Convention, "judgement" means any judgement given by a court or tribunal of a Contracting State, whatever the judgement may be called, including a decree, order, decision or writ of execution, as well as the determination of costs or expenses by an officer of the court.

## Section 1

*Recognition*

## Article 26

A judgement given in a Contracting State shall be recognised in the other Contracting States without any special procedure being required.

Any interested party who raises the recognition of a judgement as the principal issue in a dispute may, in accordance with the procedures provided for in Sections 2 and 3 of this Title, apply for a decision that the judgement be recognised.

If the outcome of proceedings in a court of a Contracting State depends on the determination of an incidental question of recognition that court shall have jurisdiction over that question.

## ARTICLE 27

A judgement shall not be recognised—

1. If such recognition is contrary to public policy in the State in which recognition is sought.

2. Where it was given in default of appearance, if the defendant was not duly served with the document which instituted the proceedings or with an equivalent document in sufficient time to enable him to arrange for his defence.

3. If the judgement is irreconcilable with a judgement given in a dispute between the same parties in the State in which recognition is sought.

4. If the court of the State of origin, in order to arrive at its judgement, has decided a preliminary question concerning the status or legal capacity of natural persons, rights in property arising out of a matrimonial relationship, wills or succession in a way that conflicts with a rule of the private international law of the State in which the recognition is sought, unless the same result would have been reached by the application of the rules of private international law of that State.

5. If the judgement is irreconcilable with an earlier judgement given in a non-contracting State involving the same cause of action and between the same parties, provided that this latter judgement fulfils the conditions necessary for its recognition in the state addressed.

## ARTICLE 28

Moreover, a judgement shall not be recognised if it conflicts with the provisions of Sections 3, 4 or 5 of Title II, or in a case provided for in Article 59.

In its examination of the grounds of jurisdiction referred to in the foregoing paragraph, the court or authority applied to shall be bound by the findings of fact on which the court of the State of origin based its jurisdiction.

Subject to the provisions of the first paragraph, the jurisdiction of the court of the State of origin may not be reviewed; the test of public policy referred to in Article 27(1) may not be applied to the rules relating to jurisdiction.

## ARTICLE 29

Under no circumstances may a foreign judgement be reviewed as to its substance.

## Article 30

A court of a Contracting State in which recognition is sought of a judgement given in another Contracting State may stay the proceedings if an ordinary appeal against the judgement has been lodged.

A court of a Contracting State in which recognition is sought of a judgement given in Ireland or the United Kingdom may stay the proceedings if enforcement is suspended in the State of origin, by reason of an appeal.

## Section 2

*Enforcement*

## Article 31

A judgement given in a Contracting State and enforceable in that State shall be enforced in another Contracting State when, on the application of any interested party, it has been declared enforceable there.

However, in the United Kingdom, such an judgement shall be enforced in England and Wales, in Scotland, or in Northern Ireland when, on the application of any interested party, it has been registered for enforcement in that part of the United Kingdom.

## Articles 32 - 49 [Omitted]

## Title IV

## Article 50

A document which has been formally drawn up or registered as an authentic instrument and is enforceable in one Contracting State shall, in another Contracting State, be declared enforceable there, on application made in accordance with the procedures provided for in Article 31 et seq. The application may be refused only if enforcement of the instrument is contrary to public policy in the State addressed.

The instrument produced must satisfy the conditions necessary to establish its authenticity in the State of origin.

The provisions of Section 3 of Title III shall apply as appropriate.

## Article 51

A settlement which has been approved by a court in the course of proceedings and is enforceable in the State in which it was concluded shall be enforceable in the State addressed under the same conditions as authentic instruments.

## Title V

### Article 52

In order to determine whether a party is domiciled in the Contracting State whose courts are seised of a matter, the Court shall apply its internal law.

If a party is not domiciled in the State whose courts are seised of the matter, then, in order to determine whether the party is domiciled in another Contracting State, the court shall apply the law of that State.

### Article 53

For the purposes of this Convention, the seat of a company or other legal person or association of natural or legal persons shall be treated as its domicile. However, in order to determine that seat, the court shall apply its rules of private international law.

In order to determine whether a trust is domiciled in the Contracting State whose courts are seised of the matter, the court shall apply its rules of private international law.

### Articles 54-56 [Omitted]

## Title VII

### Article 57

1. This Convention shall not affect any conventions to which the Contracting States are or will be parties and which in relation to particular matters, govern jurisdiction or the recognition or enforcement of judgements.

2. With a view to its uniform interpretation, paragraph 1 shall be applied in the following manner—

(a) this Convention shall not prevent a court of a Contracting State which is a party to a convention on a particular matter from assuming jurisdiction in accordance with that Convention, even where the defendant is domiciled in another Contracting State which is not a party to that Convention. The court hearing the action shall, in any event, apply Article 20 of this Convention;

(b) judgements given in a Contracting State by a court in the exercise of jurisdiction provided for in a convention on a particular matter shall be recognised and enforced in the other Contracting State in accordance with this Convention. Where a convention on a particular matter to which both the State of origin and the State addressed are parties lays down conditions for the recognition or enforcement of judgements, those conditions shall apply. In any event, the provisions of this Convention which concern the procedure for recognition and enforcement of judgements may be applied.

3. This Convention shall not affect the application of provisions which, in relation to particular matters, govern jurisdiction or the recognition or

enforcement of judgements and which are or will be contained in acts of the institutions of the European Communities or in national laws harmonised in implementation of such acts.

### ARTICLE 58 [Omitted]

### ARTICLE 59

This Convention shall not prevent a Contracting State from assuming, in a convention on the recognition and enforcement of judgements, an obligation towards a third State not to recognise judgements given in other Contracting States against defendants domiciled or habitually resident in the third State, where in cases provided for in Article 4, the judgement could only be founded on a ground of jurisdiction specified in the second paragraph of Article 3.

However, a Contracting State may not assume an obligation towards a third State not to recognise a judgement given in another Contracting State by a court basing its jurisdiction on the presence within that State of property belonging to the defendant, or the seizure by the plaintiff of property situated there—

1. if the action is brought to assert or declare proprietary or possessory rights in that property, seeks to obtain authority to dispose of it, or arises from another issue relating to such property, or

2. if the property constitutes the security for a debt which is the subject-matter of the action.

### ARTICLES 60 - 68 [OMITTED]

## SCHEDULE 3C

## TEXT OF THE LUGANO CONVENTION

[Note: The text of the Lugano Convention is the same as the Brussels Convention, except in the Articles printed below]

### TITLE II

### JURISDICTION

*Special Jurisdiction*

### ARTICLE 5

A person domiciled in a Contracting State may, in another Contracting State, be sued:

1. In matters relating to a contract, in the courts for the place of performance of the obligation in question; in matters relating to individual contracts of employment, this place is that where the employee habitually carries out his

work, or if the employee does not habitually carry out his work in any one country, this place shall be the place of business through which he was engaged;

2. in matters relating to maintenance, in the courts for the place where the maintenance creditor is domiciled or habitually resident or, if the matter is ancillary to proceedings concerning the status of a person, in the court which, according to its own law, has jurisdiction to entertain those proceedings, unless that jurisdiction is based solely on the nationality of one of the parties;

3. in matters relating to tort, delict or quasi-delict, in the courts for the place where the harmful event occurred;

4. as regards a civil claim for damages or restitution which is based on an act giving rise to criminal proceedings, in the court seised of those proceedings, to the extent that that court has jurisdiction under its own law to entertain civil proceedings;

5. as regards a dispute arising out of the operations of a branch, agency or other establishment, in the courts for the place in which the branch, agency or other establishment is situated;

6. in his capacity as settlor, trustee or beneficiary of a trust created by the operation of a statute, or by a written instrument, or created orally and evidenced in writing, in the courts of the Contracting State in which the trust is domiciled;

7. as regards a dispute concerning the payment of remuneration claimed in respect of the salvage of a cargo or freight, in the court under the authority of which the cargo or freight in question:

(a) has been arrested to secure such payment, or
(b) could have been arrested, but bail or other security has been given,

Provided that this provision shall apply only if it is claimed that the defendant has an interest in the cargo or freight or had such an interest at the time of salvage.

*Exclusive Jurisdiction*

## Article 16

The following courts shall have exclusive jurisdiction, regardless of domicile:

1.—

(a) in proceedings which have as their object rights in rem in immovable property or tenancies of immovable property, the courts of the Contracting State in which the property is situated;
(b) however, in proceedings which have as their object tenancies of immovable property concluded for temporary private use for a maximum period of six consecutive months, the courts of the Contracting State in which the defendant is domiciled shall also have jurisdiction, provided that the tenant is a natural person and neither party is domiciled in the Contracting State in which the property is situated;

2. in proceedings which have as their object the validity of the constitution, the nullity of the dissolution of companies or other legal persons or associations of natural or legal persons, or the decisions of their organs, the courts of the Contracting State in which the company, legal person or association has its seat;

3. in proceedings which have as their object the validity of entries in public registers, the courts of the Contracting State in which the register is kept;

4. in proceedings concerned with the registration of validity of patents, trade marks, designs, or other similar rights required to be deposited or registered, the courts of the Contracting State in which the deposit or registration has been applied for, has taken place or is under the terms of an international convention deemed to have taken place;

5. in proceedings concerned with the enforcement of judgements, the courts of the Contracting State in which the judgement has been or is to be enforced.

*Prorogation of Jurisdiction*

## ARTICLE 17

1. If the parties, one or more of whom is domiciled in a Contracting State, have agreed that a court or the courts of a Contracting State are to have jurisdiction to settle any disputes which have arisen or which may arise in connection with a particular legal relationship, that court or those courts shall have exclusive jurisdiction. Such an agreement conferring jurisdiction shall be either:

(a) in writing or evidenced in writing, or
(b) in a form which accords with practices which the parties have established between themselves, or
(c) in international trade or commerce, in a form which accords with a usage of which the parties are or ought to have been aware and which in such trade or commerce is widely known to, and regularly observed by, parties to contracts of the type involved in the particular trade or commerce concerned.

Where such an agreement is concluded by parties, none of whom is domiciled in a Contracting State, the courts of other Contracting States shall have no jurisdiction over their disputes unless the court or courts chosen have declined jurisdiction.

2. The court or courts of a Contracting State on which a trust instrument has conferred jurisdiction shall have exclusive jurisdiction in any proceedings brought against a settlor, trustee or beneficiary, if relations between these persons or their rights or obligations under the trust are involved.

3. Agreements or provisions of a trust instrument conferring jurisdiction shall have no legal force if they are contrary to the provisions of Article 12 or 15, or if the courts whose jurisdiction they purport to exclude have exclusive jurisdiction by virtue of Article 16.

## TITLE III

*Recognition and Enforcement*

### ARTICLE 28

Moreover, a judgement shall not be recognised if it conflicts with the provisions of Section 3, 4 or 5 of Title II or in a case provided for in Article 59.

A judgement may furthermore be refused recognition in any case provided for in Article 54B(3) or 57(4).

In its examination of the grounds of jurisdiction referred to in the foregoing paragraphs, the court or authority applied to shall be bound by the findings of fact on which the court of the State of origin based its jurisdiction.

Subject to the provisions of the first and second paragraphs, the jurisdiction of the court of the State of origin may not be reviewed; the test of public policy referred to in Article 27(1) may not be applied to the rules relating to jurisdiction.

## TITLE VII

*Relationship to the Brussels Convention and to other Conventions*

### ARTICLE 54B

1. This Convention shall not prejudice the application by the Member States of the European Communities of the Convention on Jurisdiction and the Enforcement of Judgements in Civil and Commercial Matters, signed at Brussels on 27 September 1968 and of the Protocol on interpretation of that Convention by the Court of Justice, signed at Luxembourg on 3 June 1971, as amended by the Conventions of Accession to the said Convention and the said Protocol by the States acceding to the European Communities, all of these Conventions and the Protocol being hereinafter referred to as the 'Brussels Convention'.

2. However, this Convention shall in any event be applied:
   (a) in matters of jurisdiction, where the defendant is domiciled in the territory of a Contracting State which is not a member of the European Communities, or where Article 16 or 17 of this Convention confers a jurisdiction on the courts of such a Contracting State;
   (b) in relation to a lis pendens or to related actions as provided for in Articles 21 and 22, when proceedings are instituted in a Contracting State which is not a member of the European Communities and in a Contracting State which is a member of the European Communities;
   (c) in matters of recognition and enforcement, where either the State of origin or the State addressed is not a member of the European Communities;

3. In addition to the grounds provided for in Title III recognition or enforcement may be refused if the ground of jurisdiction on which the judgement has been based differs from that resulting from this Convention and recognition or enforcement is sought against a party who is domiciled in a Contracting State which is not a member of the European Communities; unless the judgement may otherwise be recognised or enforced under any rule of law in the State addressed.

## TITLE VIII

*Final Provisions*

### ARTICLE 60

The following may be parties to this Convention:

(a) States which, at the time of the opening of this Convention for signature, are members of the European Communities or of the European Free Trade Association;

(b) States which, after the opening of this Convention for signature, become members of the European communities or of the European Free Trade Association;

(c) States invited to accede in accordance with Article 62(1)(b).

## PROTOCOL NO 2

*On the Uniform Interpretation of the Convention*

### ARTICLE 1

The courts of each Contracting State shall, when applying and interpreting the provisions of the Convention, pay due account to the principles laid down by any relevant decision delivered by courts of the other Contracting States concerning provisions of this Convention.

### ARTICLE 2

1. The Contracting Parties agree to set up a system of exchange of information concerning judgements delivered pursuant to this Convention as well as relevant judgements under the Brussels Convention. This system shall comprise:

— transmission to a central body by the competent authorities of judgements delivered by courts of last instance and the Court of Justice of the European Communities as well as judgements of particular importance which have become final and have been delivered pursuant to this Convention or the Brussels Convention,

— classification of these judgements by the central body including, as far as necessary, the drawing-up and publication of translations and abstracts,

— communication by the central body of the relevant documents to the competent national authorities of all signatories and acceding States to the Convention and to the Commission of the European Communities.

2. The central body is the Registrar of the Court of Justice of the European Communities.

### ARTICLES 3 AND 4 [Omitted]

# INTERNATIONAL TRANSPORT CONVENTIONS ACT 1983

## CHAPTER 14

*The Railway Convention*

### 1. Convention to have the force of law

(1) The Convention concerning International Carriage by Rail signed on behalf of the United Kingdom on 9th May 1980 shall have the force of law in the United Kingdom.

(2) In this Act "the Convention" means the Convention referred to in subsection (1) above including, except where the context otherwise requires;
- (a) the protocol on the privileges and immunities of the intergovernmental organisation set up by the Convention; and
- (b) the uniform rules in Appendix A and Appendix B to the Convention together with the Annexes to Appendix B.

(3) The provisions having the force of law by virtue of this section are-
- (a) the provisions of the Convention as presented to Parliament in April 1982 and set out in Command Paper 8535 as amended by—
  - (i) Part I of the Protocol of Decisions adopted by the Revision Committee constituted by the Convention in the course of its first session held at Berne from 14th to 21st December 1989, presented to Parliament in 1991 and set out in Command paper 1690, and
  - (ii) Part I of the Protocol of Decisions adopted by that Committee in the course of its second session held at Berne from 28th to 31st May 1990 as so presented and set out in Command paper 1689; and
- (b) as respects Annexes I, II and III to Appendix B to the Convention, the provisions referred to in that Command Paper;

and judicial notice shall be taken of those provisions as if they were contained in this Act.

(4) [Omitted].

### 2. [Omitted].

### 3. Fatal accidents.

(1) Where by virtue of the Convention any person has a right of action in respect of the death of a passenger by reason of his being a person whom the passenger was under a legal duty to maintain;

(a) subject to subsection (2) below, no action in respect of the passenger's death shall be brought for the benefit of that person under the Fatal Accidents Act 1976; but
(b) nothing in section 2(3) of that Act (not more than one action in respect of the same subject-matter of complaint) shall prevent an action being brought under that Act for the benefit of any other person.

(2) Nothing in subsection (1)(a) above affects the right of any person to claim for damages for bereavement under section 1A of the said Act of 1976.

(3) Section 4 of the said Act of 1976 (exclusion of certain benefits in assessment of damages) shall apply in relation to an action brought by any person under the Convention as it applied in relation to an action under that Act.

(4) Where separate proceedings are brought under the Convention and under the said Act of 1976 in respect of the death of a passenger, a court, in awarding damages under that Act, shall take into account any damages awarded in the proceedings brought under the Convention and shall have jurisdiction to make any part of its award conditional on the result of those proceedings.

(5) and (6) [Omitted].

**4.-11. and Schedules [Omitted].**

# FOREIGN LIMITATION PERIODS ACT 1984

## CHAPTER 16



### 1. Application of foreign limitation law.

(1) Subject to the following provisions of this Act, where in any action or proceedings in a court in England and Wales the law of any other country falls (in accordance with rules of private international law applicable by any such court) to be taken into account in the determination of any matter—

(a) the law of that country relating to limitation shall apply in respect of that matter for the purposes of the action or proceedings; and

(b) except where that matter falls within subsection (2) below, the law of England and Wales relating to limitation shall not so apply.

(2) A matter falls within this subsection if it is a matter in the determination of which both the law of England and Wales and the law of some other country fall to be taken into account.

(3) The law of England and Wales shall determine for the purposes of any law applicable by virtue of subsection (1)(a) above whether, and the time at which, proceedings have been commenced in respect of any matter; and, accordingly, section 35 of the Limitation Act 1980 (new claims in pending proceedings) shall apply in relation to time limits applicable by virtue of subsection (1)(a) above as it applies in relation to time limits under that Act.

(4) A court in England and Wales, in exercising in pursuance of subsection (1)(a) above any discretion conferred by the law of any other country, shall so far as practicable exercise that discretion in the manner in which it is exercised in comparable cases by the courts of that other country.

(5) In this section 'law', in relation to any country, shall not include rules of private international law applicable by the courts of that country or, in the case of England and Wales, this Act.

### 2. Exceptions to s 1.

(1) In any case in which the application of section 1 above would to any extent conflict (whether under subsection (2) below or otherwise) with public policy, that section shall not apply to the extent that its application would so conflict.

(2) The application of section 1 above in relation to any action or proceedings shall conflict with public policy to the extent that its application would cause undue hardship to a person who is, or might be made, a party to the action or proceedings.

(3) Where, under a law applicable by virtue of section 1(1)(a) above for the purposes of any action or proceedings, a limitation period is or may be extended or interrupted in respect of the absence of a party to the action or proceedings from any specified jurisdiction or country, so much of that law as provides for the extension or interruption shall be disregarded for those purposes.

(4) [Omitted].

**3. Foreign judgements on limitation points**

Where a court in any country outside England and Wales has determined any matter wholly or partly by reference to the law of that or any other country (including England and Wales) relating to limitation, then, for the purposes of the law relating to the effect to be given in England and Wales to that determination, that court shall, to the extent that it has so determined the matter, be deemed to have determined it on its merits.

**4. Meaning of law relating to limitation.**

(1) Subject to subsection (3) below, references in this Act to the law of any country (including England and Wales) relating to limitation shall, in relation to any matter, be construed as references to so much of the relevant law of that country as (in any manner) makes provision with respect to a limitation period applicable to the bringing of proceedings in respect of that matter in the courts of that country and shall include—

(a) references to so much of that law as relates to, and to the effect of, the application, extension, reduction or interruption of that period; and

(b) a reference, where under that law there is no limitation period which is so applicable, to the rule that such proceedings may be brought within an indefinite period.

(2) In subsection (1) above "relevant law", in relation to any country, means the procedural and substantive law applicable, apart from any rules of private international law, by the courts of that country.

(3) References in this Act to the law of England and Wales relating to limitation shall not include the rules by virtue of which a court may, in the exercise of any discretion, refuse equitable relief on the grounds of acquiescence or otherwise; but, in applying those rules to a case in relation to which the law of any country outside England and Wales is applicable by virtue of section 1(1)(a) above (not being a law that provides for a limitation period that has expired), a court in England and Wales shall have regard, in particular, to the provisions of the law that is so applicable.

**5.-7. [Omitted].**

# LATENT DAMAGE ACT 1986

## CHAPTER 37

*Accrual of cause of action to successive owners in respect of latent damage to property*

**3. Accrual of cause of action to successive owners in respect of latent damage to property**

(1) Subject to the following provisions of this section, where;

(a) a cause of action ("the original cause of action") has accrued to any person in respect of any negligence to which damage to any property in which he has an interest is attributable (in whole or in part); and

(b) another person acquires an interest in that property after the date on which the original cause of action accrued but before the material facts about the damage have become known to any person who, at the time when he first has knowledge of those facts, has any interest in the property;

a fresh cause of action in respect of that negligence shall accrue to that other person on the date on which he acquires his interest in the property.

(2) A cause of action accruing to any person by virtue of subsection (1) above-

(a) shall be treated as if based on breach of a duty of care at common law owed to the person to whom it accrues; and

(b) shall be treated for the purposes of section 14A of the 1980 Act (special time limit for negligence actions where facts relevant to cause of action are not known at date of accrual) as having accrued on the date on which the original cause of action accrued.

(3) [Omitted].

(4) Subsection (1) above shall not apply in any case where the person acquiring an interest in the damaged property is either-

(a) a person in whom the original cause of action vests by operation of law; or

(b) a person in whom the interest in that property vests by virtue of any order made by a court under section 538 of the Companies Act 1985 (vesting of company property in liquidator).

(5) For the purposes of subsection (1)(b) above, the material facts about the damage are such facts about the damage as would lead a reasonable person who has an interest in the damaged property at the time when those facts become known to him to consider it sufficiently serious to justify his instituting proceedings for damages against a defendant who did not dispute liability and was able to satisfy a judgement.

(6) For the purposes of this section a person's knowledge includes knowledge which he might reasonably have been expected to acquire—

(a) from facts observable or ascertainable by him; or

(b) from facts ascertainable by him with the help of appropriate expert advice which it is reasonable for him to seek;

but a person shall not be taken by virtue of this subsection to have knowledge of a fact ascertainable by him only with the help of expert advice so long as he has taken all reasonable steps to obtain (and, where appropriate to act on) that advice.

(7) [Omitted].

# CONTRACTS (APPLICABLE LAW) ACT 1990

## CHAPTER 36

### 1. Meaning of 'the Conventions'.

In this Act—

(a) "the Rome Convention" means the Convention on the law applicable to contractual obligations opened for signature in Rome on 19th June 1980 and signed by the United Kingdom on 7th December 1981;

(b) "the Luxembourg Convention" means the Convention on the accession of the Hellenic Republic to the Rome Convention signed by the United Kingdom in Luxembourg on 10th April 1984; and

(c) "the Brussels Protocol" means the first Protocol on the interpretation of the Rome Convention by the European Court signed by the United Kingdom in Brussels on 19th December 1988;

and the Rome Convention, the Luxembourg Convention and the Brussels Protocol are together referred to as "the Conventions".

### 2. Conventions to have force of law.

(1) Subject to subsections (2) and (3) below, the Conventions shall have the force of law in the United Kingdom.

(2) Articles 7(1) and 10(1)(e) of the Rome Convention shall not have the force of law in the United Kingdom.

(3) Notwithstanding Article 19(2) of the Rome Convention, the Conventions shall apply in the case of conflicts between the laws of different parts of the United Kingdom.

(4) [Omitted].

### 3. Interpretation of Conventions.

(1) Any question as to the meaning or effect of any provision of the Conventions shall, if not referred to the European Court in accordance with the Brussels Protocol, be determined in accordance with the principles laid down by, and any relevant decision of, the European Court.

(2) Judicial notice shall be taken of any decision of, or expression of opinion by, the European Court on any such question.

(3) Without prejudice to any practice of the courts as to the matters which may be considered apart from this subsection-

(a) the report on the Rome Convention by Professor Mario Giuliano and Professor Paul Lagarde which is reproduced in the Official Journal of the Communities of 31st October 1980 may be considered in ascertaining the meaning or effect of any provision of that Convention; and

(b) any report on the Brussels Protocol which is reproduced in the Official Journal of the Communities may be considered in ascertaining the meaning of effect of any provision of that Protocol.

**4.-9. [Omitted].**

## SCHEDULE 1

## THE ROME CONVENTION

## TITLE 1

## SCOPE OF THE CONVENTION

### ARTICLE 1

*Scope of the Convention*

1. The rules of this Convention shall apply to contractual obligations in any situation involving a choice between the laws of different countries.

2. They shall not apply to:
- (a) questions involving the status or legal capacity of natural persons, without prejudice to Article 11;
- (b) contractual obligations relating to:
  - — wills and succession,
  - — rights in property arising out of a matrimonial relationship,
  - — rights and duties arising out of a family relationship, parentage, marriage or affinity, including maintenance obligations in respect of children who are not legitimate;
- (c) obligations arising under bills of exchange, cheques and promissory notes and other negotiable instruments to the extent that the obligations under such other negotiable instruments arise out of their negotiable character;
- (d) arbitration agreements and agreements on the choice of court;
- (e) questions governed by the law of companies and other bodies corporate or unincorporate such as the creation, by registration or otherwise, legal capacity, internal organisation or winding up of companies and other bodies corporate or unincorporate and the personal liability of officers and members as such for the obligations of the company or body;
- (f) the question whether an agent is able to bind a principal, or an organ to bind a company or body corporate or unincorporate, to a third party;
- (g) the constitution of trusts and the relationship between settlors, trustees and beneficiaries;
- (h) evidence and procedure, without prejudice to Article 14.

3. The rules of this Convention do not apply to contracts of insurance which cover risks situated in the territories of the Member States of the European Economic Community. In order to determine whether a risk is situated in these territories the court shall apply its internal law.

4. The preceding paragraph does not apply to contracts of re-insurance.

## ARTICLE 2

*Application of law of non-contracting States*

Any law specified by this Convention shall be applied whether or not it is the law of a Contracting State.

## TITLE II

## UNIFORM RULES

## ARTICLE 3

*Freedom of choice*

1. A contract shall be governed by the law chosen by the parties. The choice must be express or demonstrated with reasonable certainty by the terms of the contract or the circumstances of the case. By their choice the parties can select the law applicable to the whole or a part only of the contract.

2. The parties may at any time agree to subject the contract to a law other than that which previously governed it, whether as a result of an earlier choice under this Article or of other provisions of this Convention. Any variation by the parties of the law to be applied made after the conclusion of the contract shall not prejudice its formal validity under Article 9 or adversely affect the rights of third parties.

3. The fact that the parties have chosen a foreign law, whether or not accompanied by the choice of a foreign tribunal, shall not, where all the other elements relevant to the situation at the time of the choice are connected with one country only, prejudice the application of rules of the law of that country which cannot be derogated from by contract, hereinafter called "mandatory rules".

4. The existence and validity of the consent of the parties as to the choice of the applicable law shall be determined in accordance with the provisions of Articles 8, 9 and 11.

## ARTICLE 4

*Applicable law in the absence of choice*

1. To the extent that the law applicable to the contract has not been chosen in accordance with Article 3, the contract shall be governed by the law of the country with which it is most closely connected. Nevertheless, a severable part of the contract which has a closer connection with another country may by way of exception be governed by the law of that other country.

2. Subject to the provisions of paragraph 5 of this Article, it shall be presumed that the contract is most closely connected with the country where the party who is to effect the performance which is characteristic of the contract has, at the time of conclusion of the contract, his habitual residence, or, in the case of a body corporate or unincorporate, its central administration. However, if the contract is entered into in the course of that party's trade or profession, that country shall be the country in which the principal place of business is situated or, where under the terms of the contract the performance is to be effected through a place of business other than the principal place of business, the country in which that other place of business is situated.

3. Notwithstanding the provisions of paragraph 2 of this Article, to the extent that the subject matter of the contract is a right in immovable property or a right to use immovable property it shall be presumed that the contract is most closely connected with the country where the immovable property is situated.

4. A contract for the carriage of goods shall not be subject to the presumption in paragraph 2. In such a contract if the country in which, at the time the contract is concluded, the carrier has his principal place of business is also the country in which the place of loading or the place of discharge or the principal place of business of the consignor is situated, it shall be presumed that the contract is most closely connected with that country. In applying this paragraph single voyage charter-parties and other contracts the main purpose of which is the carriage of goods shall be treated as contracts for the carriage of goods.

5. Paragraph 2 shall not apply if the characteristic performance cannot be determined, and the presumptions in paragraphs 2, 3 and 4 shall be disregarded if it appears from the circumstances as a whole that the contract is more closely connected with another country.

## ARTICLE 5

*Certain consumer contracts*

1. This Article applies to a contract the object of which is the supply of goods or services to a person ("the consumer") for a purpose which can be regarded as being outside his trade or profession, or a contract for the provision of credit for that object.

2. Notwithstanding the provisions of Article 3, a choice of law made by the parties shall not have the result of depriving the consumer of the protection afforded to him by the mandatory rules of the law of the country in which he has his habitual residence:

— if in that country the conclusion of the contract was preceded by a specific invitation addressed to him or by advertising, and he had taken in that country all the steps necessary on his part for the conclusion of the contract, or

— if the other party or his agent received the consumer's order in that country, or

— if the contract is for the sale of goods and the consumer travelled from that country to another country and there gave his order, provided that the consumer's journey was arranged by the seller for the purpose of inducing the consumer to buy.

3. Notwithstanding the provisions of Article 4, a contract to which this Article applies will, in the absence of choice in accordance with Article 3, be governed by the law of the country in which the consumer has his habitual residence if it is entered into in the circumstances described in paragraph 2 of this Article.

4. This Article shall not apply to:
(a) a contract of carriage;
(b) a contract for the supply of services where the services are to be supplied to the consumer exclusively in a country other than that in which he has his habitual residence.

5. Notwithstanding the provisions of paragraph 4, this Article shall apply to a contract which, for an inclusive price, provides for a combination of travel and accommodation.

## ARTICLE 6

### *Individual employment contracts*

1. Notwithstanding the provisions of Article 3, in a contract of employment a choice of law made by the parties shall not have the result of depriving the employee of the protection afforded to him by the mandatory rules of the law which would be applicable under paragraph 2 in the absence of choice.

2. Notwithstanding the provisions of Article 4, a contract of employment shall, in the absence of choice in accordance with Article 3, be governed:
(a) by the law of the country in which the employee habitually carries out his work in performance of the contract, even if he is temporarily employed in another country; or
(b) if the employee does not habitually carry out his work in any one country, by the law of the country in which the place of business through which he was engaged is situated;
unless it appears from the circumstances as a whole that the contract is more closely connected with another country, in which case the contract shall be governed by the law of that country.

## ARTICLE 7

### *Mandatory rules*

1. When applying under this Convention the law of a country, effect may be given to the mandatory rules of the law of another country with which the situation has a close connection, if and in so far as, under the law of the latter country, those rules must be applied whatever the law applicable to the contract. In considering whether to give effect to these mandatory rules, regard shall be had to their nature and purpose and to the consequences of their application or non-application.

2. Nothing in this Convention shall restrict the application of the rules of the law of the forum in a situation where they are mandatory irrespective of the law otherwise applicable to the contract.

## ARTICLE 8

*Material validity*

1. The existence and validity of a contract, or of any term of a contract, shall be determined by the law which would govern it under this Convention if the contract or term were valid.

2. Nevertheless a party may rely upon the law of the country in which he has his habitual residence to establish that he did not consent if it appears from the circumstances that it would not be reasonable to determine the effect of his conduct in accordance with the law specified in the preceding paragraph.

## ARTICLE 9

*Formal validity*

1. A contract concluded between persons who are in the same country is formally valid if it satisfies the formal requirements of the law which governs it under this Convention or of the law of the country where it is concluded.

2. A contract concluded between persons who are in different countries is formally valid if it satisfies the formal requirements of the law which governs it under this Convention or of the law of one of those countries.

3. Where a contract is concluded by an agent, the country in which the agent acts is the relevant country for the purposes of paragraphs 1 and 2.

4. An act intended to have legal effect relating to an existing or contemplated contract is formally valid if it satisfies the formal requirements of the law which under this Convention governs or would govern the contract or of the law of the country where the act was done.

5. The provisions of the preceding paragraphs shall not apply to a contract to which Article 5 applies, concluded in the circumstances described in paragraph 2 of Article 5. The formal validity of such a contract is governed by the law of the country in which the consumer has his habitual residence.

6. Notwithstanding paragraphs 1 to 4 of this Article, a contract the subject matter of which is a right in immovable property or a right to use immovable property shall be subject to the mandatory requirements of form of the law of the country where the property is situated if by that law those requirements are imposed irrespective of the country where the contract is concluded and irrespective of the law governing the contract.

## ARTICLE 10

*Scope of the applicable law*

1. The law applicable to a contract by virtue of Articles 3 to 6 and 12 of this Convention shall govern in particular:

(a) interpretation;
(b) performance;
(c) within the limits of the powers conferred on the court by its procedural law, the consequences of breach, including the assessment of damages in so far as it is governed by rules of law;
(d) the various ways of extinguishing obligations and prescription and limitation of actions;
(e) the consequences of nullity of the contract.

2. In relation to the manner of performance and the steps to be taken in the event of defective performance regard shall be had to the law of the country in which performance takes place.

## ARTICLE 11

*Incapacity*

In a contract concluded between persons who are in the same country, a natural person who would have capacity under the law of that country may invoke his incapacity resulting from another law only if the other party to the contract was aware of this incapacity at the time of the conclusion of the contract or was not aware thereof as a result of negligence.

## ARTICLE 12

*Voluntary assignment*

1. The mutual obligations of assignor and assignee under a voluntary assignment of a right against another person ("the debtor") shall be governed by the law which under this Convention applies to the contract between the assignor and assignee.

2. The law governing the right to which the assignment relates shall determine its assignability, the relationship between the assignee and the debtor, the conditions under which the assignment can be invoked against the debtor and any question whether the debtor's obligations have been discharged.

## ARTICLE 13

*Subrogation*

1. Where a person ('the creditor') has a contractual claim upon another ('the debtor'), and a third person has a duty to satisfy the creditor, or has in fact satisfied the creditor in discharge of that duty, the law which governs the third person's duty to satisfy the creditor shall determine whether the third person is entitled to exercise against the debtor the rights which the creditor had against the debtor under the law governing their relationship and, if so, whether he may do so in full or only to a limited extent.

2. The same rule applies where several persons are subject to the same contractual claim and one of them has satisfied the creditor.

## Article 14

*Burden of proof, etc.*

1. The law governing the contract under this Convention applies to the extent that it contains, in the law of contract, rules which raise presumptions of law or determine the burden of proof.

2. A contract or an act intended to have legal effect may be proved by any mode of proof recognised by the law of the forum or by any of the laws referred to in Article 9 under which that contract or act is formally valid, provided that such mode of proof can be administered by the forum.

## Article 15

*Exclusion of renvoi*

The application of the law of any country specified by this Convention means the application of the rules of law in force in that country other than its rules of private international law.

## Article 16

*'Ordre public'*

The application of a rule of the law of any country specified by this Convention may be refused only if such application is manifestly incompatible with the public policy (*'ordre public'*) of the forum.

## Article 17

*No retrospective effect*

This Convention shall apply in a Contracting State to contracts made after the date on which this Convention has entered into force with respect to that State.

## Article 18

*Uniform interpretation*

In the interpretation and application of the preceding uniform rules, regard shall be had to their international character and to the desirability of achieving uniformity in their interpretation and application.

## ARTICLE 19

*States with more than one legal system*

1. Where a State comprises several territorial units each of which has its own rules of law in respect of contractual obligations, each territorial unit shall be considered as a country for the purposes of identifying the law applicable under this Convention.

2. A State within which different territorial units have their own rules of law in respect of contractual obligations shall not be bound to apply this Convention to conflicts solely between the laws of such units.

## ARTICLE 20

*Precedence of Community law*

This Convention shall not affect the application of provisions which, in relation to particular matters, lay down choice of law rules relating to contractual obligations and which are or will be contained in acts of the institutions of the European Communities or in national laws harmonised in implementation of such acts.

## ARTICLE 21

*Relationship with other conventions*

This Convention shall not prejudice the application of international conventions to which a Contracting State is, or becomes, a party.

## ARTICLES 22 - 26 [Omitted].

## ARTICLE 27

1. This Convention shall apply to the European territories of the Contracting States, including Greenland, and to the entire territory of the French Republic.

2. Notwithstanding paragraph 1:
   - (a) this Convention shall not apply to the Faroe Islands, unless the Kingdom of Denmark makes a declaration to the contrary;
   - (b) this Convention shall not apply to any European territory situated outside the United Kingdom for the international relations of which the United Kingdom is responsible, unless the United Kingdom makes a declaration to the contrary in respect of any such territory;
   - (c) this Convention shall apply to the Netherlands Antilles, if the Kingdom of the Netherlands makes a declaration to that effect.

3. Such declarations may be made at any time by notifying the Secretary-General of the Council of the European Communities.

4. Proceedings brought in the United Kingdom on appeal from courts in one of the territories referred to in paragraph 2(b) shall be deemed to be proceedings taking place in those courts.

### ARTICLES 28 - 33 [OMITTED].

## SCHEDULE 2

### THE LUXEMBOURG CONVENTION

### ARTICLE 1

The Hellenic Republic hereby accedes to the Convention on the law applicable to contractual obligations, opened for signature in Rome on 19 June 1980.

### ARTICLES 2 - 6 [OMITTED].

## SCHEDULE 3

### THE BRUSSELS PROTOCOL

### ARTICLE 1

The Court of Justice of the European Communities shall have jurisdiction to give rulings on the interpretation of—

(a) the Convention on the law applicable to contractual obligations, opened for signature in Rome on 19 June 1980, hereinafter referred to as "the Rome Convention";

(b) the Convention on accession to the Rome Convention by the States which have become Members of the European Communities since the date on which it was opened for signature;

(c) this Protocol.

### ARTICLES 2 - 11 [OMITTED].

# CARRIAGE OF GOODS BY SEA ACT 1992

## CHAPTER 50

### 1. Shipping documents etc. to which Act applies.

(1) This Act applies to the following documents, that is to say—
- (a) any bill of lading;
- (b) any sea waybill; and
- (c) any ship's delivery order.

(2) References in this Act to a bill of lading -
- (a) do not include references to a document which is incapable of transfer either by endorsement or, as a bearer bill, by delivery without endorsement; but
- (b) subject to that, do include references to a received for shipment bill of lading.

(3) References in this Act to a sea waybill are references to any document which is not a bill of lading but-
- (a) is such a receipt for goods as contains or evidences a contract for the carriage of goods by sea; and
- (b) identifies the person to whom delivery of the goods is to be made by the carrier in accordance with that contract.

(4) References in this Act to a ship's delivery order are references to any document which is neither a bill of lading nor a sea waybill but contains an undertaking which—
- (a) is given under or for the purposes of a contract for the carriage by sea of the goods to which the document relates, or of goods which include those goods; and
- (b) is an undertaking by the carrier to a person identified in the document to deliver the goods to which the document relates to that person.

(5) The Secretary of State may by regulations make provision for the application of this Act to cases where a telecommunication system or any other information technology is used for effecting transactions corresponding to-
- (a) the issue of a document to which this Act applies;
- (b) the endorsement, delivery or other transfer of such a document; or
- (c) the doing of anything else in relation to such a document.

(6) [Omitted].

### 2. Rights under shipping documents.

(1) Subject to the following provisions of this section, a person who becomes—
- (a) the lawful holder of a bill of lading;
- (b) the person who (without being an original party to the contract of carriage) is the person to whom delivery of the goods to which a sea waybill relates is to be made by the carrier in accordance with that contract; or

(c) the person to whom delivery of the goods to which a ship's delivery order relates is to be made in accordance with the undertaking contained in the order,

shall (by virtue of becoming the holder of the bill or, as the case may be, the person to whom delivery is to be made) have transferred to and vested in him all rights of suit under the contract of carriage as if he had been a party to that contract.

(2) Where, when a person becomes the lawful holder of a bill of lading, possession of the bill no longer gives a right (as against the carrier) to possession of the goods to which the bill relates, that person shall not have any rights transferred to him by virtue of subsection (1) above unless he becomes the holder of the bill-

(a) by virtue of a transaction effected in pursuance of any contractual of other arrangements made before the time when such a right to possession ceased to attach to possession of the bill; or

(b) as a result of the rejection to that person by another person of goods or documents delivered to the other person in pursuance of any such arrangements.

(3) The rights vested in any person by virtue of the operation of subsection (1) above in relation to a ship's delivery order-

(a) shall be so vested subject to the terms of the order; and

(b) where the goods to which the order relates form a part only of the goods to which the contract of carriage relates, shall be confined to rights in respect of the goods to which the order relates.

(4) Where, in the case of any document to which this Act applies-

(a) a person with any interest or right in or in relation to goods to which the document relates sustains loss or damage in consequence of a breach of the contract of carriage; but

(b) subsection (1) above operates in relation to that document so that rights of suit in respect of that breach are vested in another person,

the other person shall be entitled to exercise those rights for the benefit of the person who sustained the loss or damage to the same extent as they could have been exercised if they had been vested in the person for whose benefit they are exercised.

(5) Where rights are transferred by virtue of the operation of subsection (1) above in relation to any document, the transfer for which that subsection provides shall extinguish any entitlement to those rights which derives-

(a) where that document is a bill of lading, from a person's having been an original party to the contract of carriage; or

(b) in the case of any document to which this Act applies, from the previous operation of that subsection in relation to that document;

but the operation of that subsection shall be without prejudice to any rights which derive from a person's having been an original party to the contract contained in, or evidenced by, a sea waybill and, in relation to a ship's delivery order, shall be without prejudice to any rights deriving otherwise than from the previous operation of that subsection in relation to that order.

**3. Liabilities under shipping documents.**

(1) Where subjection (1) of section 2 of this Act operates in relation to any document to which this Act applies and the person in whom rights are vested by virtue of that subsection-

(a) takes or demands delivery from the carrier of any of the goods to which the document relates;

(b) makes a claim under the contract of carriage against the carrier in respect of any of those goods; or

(c) is a person who, at a time before those rights were vested in him, took or demanded delivery from the carrier of any of those goods,

that person shall (by virtue of taking or demanding delivery or making the claim or, in a case falling within paragraph (c) above, of having the rights vested in him) become subject to the same liabilities under that contract as if he had been a party to that contract.

(2) Where the goods to which a ship's delivery order relates form a part only of the goods to which the contract of carriage relates, the liabilities to which any person is subject by virtue of the operation of this section in relation to that order shall exclude liabilities in respect of any goods to which the order does not relate.

(3) This section, so far as it imposes liabilities under any contract on any person, shall be without prejudice to the liabilities under the contract of any person as an original party to the contract.

**4. Representations in bills of lading**

A bill of lading which—

(a) represents goods to have been shipped on board a vessel or to have been received for shipment on board a vessel; and

(b) has been signed by the master of the vessel or by a person who was not the master but has the express, implied or apparent authority of the carrier to sign bills of lading,

shall, in favour of a person who has become the lawful holder of the bill, be conclusive evidence against the carrier of the shipment of the goods or, as the case may be, of their receipt for shipment.

**5. Interpretation etc.**

(1) In this Act—

'bill of lading', 'sea waybill' and 'ship's delivery order' shall be construed in accordance with section 1 above;

'the contract of carriage'—

(a) in relation to a bill of lading or sea waybill, means the contract contained in or evidenced by that bill or waybill; and

(b) in relation to a ship's delivery order, means the contract under or for the purposes of which the undertaking contained in the order is given;

'holder', in relation to a bill of lading, shall be construed in accordance with subsection (2) below;

'information technology' includes any computer or other technology by means of which information or other matter may be recorded or communicated without being reduced to documentary form; and

'telecommunication system' has the same meaning as in the Telecommunications Act 1984.

(2) References in this Act to the holder of a bill of lading are references to any of the following persons, that is to say—

(a) a person with possession of the bill who, by virtue of being the person identified in the bill, is the consignee of the goods to which the bill relates;

(b) a person with possession of the bill as a result of the completion, by delivery of the bill, of any endorsement of the bill or, in the case of a bearer bill, of any other transfer of the bill;

(c) a person with possession of the bill as a result of any transaction by virtue of which he would have become a holder falling within paragraph (a) or (b) above had not the transaction been effected at a time when possession of the bill no longer gave a right (as against the carrier) to possession of the goods to which the bill relates;

and a person shall be regarded for the purposes of this Act as having become the lawful holder of a bill of lading wherever he has become the holder of the bill in good faith.

(3) References in this Act to a person's being identified in a document include references to his being identified by a description which allows for the identity of the person in question to be varied, in accordance with the terms of the document, after its issue; and the reference in section 1(3)(b) of this Act to a document's identifying a person shall be construed accordingly.

(4) Without prejudice to sections 2(2) and 4 above, nothing in this Act shall preclude its operation in relation to a case where the goods to which a document relates-

(a) cease to exist after the issue of the document; or

(b) cannot be identified (whether because they are mixed with other goods or for any other reason);

and references in this Act to the goods to which a document relates shall be construed accordingly.

(5) The preceding provisions of this Act shall have effect without prejudice to the application, in relation to any case, of the rules (the Hague-Visby Rules) which for the time being have the force of law by virtue of section 1 of the Carriage of Goods by Sea Act 1971.

**6. [Omitted].**

SECTION II

# CONVENTIONS

# GENEVA PROTOCOL ON ARBITRATION CLAUSES 1923

See First Schedule Arbitration Act 1950 for text of the Convention

# INTERNATIONAL CONVENTION FOR THE UNIFICATION OF CERTAIN RULES RELATING TO BILLS OF LADING, BRUSSELS, 1924 (THE HAGUE RULES)

## ARTICLE 1

In this convention the following words are employed with the meanings set out below:

(a). 'Carrier' includes the owner of the vessel or the charterer who enters into a contract of carriage with a shipper.

(b) 'Contract of carriage' applies only to contracts of carriage covered by a bill of lading or any similar document of title, in so far as such document relates to the carriage of goods by sea; it also applies to any bill of lading or any similar document as aforesaid issued under or pursuant to a charter party from the moment at which such instrument regulates the relations between a carrier and a holder of the same.

(c) 'Goods' includes goods, wares, merchandise, and articles of every kind whatsoever except live animals and cargo which by the contract of carriage is stated as being carried on deck and is so carried.

(d) 'Ship' means any vessel used for the carriage of goods by sea.

(e) 'Carriage of goods' covers the period from the time when the goods are loaded on to the time they are discharged from the ship.

## ARTICLE 2

Subject to the provisions of Article 6, under every contract of carriage of goods by sea the carrier, in relation to the loading, handling, stowage, carriage, custody, care, and discharge of such goods shall be subject to the responsibilities and liabilities, and entitled to the rights and immunities hereinafter set forth.

## ARTICLE 3

1. The carrier shall be bound before and at the beginning of the voyage to exercise due diligence to:

(a) Make the ship seaworthy;

(b) Properly man, equip, and supply the ship;

(c) Make the holds, refrigerating and cool chambers, and all other parts of the ship in which goods are carried, fit and safe for their reception, carriage, and preservation.

2. Subject to the provisions of Article 4, the carrier shall properly and carefully load, handle, stow, carry, keep, care for, and discharge the goods carried.

3. After receiving the goods into his charge, the carrier or the master or agent of the carrier shall, on demand of the shipper, issue to the shipper a bill of lading showing among other things:

(a) The leading marks necessary for identification of the goods as the same are furnished in writing by the shipper before the loading of such goods starts, provided such marks are stamped or otherwise shown clearly upon the goods if uncovered, or on the cases or coverings in which such goods are contained, in such a manner as should ordinarily remain legible until the end of the voyage;

(b) Either the number of packages or pieces, or the quantity; or weight, as the case may be, as furnished in writing by the shipper;

(c) The apparent order and condition of the goods.

Provided that no carrier, master, or agent of the carrier shall be bound to state or show in the bill of lading any marks, number, quantity, or weight which he has reasonable grounds for suspecting not accurately to represent the goods actually received or which he has had no reasonable means of checking.

4. Such a bill of lading shall be *prima facie* evidence of the receipt by the carrier of the goods as therein described in accordance with paragraph 3 a, b, and c.

5. The shipper shall be deemed to have guaranteed to the carrier the accuracy at the time of shipment of the marks, number, quantity, and weight, as furnished by him, and the shipper shall indemnify the carrier against all loss, damages, and expenses arising or resulting from inaccuracies in such particulars. The right of the carrier to such indemnity shall in no way limit his responsibility and liability under the contract of carriage to any person other than the shipper.

6. Unless notice of loss or damage and the general nature of such loss or damage be given in writing to the carrier or his agent at the port of discharge before or at the time of the removal of the goods into the custody of the person entitled to delivery thereof under the contract of carriage, such removal shall be *prima facie* evidence of the delivery by the carrier of the goods as described in the bill of lading.

If the loss or damage is not apparent, the notice must be given within three days of the delivery.

The notice in writing need not be given if the state of the goods has at the time of their receipt been the subject of joint survey or inspection.

In any event the carrier and the ship shall be discharged from all liability in respect of loss or damage unless suit is brought within one year after delivery of the goods or the date when the goods should have been delivered.

In the case of any actual or apprehended loss or damage the carrier and the receiver shall give all reasonable facilities to each other for inspecting and tallying the goods.

7. After the goods are loaded, the bill of lading to be issued by the carrier, master, or agent of the carrier to the shipper shall, if the shipper so demands, be a 'shipped' bill of lading, provided that if the shipper shall have previously taken up any document of title to such goods, he shall surrender the same as against the issue of the 'shipped' bill of lading. At the option of the carrier such document of title may be noted at the port of shipment by the carrier, master, or agent with the name or names of the ship or ships upon which he goods have been shipped and the date or dates of shipment, and when so noted, if it shows

the particulars mentioned in paragraph 3 or Article 3, it shall for the purpose of this Article be deemed to constitute a 'shipped' bill of lading.

8. Any clause, covenant, or agreement in a contract of carriage relieving the carrier or the ship from liability for loss or damage to or in connection with goods arising from negligence, fault, or failure in the duties and obligations provided in this Article, or lessening such liability otherwise than as provided in this convention, shall be null and void and of no effect. A benefit of insurance in favour of the carrier or similar clause shall be deemed to be a clause relieving the carrier from liability.

## ARTICLE 4

1. Neither the carrier nor the ship shall be liable for loss or damage arising or resulting from unseaworthiness unless caused by want of due diligence on the part of the carrier to make the ship seaworthy and to secure that the ship is properly manned, equipped, and supplied and to make the holds, refrigerating and cool chambers, and all other parts of the ship in which goods are carried fit and safe for their reception, carriage, and preservation in accordance with the provisions of paragraph 1 of Article 3. Whenever loss or damage has resulted from unseaworthiness, the burden of proving the exercise of due diligence shall be on the carrier or other person claiming exemption under this Article.

2. Neither the carrier nor the ship shall be responsible for loss or damage arising or resulting from:

(a) Act, neglect, or default of the master, mariner, pilot, or the servants of the carrier in the navigation or in the management of the ship.
(b) Fire, unless caused by the actual fault or privity of the carrier.
(c) Perils, dangers, and accidents of the sea or other navigable waters.
(d) Act of God.
(e) Act of war.
(f) Act of public enemies.
(g) Arrest or restraint of princes, rulers, or people or seizure under legal process.
(h) Quarantine restrictions.
(i) Act or omission of the shipper or owner of the goods, his agent, or representative.
(j) Strikes or lock-outs or stoppage or restraint of labour from whatever cause, whether partial or general.
(k) Riots and civil commotions.
(l) Saving or attempting to save life or property at sea.
(m) Wastage in bulk or weight or any other loss or damage arising from inherent defect, quality, or vice of the goods.
(n) Insufficiency of packing.
(o) Insufficiency or inadequacy of marks.
(p) Latent defects not discoverable by due diligence.
(q) Any other cause arising without the actual fault or privity of the carrier, or without the fault or neglect of the agents or servants of the carrier, but the burden of proof shall be on the person claiming the benefit of this exception to show that neither the actual fault or privity of the carrier nor the fault or neglect of the agents or servants of the carrier contributed to the loss or damage.

3. The shipper shall not be responsible for loss or damage sustained by the carrier or the ship arising or resulting from any cause without the act, fault, or neglect of the shipper, his agents, or his servants.

4. Any deviation in saving or attempting to save a life or property at sea or any reasonable deviation shall not be deemed to be an infringement or breach of this convention or of the contract of carriage, and the carrier shall not be liable for any loss or damage resulting therefrom.

5. Neither the carrier nor the ship shall in any event be or become liable for any loss or damage to or in connection with goods in an amount exceeding 100 pounds sterling per package or unit or the equivalent of that sum in other currency unless the nature and value of such goods have been declared by the shipper before shipment and inserted in the bill of lading.

This declaration if embodied in the bill of lading shall be *prima facie* evidence but shall not be binding or conclusive on the carrier.

By agreement between the carrier, master, or agent of the carrier and the shipper another maximum amount than that mentioned in this paragraph may be fixed, provided that such maximum shall not be less than the figure above named.

Neither the carrier nor the ship shall be responsible in any event for loss or damage to, or in connection with, goods if the nature or value thereof has been knowingly mis-stated by the shipper in the bill of lading.

6. Goods of an inflammable, explosive, or dangerous nature to the shipment whereof the carrier, master, or agent of the carrier has not consented with knowledge of their nature and character may at any time before discharge be landed at any place or destroyed or rendered innocuous by the carrier without compensation, and the shipper of such goods shall be liable for all damages and expenses directly or indirectly arising out of or resulting from such shipment. If any such goods shipped with such knowledge and consent shall become a danger to the ship or cargo, they may in like manner be landed at any place or destroyed or rendered innocuous by the carrier without liability on the part of the carrier except to general average, if any.

## Article 5

A carrier shall be at liberty to surrender in whole or in part all or any of his rights and immunities, or to increase any of his responsibilities and liabilities under this convention provided such surrender or increase shall be embodied in the bill of lading issued to the shipper.

The provisions of this convention shall not be applicable to charter-parties, but if bills of lading are issued in the case of a ship under a charter-party they shall comply with the terms of this convention. Nothing in these rules shall be held to prevent the insertion in a bill of lading of any lawful provision regarding general average.

## Article 6

Notwithstanding the provisions of the preceding Articles, a carrier, master, or agent of the carrier and a shipper shall in regard to any particular goods be at liberty to enter into any agreement in any terms as to the responsibility and liability of the carrier for such goods, and as to the rights and immunities of the carrier in respect of such goods, or concerning his obligation as to seaworthiness so far as this stipulation is not contrary to public policy, or concerning the care or diligence of his servants or agents in regard to the loading, handling, stowage, carriage, custody, care, and discharge of the goods carried by sea, provided that in this case no bill of lading has been or shall be issued and that the terms agreed shall be embodied in a receipt which shall be a non-negotiable document and shall be marked as such.

Any agreement so entered into shall have full legal effect:

Provided that this Article shall not apply to ordinary commercial shipments made in the ordinary course of trade, but only to other shipments where the character or condition of the property to be carried or the circumstances, terms, and conditions under which the carriage is to be performed are such as reasonably to justify a special agreement.

## Article 7

Nothing herein contained shall prevent a carrier or a shipper from entering into any agreement stipulation, condition, reservation, or exemption as to the responsibility and liability of the carrier or the ship for the loss or damage to, or in connection with, the custody and care and handling of goods prior to the loading on, and subsequent to the discharge from, the ship on which the goods are carried by sea.

## Article 8

The provisions of this convention shall not affect the rights and obligations of the carrier under any statute for the time being in force relating to the limitation of the liability of owners of seagoing vessels.

## Article 9

The monetary units mentioned in this convention are to be taken to be gold value. Those contracting states in which the pound sterling is not a monetary unit reserve to themselves the right of translating the sums indicated in this convention in terms of pound sterling into terms of their own monetary system in round figures. The national laws may reserve to the debtor the right of discharging his debt in national currency according to the rate of exchange prevailing on the day of their arrival of the ship at the port of discharge of the goods concerned.

## Article 10

The provisions of this convention shall apply to all bills of lading issued in any of the contracting States.

## Articles 11-16 [Omitted].

## GENEVA CONVENTION ON THE EXECUTION OF FOREIGN ARBITRAL AWARDS 1927

See Second Schedule Arbitration Act 1950 for text of the Convention

# CONVENTION FOR THE UNIFICATION OF CERTAIN RULES RELATING TO INTERNATIONAL CARRIAGE BY AIR, WARSAW, 1929 (WARSAW CONVENTION)

## CHAPTER I

*Scope — Definitions*

### ARTICLE I

1. This Convention applies to all international carriage of persons, luggage or goods performed by aircraft for reward. It applies equally to gratuitous carriage by aircraft performed by an air transport undertaking.

2. For the purpose of this Convention the expression 'international carriage' means any carriage in which, according to the contract made by the parties, the place of departure and the place of destination, whether or not there be a break in the carriage or a transhipment, are situated either within the territories of two High Contracting Parties, or within the territory of a single High Contracting party, if there is an agreed stopping place within a territory subject to the sovereignty, suzerainty, mandate or authority of another Power, even though that Power is not a party to this convention. A carriage without such an agreed stopping place between territories subject to the sovereignty, suzerainty, mandate or authority of the same High Contracting Party is not deemed to be international for the purposes of this Convention.

3. A carriage to be performed by several successive air carriers is deemed, for the purposes of this convention, to be one undivided carriage, if it has been regarded by the parties as a single operation, whether it had been agreed upon under the form of a single contract or of a series of contracts, and it does not lose its international character merely because one contract or a series of contracts is to be performed entirely within a territory subject to the sovereignty, suzerainty, mandate or authority of the same High Contracting Party.

### ARTICLE 2

1. This Convention applies to carriage performed by the State or by legally constituted public bodies provided it falls within the conditions laid down in Article I.

2. This Convention does not apply to carriage performed under the terms of any international postal Convention.

## CHAPTER II

### DOCUMENTS OF CARRIAGE

### SECTION 1— PASSENGER TICKET

#### ARTICLE 3 [Omitted].

### SECTION 2 — LUGGAGE TICKET

#### ARTICLE 4 [Omitted].

### SECTION 3 — AIR CONSIGNMENT NOTE

#### ARTICLE 5

1. Every carrier of goods has the right to require the consignor to make out and over to him a document called an 'air consignment note'; every consignor has the right to require the carrier to accept this document.

2. The absence, irregularity or loss of this document does not affect the existence or the validity of the contract of carriage which shall, subject to the provisions of Article 9, be none the less governed by the rules of this Convention.

#### ARTICLE 6

1. The air consignment note shall be made out by the consignor in three original parts and be handed over with the goods.

2. The first part shall be marked 'for the carrier,' and shall be signed by the consignor. The second part shall be marked 'for the consignee', it shall be signed by the consignor and by the carrier and shall accompany the goods. The third part shall be signed by the carrier and handed by him to the consignor after the goods have been accepted.

3. The carrier shall sign on acceptance of the goods.

4. The signature of the carrier may be stamped; that of the consignor may be printed or stamped.

5. If, at the request of the consignor, the carrier makes out the air consignment note, he shall be deemed, subject to proof to the contrary, to have done so on behalf of the consignor.

## ARTICLE 7

The carrier of goods has the right to require the consignor to make out separate consignment notes when there is more than one package.

## ARTICLE 8

The air consignment note shall contain the following particulars:

(a) The place and date of its execution;
(b) The place of departure and of destination;
(c) The agreed stopping places, provided that the carrier may reserve the right to alter the stopping places in case of necessity, and that if he exercises that right the alteration shall not have the affect of depriving the carriage of its international character;
(d) The name and address of the consignor;
(e) The name and address of the first carrier;
(f) The name and address of the consignee, if the case so requires;
(g) The nature of the goods;
(h) The number of the packages, the method of packing and the particular marks or numbers upon them;
(i) The weight, the quantity and the volume or dimensions of the goods;
(j) The apparent condition of the goods and of the packing;
(k) The freight, if it has been agreed upon, the date and place of payment, and the person who is to pay it;
(l) If the goods are sent for payment on delivery, the price of the goods, and, if the case so requires, the amount of the expenses incurred;
(m) The amount of the value declared in accordance with Article 22 (2);
(n) The number of parts of the air consignment note;
(o) The document handed to the carrier to accompany the air consignment note;
(p) The time fixed for the completion of the carriage and a brief note of the route to be followed, if these matters have been agreed upon;
(q) A statement that the carriage is subject to the rules relating to liability established by this Convention.

## ARTICLE 9

If the carrier accepts goods without an air consignment note having been made out, or if the air consignment note does not contain all the particulars set out in Article 8 (a) to (i) inclusive and (q), the carrier shall not be entitled to avail himself of the provisions of this Convention which exclude or limit his liability.

## ARTICLE 10

1. The consignor is responsible for the correctness of the particulars and statements relating to the goods which he inserts in the air consignment note.

2. The consignor will be liable for all damage suffered by the carrier or any other person by reason of the irregularity, incorrectness or incompleteness of the said particulars and statements.

## Article 11

1. The air consignment note is *prima facie* evidence of the conclusion of the contract, of the receipt of the goods and of the conditions of carriage.

2. The statements in the air consignment note relating to the weight, dimensions and packing of the goods, as well as those relating to the number of packages, are *prima facie* evidence of the facts stated; those relating to the quantity, volume and condition of the goods do not constitute evidence against the carrier except so far as they both have been, and are stated in the air consignment note to have been, checked by him in the presence of the consignor, or relate to the apparent condition of the goods.

## Article 12

1. Subject to his liability to carry out all his obligations under the contract of carriage, the consignor has the right to dispose of the goods by withdrawing them at the aerodrome of departure or destination, or by stopping them in the course of the journey on any landing, or by calling for them to be delivered at the place of destination or in the course of the journey to a person other than the consignee named in the air consignment note, or by requiring them to be returned to the aerodrome of departure. He must not exercise this right of disposition in such a way as to prejudice the carrier or other consignors and he must repay any expenses occasioned by the exercise of this right.

2. If it is impossible to carry out the orders of the consignor the carrier must so inform him forthwith.

3. If the carrier obeys the orders of the consignor for the disposition of the goods without requiring the production of the part of the air consignment note delivered to the latter, he will be liable, without prejudice to his right of recovery from the consignor, for any damage which may be caused thereby to any person who is lawfully in possession of that part of the air consignment note.

4. The right conferred on the consignor ceases at the moment when that of the consignee begins in accordance with Article 13. Nevertheless, if the consignee declines to accept the consignment note or the goods, or if he cannot be communicated with, the consignor resumes his right of disposition.

## Article 13

1. Except in the circumstances set out in the preceding Article, the consignee is entitled, on arrival of the goods at the place of destination, to require the carrier to hand over to him the air consignment note and to deliver the goods to him, on payment of the charges due and on complying with the conditions of carriage set out in the air consignment note.

2. Unless it is otherwise agreed, it is the duty of the carrier to give notice to the consignee as soon as the goods arrive.

3. If the carrier admits the loss of the goods have not arrived at the expiration of seven days after date on which they ought to have arrived, the consignee is entitled to put into force against the carrier the rights which flow from the contract of carriage.

### ARTICLE 14

The consignor and the consignee can respectively enforce all the rights given them by Articles 12 and 13, each in his own name, whether he is acting in his own interest or in the interest of another, provided that he carries out the obligations imposed by the contract.

### ARTICLE 15

1. Articles 12, 13 and 14 do not affect either the relations of the consignor or the consignee with each other or the mutual relations of third parties whose rights are derived either from the consignor or from the consignee.

2. The provisions of Articles 12, 13 and 14 can only be varied by express provision in the air consignment note.

### ARTICLE 16

1. The consignor must furnish such information and attach to the air consignment note such documents as are necessary to meet the formalities of customs, octroi or police before the goods can be delivered to the consignee. The consignor is liable to the carrier for any damage occasioned by the absence, insufficiency or irregularity of any such information or documents, unless the damage is due to the fault of the carrier or his agents.

2. The carrier is under no obligation to enquire into the correctness or sufficiency of such information or documents.

## CHAPTER III

## LIABILITY OF THE CARRIER

### ARTICLE 17

The carrier is liable for damage sustained in the event of the death or wounding of a passenger or any other bodily injury suffered by a passenger, if the accident which caused the damage so sustained took place on board the aircraft or in the course of any of the operations of embarking or disembarking.

## ARTICLE 18

1. The carrier is liable for damage sustained in the event of the destruction or loss of, or of damage to, any registered luggage or any goods, if the occurrence which caused the damage so sustained took place during the carriage by air.

2. The carriage by air within the meaning for the preceding paragraph comprises the period during which the luggage or goods are in charge of the carrier, whether in an aerodrome or on board an aircraft, or, in the case of a landing outside an aerodrome, in any place whatsoever.

3. The period of the carriage by air does not extend to any carriage by land, by sea or by river performed outside an aerodrome. If, however, such a carriage takes place in the performance of a contract for carriage by air, for the purpose of loading, delivery or trans-shipment, any damage is presumed, subject to proof to the contrary, to have been the result of an event which took place during the carriage by air.

## ARTICLE 19

The carrier is liable for damage occasioned by delay in the carriage by air of passengers, luggage or goods.

## ARTICLE 20

1. The carrier is not liable if he proves that he and his agents have taken all necessary measures to avoid the damage or that it was impossible for him or them to take such measures.

2. In the carriage of goods and luggage the carrier is not liable if he proves that the damage was occasioned by negligent pilotage or negligence in the handling of the aircraft or in navigation and that, in all other respects, he and his agents have taken all necessary measures to avoid the damage.

## ARTICLE 21

If the carrier proves that the damage was caused by or contributed to by the negligence of the injured person the court may, in accordance with the provisions of its own law, exonerate the carrier wholly or partly from his liability.

## ARTICLE 22

1. In the carriage of passengers the liability of the carrier for each passenger is limited to the sum of 125,000 francs. Where, in accordance with the law of the Court seised of the case, damages may be awarded in the form of periodical payments, the equivalent capital value of the said payment shall not exceed 125,000 francs. Nevertheless, by special contract, the carrier and the passenger may agree to a higher limit of liability.

2. In the carriage of registered luggage and of goods, the liability of the carrier is limited to a sum of 250 francs per kilogram, unless the consignor has made, at the time when the package was handed over to the carrier, a special declaration of the value at delivery and has paid a supplementary sum if the case so requires. In that case the carrier will be liable to pay a sum not exceeding the declared sum, unless he proves that the sum is greater than the actual value to the consignor at delivery.

3. As regards objects of which the passenger takes charge himself the liability of the carrier is limited to 5000 francs per passenger.

4. The sums mentioned above shall be deemed to refer to the French franc consisting of 65 1/2 milligrams gold of millesimal fineness 900. These sums may be converted into any national currency in round figures.

## Article 23

Any provision tending to relieve the carrier of liability or to fix a lower limit than that which is laid down in this convention shall be null and void, but the nullity of any such provision does not involve the nullity of the whole contract, which shall remain subject to the provisions of this Convention.

## Article 24

1. In the cases covered by Articles 18 and 19 any action for damages, however founded, can only be brought subject to the conditions and limits set out in this Convention.

2. In the cases covered by Article 17 the provisions of the preceding paragraph also apply, without prejudice to the questions as to who are the persons who have the right to bring suit and what are their respective rights.

## Article 25

1. The carrier shall not be entitled to avail himself of the provisions of this Convention which exclude or limit his liability, if the damage is caused by his wilful misconduct or by such default on his part as, in accordance with the law of the Court seised of the case, is considered to be equivalent to wilful misconduct.

2. Similarly the carrier shall not be entitled to avail himself of the said provisions, if the damage is caused as aforesaid by any agent of the carrier acting within the scope of his employment.

## Article 26

1. Receipt by the person entitled to delivery of luggage or goods without complaint is *prima facie* evidence that the same have been delivered in good condition and in accordance with the document of carriage.

2. In the case of damage, the person entitled to delivery must complain to the carrier forthwith after the discovery of the damage, and, at the latest, within three days from the date of receipt in the case of luggage and seven days from the date of receipt in the case of goods. In the case of delay the complaint must be made at the latest within fourteen days from the date on which the luggage or goods have been placed at his disposal.

3. Every complaint must be made in writing upon the document of carriage or by separate notice in writing despatched within the times aforesaid.

4. Failing complaint within the times aforesaid, no action shall lie against the carrier, save in the case of fraud on his part.

## ARTICLE 27

In the case of the death of the person liable, an action for damages lies in accordance with the terms of this Convention against those legally representing his estate.

## ARTICLE 28

1. An action for damages must be brought, at the option of the plaintiff, in the territory of one of the High contracting Parties, either before the Court having jurisdiction where the carrier is ordinarily resident, or has his principal place of business, or has an establishment by which the contract has been made or before the Court having jurisdiction at the place of destination.

2. Questions of procedure shall be governed by the law of the Court seised of the case.

## ARTICLE 29

1. The right to damages shall be extinguished if an action is not brought within two years, reckoned from the date of arrival at the destination, or from the date on which the aircraft ought to have arrived, or from the date on which the carriage stopped.

2. The method of calculating the period of limitation shall be determined by the law of the court seised of the case.

## ARTICLE 30

1. In the case of carriage to be performed by various successive carriers and falling within the definition set out in the third paragraph of Article I, each carrier who accepts passengers, luggage or goods is subjected to the rules set out in this Convention, and is deemed to be one of the contracting parties to the contract of carriage in so far as the contract deals with that part of the carriage which is performed under his supervision.

2. In the case of carriage of this nature, the passenger or his representative can take action only against the carrier who performed the carriage during which the accident or the delay occurred, save in the case where, by express agreement, the first carrier has assumed liability for the whole journey.

3. As regards luggage or goods, the passenger or consignor will have a right of action against the first carrier, and the passenger or consignee who is entitled to delivery will have a right of action against the last carrier, and further, each may take action against the carrier who performed the carriage during which the destruction, loss, damage or delay took place. These carriers will be jointly and severally liable to the passenger or to the consignor or consignee.

## CHAPTER IV

### Provisions to Combined Carriage

### Article 31

1. In the case of combined carriage performed partly by air and partly by any other mode of carriage, the provisions of the Convention apply only to the carriage by air, provided that the carriage by air falls within the terms of Article 1.

2. Nothing in this Convention shall prevent the parties in the case of combined carriage from inserting in the document of air carriage conditions relating to other modes of carriage, provided that the provisions of this Convention are observed as regards the carriage by air.

## CHAPTER V

### General and Final Provisions

### Article 32

Any clause contained in the contract and all special agreements entered into before the damage occurred by which the parties purport to infringe the rules laid down by this Convention, whether by deciding the law to be applied, or by altering the rules as to jurisdiction, shall be null and void. Nevertheless for the carriage of goods arbitration clauses are allowed, subject to this Convention, if the arbitration is to take place within one of the jurisdictions referred to in the first paragraph of Article 28.

### Article 33

Nothing contained in this Convention shall prevent the carrier either from refusing to enter into any contract of carriage, or from making regulations which do not conflict with the provisions of this Convention.

## ARTICLE 34

This Convention does not apply to international carriage by air performed by way of experimental trial by air navigation undertakings with the view to the establishment of a regular line of air navigation, nor does it apply to carriage performed in extraordinary circumstances outside the normal scope of an air carrier's business.

## ARTICLE 35

The expression 'days' when used in this Convention means current days not working days.

## ARTICLES 36-41 [OMITTED].

# CONVENTION PROVIDING A UNIFORM LAW FOR BILLS OF EXCHANGE AND PROMISSORY NOTES, GENEVA, 1930

ARTICLES I - XI [Omitted].

## ANNEX I

## UNIFORM LAW ON BILLS OF EXCHANGE AND PROMISSORY NOTES

## TITLE I

*Bills of Exchange*

### CHAPTER I.— ISSUE AND FORM OF A BILL OF EXCHANGE

### ARTICLE 1

A bill of exchange contains:

1. The term 'bill of exchange' inserted in the body of the instrument and expressed in the language employed in drawing up the instrument;
2. An unconditional order to pay a determinate sum of money;
3. The name of the person who is to pay (drawee);
4. A statement of the time of payment;
5. A statement of the place where payment is to be made;
6. The name of the person to whom or to whose order payment is to be made;
7. A statement of the date and of the place where the bill is issued;
8. The signature of the person who issues the bill (drawer).

### ARTICLE 2

An instrument in which any of the requirements mentioned in the preceding Article is wanting is invalid as a bill of exchange, except in the cases specified in the following paragraphs:

A bill of exchange in which the time of payment is not specified is deemed to be payable at sight.

In default of special mention, the place specified beside the name of the drawee is deemed to be the place of payment, and at the same time the place of the domicile of the drawee.

A bill of exchange which does not mention the place of its issue is deemed to have been drawn in the place mentioned beside the name of the drawer.

## ARTICLE 3

A bill of exchang may be drawn payable to drawer's order.

It may be drawn on the drawer himself.

It may be drawn for account of a third person.

## ARTICLE 4

A bill of exchange may be payable at the domicile of a third person either in the locality where the drawee has his domicile or in another locality.

## ARTICLE 5

When a bill of exchange is payable at sight, or at a fixed period after sight, the drawer may stipulate that the sum payable shall bear interest. In the case of any other bill of exchange, this stipulation is deemed not to be written *(non écrite)*.

The rate of interest must be specified in the bill; in default of such specification, the stipulation shall be deemed not to be written (*non écrite*).

Interest runs from the date of the bill of exchange, unless some other date is specified.

## ARTICLE 6

When the sum payable by a bill of exchange is expressed in words and also in figures, and there is a discrepancy between the two, the sum denoted by the words is the amount payable. Where the sum payable by a bill of exchange is expressed more than once in words or more than once in figues, and there is a discrepancy, the smaller sum is the sum payable.

## ARTICLE 7

If a bill of exchange bears signatures of persons incapable of binding themselves by a bill of exchange, or forged signatures, or signatures of fictitious persons, or signatures which for any other reason cannot bind the persons who signed the bill of exchange or on whose behalf it was signed, the obligations of the other persons who signed it are none the less valid.

## ARTICLE 8

Whosoever puts his signature on a bill of exchange as representing a person for whom he had no power to act is bound himself as a party to the bill and, if he pays, has the same rights as the person for whom he purported to act. The same rule applies to a representative who has exceeded his powers.

## ARTICLE 9

The drawer guarantees both acceptance and payment.

He may release himself from guaranteeing acceptance; every stipulation by which he releases himself from the guarantee of payment is deemed not to be written (*non écrite*).

### ARTICLE 10

If a bill of exchange, which was incomplete when issued, has been completed otherwise than in accordance with the agreements entered into, the non-observance of such agreements may not be set up against the holder unless he has acquired the bill of exchange in bad faith or, in acquiring it, has been guilty of gross negligence.

## CHAPTER II — ENDORSEMENT

### ARTICLE 11

Every bill of exchange, even if not expressly drawn to order, may be transferred by means of endorsement.

When the drawer has inserted in a bill of exchange the words 'not to order' or an equivalent expression, the instrument can only be transferred according to the form, and with the effects of an ordinary assignment.

The bill may be endorsed even in favour of the drawee, whether he has accepted or not, or of the drawer, or of any other party to the bill. These persons may re-endorse the bill.

### ARTICLE 12

An endorsement must be unconditional. Any condition to which it is made subject is deemed not to be written (*non écrite*).

A partial endorsement is null and void.

An endorsement 'to bearer' is equivalent to an endorsement in blank.

### ARTICLE 13

An endorsement must be written on the bill of exchange or on a slip affixed thereto (*allonge*). It must be signed by the endorser.

The endorsement may leave the beneficiary unspecified or may consist simply of the signature of the endorser (endorsement in blank). In the latter case, the endorsement, to be valid, must be written on the back of the bill of exchang or on the slip attached thereto (*allonge*).

### ARTICLE 14

An endorsement transfers all the rights arising out of a bill of exchange.

If the endorsement is in blank, the holder may:

1. Fill up the blank either with his own name or with the name of some other person;
2. Re-endorse the bill in blank, or to some other person;
3. Transfer the bill to a third prson without filling up the blank , and without endorsing it.

## Article 15

In the absence of any contrary stipulation, the endorser guarantees acceptance and payment. He may prohibit any further endorsement; in this case, he gives no guarantee to the persons to whom the bill is subsequently endorsed.

## Article 16

The possessor of a bill of exchange is deemed to be the lawful holder if he establishes his title to the bill through an uninterrupted series of endorsements, even if the last endorsement is in blank. In this connection, cancelled endorsements are deemed not to be written (*non écrits*). When an endorsement in blank is followed by another endorsement, the person who signed this last endorsement is deemed to have acquired the bill by the endorsement in blank.

Where a person has been dispossessed of a bill of exchanged, in any manner whatsoever, the holder who establishes his right thereto in the manner mentioned in the preceding paragraph is not bound to give up the bill unless he has acquired it in bad faith, or unless in acquiring it he has been guilty of gross negligence.

## Article 17

Persons sued on a bill of exchange cannot set up against the holder defences founded on their personal relations with the drawer or with previous holders, unless the holder, in acquiring the bill, has knowingly acted to the detriment of the debtor.

## Article 18

When an endorsement contains the statements 'value in collection' ('*valeur en recouvrement*'), 'for collection' ('*pour encaissement*'), 'by procuration' ('*par procuration*') or any other phrase implying a simple mandate, the holder may exercise all rights arising out of the bill of exchange, but he can only endorse it in his capacity as agent.

In this case, the parties liable can only set up against the holder defences which could be set up against the endorser.

The mandate contained in an endorsement by procuration does not terminate by reason of the death of the party giving the mandate or by reason of his becoming legally incapable.

### Article 19

When an endorsement contains the statements 'value in security' ('*valeur en garantie*'), 'value in pledge' ('*valeur en gage*'), or any other statement implying a pledge, the holder may exercise all the rights arising out of the bill of exchange, but an endorsement by him has the effects only of an endorsement by an agent.

The parties liable cannot set up against the holder defences founded on their personal relations with the endorser, unless the holder, in receiving the bill, has knowingly acted to the detriment of the debtor.

### Article 20

An endorsement after maturity has the same effects as an endorsement before maturity. Nevertheless, an endorsement after protest for non-payment, or after the expiration of the limit of time fixed for drawing up the protest, operates only as an ordinary assignment.

Failing proof to the contrary, an endorsement without date is deemed to have been placed on the bill before the expiration of the limit of time fixed for drawing up the protest.

## Chapter III — Acceptance

### Article 21

Until maturity, a bill of exchang may be presented to the drawee for acceptance at his domicile, either by the holder or by a person who is merely in possession of the bill.

### Article 22

In any bill of exchange, the drawer may stipulate that it shall be presented for acceptance with or without fixing a limit of time for presentment.

Except in the case of a bill payable at the address of a third party or in a locality other than that of the domicile of the drawee, or, except in the case of a bill drawn payable at a fixed period after sight, the drawer may prohibit presentment for acceptance.

He may also stipulate that presentment for acceptance shall not take place before a named date.

Unless the drawer has prohibited acceptance, every endorser may stipulate that the bill shall be presented for acceptance, with or without fixing a limit of time for presentment.

### Article 23

Bills of exchange payable at a fixed period after sight must be presented for acceptance within one year of their date. The drawer may abridge or extend this period. These periods may be abridged by the endorsers.

## Article 24

The drawee may demand that a bill shall be presented to him a second time on the day after the first presentment. Parties interested are not allowed to set up that this demand has not been complied with unless this request is mentioned in the protest.

The holder is not obliged to surrender to the drawee a bill presented for acceptance.

## Article 25

An acceptance is written on the bill of exchange. It is expressed by the word 'accepted' or any other equivalent term. It is signed by the drawee. The simple signature of the drawee on the face of the bill constitutes an acceptance.

When the bill is payable at a certain time after sight, or when it must be presented for acceptance within a certain limit of time in accordance with a special stipulation, the acceptance must be dated as of the day when the acceptance is given, unless the holder requires it shall be dated as of the day of presentment. If it is undated, the holder, in order to preserve his right of recourse against the endorsers and the drawer, must authenticate the omission by a protest drawn up within the proper time.

## Article 26

An acceptance is unconditional, but the drawee may restrict it to part of the sum payable.

Every other modification introduced by an acceptance into the tenor of the bill of exchange operates as a refusal to accept. Nevertheless, the acceptor is bound according to the terms of his acceptance.

## Article 27

When the drawer of a bill has indicated a place of payment other than the domicile of the drawee without specifying a third party at whose address payment must be made, the drawee may name such third party at the time of acceptance. In default of this indication, the acceptor is deemed to have undertaken to pay the bill himself at the place of payment.

If a bill is payable at the domicile of the drawee, the latter may in his acceptance indicate an address in the same place where payment is to be made.

## Article 28

By accepting, the drawee undertakes to pay the bill of exchange at its maturity.

In default of payment, the holder, even if he is the drawer, has a direct action on the bill of exchange against the acceptor for all that can be demanded in accordance with Articles 48 and 49.

### Article 29

Where the drawee who has put his acceptance on a bill has cancelled it before restoring the bill, acceptance is deemed to be refused. Failing proof to the contrary, the cancellation is deemed to have taken place before the bill was restored.

Nevertheless, if the drawee has notified his acceptance in writing to the holder or to any party who has signed the bill, he is liable to such parties according to the terms of his acceptance.

## Chapter IV — '*Avals*'

### Article 30

Payment of a bill of exchange may be guaranteed by an '*aval*' as to the whole or part of its amount.

This guarantee may be given by a third person or even by a person who has signed as a party to the bill.

### Article 31

The '*aval*' is given either on the bill itself or on an '*allonge*'.

It is expressed by the words 'good as *aval*' ('*bon pour aval*') or by any other equivalent formula. It is signed by the giver of the '*aval*'.

It is deemed to be constituted by the mere signature of the giver of the '*aval*' placed on the face of the bill, except in the case of the signature of the drawee or of the drawer.

An '*aval*' must specirfy for whose account it is given. In default of this it is deemed to be given for the drawer.

### Article 32

The giver of an '*aval*' is bound in the same manner as the person for whom he has become guarantor.

His undertaking is valid even when the liability which he has guaranteed is inoperative for any reason other than defect of form.

He has, when he pays a bill of exchange, the rights arising out of the bill of exchange against the person guaranteed and against those who are liable to the latter on the bill of exchange.

## Chapter V — Maturity

### Article 33

A bill of exchange may be drawn payable:

At sight;
At a fixed period after sight;
At a fixed period after date;
At a fixed date.

Bills of exchange at other maturities or payable by instalments are null and void.

## ARTICLE 34

A bill of exchange at sight is payable on presentment. It must ve presented for payment within a year of its date. The drawer may abridge or extend this period. These periods may be abridged by the endorsers.

The drawer may prescribe that a bill of exchange payable at sight must not be presented for payment before a named date. In this case, the period for presentation begins from the said date.

## ARTICLE 35

The maturity of a bill of exchange payable at a fixed period after sight is determined either by the date of the acceptance or by the date of the protest.

In the absence of the protest, an undated acceptance is deemed, so far as regards the acceptor, to have been given on the last day of the limit of time for presentment for acceptance.

## ARTICLE 36

Where a bill of exchange is drawn at one or more months after date or after sight, the bill matures on the corresponding date of the month when payment must be made. If there be no corresponding date, the bill maturs onthe last day of this month.

When a bill of exchange is drawn at one or more months and a-half after date or sight, entire months must first be calculated.

If the maturity is fixed at the commencement, in the middle (mid-January or mid-February, etc.,) or at the end of the month, the first, fifteenth or last day of the month is to be understood.

The expressions 'eight days' or 'fifteen days' indicate not one or two weeks, but a period of eight or fifteen actual days.

The expression 'half-month' means a period of fifteen days.

## ARTICLE 37

When a bill of exchange is payable on a fixed day in a place where the calendar is different from the calendar in the place of issue, the day of maturity is deemed to be fixed according to the calendar of the place of payment.

When a bill of exchange drawn between two places having different calendars is payable at a fixed period after date, the day of issue is referred to the corresponding day of the calendar in the place of payment, and the maturity is fixed accordingly.

The time for presenting bills of exchange is calculated in accordance with the rules of the preceding paragraph.

These rules do not apply if a stipulation in the bill or even the simple terms of the instrument indicate an intention to adopt some different rule.

## Chapter VI — Payment

### Article 38

The holder of a bill of exchange payable on a fixed day or at a fixed period after date or after sight must present the bill for payment either on the day on which it is payable or on one of the two business days which follow.

The presentment of a bill of exchange at a clearing-house is equivalent to a presentment for payment.

### Article 39

The drawee who pays a bill of exchange may require that it shall be given up to him receipted by the holder.

The holder may not refuse partial payment.

In case of partial payment the drawee may require that mention of this payment shall be made on the bill, and that a receipt therefor shall be given to him.

### Article 40

The holder of a bill of exchange cannot be compelled to receive a payment thereof before maturity.

The drawee who pays before maturity does so at his own risk and peril. He who pays at maturity is validly discharged, unless he has been guilty of fraud or gross negligence. He is bound to verify the regularity of the series of endorsements, but not the signature of the endorsers.

### Article 41

When a bill of exchange is drawn payable in a currency which is not that of the place of payment, the sum payable may be paid in the currency of the country, according to its value on the date of maturity. If the debtor is in default, the holder may at his option demand that the amount of the bill be paid in the currency of the country according to the rate on the day of maturity or the day of payment.

The usages of the place of payment determine the value of foreign currency. Nevertheless, the drawer may stipulate that the sum payable shall be calculated according to a rate expressed in the bill.

The foregoing rules shall not apply to the case in which the drawer has stipulated that payment must be made in a certain specified currency (stipulation for effective payment in foreign currency).

If the amount of the bill of exchange is specified in a currency having the same denomination, but a different value in the country of issue and the country of payment, reference is deemed to be made to the currency of the place of payment.

## ARTICLE 42

When a bill of exchang e is not presented for payment within the limit of time fixed by Article 38, every debtor is authorised to deposit the amount with the competent authority at the charge, risk and peril of the holder.

# CHAPTER VII. — RECOURSE FOR NON-AACCEPTANCE OR NON-PAYMENT

## ARTICLE 43

The holder may exercise his right of recourse against the endorsers, the drawer and the other parties liable:

At maturity:

If payment has not been made;

Even before maturity;

1. If there has been total or partial refusal to accept;
2. In the event of the bankruptcy (*faillite*) of the drawee, whether he has accepted or not, or in the event of a stoppage of payment on his part, even when not declared by a judgment, or wher execution has been levied against his goods without result;
3. In the event of the bankruptcy (*faillite*) of the drawer of a non-acceptable bill.

## ARTICLE 44

Default of acceptance or on payment must be evidenced by an authentic act (protest for non-acceptance or non-payment).

Protest for non-acceptance must be made within the limit of time fixed for presentment for acceptance. If in the case contemplated by Article 24, paragraph I, the first presentment takes place on the last day of that time, the protest may nevertheless be drawn up on the next day.

Protest for non-payment of a bill of exchange payable on a fixed day or at a fixed period after date or sight must be made on one of the two business days following the day on which the bill is payable. In the case of a bill payable at sight, the protest must be drawn up under the conditions specified in the foregoing paragraph for the drawing up of a protest for non-acceptance.

Protest for non-acceptance dispenses with presentment for payment and protest for non-payment.

If there is a stoppage of payment on the part of the drawee, whether he has accepted or not, or if execution has been levied against his goods without result, the holder cannot exercise his right of recourse until after presentment of the bill to the drawee for payment and after the protest has been drawn up.

If the drawee, whether he accepted or not, is declared bankrupt (*faillite déclarée*), or in the event of the declared bankruptcy of the drawer of a non-acceptable bill, the production of the judgment declaring the bankruptcy suffices to enable the holder to exercise his right of recourse.

## Article 45

The holder must give notice of non-acceptance or non-payment to his endorser and to the drawer within the four business days which follow the day for protest or, in case of a stipulation '*retour sans frais*', the day for presentment. Every endorser must, within the two business days following the day on which he receives notice, notify his endorser of the notice he has received, mentioning the names and addresses of those who have given the previous notices, and so on through the series until the drawer is reached. The periods mentioned above run from the receipt of the preceding notice.

When, in conformity with the preceding paragraph, notice is given to a person who has signed a bill of exchange, the same notice must be given within the same limit of time to his *avaliseur*.

Where an endorser either has not specified his address or has specified it in an illegible manner, it is sufficient that notice should be given to the preceding endorser.

A person who must give notice may give it in any form whatever, even by simply returning the bill of exchange.

He must prove that he has given notice within the time allowed. this time-limit shall be regarded as having been observed if a letter giving the notice has been posted within the prescribed time.

A person who does not give notice within the limit of time mentioned above does not forfeit his rights. He is responsible for the injury, if any, caused by his negligence, but the damages shall not exceed the amount of the bill of exchange.

## Article 46

The drawer, an endorser, or a person guaranteeing payment by *aval* (*avaliseur*) may, by the stipulation '*retour sans frais*', '*sans protet*', or any other equivalent expression written on the instrument and signed, release the holder from having a protest of non-acceptance or non-payment drawn up in order to excercise his right of recourse.

This stipulation does not release the holder from presenting the bill within the prescribed time, or from the notices he has to give. The burden of proving the non-observance of the limits of time lies on the person who seeks to set it up against the holder.

If the stipulation is written by the drawer, it is operative in respect of all persons who have signed the bill; if it is written by an endorser or an *avaliseur,* it is operative only in respect of such endorser or *avaliseur.* If, in spite of the stipulation written by the drawer, the holder has the protest drawn up, he must bear the expenses thereof. When the stipulation emanates from an endorser or *avaliseur,* the costs of the protest, if one is drawn up, may be recovered from all the persons who have signed the bill.

## Article 47

All drawers, acceptors, endorsers or guarantors by *aval* of a bill of exchange are jointly and severally liabler to the holder.

The holder has the right of proceeding against all these persons individually or collectively without being required to observe the order in which they have become bound.

The same right is possessed by any person signing the bill who has taken it up and paid it.

Proceedings against one of the parties liable do not prevent proceedings against the others, even though they may be subsequent to the party first proceeded against.

## ARTICLE 48

The holder may recover from the person against whom he exercises his right of recourse:

1. The amount of the unaccepted or unpaid bill of exchange with interest, if interest has been stipulated for;
2. Interest at the rate of 6 per cent from the date of maturity;
3. The expenses of protest and of the notices given as well as other expenses.

If the right of recourse is exercised before maturity, the amount of the bill shall be subject to a discount. This discount shall be calculated according to the official rate of discount (bank-rate) ruling on the date when recourse is exercised at the place of domicile of the holder.

## ARTICLE 49

A party who takes up and pays a bill of exchange can recover from the parties liable to him:

1. The entire sum which he has paid;
2. Interest on the said sum calculated at the rate of 6 per cent, starting from the day when he made payment;
3. Any expenses which he has incurred.

## ARTICLE 50

Every party liable against whom a right of recourse is or may be exercised, can require against payment, that the bill shall be given up to him with the protest and a receipted account.

Every endorser who has taken up and paid a bill of exchange may cancel his own endorsement and those of subsequent endorsers.

## ARTICLE 51

In the case of the exercise of the right of recourse after a partial acceptance, the party who pays the sum in respect of which the bill has not been accepted can require that this payment shall be specified on the bill and that he shall be given a receipt therefor. The holder must also give him a certified copy of the bill, together with the protest, in order to enable subsequent recourse to be exercised.

## ARTICLE 52

Every person having the right of recourse may, in the absence of agreement to the contrary, reimburse himself by means of a fresh bill (redraft) to be drawn at sight on one of the parties liable to him and payable at the domicile of that party.

The redraft includes, in addition to the sums mentioned in Articles 48 and 49, brokerage and the cost of stamping the redraft.

If the redraft is drawn by the holder, the sum payable is fixed according to the rate for a sight bill drawn at the place where the original bill was payable upon the party liable at the place of his domicile. If the redraft is drawn by an endorser, the sum payable is fixed according to the rate for a sight bill drawn at the place where the drawer of the redraft is domiciled upon the place of domicile of the party liable.

## ARTICLE 53

After the expiration of the limits of time fixed:

For the presentment of a bill of exchange drawn at sight or at a fixed period after sight;

For drawing up the protest for non-acceptance or non-payment;

For presentment for payment in the case of a stipulation *retour sans frais*,

the holder loses his rights of recourse against the endorsers, against the drawer and against the other parties liable, with the exception of the acceptor.

In default of presentment for acceptance within the limit of time stipulated by the drawer, the holder loses his right of recourse for non-payment, as well as for non-acceptance, unless it appears from the terms of the stipulation that the drawer only meant to release himself from the guarantee of acceptance.

If the stipulation for a limit of time for presentment is contained in an endorsement, the endorser alone can avail himself of it.

## ARTICLE 54

Should the presentment of the bill of exchange or the drawing up of the protest within the prescribed limits of time be prevented by an insurmountable obstacle (legal prohibition (*prescription légale*) by any State or other case of *vis major*), these limits of time shall be extended. The holder is bound to give notice without delay of the case of *vis major* to his endorser and to specify this notice, which he must date and sign, on the bill or on an *allonge*; in other respects the provisions of Article 45 shall apply.

When *vis major* has terminated, the holder must without delay present the bill of exchange for acceptance or payment and, if need be, draw up the protest.

If *vis major* continues to operate beyond thirty days after maturity, recourse may be exercised, and neither presentment nor the drawing up of a protest shall be necessary.

In the case of bills of exchange drawn at sight or at a fixed period after sight, the time-limit of thirty days shall run from the date on which the holder, even before the expiration of the time for presentment, has given notice of *vis major* to his endorser. In the case of bill sof exchange drawn at a certain time after sight, the above time-limit of thirty days shall be added to the period after sight specified in the bill of exchange.

Facts which are purely personal to the holder or to the person whom he has entrusted with the presentment of the bill or drawing up of the bill or drawing up of the protest are not deemed to constitute cases of *vis major*.

## CHAPTER VIII — INTERVENTION FOR HONOUR

### I. GENERAL PROVISIONS

#### ARTICLE 55

The drawer, an endorser, or a person giving an *aval* may specify a person who is to accept or pay in case of need.

A bill of exchange may, subject as hereinafter mentioned, be accepted or paid by a person who intervenes for the honour of any debtor against whom a right of recourse exists.

The person intervening may be a third party, even the drawee, or, save the acceptor, a party already liable on the bill of exchange.

The person intervening is bound to give, within two business days, notice of his intervetion to the party for whose honour he heas intervened. In default, he is responsible for the injury, if any, due to his negligence, but the damages shall not exceed the amount of the bill of exchange.

### 2. ACCEPTANCE BY INTERVENTION (FOR HONOUR)

#### ARTICLE 56

There may be acceptance by intervention in all cases where the holder has a right of recourse before maturity on a bill which is capable of acceptance.

When the bill of exchange indicates a person who is designated to accept or pay it in case of need at the place of payment, the holder may not exercise his rights of recourse before maturity against the person naming such referee in case of need and against subsequent signatories, unless he has presented the bill of exchange to the referee in case of need and until, if acceptance is refused by the latter, this refusal has been authenticated by a protest.

In other cases of intervention the holder may refuse an acceptance by intervention. Nevertheless, if he allows it, he loses his right of recourse before maturity against the person on whose behalf such acceptance was given and against subsequent signatories.

#### ARTICLE 57

Acceptance by intervention is specified on the bill of exchange. It is signed by the person intervening. It mentions the person for whose honour it has been given and, in default of such mention, the acceptance is deemed to have been given for the honour of the drawer.

#### ARTICLE 58

The acceptor by intervention is liable to the holder and to the endorsers, subsequent to the party for whose honour he intervened, in the same manner as such party.

Notwithstanding an acceptance by intervention, the party for whose honour it has been given and the parties liable to him may require the holder, in exchange for payment of the sum mentioned in Article 48, to deliver the bill, the protest, and a receipted account, if any.

### 3. Payment by Intervention

#### Article 59

Payment by intervention may take place in all cases where, either at maturity or before maturity, the holder has a right of recourse on the bill.

Payment must include the whole amount payable by the party for whose honour it is made.

It must be made at the latest on the day following the last day allowed for drawing up the protest for non-payment.

#### Article 60

If a bill of exchang has been accepted by persons intervening who are domiciled in the place of payment, or if persons domiciled therein have been named as referees in case of need, the holder must present the bill to all these persons and, if necessary, have a protest for non-payment drawn up at latest on the day following the last day allowed for drawing up the protest.

In default of protest within this limit of time, the party who has named the referee in case of need, or for whose account the bill has been accepted, and the subsequent endorsers are discharged.

#### Article 61

The holder who refuses payment by intervention loses his right of recourse against any persons who would have been discharged thereby.

#### Article 62

Payment by intervention must be authenticated by a receipt given on the bill of exchange mentioning the person for whose honour payment has been made. In default of such mention, payment is deemed to have been made for the honour of the drawer.

The bill of exchange and the protest, if any, must be given up to the person paying by intervention.

#### Article 63

The person paying by intervention acquires the rights arising out of the bill of exchange against the party for whose honour he has paid and against persons who are liable to the latter on the bill of exchange. Nevertheless, he cannot re-endorse the bill of exchange.

Endorsers subsequent to the party for whose honour payment has been made are discharged.

In case of competition for payment by intervention, the payment which effects the greater number of releases has the preference. Any person who, with a knowledge of the facts, intervenes in a manner contrary to this rule, loses his right of recourse against those who would have been discharged.

## CHAPTER IX — PARTS OF A SET, AND COPIES

### I. PARTS OF A SET

### ARTICLE 64

A bill of exchange can be drawn in a set of two or more identical parts.

These parts must be numbered in the body of the instrument itself; in default, each part is considered as a separate bill of exchange.

Every holder of a bill which does not specify that it has been drawn as a sole bill may, at his own expense, require the delivery of two or more parts. For this purpose he must apply to his immediate endorser, who is bound to assist him in proceeding against his own endorser, and so on in the series until the drawer is reached. The endorsers are bound to reproduce their endorsements on the new parts of the set.

### ARTICLE 65

Payment made on one part of a set operates as a discharge, even though there is no stipulation that this payment annuls the effect on the other parts. Nevertheless, the drawee is liable on each accepted part which he has not recovered.

An endorser who has transferred parts of a set to different persons, as well as subsequent endorsers, are liable on all the parts bearing their signature which have not been restored.

### ARTICLE 66

A party who has sent one part for acceptance must indicate on the other parts the name of the person in whose hands this part is to be found. That person is bound to give it up to the lawful holder of another part.

If he refuses, the holder cannot exercise his right of recourse until he has had a protest drawn us specifying:

1. That the part sent for acceptance has not been given up to him on his demand;
2. that acceptance or payment could not be obtained on another of the parts.

### 2. Copies

### Article 67

Every holder of a bill of exchange has the right to make copies of it. A copy must reproduce the original exactly, with the endorsements and all other statements to be found therein. It must specify where the copy ends. It may be endorsed and guaranteed by *aval* in the same manner and with the same effects as the original.

### Article 68

A copy must specify the person in possession of the original instrument. The latter is bound to hand over the said instrument to the lawful holder of the copy.

If he refuses, the holder may not exercise his right of recourse against the persons who have endorsed the copy or guaranteed it by *aval* until he has had a protest drawn up specifying that the original has not been given up to him on his demand.

Where the original instrument, after the last endorsement before the making of the copy contains a clause 'commencing from here an endorsement is only valid if made on the copy' or some equivalent formula, a subsequent endorsement on the original is null and void.

## Chapter X.—- Alterations

### Article 69

In case of alteration of the text of a bill of exchange, parties who have signed subsequent to the alteration are bound according to the terms of the altered text; parties who have signed before the alteration are bound according to the terms of the original text.

## CHAPTER XI. - LIMITATION OF ACTIONS

### Article 70

All actions arising out of a bill of exchange against the acceptor are barred after three years, reckoned from the date of maturity.

Actions by the holder against the endorsers and against the drawer are barred after one year from the date of a protest drawn up within proper time, or from the date of maturity where there is a stipulation *retour sans frais*.

Actions by endorsers against each other and against the drawer are barred after six months, reckoned from the day when the endorser took up and paid the bill or from the day when he himself was sued.

## ARTICLE 71

Interruption of the period of limitation is only effective against the person in respect of whom the period has been interrupted.

## CHAPTER XII. — GENERAL PROVISIONS

## ARTICLE 72

Payment of a bill of exchange which falls due on a legal holiday (*jour férié légal*) cannot be demanded until the next business day. So, too, all other proceedings relating to a bill of exchange, in particular presentment for acceptance and protest, can only be taken on a business day.

Where any of these proceedings must be taken within a certain limit of time the last day of which is a legal holiday (*jour férié légal*), the limit of time is extended until the first business day which follows the expiration of that time. Intermediate holidays (*jours fériés)* are included in computing limits of time.

## ARTICLE 73

Legal or contractual limits of time do not include the day on which the period commences.

## ARTICLE 74

No days of grace, whether legal or judicial, are permitted.

# TITLE II

# PROMISSORY NOTES

## ARTICLE 75

A promissory note contains:

1. The term 'promissory note' inserted in the body of the instrument and expressed in the language employed in drawing up the instrument;
2. An unconditional promise to pay a determinate sum of money;
3. A statement of the time of payment;
4. A statement of the place where payment is to be made;
5. The name of the person to whom or to whose order payment is to be made;
6. A statement of the date and of the place where the promissory note is issued;
7. The signature of the person who issues the instrument (maker).

## ARTICLE 76

An instrument in which any of the requirements mentioned in the preceding Article are wanting is invalid as a promissory note except in the cases specified in the following paragraphs.

A promissory note in which the time of payment is not specified is deemed to be payable at sight.

In default of special mention, the place where the instrument is made is deemed to be the place of payment and at the same time the place of the domicile of the maker.

A promissory note which does not mention the place of its issue is deemed to have been made in the place mentioned beside the name of the maker.

## ARTICLE 77

The following provisions relating to bills of exchange apply to promissory notes so far as they are not inconsistent with the nature of these instruments, viz:

Endorsement (Article 11 to 20);
Time of payment (Articles 33 to 37);
Payment (Articles 38 to 42);
Recourse in case of non-payment (Articles 43 to 50, 52 to 54);
Payment by intervention (Articles 55, 59 to 63);
Copies (Articles 67 and 68);
Alterations (Article 69);
Limitation of actions (Articles 70 and 71);
Holidays, computation of limits of time and prohibition of days of grace (Articles 72, 73 and 74).

The following provisions are also applicable to a promissory note: The provisions concerning a bill of exchange payable at the address of a third party or in a locality other than that of the domicile of the drawee (Articles 4 and 27): stipulation for interest (Article 5); discrepancies as regards the sum payable (Article 6); the consequences of signature under the conditions mentioned in Article 7, the consequences of signature by a person who acts without authority or who exceeds his authority (Article 8); and provisions concerning a bill of exchange in blank (Article 10).

The following provisions are also applicable to a promissory note: Provisions relating to guarantee by *aval* (Articles 30-32); in the case provided for in Article 31, last paragraph, if the *aval* does not specify on whose behalf it has been given, it is deemed to have been given on behalf of the maker of the promissory note.

## ARTICLE 78

The maker of a promissory note is bound in the same manner as an acceptor of a bill of exchange.

Promissory notes payable at a certain time after sight must be presented for the visa of the maker within the limits of time fixed by Article 23. The limit of time runs from the date of which marks the commencement of the period of time after sight.

## ANNEX II — ARTICLES 1-23 [OMITTED].

# CONVENTION ON THE LAW APPLICABLE TO INTERNATIONAL SALES OF GOODS, THE HAGUE, 1955

## ARTICLE PREMIER

This Convention shall apply to international sales of goods.

It shall not apply to sales of securities, to sales of ships and of registered boats or aircraft, or to sales upon judicial order or by way of execution. It shall apply to sales based on documents.

For the purposes of this Convention, contracts to deliver goods to be manufactured or produced shall be placed on the same footing as sales, provided the party who assumes delivery is to furnish the necessary raw materials for their manufacture or production.

The mere declaration of the parties, relative to the application of a law or the competence of a judge or arbitrator, shall not be sufficient to confer upon a sale the international character provided for in the first paragraph of this Article.

## ARTICLE 2

A sale shall be governed by the domestic law of the country designated by the Contracting Parties.

Such designation must be contained in an express clause, or unambiguously result from the the provisions of the contract.

Conditions affecting the consent of the parties to the law declared applicable shall be determined by such law.

## ARTICLE 3

In default of a law declared applicable by the parties under the conditions provided in the preceding Article, a sale shall be governed by the domestic law of the country in which the vendor has his habitual residence at the time when he receives the order. If the order is received by an establishment of the vendor, the sale shall be governed by the domestic law of the country in which the establishment is situated.

Nevertheless, a sale shall be governed by the domestic law of the country in which the purchaser has his habitaul residence, or in which he has the establishment that has given the order, if the order has been received in such country, whether by the vendor or by his representative, agent or commercial traveller.

In case of a sale at an exchange or at a public auction, the sale shall be governed by the domestic law of the country in which the exchange is situated or the auction takes place.

## ARTICLE 4

In the absence of an express clause to the contrary, the domestic law of the country in which inspection of goods delivered pursuant to a sale is to take place shall apply in respect of the form in which and the periods within which the inspection must take place, the notifications concerning the inspection and the measures to be taken in case of refusal of the goods.

## ARTICLE 5

This Convention shall not apply to:

1. The capacity of the parties;
2. The form of the contract;
3. The transfer of ownership, provided that the various obligations of the parties, and especially those relating to risks, shall be subject to the law applicable to the sale pursuant to this Convention;
4. The effects of the sale as regards all persons other than the parties.

## ARTICLE 6

In each of the Contracting States, the application of the law determined by this convention may be excluded on a ground of public policy.

## ARTICLE 7

The contracting States have agreed to incorporate the provisions of Articles 1-6 of this Convention in the national law of their respective countries.

## ARTICLES 8 - 12 [OMITTED].

# Hague Protocol to Amend the Convention for the Unification of Certian Rules Relating to International Carriage by Air signed at Warsaw of 12 October 1929 (The Hague Protocol) 1955

See Schedule I Carriage by Air Act 1961 for text of the Convention

## Convention on the Contract for the International Carriage of Goods by Road, Geneva, 1956

See Schedule Carriage of Goods by Road Act 1965 for text of the Convention

# CONVENTION ON THE RECOGNITION AND ENFORCEMENT OF FOREIGN ARBITRAL AWARDS, NEW YORK, 1958

## ARTICLE I

1. This Convention shall apply to the recognition and enforcement of arbitral awards made in the territory of a State other than the State where the recognition and enforcement of such awards are sought, and arising out of differences between persons, whether physical or legal. It shall also apply to arbitral awards not considered as domestic awards in the State where their recognition and enforcement are sought.

2. The term 'arbitral awards' shall include not only awards made by arbitrators appointed for each case but also those made by permanent arbitral bodies to which the parties have submitted.

3. When signing, ratifying or acceding to this convention, or notifying extension under Article X hereof, any State may on the basis of reciprocity declare that it will apply the Convention to the recognition and enforcement of awards made only in the territory of another Contracting State. It may also declare that it will apply the Convention only to differences arising out of legal relationships, whether contractual or not, which are considered as commercial under the national law of the State making such declaration.

## ARTICLE II

1. Each Contracting State shall recognize an agreement in writing under which the parties undertake to submit to arbitration all or any differences which have arisen or which may arise between them in respect of a defined legal relationship, whether contractual or not, concerning a subject matter capable of settlement by arbitration.

2. The term 'agreement in writing' shall include an arbitral clause in a contract or an arbitration agreement, signed by the parties or contained in an exchange of letters or telegrams.

3. The court of a Contracting State, when seised of an action in a matter in respect of which the parties have made an agreement within the meaning of this Article, at the request of one of the parties, refer the parties to arbitration, unless it finds that the said agreement is null and void, inoperative or incapable of being performed.

## ARTICLE III

Each Contracting State shall recognize arbitral awards as binding and enforce them in accordance with the rules of procedure of the territory where the award is relied upon, under the conditions laid down in the following Articles. There shall not be imposed substantially more onerous conditions or higher fees or charges on the recognition or enforcement of arbitral awards to which this Convention applies than are imposed on the recognition or enforcement of domestic arbitral awards.

## Article IV

1 To obtain the recognition and enforcement mentioned in the preceding Article, the party applying for recognition and enforcement shall, at the time of the application, supply:

(a) The duly authenticated original award or a duly certified copy thereof;

(b) The original agreement referred to in Article II or a duly certified copy thereof.

2 If the said award or agreement is not made in an official language of the country in which the award is relied upon, the party applying for recognition and enforcement of the award shall produce a translation of these documents into such language. The translation shall be certified by an official or sworn translator or by a diplomatic or consular agent.

## Article V

1 Recognition and enforcement of the award may be refused, at the request of the party against whom it is invoked, only if that party furnishes to the competent authority where the recognition and enforcement is sought, proof that:

(a) The parties to the agreement referred to in Article II were, under the law applicable to them, under some incapacity, or the said agreement is not valid under the law to which the parties have subjected it or, failing any indication thereon, under the law of the country where the award was made; or

(b) The party against whom the award is invoked was not given proper notice of the appointment of the arbitrator or of the arbitration proceedings or was otherwise unable to present his case; or

(c) The award deals with a difference not contemplated by or not falling within the terms of the submission to arbitration, or it contains decisions on matters beyond the scope of the submission to arbitration, provided that, if the decisions on matters submitted to arbitration can be separated from those not so submitted , that part of the award which contains decisions on matters submitted to arbitration may be recognized and enforced; or

(d) The composition of the arbitral authority or the arbitral procedure was not in accordance with the agreement of the parties, or, failing such agreement, was not in accordance with the law of the country where the arbitration took place; or

(e) The award has not yet become binding on the parties, or has been set aside or suspended by a competent authority of the country in which, or under the law of which, that award was made.

2 Recognition and enforcement of an arbitral award may also be refused if the competent authority in the country where recognition and enforcement is sought finds that:

(a) The subject matter of the difference is not capable of settlement by arbitration under the law of that country; or

(b) The recognition or enforcement of the award would be contrary to the public policy of that country.

## Articles VI-XVI [Omitted].

## Convention supplementary to the Warsaw Convention for the Unification of Certain Rules relating to International Carriage by Air performed by a Person other than the Contracting Carrier (Guadalajara) 1961

See Schedule Carriage by Air (Supplementary Provisions) Act 1962

# EUROPEAN CONVENTION ON INTERNATIONAL COMMERCIAL ARBITRATION, GENEVA, 1961

## ARTICLE I

### SCOPE OF THE CONVENTION

1. This Convention shall apply:
   (a) to arbitration agreements concluded for the purpose of settling disputes arising from international trade between physical or legal persons having, when concluding the agreement, their habitual place of residence or their seat in difference contracting states;
   (b) to arbitral procedures and awards based on agreements referred to in paragraph 1 a above.

2. For the purpose of this Convention,
   (a) the term 'arbitration agreement' shall mean either an arbitral clause in a contract or an arbitration agreement, the contract or arbitration agreement being signed by the parties, or contained in an exchange of letters, telegrams, or in a communication by teleprinter and, in relations between States whose laws do not require that an arbitration agreement be made in writing, any arbitration agreement concluded in the form authorized by these laws;
   (b) the term 'arbitration' shall mean not only settlement by arbitrators appointed for each case (*ad hoc* arbitration) but also by permanent arbitral institutions;
   (c) the term 'seat' shall mean the place of the situation of the establishment that has made the arbitration agreement.

## ARTICLE II

### RIGHT OF LEGAL PERSONS OF PUBLIC LAW TO RESORT TO ARBITRATION

1. In the cases referred to in Article I, paragraph 1, of this Convention, legal persons considered by the law which is applicable to them as 'legal persons of public law' have the right to conclude valid arbitration agreements.

2. On signing, ratifying or acceding to this convention any State shall be entitled to declare that it limits the above faculty to such conditions as may be stated in its declaration.

## ARTICLE III

### RIGHT OF FOREIGN NATIONALS TO BE DESIGNATED AS ARBITRATORS

In arbitration covered by this Convention, foreign nationals may be designated as arbitrators.

## ARTICLE IV

### ORGANIZATION OF THE ARBITRATION

1. The parties to an arbitration agreement shall be free to submit their disputes:
   - (a) to a permanet arbitral institution; in this case, the arbitration proceedings shall be held in conformity with the rules of the said institution;
   - (b) to an *ad hoc* arbitral procedure; in this case, they shall be free *inter alia*
     - (i) to appoint arbitrators or to establish means for their appointment in the event of an actual dispute;
     - (ii) to determine the place of arbitration; and
     - (iii) to lay down the procedure to be followed by the arbitrators.

2. Where the parties have agreed to submit any disputes to an ad hoc arbitration, and where within thirty days of the notification of the request for arbitration to the respondent one of the parties fails to appoint his arbitrator, the latter shall, unless otherwise provided, be appointed at the request of the other party by the President of the competent Chamber of Commerce of the country of the defaulting party's habitual place of residence or seat at the time of the introduction of the request for arbitration. This paragraph shall also apply to the replacement of the arbitrator(s) appointed by one of the parties or by the President of the Chamber of Commerce above referred to.

3. Where the parties have agreed to submit any disputes to an *ad hoc* arbitration by one or more arbitrators and the arbitration agreement contains no indication regarding the organization of the arbitration, as mentioned in paragraph 1 of this Article, the necessary steps shall be taken by the arbitrator(s) already appointed, unless the parties are able to agree thereon and without prejudice to the case referred to in in paragraph 2 above. Where the parties cannot agree on the appointment of the sole arbitrator or where the arbitrators appointed cannot agree on the measures to be taken, the claimant shall apply for the necessary action, where the place of arbitration has been agreed upon by the parties, at his option to the President of the Chamber of Commerce of the place of arbitration agreed upon or to the President of the competent Chamber of Commerce of the respondent's habitual place of residence or seat at the time of the introduction of the request for arbitration. Where such a place has not been agreed upon, the claimant shall be entitled at his option to apply for the necessary action either to the President of the competent Chamber of Commerce of the country of the respondent's habitual place of residence or seat at the time of the introduction of the request for arbitration, or to the Special Committee whose composition and procedure are specified in the Annex to this Convention. Where the claimant fails to exercise the rights given to him under this paragraph the respondent or the arbitrator(s) shall be entitled to do so.

4 When seised of a request the President or the Special Committee shall be entitled as need be:
   - (a) to appoint the sole arbitrator, presiding arbitrator, umpire, or referee;
   - (b) to replace the arbitrator(s) appointed under any procedure other than that referred to in paragraph 2 above;
   - (c) to determine the place of arbitration, provided that the arbitrator(s) may fix another place of arbitration:

(d) to establush directly or by reference to the rules and statutes of a permanent arbitral institution the rules of procedure to be followed by the arbitrator(s), provided that the arbitrators have not established these rules themselves in the absence of any agreement thereon between the parties.

5. Where the parties have agreed to submit their disputes to a permanent arbitral institution without determining the institution in question and cannot agree thereon, the claimant may request the determination of such institution in conformity with the procedure referred to in paragraph 3 above.

6. Where the arbitration agreement does not specify the mode of arbitration (arbitration by a permanent arbitral institution or an *ad hoc* arbitration) to which the parties have agreed to submit their dispute, and where the parties cannot agree thereon, the claimant shall be entitled to have recourse in this case to the procedure referred to in paragraph 3 above to determine thequestion. The President of the competent Chamber of Commerce or the Special Committee, shall be entitled either to refer the parties to a permanent arbitral institution or to request the parties to appoint their arbitrators within such time-limits as the President of the competent Chamber of Commerce or the Special Committee may have fixed and to agree within such time-limits on the necessary measures for the functioning of the arbitration. In the latter case, the provisions of paragraphs 2, 3 and 4 of this Article shall apply.

7. Where within a period of sixty days from the moment when he was requested to fulfil one of the functions set out in paragraphs 2, 3, 4, 5 and 6 of this Article, the President of the Chamber of Commerce designated by virtue of these paragraphs has not fulfilled one of these functions, the party requesting shall be entitled to ask the Special Committee to do so.

## Article V

### Plea as to Arbitral Jurisdiction

1. The party which intends to raise a plea as to the arbitrator's jurisdiction based on the fact that the arbitration agreement was either non-existent or null and void or had lapsed shall do so during the arbitration proceedings, not later than the delivery of its statement of claim or defence relating to the substance of the dispute; those based on the fact that an arbitrator has exceeded his terms of reference shall be raised during the arbitration proceedings as soon as the question on which the arbitrator is alleged to have no jurisdiction is raised during the arbitral procedure. Where the delay in raising the plea is due to a cause which the arbitrator deems justified, the arbitrator shall declare the plea admissible.

2. Pleas to the jurisdiction referred to in paragraph 1 above that have not been raised during the time-limits there referred to, may not be entered either during a subsequent stage of the arbitral proceedings where they are pleas left to the sole discretion of the parties under the law applicable by the arbitrator, or during subsequent court proceedings concerning the substance or the enforcement of the award where such pleas are left to the discretion of the parties under the rule of conflict of the court seised of the substance of the

dispute or the enforcement of the award. The arbitrator's decision on the delay in raising the plea, will, however, be subject to judicial control.

3. Subject to any subsequent judicial control provided for under the *lex fori*, the arbitrator whose jurisdiction is called in question shall be entitled to proceed with the arbitration, to rule on his own jurisdiction and to decide upon the existence or the validity of the arbitration agreement or of the contract of which the agreement forms part.

## ARTICLE VI

### JURISDICTION OF COURTS OF LAW

1. A plea as to the jurisdiction of the court made before the court seised by either party to the arbitration agreement, on the basis of the fact that an arbitration agreement exists shall, under penalty of estoppel, be presented by the respondent before or at the same time as the presentation of his substantial defence, depending upon whether the law of the court seised regards this plea as one of procedure or of substance.

2. In taking a decision concerning the existing or the validity of an arbitration agreement, courts of Contracting States shall examine the validity of such agreement with reference to the capacity of the parties, under the law applicable to them, and with reference to other questions—

(a) under the law to which the parties have subjected their arbitration agreement;
(b) failing any indication thereon, under the law of the country in which the award is to be made;
(c) failing any indication as to the law to which the parties have subjected the agreement, and where at the time when the question is raised in court the country in which the award is to be made cannot be determined, under the competent law by virtue of the rules of conflict of the court seised of the dispute.

The court may also refuse recognition of the arbitration agreement if under the law of their country the dispute is not capable of settlement by arbitration.

3. Where either party to an arbitration agreement has initiated arbitration proceedings before any resort is had to a court, courts of contracting States subsequently asked to deal with the same subject-matter between the same parties or with the question whether the arbitration agreement was non-existent or null and void or had lapsed, shall stay their ruling on the arbitrator's jurisdiction until the arbitral award is made, unless they have good and substantial reasons to the contrary.

4. A request for interim measures or measures of conservation addressed to a judicial authority shall not be deemed incompatible with the arbitration agreement, or regarded as a submission of the substance of the case to the court.

## Article VII

### Applicable Law

1. The parties shall be free to determine, by agreement, the law to be applied by the arbitrators to the substance of the dispute. Failing any indication by the parties as to the applicable law, the arbitrators shall apply the proper law under the rule of conflict that the arbitrators deem applicable. In both cases the arbitrators shall take account of the terms of the contract and trade usages.

2. The arbitrators shall act as *amiables compositeurs* if the parties so decide and if they may do so under the law applicable to the arbitration.

## Article VIII

### Reasons for the Award

The parties shall be presumed to have agreed that reasons shall be given for the award unless they

(a) either expressly declare that reasons shall not be given; or

(b) have assented to an arbitral procedure under which it is not customary to give reasons for awards, provided that in this case neither party requests before the end of the hearing, or if there has not been a hearing then before the making of the award, that reasons be given.

## Article IX

### Setting aside of the Arbitral Award

1. The setting aside in a Contracting State of an arbitral award covered by this convention shall only constitute a ground for the refusal or recognition or enforcement in another Contracting State where such setting aside took place in a State in which, or under the law of which, the award has been made and for one of the following reasons:

(a) the parties to the arbitration agreement were under the law applicable to them, under some incapacity or the said agreement is not valid under the law to which the parties have subjected it or, failing any indication thereon, under the law of the country where the award was made, or

(b) the party requesting the setting aside of the award was not given proper notice of appointment of the arbitrator or of the arbitration proceedings or was otherwise unable to present his case; or

(c) the award deals with a difference not contemplated by or not falling within the terms of the submission to arbitration, or it contains decision on matters beyond the scope of the submission to arbitration, provided that, if the decisions on matters submitted to arbitration can be separated from those not so submitted, that part of the award which contains decisions on matters submitted to arbitration need not be set aside;

(d) the composition of the arbitral authority or the arbitral procedure was not in accordance with the agreement of the parties, or failing such agreement, with the provisions of Article IV of this Convention.

2. In relations between contracting States that are also parties to the New York convention on the Recognition and Enforcement of Foreign Arbitral Awards of 10th June 1958, paragraph 1 of this Article limits the application of Article V (1) (e) of the New York Convention solely to the cases of setting aside set out under paragraph 1 above.

## ARTICLE X [OMITTED].

# AGREEMENT RELATING TO APPLICATION OF THE EUROPEAN CONVENTION ON INTERNATIONAL COMMERCIAL ARBITRATION, PARIS, 1962

## ARTICLE 1

In relations between physical or legal persons whose habitual residence or seat is in States Parties to the present Agreement, paragraphs 2 to 7 of Article IV of the European convention on International Commercial Arbitration, opened for signature at Geneva on 21st April 1961, are replaced by the following provision:

'If the arbitral Agreement contains no indication regarding the measures referred to in paragraph 1 of Article IV of the European Convention on International Commercial Arbitration as a whole, or some of these measures, any difficulties arising with regard to the constitution or functioning of the arbitral tribunal shall be submitted to the decision of the competent authority at the request of the party instituting proceedings.'

## ARTICLES 2-6 [OMITTED].

# Convention relating to a Uniform Law on the International Sale of Goods, The Hague, 1964

See Schedule 1 of Uniform Law on International Sales Act 1967 for text of the Convention

## Convention relating to a Uniform Law on the Formation of Contracts for the International Sale of Goods, The Hague, 1964

See Schedule 2 of Uniform Laws on International Sales Act 1967 for text of the Convention

# CONVENTION ON THE SERVICE ABROAD OF JUDICIAL AND EXTRAJUDICIAL DOCUMENTS IN CIVIL OR COMMERCIAL MATTERS, THE HAGUE, 1965

## ARTICLE 1

The present convention shall apply in all cases, in civil or commercial matters, where there is occasion to transmit a judicial or extrajudicial document for service abroad.

This Convention shall not apply where the address of the person to be served with the document is not known.

## CHAPTER I

## JUDICIAL DOCUMENTS

## ARTICLE 2

Each contracting State shall designate a Central Authority which will undertake to receive requests for service coming from other contracting States and to proceed in conformity with the provisions of Articles 3 to 6.

Each State shall organise the Central Authority in conformity with its own law.

## ARTICLE 3

The authority or judicial officer competent under the law of the State in which the documents originate shall forward to the Central Authority of the State addressed a request conforming to the model annexed to the present convention, without any requirement of legalisation or other equivalent formality.

The document to be served or a copy thereof shall be annexed to the request. The request and the document shall both be furnished in duplicate.

## ARTICLE 4

If the Central Authority considers that the request does not comply with the provisions of the present Convention it shall promptly inform the applicant and specify its objections to the request.

## ARTICLE 5

The Central Authority of the State addressed shall itself serve the document or shall arrange to have it served by an appropriate agency, either—

(a) by a method prescribed by its internal law for the service of documents in domestic actions upon persons who are within its territory, or

(b) by a particular method requested by the applicant, unless such a method is incompatible with the law of the State addressed.

Subject to sub-paragraph (b) of the first paragraph of this Article, the document may always be served by delivery to an addressee who accepts it voluntarily.

If the document is to be served under the first paragraph above, the Central authority may require the document to be written in, or translated into, the official language or one of the official languages of the State addressed.

The part of the request, in the form attached to the present Convention, which contains a summary of the document to be served, shall be served with the document.

## ARTICLE 6

The Central Authority of the State addressed or any authority which it may have designated for that purpose, shall complete a certificate in the form of the model annexed to the present Convention.

The certificate shall state that the document has been served and shall include the method, the place and the date of service and the person to whom the document was delivered. If the document has not been served, the certificate shall set out the reasons which have prevented service.

The applicant may require that a certificate not completed by a Central Authority or by a judicial authority shall be countersigned by one of these authorities.

The certificate shall be forwarded directly to the applicant.

## ARTICLE 7

The standard terms in the model annexed to the present convention shall in all cases be written either in French or in English. They may also be written in the official language, or in one of the official languages, of the State in which the documents originate.

The corresponding blanks shall be completed either in the language of the State addressed or in French or in English.

## ARTICLE 8

Each contracting State shall be free to effect service of judicial documents upon persons abroad, without application of any compulsion, directly through its diplomatic or consular agents.

Any State may declare that it is opposed to such service within its territory, unless the document is to be served upon a national of the State in which the documents originate.

## Article 9

Each contracting State shall be free, in addition, to use consular channels to forward documents, for the purpose of service, to those authorities of another contracting State which are designated by the latter for this purpose.

Each contracting State may, if exceptional circumstances so require, use diplomatic channels for the same purpose.

## Article 10

Provided the State of destination does not object, the present Convention shall not interfere with—

(a) the freedom to send judicial documents, by postal channels, directly to persons abroad,

(b) the freedom of judicial officers, officials or other competent persons of the State of origin to effect service of judicial documents directly through the judicial officers, officials or other competent persons of the State of destination,

(c) the freedom of any person interested in a judicial proceeding to effect service of judicial documents directly through the judicial officers, officials or other competent persons of the State of destination.

## Article 11

The present Convention shall not prevent two or more contracting States from agreeing to permit, for the purpose of service of judicial documents, channels of transmission other than those provided for in the preceding Articles and, in particular, direct communication between their respective authorities.

## Article 12

The service of judicial documents coming from a contracting State shall not give rise to any payment or reimbursement of taxes or costs for the services rendered by the State addressed.

The applicant shall pay or reimburse the costs occasioned by -

(a) the employment of a judicial officer or of a person competent under the law of the State of destination,

(b) the use of a particular method of service.

## Article 13

Where a request for service complies with the terms of the present convention, the State addressed may refuse to comply therewith only if it deems that compliance would infringe its sovereignty or security.

It may not refuse to comply solely on the ground that, under its internal law, it claims exclusive jurisdiction over the subject-matter of the action or that its internal law would not permit the action upon which the application is based.

The Central Authority shall, in case of refusal, promptly inform the applicant and state the reasons for the refusal.

## Article 14

Difficulties which may arise in connection with the transmission of judicial documents for service shall be settled through diplomatic channels.

## Article 15

Where a writ of summons or an equivalent document had to be transmitted abroad for the purpose of service, under the provisions of the present Convention, and the defendant has not appeared, judgement shall not be given until it is established that—

(a) the document was served by a method prescribed by the internal law of the State addressed for the service of documents in domestic actions upon persons who are within its territory, or

(b) the document was actually delivered to the defendant or to his residence by another method provided for by this Convention,

and that in either of these cases the service or the delivery was effected in sufficient time to enable the defendant to defend.

Each contracting State shall be free to declare that the judge, notwithstanding the provisions of the first paragraph of this Article, may give judgement even if no certificate of service or delivery has been received, if all the following conditions are fulfilled—

(a) the document was transmitted by one of the methods provided for in this convention,

(b) a period of time of not less than six months, considered adequate by the judge in the particular case, has elapsed since the date of the transmission of the document,

(c) no certificate of any kind has been received, even though every reasonable effort has been made to obtain it through the competent authorities of the State addressed.

Notwithstanding the provisions of the preceding paragraphs the judge may order, in case of urgency, any provisional or protective measures.

## Article 16

When a writ of summons or an equivalent document had to be transmitted abroad for the purpose of service, under the provisions of the present Convention, and a judgement has been entered against a defendant who has not appeared, the judge shall have the power to relieve the defendant from the effects of the expiration of the time for appeal from the judgement if the following conditions are fulfilled—

(a) the defendant, without any fault on his part, did not have knowledge of the document in sufficient time to defend, or knowledge of the judgement in sufficient time to appeal, and

(b) the defendant has disclosed a *prima facie* defence to the action on the merits.

An application for relief may be filled only within a reasonable time after the defendant has knowledge of the judgement.

Each Contracting State may declare that the application will not be entertained if it is filed after the expiration of a time to be stated in the declaration, but which shall in no case be less than one year following the date of the judgement.

## Chapter II

## Extrajudicial Documents

### Article 17

Extrajudicial documents emanating from authorities and judicial officers of a contracting State may be transmitted for the purpose of service in another contracting State by the methods and under the provisions of the present Convention.

## Chapter III

## General Clauses

### Article 18

Each contracting State may designate other authorities in addition to the Central Authority and shall determine the extent of their competence. The applicant shall, however, in all cases, have the right to address a request directly to the Central Authority. Federal States shall be free to designate more than one Central Authority.

### Article 19

To the extent that the internal law of a contracting State permits methods of transmission, other than those provided for in the preceding Articles, of documents coming from abroad, for service within its territory, the present Convention shall not affect such provisions.

### Article 20

The present Convention shall not prevent an agreement between any two or more contracting States to dispense with —

(a) the necessity for duplicate copies of transmitted documents as required by the second paragraph of Article 3,

(b) the language requirements of the third paragraph of Article 5 and Article 7,

(c) the provisions of the fourth paragraph of Article 5;

(d) the provisions of the second paragraph of Article 12.

## Annex to the Convention

*Forms*

### *Request for Service Abroad of Judicial or Extrajudicial Documents*

Convention on the service abroad of judicial and extrajudicial documents in civil or commercial matters, signed at The Hague, _ _ _ _ _ _ _ _ _ 196

| Identity and address of the applicant | Address of receiving authority |
|---|---|
| | |

The undersigned applicant has the honour to transmit — in duplicate — the documents listed below and, in conformity with Article 5 of the above-mentioned Convention, requests prompt service of one copy thereof on the addressee, i.e.

(identity and address) _ _ _ _ _ _ _ _ _ _ _ _ _ _ _ _ _ _ _ _ _ _ _ _ _ _ _ _ _ _ _ _ _ _ _ _ _ _ _ _

_ _ _ _ _ _ _ _ _ _ _ _ _ _ _ _ _ _ _ _ _ _ _ _ _ _ _ _ _ _ _ _ _ _ _ _ _ _ _ _ _ _ _ _ _ _ _ _ _ _ _ _ _ _ _ _ _ _ _ _

(a) in accordance with the provisions of sub-paragraph a of the first paragraph of Article 5 of the convention*

(b) in accordance with the following particular method (sub-paragraph b of the first paragraph of Article 5) *: _ _ _ _ _ _ _ _ _ _ _ _ _ _ _ _ _ _ _ _ _ _ _ _ _ _ _

_ _ _ _ _ _ _ _ _ _ _ _ _ _ _ _ _ _ _ _ _ _ _ _ _ _ _ _ _ _ _ _ _ _ _ _ _ _ _ _ _ _ _ _ _ _ _ _ _ _ _ _ _ _ _ _ _ _ _ _

(c) by delivery to the addressee, if he accepts it voluntarily (second paragraph of Article 5)*.

The authority is requested to return or to have returned to the applicant a copy of the documents — and of the annexes* — with a certificate as provided on the reverse side.

*List of documents*

_ _ _ _ _ _ _ _ _ _ _ _ _ _ _ _ _ _ _ _ _ _ _ _ _ _ _ _

_ _ _ _ _ _ _ _ _ _ _ _ _ _ _ _ _ _ _ _ _ _ _ _ _ _ _ _

_ _ _ _ _ _ _ _ _ _ _ _ _ _ _ _ _ _ _ _ _ _ _ _ _ _ _ _

_ _ _ _ _ _ _ _ _ _ _ _ _ _ _ _ _ _ _ _ _ _ _ _ _ _ _ _

Done at _ _ _ _ _ _ _ _ _ _ _ _ _, the _ _ _ _ _ _ _ _ _

Signature and/or stamp

* Delete if inappropriate.

*Reverse of the request*

*CERTIFICATE*

The undersigned authority has the honour to certify, in conformity with Article 6 of the Convention,

1) that the document has been served*

- the (date) ............................................................

- at (place, street, number) ............................................................

............................................................

-in one of the following methods authorised by Article 5 -

(a) in accordance with the provisions of sub-paragraph a of the first para of Article 5 of the Convention*.

(b) in accordance with the following particular method*. ............................................................

............................................................

(c) by delivery to the addressee, who accepted it voluntarily*.

The documents referred to in the request have been delivered to:

—(identity and description of person) ............................................................

............................................................

—relationship to the addressee (family, business or other): ............................................................

............................................................

2) that the document has not been served, by reason of the following facts*:

............................................................

............................................................

In conformity with the second paragraph of Article 12 of the Convention, the applicant is requested to pay or reimburse the expenses detailed in the attached statement*.

*Annexes*

Documents returned: ............................................................

............................................................

............................................................

In appropriate cases, documents establishing the service: ............................................................

............................................................

............................................................

Done at ................, the ................

Signature and/or stamp.

* Delete if inappropriate

## *SUMMARY OF THE DOCUMENT TO BE SERVED*

Convention on the service abroad of judicial and extrajudicial documents in civil or commercial matters, signed at The Hague, the ____________196

(Article 5, fourth paragraph)

Name and address of the requesting authority: ______________________________

______________________________________________

Particulars of the parties*: ______________________________

______________________________________________

JUDICIAL DOCUMENT **

Nature and purpose of the document: ______________________________

______________________________________________

Nature and purpose of the proceedings and, where appropriate, the amount in dispute: ______________________________

______________________________________________

Date and place for entering appearance**: ______________________________

______________________________________________

Court which has given judgement**: ______________________________

______________________________________________

Date of judgement**: ______________________________

Time limits stated in the document**: ______________________________

______________________________________________

EXTRAJUDICIAL DOCUMENT**

Nature and purpose of the document: ______________________________

______________________________________________

Time limits stated in the document**: ______________________________

______________________________________________

* If appropriate, identity and address of the person interested in the transmission of the document.

** Delete if inappropriate.

# Brussels Protocol amending the Hague rules relating to Bills of Lading 1968 (Hague - Visby Rules)

See Schedule Carriage of Goods by Sea Act 1972 for text of the Convention

# Convention of Jurisdiction and Enforcement of Judgements in Civil and Commercial Matters (as amended) Brussels 1968

See Schedule 1 of Civil Jurisdiction and Judgements Act 1982
for text of convention

# UNITED NATIONS CONVENTION ON THE LIMITATION PERIOD IN THE INTERNATIONAL SALE OF GOODS, NEW YORK, 1974

## PART I. SUBSTANTIVE PROVISIONS

*Sphere of application*

### ARTICLE 1

1. This Convention shall determine when claims of a buyer and a seller against each other arising from a contract of international sale of goods or relating to its breach, termination or invalidity can no longer be exercised by reason on the expiration of a period of time. Such period of time is hereinafter referred to as 'the limitation period'.

2. This Convention shall not affect a particular time-limit within which one party is required, as a condition for the acquisition or exercise of his claim to give notice to the other party or perform any act other than the institution of legal proceedings.

3. In this Convention:
   (a) 'buyer', 'seller' and 'party' mean persons who buy or sell, or agree to buy or sell, goods, and the successors to and assigns of their rights or obligations under the contract of sale;
   (b) 'creditor' means a party who asserts a claim, whether or not such a claim is for a sum of money;
   (c) 'debtor' means a party against whom a creditor asserts a claim.
   (d) 'breach of contract' means the failure of a party to perform the contract or any performance not in conformity with the contract
   (e) 'legal proceedings' includes judicial, arbitral and administrative proceedings:
   (f) 'person' includes corporation, company, partnership, association or entity, whether private or public, which can sue or be sued;
   (g) 'writing' includes telegram and telex;
   (h) 'year' means a year according to the Gregorian calendar.

### ARTICLE 2

For the purposes of this convention:
   (a) a contract of sale of goods shall be considered international if, at the time of the conclusion of the contract, the buyer and the seller have their places of business in different States:
   (b) the fact that the parties have their places of business in different States shall be disregarded whenever this fact does not appear either from the contract or from any dealings between, or from information disclosed by, the parties at any time before or at the conclusion of the contract;

(c) where a party to a contract of sale of goods has places of business in more than one State, the place of business shall be that which has the closest relationship to the contract and its performance, having regard to the circumstances known to or contemplated by the parties at the time of the conclusion of the contract;
(d) where a party does not have a place of business, reference shall be made to his habitual residence;
(e) neither the nationality of the parties nor the civil or commercial character of the parties or of the contract shall be taken into consideration.

## Article 3

1. This Convention shall apply only if, at the time of the conclusion of the contract, the places of business of the parties to a contract of international sale of goods are in Contracting States.

2. Unless this Convention provides otherwise, it shall apply irrespective of the law which would otherwise by applicable by virtue of the rules of private international law.

3. This Convention shall not apply when the parties have expressly excluded its application.

## Article 4

This Convention shall not apply to sales:
(a) of goods bought for personal, family or household use;
(b) by auction;
(c) on execution or otherwise by authority of law;
(d) of stocks, shares, investment securities, negotiable instruments or money;
(e) of ships, vessels or aircraft;
(f) of electricity.

## Article 5

This Convention shall not apply to claims based upon:
(a) death of, or personal injury to, any person;
(b) nuclear damage caused by the goods sold;
(c) a lien, mortgage or other security interest in property;
(d) a judgement or award made in legal proceedings;
(e) a document on which direct enforcement or execution can be obtained in accordance with the law of the place where such enforcement or execution is sought;
(f) a bill of exchange, cheque or promissory note.

## ARTICLE 6

1. This Convention shall not apply to contracts in which the preponderant part of the obligations of the seller consists in the supply of labour or other services.

2. Contracts for the supply of goods to be manufactured or produced shall be considered to be sales, unless the party who orders the goods undertakes to supply a substantial part of the materials necessary for such manufacture or production.

## ARTICLE 7

In the interpretation and application of the provisions of this convention, regard shall be had to its international character and to the need to promote uniformity.

*The duration and commencement of the limitation period.*

## ARTICLE 8

The limitation period shall be four years.

## ARTICLE 9

1. Subject to the provisions of Articles 10, 11 and 12 the limitation period shall commence on the date on which the claim accrues.

2. The commencement of the limitation period shall not be postponed by:
   (a) a requirement that the party be given a notice as described in para 2 of Article 1, or
   (b) a provision in an arbitration agreement that no right shall arise until an arbitration award has been made.

## ARTICLE 10

1. A claim arising from a breach of contract shall accrue on the date on which such breach occurs.

2. A claim arising from a defect or other lack of conformity shall accrue on the date on which the goods are actually handed over to, or their tender is refused by, the buyer.

3. A claim based on fraud committed before or at the time of the conclusion of the contract or during its performance shall accrue on the date on which the fraud was or reasonably could have been discovered.

## ARTICLE 11

If the seller has given an express undertaking relating to the goods which is stated to have effect for a certain period of time, whether expressed in terms of a specific period of time or otherwise, the limitation period in respect of any claim arising from the undertaking shall commence on the date on which the buyer notifies the seller of the fact on which the claim is based, but not later than on the date of the expiration of the period of the undertaking.

## Article 12

1. If, in circumstances provided for by the law applicable to the contract, one party is entitled to declare the contract terminated before the time for performance is due, and exercises this right, the limitation period in respect of a claim based on any such circumstances shall commence on the date on which the declaration is made to the other party. If the contract is not declared to be terminated before performance becomes due, the limitation period shall commence on the date on which performance is due.

2. The limitation period in respect of a claim arising out of a breach by one party of a contract for the delivery of or payment for goods by instalments shall, in relation to each separate instalment, commence on the date on which the particular breach occurs. If, under the law applicable to the contract, one party is entitled to declare the contract terminated by reason of such breach, and exercises this right, the limitation period in respect of all relevant instalments shall commence on the date on which the declaration is made to the other party.

*Cessation and extension of the limitation period*

## Article 13

The limitation period shall cease to run when the creditor performs any act which, under the law of the court where the proceedings are instituted, is recognised as commencing judicial proceedings against the debtor or as asserting his claim in such proceedings already instituted against the debtor, for the purpose of obtaining satisfaction or recognition of his claim.

## Article 14

1. Where the parties have agreed to submit to arbitration, the limitation period shall cease to run when either party commences arbitral proceedings in the manner provided for in the arbitration agreement or by the law applicable to such proceedings.

2. In the absence of any such provision, arbitral proceedings shall be deemed to commence on the date on which a request that the claim in dispute be referred to arbitration is delivered at the habitual residence or place of business of the other party or, if he has no such residence or place of business, then at his last known residence or place of business.

## Article 15

If any legal proceedings other than those mentioned in Articles 13 and 14, including legal proceedings commenced upon the occurrence of:

(a) the death or incapacity of the debtor

(b) the bankruptcy or any state of insolvency affecting the whole of the property of the debtor, or

(c) the dissolution or liquidation of a corporation, company, partnership, association or entity when it is the debtor.

The limitation period shall cease to run when the creditor asserts his claim in such proceedings for the purpose of obtaining satisfaction or recognition of the claim, subject to the law governing the proceedings.

## Article 16

For the purposes of Articles 13, 14 and 15, any act performed by way of counterclaim shall be deemed to have been performed on the same date as the act performed in relation to the claim against which the counterclaim is raised, provided that both the claim and the counterclaim relate to the same contract or to several contracts concluded in the course of the same transaction.

## Article 17

1. Where a claim has been asserted in legal proceedings within the limitation period in accordance with Articles 13, 14, 15 or 16, but such legal proceedings have ended without a decision binding on the merits of the claim, the limitation period shall be deemed to have continued to run.

2. If, at the time such legal proceedings ended, the limitation period has expired or has less than one year to run, the creditor shall be entitled to a period of one year from the date on which the legal proceedings ended.

## Article 18

1. Where legal proceedings have been commenced against one debtor, the limitation period prescribed in this Convention shall cease to run against any other party jointly and severally liable with the debtor, provided that the creditor informs such party in writing within that period that the proceedings have been commenced.

2. Where legal proceedings have been commenced by a subpurchaser against the buyer, the limitation period prescribed in this Convention shall cease to run in relation to the buyer's claim over against the seller, if the buyer informs the seller in writing within that period that the proceedings have been commenced.

3. Where the legal proceedings referred to in paragraphs 1 and 2 of this Article have ended, the limitation period in respect of the claim of the creditor

or the buyer against the party jointly and severally liable or against the seller shall be deemed not to have ceased running by virtue of paragraphs 1 and 2 of this Article, but the creditor or the buyer shall be entitled to an additional year from the date on which the legal proceedings ended, if at that time the limitation period had expired or had less than one year to run.

## ARTICLE 19

Where the creditor performs, in the State in which the debtor has his place of business and before the expiration of the limitation period, any act, other than the acts described in Articles 13, 14, 15 and 16, which under the law of that State has the effect of recommencing a limitation period, a new limitation period of four years shall commence on the date prescribed by that law.

## ARTICLE 20

1. Where the debtor, before the expiration of the limitation period, acknowledges in writing his obligation to the creditor, a new limitation period of four years shall commence to run from the date of such acknowledgement.

2. Payment of interest or partial performance of an obligation by the debtor shall have the same effect as an acknowledgement under paragraph 1 of this Article if it can reasonably be inferred from such payment or performance that the debtor acknowledges that obligation.

## ARTICLE 21

Where, as a result of a circumstance which is beyond the control of the creditor and which he could neither avoid nor overcome, the creditor has been prevented from causing the limitation period to cease to run, the limitation period shall be extended so as not to expire before the expiration of one year from the date on which the relevant circumstance ceased to exist.

*Modification of the limitation period by the parties*

## ARTICLE 22

1. The limitation period cannot be modified or affected by any declaration or agreement between the parties, except in the cases provided for in paragraph 2 of this Article.

2. The debtor may at any time during the running of the limitation period extend the period by a declaration in writing to the creditor. This declaration may be renewed.

3. The provisions of this Article shall not affect the validity of a clause in the contract of sale which stipulates that arbitral proceedings shall be commenced within a shorter period of limitation than that prescribed by this Convention, provided that such clause is valid under the law applicable to the contract of sale.

*General limit of the limitation period*

## ARTICLE 23

Notwithstanding the provisions of this Convention, a limitation period shall in any event expire not later than 10 years from the date on which it commenced to run under Articles 9, 10 11 and 12 of this Convention.

*Consequences of expiration of the limitation period*

## ARTICLE 24

Expiration of the limitation period shall be taken into consideration in any legal proceedings only if invoked by a party to such proceedings.

## ARTICLE 25

1. Subject to the provisions of paragraph 2 of this Article and of Article 24, no claim shall be recognised or enforced in any legal proceedings commenced after the expiration of the limitation period.

2. Notwithstanding the expiration of the limitation period, one party may rely on his claim as a defence or for the purpose of set-off against a claim asserted by the other party, provided that in the latter case this may only be done:

(a) if both claims relate to the same contract or to several contracts concluded in the course of the same transaction; or

(b) if the claims could have been set-off at any time before the expiration of the limitation period.

## ARTICLE 26

Where the debtor performs his obligation after the expiration of the limitation period, he shall not on that ground be entitled in any way to claim restitution even if he did not know at the time when he performed his obligation that the limitation period had expired.

## ARTICLE 27

The expiration of the limitation period with respect to a principal debt shall have the same effect with respect to an obligation to pay interest on that debt.

*Calculation of the period*

## ARTICLE 28

1. The limitation period shall be calculated in such a way that it shall expire at the end of the day which corresponds to the date on which the period commenced to run. If there is no such corresponding date, the period shall expire at the end of the last day of the last month of the limitation period.

2. The limitation period shall be calculated by reference to the date of the place where the legal proceedings are instituted.

## ARTICLE 29

Where the last day of the limitation period falls on an official holiday or other *dies non juridicus* precluding the appropriate legal action in the jurisdiction where the creditor institutes legal proceedings or asserts a claim as envisaged in Article 13, 14, or 15, the limitation period shall be extended so as not to expire until the end of the first day following that official holiday or *dies non juridicus* on which such proceedings could be instituted or on which such a claim could be asserted in that jurisdiction.

*International effect*

## ARTICLE 30

The acts and circumstances referred to in Articles 13 through 19 which have taken place in one Contracting State shall have effect for the purposes of this Convention in another Contracting State, provided that the creditor has taken all reasonable steps to ensure that the debtor is informed of the relevant act or circumstances as soon as possible.

PART II, ARTICLES 31-33 [OMITTED].

PART III, ARTICLES 34-40 [OMITTED].

PART IV, ARTICLES 41-46 [OMITTED].

## Convention on Limitation of Liability for Maritime Claims, 1976

See Schedule Merchant Shipping Act 1979 for the text of the Convention

# UNITED NATIONS CONVENTION ON THE CARRIAGE OF GOODS BY SEA, HAMBURG, 1978 (HAMBURG RULES)

## PART I. GENERAL PROVISIONS

### ARTICLE 1. DEFINITIONS

In this Convention:
1. 'Carrier' means any person by whom or in whose name a contract of carriage of goods by sea has been concluded with a shipper.

2. 'Actual carrier' means any person to whom the performance of the carriage of the goods, or of part of the carriage, has been entrusted by the carrier, and includes any other person to whom such performance has been entrusted.

3. 'Shipper' means any person by whom or in whose name or on whose behalf a contract of carriage of goods by sea has been concluded with a carrier, or any person by whom or in whose name or on whose behalf the goods are actually delivered to the carrier in relation to the contract of carriage by sea.

4. 'Consignee' means the person entitled to take delivery of the goods.

5. 'Goods' includes live animals; where the goods are consolidated in a container, pallet or similar article of transport or where they are packed, 'goods' includes such article of transport or packaging if supplied by the shipper.

6. 'Contract of carriage by sea' means any contract whereby the carrier undertakes against payment of freight to carry goods by sea from one port to another; however, a contract which involves carriage by sea and also carriage by some other means is deemed to be a contract of carriage by sea for the purposes of this Convention only in so far as it relates to the carriage by sea.

7. 'Bill of lading' means a document which evidences a contract of carriage by sea and the taking over or loading of the goods by the carrier, and by which the carrier undertakes to deliver the goods against surrender of the document. A provision in the document that the goods are to be delivered to the order of a named person, or to order, or to bearer, constitutes such an undertaking.

8. 'Writing' includes, *inter alia*, telegram and telex.

### ARTICLE 2. SCOPE OF APPLICATION

1. The provisions of this Convention are applicable to all contracts of carriage by sea between two different States, if:
   (a) the port of loading as provided for in the contract of carriage by sea is located in a Contracting State, or

(b) the port of discharge as provided for in the contract of carriage by sea is located in a Contracting State, or
(c) one of the optional ports of discharge provided for in the contract of carriage by sea is the actual port of discharge and such port is located in a Contracting State, or
(d) the bill of lading or other document evidencing the contract of carriage by sea is issued in a Contracting State, or
(e) the bill of lading or other document evidencing the contract of carriage by sea provides that the provisions of this Convention or the legislation of any State giving effect to them are to govern the contract.

2. The provisions of this Convention are applicable without regard to the nationality of the ship, the carrier, the actual carrier, the shipper, the consignee or any other interested person.

3. The provisions of this Convention are not applicable to charter-parties. However, where a bill of lading is issued pursuant to a charter-party, the provisions of the Convention apply to such a bill of lading if it governs the relation between the carrier and the holder of the bill of lading, not being the charterer.

4. If a contract provides for future carriage of goods in a series of shipments during an agreed period, the provisions of this Convention apply to each shipment. However, where a shipment is made under a charter-party, the provisions of paragraph 3 of this Article apply.

### ARTICLE 3. INTERPRETATION OF THE CONVENTION

In the interpretation and application of the provisions of this Convention regard shall be had to its international character and to the need to promote uniformity.

## PART II. LIABILITY OF THE CARRIER

### ARTICLE 4. PERIOD OF RESPONSIBILITY

1. The responsibility of the carrier for the goods under this Convention covers the period during which the carrier is in charge of the goods at the port of loading, during the carriage and at the port of discharge.

2. For the purpose of paragraph 1 of this Article, the carrier is deemed to be in charge of the goods
(a) from the time he has taken over the goods from;
  (i) the shipper, or a person acting on his behalf; or
  (ii) an authority or other third party to whom, pursuant to law or regulations applicable at the port of loading, the goods must be handed over for shipment;
(b) until the time he has delivered the goods:
  (i) by handing over the goods to the consignee; or

(ii) in cases where the consignee does not receive the goods from the carrier, by placing them at the disposal of the consignee in accordance with the contract or with the law or with the usage of the particular trade, applicable at the port of discharge; or

(iii) by handing over the goods to an authority or other third party to whom, pursuant to law or regulations applicable at the port of discharge, the goods must be handed over.

3. In paragraphs 1 and 2 of this Article, reference to the carrier or to the consignee means, in addition to the carrier or the consignee, the servants or agents, respectively of the carrier or the consignee.

## ARTICLE 5. BASIS OF LIABILITY

1. The carrier is liable for loss resulting from loss of or damage to the goods, as well as from delay in delivery, if the occurrence which caused the loss, damage or delay took place while the goods were in his charge as defined in Article 4, unless the carrier proves that he, his servants or agents took all measures that could reasonably be required to avoid the occurrence and its consequences.

2. Delay in delivery occurs when the goods have not been delivered at the port of discharge provided for in the contract of carriage by sea within the time expressly agreed upon or, in the absence of such agreement, within the time which it would be reasonable to require of a diligent carrier, having regard to the circumstances of the case.

3. The person entitled to make a claim for the loss of goods may treat the goods as lost if they have not been delivered as required by Article 4 within 60 consecutive days following the expiry of the time for delivery according to paragraph 2 of this Article.

4.—

(a) The carrier is liable

(i) for loss of or damage to the goods or delay in delivery caused by fire, if the claimant proves that the fire arose from fault or neglect on the part of the carrier, his servants or agents;

(ii) for such loss, damage or delay in delivery which is proved by the claimant to have resulted from the fault or neglect of the carrier, his servants or agents, in taking all measures that could reasonably be required to put out the fire and avoid or mitigate its consequences.

(b) In case of fire on board the ship affecting the goods, if the claimant or the carrier so desires, a survey in accordance with shipping practices must be held into the cause and circumstances of the fire, and a copy of the surveyor's report shall be made available on demand to the carrier and the claimant.

5. With respect to live animals, the carrier is not liable for loss, damage or delay in delivery resulting from any special risks inherent in that kind of carriage. If the carrier proves that he has complied with any special instructions given to him by the shipper respecting the animals and that, in the circumstances of the case, the loss, damage or delay in delivery could be

attributed to such risks, it is presumed that the loss, damage or delay in delivery was so caused, unless there is proof that all or a part of the loss, damage or delay in delivery resulted from fault or neglect on the part of the carrier, his servants or agents.

6. The carrier is not liable, except in general average, where loss, damage or delay in delivery resulted from measures to save life or from reasonable measures to save property at sea.

7. Where fault or neglect on the part of the carrier, his servants or agents combines with another cause to produce loss, damage or delay in delivery the carrier is liable only to the extent that the loss, damage or delay in delivery is attributable to such fault or neglect, provided that the carrier proves the amount of the loss, damage or delay in delivery not attributable thereto.

## ARTICLE 6. LIMITS OF LIABILITY

1.—

(a) The liability of the carrier for loss resulting from loss of or damage to goods according to the provisions of Article 5 is limited to an amount equivalent to 835 units of account per package or other shipping unit or 2.5 units of account per kilogram of gross weight of the goods lost or damaged, whichever is the higher.

(b) The liability of the carrier for delay in delivery according to the provisions of Article 5 is limited to an amount equivalent to two and a half times the freight payable for the goods delayed, but not exceeding the total freight payable under the contract of carriage of goods by sea.

(c) In no case shall the aggregate liability of the carrier, under both subparagraphs a and b of this para, exceed the limitation which would be established under subparagraph a of this para for total loss of the goods with respect to which such liability was incurred.

2. For the purpose of calculating which amount is the higher in accordance with paragraph 1 a of this Article, the following rules apply;

(a) Where a container, pallet or similar article of transport is used to consolidate goods, the package or other shipping units enumerated in the bill of lading, if issued, or otherwise in any other document evidencing the contract of carriage by sea, as packed in such article of transport are deemed packages or shipping units. Except as aforesaid the goods in such article of transport are deemed one shipping unit.

(b) In cases where the article of transport itself has been lost or damaged, that article of transport, if not owned or otherwise supplied by the carrier, is considered one separate shipping unit.

3. Unit of account means the unit of account mentioned in Article 26.

4. By agreement between the carrier and the shipper, limits of liability exceeding those provided for in paragraph 1 may be fixed.

## Article 7. Application to non-contractual claims

1. The defences and limits of liability provided for in this Convention apply in any action against the carrier in respect of loss or damage to the goods covered by the contract of carriage by sea, as well as of delay in delivery whether the action is founded in contract, in tort or otherwise.

2. If such an action is brought against a servant or agent of the carrier, such servant or agent, if he proves that he acted within the scope of his employment, is entitled to avail himself of the defences and limits of liability which the carrier is entitled to invoke under this Convention.

3. Except as provided in Article 8, the aggregate of the amounts recoverable from the carrier and from any persons referred to in paragraph 2 of this Article shall not exceed the limits of liability provided for in this convention.

## Article 8. Loss of right to limit responsibility

1. The carrier is not entitled to the benefit of the limitation of liability provided for in Article 6 if it is proved that the loss, damage or delay in delivery resulted from an act or omission of the carrier done with the intent to cause such loss, damage or delay, or recklessly and with knowledge that such loss, damage or delay would probably result.

2. Notwithstanding the provisions of paragraph 2 of Article 7, a servant or agent of the carrier is not entitled to the benefit of the limitation of liability provided for in Article 6 if it is proved that the loss, damage or delay in delivery resulted from an act or omission of such servant or agent, done with the intent to cause such loss, damage or delay, or recklessly and with knowledge that such loss, damage or delay would probably result.

## Article 9. Deck cargo

1. The carrier is entitled to carry the goods on deck only is such carriage is in accordance with an agreement with the shipper or with the usage of the particular trade or is required by statutory rules or regulations.

2. If the carrier and the shipper have agreed that the goods shall or may be carried on deck, the carrier must insert in the bill of lading or other document evidencing the contract of carriage by sea a statement to that effect. In the absence of such a statement the carrier has the burden of proving that an agreement for carriage on deck has been entered into; however, the carrier is not entitled to invoke such an agreement against a third party, including a consignee, who has acquired the bill of lading in good faith.

3. Where the goods have been carried on deck contrary to the provisions of paragraph 1 of this Article or where the carrier may not under paragraph 2 of this Article invoke an agreement for carriage on deck, the carrier, notwithstanding the provisions of paragraph 1 of Article 5, is liable for loss of or damage to the goods, as well as for delay in delivery, resulting solely from

the carriage on deck, and the extent of his liability is to be determined in accordance with the provisions of Article 6 or Article 8 of this Convention, as the case may be.

4. Carriage of goods on deck contrary to express agreement for carriage under deck is deemed to be an act or omission of the carrier within the meaning of Article 8.

## ARTICLE 10. LIABILITY OF THE CARRIER AND ACTUAL CARRIER

1. Where the performance of the carriage or part thereof has been entrusted to an actual carrier, whether or not in pursuance of a liberty under the contract of carriage by sea to do so, the carrier nevertheless remains responsible for the entire carriage according to the provisions of this Convention. The carrier is responsible, in relation to the carriage performed by the actual carrier, for the acts and omissions of the actual carrier and of his servants and agents acting within the scope of their employment.

2. All the provisions of this Convention governing the responsibility of the carrier also apply to the responsibility of the actual carrier for the carriage performed by him. The provisions of paragraphs 2 and 3 of Article 7 and of paragraph 2 of Article 8 apply if an action is brought against a servant or agent of the actual carrier.

3. Any special agreement under which the carrier assumes obligations not imposed by this Convention or waives rights conferred by this Convention affects the actual carrier only if agreed to by him expressly and in writing. Whether or not the actual carrier has so agreed, the carrier nevertheless remains bound by the obligations or waivers resulting from such special agreement.

4. Where and to the extent that both the carrier and the actual carrier are liable, their liability is joint and several.

5. The aggregate of the amounts recoverable from the carrier; the actual carrier and their servants and agents shall not exceed the limits of liability provided for in this Convention.

6. Nothing in this Article shall prejudice any right of recourse as between the carrier and the actual carrier.

## ARTICLE 11. THROUGH CARRIAGE

1. Notwithstanding the provisions of paragraph 1 of Article 10, where a contract of carriage by sea provides explicitly that a specified part of the carriage covered by the said contract is to be performed by a named person other than the carrier, the contract may also provide that the carrier is not liable for loss, damage or delay in delivery caused by an occurrence which takes place while the goods are in the charge of the actual carrier during such part of the carriage. Nevertheless, any stipulation limiting or excluding such liability is without effect if no judicial proceedings can be instituted against the actual carrier in a court competent under paragraph 1 or 2 of Article 21. The burden of proving

that any loss, damage or delay in delivery has been caused by such an occurrence rests upon the carrier.

2. The actual carrier is responsible in accordance with the provisions of paragraph 2 of Article 10 for loss, damage or delay in delivery caused by an occurrence which takes place while the goods are in his charge.

## PART III. LIABILITY OF THE SHIPPER

### ARTICLE 12. GENERAL RULE

The shipper is not liable for loss sustained by the carrier or the actual carrier, or for damage sustained by the ship, unless such loss or damage was caused by the fault or neglect of the shipper, his servants or agents, Nor is any servant or agent of the shipper liable for such loss or damage unless the loss or damage was caused by fault or neglect on his part.

### ARTICLE 13. SPECIAL RULES ON DANGEROUS GOODS.

1. The shipper must mark or label in a suitable manner dangerous goods as dangerous.

2. Where the shipper hands over dangerous goods to the carrier or an actual carrier, as the case may be, the shipper must inform him of the dangerous character of the goods and, if necessary, of the precautions to be taken. If the shipper fails to do so and such carrier or actual carrier does not otherwise have knowledge of their dangerous character:

(a) the shipper is liable to the carrier and any actual carrier for the loss resulting from the shipment of such goods, and

(b) the goods may at any time be unloaded, destroyed or rendered innocuous, as the circumstances may require, without payment of compensation.

3. The provisions of paragraph 2 of this Article may not be invoked by any person if during the carriage he has taken the goods in his charge with knowledge of their dangerous character.

4. If, in cases where the provisions of paragraph 2, subparagraph b, of this Article do not apply or may not be invoked, dangerous goods become an actual danger to life or property, they may unloaded, destroyed or rendered innocuous, as the circumstances may require, without payment of compensation except where there is an obligation to contribute in general average or where the carrier is liable in accordance with the provisions of Article 5.

## Part IV. Transport Documents

### Article 14. Issue of bill of lading

1. When the carrier or the actual carrier takes the goods in his charge, the carrier must, on demand of the shipper, issue to the shipper a bill of lading.

2. The bill of lading may be signed by a person having authority from the carrier. A bill of lading signed by the master of the ship carrying the goods is deemed to have been signed on behalf of the carrier.

3. The signature on the bill of lading may be in handwriting, printed in facsimile, perforated, stamped, in symbols, or made by any other mechanical or electronic means, if not inconsistent with the law of the country where the bill of lading is issued.

### Article 15. Contents of bill of lading.

1. The bill of lading must include, *inter alia*, the following particulars:

(a) the general nature of the goods, the leading marks necessary for identification of the goods, an express statement, if applicable, as to the dangerous character of the goods, the number of packages or pieces, and the weight of the goods or their quantity otherwise expressed, all such particulars as furnished by the shipper;
(b) the apparent condition of the goods;
(c) the name and principal place of business of the carrier;
(d) the name of the shipper;
(e) the consignee if named by the shipper;
(f) the port of loading under the contract of carriage by sea and the date on which the goods were taken over by the carrier at the port of loading;
(g) the port of discharge under the contract of carriage by sea;
(h) the number of originals of the bill of lading, if more than one;
(i) the place of issuance of the bill of lading;
(j) the signature of the carrier or a person acting on his behalf;
(k) the freight to the extent payable by the consignee or other indication that freight is payable by him;
(l) the statement referred to in paragraph 3 of Article 23;
(m) the statement, if applicable, that the goods shall or may be carried on deck;
(n) the date or the period of delivery of the goods at the port of discharge if expressly agreed upon between the parties; and
(o) any increased limit or limits of liability where agreed in accordance with paragraph 4 of Article 6.

2. After the goods have been loaded on board, if the shipper so demands, the carrier must issue to the shipper a 'shipped' bill of lading which, in addition to the particulars required under paragraph 1 of this Article, must state that the goods are on board a named ship or ships, and the date or dates of loading. If the carrier has previously issued to the shipper a bill of lading or other document of title with respect to any of such goods, on request of the carrier, the shipper must surrender such document in exchange for a 'shipped' bill of

lading. The carrier may amend any previously issued document in order to meet the shipper/s demand for a 'shipped' bill of lading if, as amended, such document includes all the information required to be contained in a 'shipped' bill of lading.

3. The absence in the bill of lading of one or more particulars referred to in this Article does not affect the legal character of the document as a bill of lading provided that it nevertheless meets the requirements set out in paragraph 7 of Article 1.

## Article 16. Bills of lading: reservations and evidentiary effect

1. If the bill of lading contains particulars concerning the general nature, leading marks, number of packages or pieces, weight or quantity of the goods which the carrier or other person issuing the bill of lading on his behalf knows or has reasonable grounds to suspect do not accurately represent the goods actually taken over or, where a 'shipped' bill of lading is issued, loaded, or if he had no reasonable means of checking such particulars, the carrier or such other person must insert in the bill of lading a reservation specifying these inaccuracies, grounds of suspicion or the absence of reasonable means of checking.

2. If the carrier or other person issuing the bill of lading on his behalf fails to note on the bill of lading the apparent condition of the goods, he is deemed to have noted on the bill of lading that the goods were in apparent good condition.

3. Except for particulars in respect of which and to the extent to which a reservation permitted under paragraph 1 of this Article has been entered:

(a) the bill of lading is *prima facie* evidence of the taking over or, where a 'shipped' bill of lading is issued, loading, by the carrier of the goods as described in the bill of lading; and

(b) proof to the contrary by the carrier is not admissible if the bill of lading has been transferred to a third party, including a consignee, who in good faith has acted in reliance on the description of the goods therein.

4. A bill of lading which does not, as provided in paragraph 1 subparagraph h of Article 15, set forth the freight or otherwise indicate that freight is payable by the consignee or does not set forth demurrage incurred at the port of loading payable by the consignee, is *prima facie* evidence that no freight or such demurrage is payable by him. However, proof to the contrary by the carrier is not admissible when the bill of lading has been transferred to a third party, including a consignee, who in good faith has acted in reliance on the absence in the bill of lading of any such indication.

## Article 17. Guarantees by the shipper

1. The shipper is deemed to have guaranteed to the carrier the accuracy of particulars relating to the general nature of the goods, their marks, number, weight and quantity as furnished by him for insertion in the bill of lading. The shipper must indemnify the carrier against the loss resulting from inaccuracies in such particulars. The shipper remains liable even if the bill of lading has been

transferred by him. The right of the carrier to such indemnity in no way limits his liability under the contract of carriage by sea to any person other than the shipper.

2. Any letter of guarantee or agreement by which the shipper undertakes to indemnify the carrier against loss resulting from the issuance of the bill of lading by the carrier, or by a person acting on his behalf, without entering a reservation relating to particulars furnished by the shipper for insertion in the bill of lading, or to the apparent condition of the goods, is void and of no effect as against any third party, including a consignee, to whom the bill of lading has been transferred.

3. Such letter of guarantee or agreement is valid as against the shipper unless the carrier or the person acting on his behalf, by omitting the reservation referred to in paragraph 2 of this Article, intends to defraud a third party, including a consignee, who acts in reliance on the description of the goods in the bill of lading. In the latter case, if the reservation omitted relates to particulars furnished by the shipper for insertion in the bill of lading the carrier has no right of indemnity from the shipper pursuant to paragraph 1 of this Article.

4. In the case of intended fraud referred to in paragraph 3 of this Article the carrier is liable, without the benefit of the limitation of liability provided for in this Convention, for the loss incurred by a third party, including a consignee, because he has acted in reliance on the description of the goods in the bill of lading.

## ARTICLE 18. DOCUMENTS OTHER THAN BILLS OF LADING

Where a carrier issues a document other than a bill of lading to evidence the receipt of the goods to be carried, such a document is *prima facie* evidence of the conclusion of the contract of carriage by sea and the taking over by the carrier of the goods as therein described.

# PART V. CLAIMS AND ACTIONS

## ARTICLE 19. NOTICE OF LOSS, DAMAGE OR DELAY

1. Unless notice of loss or damage, specifying the general nature of such loss or damage, is given in writing by the consignee to the carrier not later than the working day after the day when the goods were handed over to the consignee, such handing over is *prima facie* evidence of the delivery by the carrier of the goods as described in the document of transport or, if no such document has been issued, in good condition.

2. Where the loss or damage is not apparent, the provisions of paragraph 1 of this Article apply correspondingly if notice in writing is not given within 15 consecutive days after the day when the goods were handed over to the consignee.

3. If the state of the goods at the time they were handed over to the consignee has been the subject of a joint survey or inspection by the parties,

notice in writing need not be given of loss or damage ascertained during such survey or inspection.

4. In the case of any actual or apprehended loss or damage the carrier and the consignee must give all reasonable facilities to each other for inspecting and tallying the goods.

5. No compensation shall be payable for loss resulting from delay in delivery unless a notice has been given in writing to the carrier within 60 consecutive days after the day when the goods were handed over to the consignee.

6. If the goods have been delivered by an actual carrier, any notice given under this Article to him shall have the same effect as if it had been given to the carrier and any notice given to the carrier shall have effect as if given to such actual carrier.

7. Unless notice of loss or damage, specifying the general nature of the loss or damage, is given in writing by the carrier or actual carrier to the shipper not later than 90 consecutive days after the occurrence of such loss or damage or after the delivery of the goods in accordance with paragraph 2 of Article 4, whichever is later, the failure to give such notice is *prima facie* evidence that the carrier or the actual carrier has sustained no loss or damage due to the fault or neglect of the shipper, his servants or agents.

8. For the purpose of this Article, notice given to a person acting on the carrier's or the actual carrier's behalf, including the master or the officer in charge of the ship, or to a person acting on the shipper's behalf is deemed to have been given to the carrier, to the actual carrier or to the shipper, respectively.

## ARTICLE 20. LIMITATION OF ACTIONS

1. Any action relating to carriage of goods under this convention is time-barred if judicial or arbitral proceedings have not been instituted within a period of two years.

2. The limitation period commences on the day on which the carrier has delivered the goods or part thereof or, in cases where no goods have been delivered, on the last day on which the goods should have been delivered.

3. The day on which the limitation period commences is not included in the period.

4. The person against whom a claim is made may at any time during the running of the limitation period extend that period by a declaration in writing to the claimant. This period may be further extended by another declaration or declarations.

5. An action for indemnity by a person held liable may be instituted even after the expiration of the limitation period provided for in the preceding paragraphs if instituted within the time allowed by the law of the state where proceedings are instituted. However, the time allowed shall not be less than 90

days commencing from the day when the person instituting such action for indemnity has settled the claim or has been served with process in the action against himself.

## Article 21. Jurisdiction

1. In judicial proceedings relating to carriage of goods under this convention the plaintiff, at his option, may institute an action in a court which, according to the law of the State where the court is situated, is competent and within the jurisdiction of which is situated one of the following places:

(a) the principal place of business or, in the absence thereof, the habitual residence of the defendant; or
(b) the place where the contract was made provided that the defendant has there a place of business, branch of agency through which the contract was made; or
(c) the port of loading or the port of discharge; or
(d) any additional place designated for that purpose in the contract of carriage by sea.

2.—

(a) Notwithstanding the preceding provisions of this Article, an action may be instituted in the courts of any port or place in a Contracting State at which the carrying vessel or any other vessel of the same ownership may have been arrested in accordance with applicable rules of the law of that State and of international law. However, in such a case, at the petition of the defendant, the claimant must remove the action, at his choice, to one of the jurisdictions referred to in paragraph 1 of this Article for the determination of the claim, but before such removal the defendant must furnish security sufficient to ensure payment of any judgement that may subsequently be awarded to the claimant in the action.
(b) All questions relating to the sufficiency or otherwise of the security shall be determined by the court of the port or place of the arrest.

3. No judicial proceedings relating to carriage of goods under this convention may be instituted in a place not specified in paragraph 1 or 2 of this Article. The provisions of this paragraph do not constitute an obstacle to the jurisdiction of the Contracting States for provisional or protective measures.

4.—

(a) Where an action has been instituted in a court competent under paragraph 1 or 2 of this Article or where judgement has been delivered by such a court, no new action may be started between the same parties on the same grounds unless the judgement of the court before which the first action was instituted is not enforceable in the country in which the new proceedings are instituted;
(b) for the purpose of this Article the institution of measures with a view to obtaining enforcement of a judgement is not to be considered as the starting of a new action;
(c) for the purpose of this Article, the removal of an action to a different court within the same country, or to a court in another country, in accordance with paragraph 2 a of this Article, is not to be considered as the starting of a new action.

5. Notwithstanding the provisions of the preceding paragraphs, an agreement made by the parties, after a claim under the contract of carriage by sea has arisen, which designates the place where the claimant may institute an action, is effective.

## Article 22. Arbitration

1. Subject to the provisions of this Article, parties may provide by agreement evidenced in writing that any dispute that may arise relating to carriage of goods under this Convention shall be referred to arbitration.

2. Where a charter-party contains a provision that disputes arising thereunder shall be referred to arbitration and a bill of lading issued pursuant to the charter-party does not contain a special annotation providing that such provision shall be binding upon the holder of the bill of lading, the carrier may not invoke such provision as against a holder having acquired the bill of lading in good faith.

3. The arbitration proceedings shall, at the option of the claimant, be instituted at one of the following places;
   (a) a place in a state within whose territory is situated:
      (i) the principal place of business of the defendant or, in the absence thereof, the habitual residence of the defendant; or
      (ii) the place where the contract was made, provided that the defendant has there a place of business, branch or agency through which the contract was made; or
      (iii) the port of loading or the port of discharge; or
   (b) any place designated for that purpose in the arbitration clause or agreement.

4. The arbitrator or arbitration tribunal shall apply the rules of this Convention.

5. The provisions of paragraphs 3 and 4 of this Article are deemed to be part of every arbitration clause or agreement, and any term, of such clause or agreement which is inconsistent therewith is null and void.

6. Nothing in this Article affects the validity of an agreement relating to arbitration made by the parties after the claim under the contract of carriage by sea has arisen.

## Part VI. Supplement Provision

## Article 23. Contractual stipulations

1. Any stipulation in a contract of carriage by sea, in a bill of lading, or in any other document evidencing the contract of carriage by sea is null and void to the extent that it derogates, directly or indirectly, from the provisions of this Convention. The nullity of such a stipulation does not affect the validity of the other provisions of the contract or document of which it forms a part. A clause assigning benefit of insurance of the goods in favour of the carrier, or any similar clause, is null and void.

2. Notwithstanding the provisions of paragraph 1 of this Article, a carrier may increase his responsibilities and obligations under this Convention.

3. Where a bill of lading or any other document evidencing the contract of carriage by sea is issued, it must contain a statement that the carriage is subject to the provisions of this Convention which nullify any stipulation derogating therefrom to the detriment of the shipper or the consignee.

4. Where the claimant in respect of the goods has incurred loss as a result of a stipulation which is null and void by virtue of the present Article, or as a result of the omission of the statement referred to in paragraph 3 of this Article, the carrier must pay compensation to the extent required in order to give the claimant compensation in accordance with the provisions of this Convention for any loss of or damage to the goods as well as for delay in delivery. The carrier must, in addition, pay compensation for costs incurred by the claimant for the purpose of exercising his right, provided that costs incurred in the action where the foregoing provision is invoked are to be determined in accordance with the law of the State where proceedings are instituted.

## ARTICLE 24. GENERAL AVERAGE

1. Nothing in this Convention shall prevent the application of provisions in the contract of carriage by sea or national law regarding the adjustment of general average.

2. With the exception of Article 20, the provisions of this Convention relating to the liability of the carrier for loss of or damage to the goods also determine whether the consignee may refuse contribution in general average and the liability of the carrier to indemnify the consignee in respect of any such contribution made or any salvage paid.

## ARTICLE 25. OTHER CONVENTIONS

1. This Convention does not modify the rights or duties of the carrier, the actual carrier and their servants and agents, provided for in international conventions or national law relating to the limitation of liability of owners of seagoing ships.

[2.-4. Omitted.]

5. Nothing contained in this Convention prevents a Contracting State from applying any other international convention which is already in force at the date of this Convention and which applies mandatorily to contracts of carriage of goods primarily by a mode of transport other than transport by sea. This provision also applies to any subsequent revision or amendment of such international convention.

## ARTICLE 26. UNIT OF ACCOUNT

1. The unit of account referred to in Article 6 of this Convention is the Special Drawing Right as defined by the International Monetary Fund. The amounts

mentioned in Article 6 are to be converted into the national currency of a State according to the value of such currency at the date of judgement or the date agreed upon by the parties. The value of a national currency, in terms of the Special Drawing Right, of a Contracting State which is a member of the International Monetary Fund is to be calculated in accordance with the method of valuation applied by the International Monetary Fund in effect at the date in question for its operations and transactions. The value of a national currency in terms of the Special Drawing Right of a Contracting State which is not a member of the International Monetary Fund is to be calculated in a manner determined by that State.

2. Nevertheless, those States which are not members of the International Monetary Fund and whose law does not permit the application of the provisions of paragraph 1 of this Article may, at the time of signature, or at the time of ratification, acceptance, approval or accession or at any time thereafter, declare that the limits of liability provided for in this Convention to be applied in their territories shall be fixed as:

> 12,500 monetary units per package or other shipping unit or 37.5 monetary units per kilogram of gross weight of the goods.

3. The monetary unit referred to in paragraph 2 of this Article corresponds to sixty-five and a half milligrams of gold of millesimal fineness nine hundred. the conversion of the amounts referred to in paragraph 2 into the national currency is to be made according to the law of the state concerned.

4. The calculation mentioned in the last sentence of paragraph 1 and the conversion mentioned in paragraph 3 of this Article is to be made in such a manner as to express in the national currency of the Contracting State as far as possible the same real value for the amounts in Article 6 as is expressed there in units of account. Contracting States must communicate to the depositary the manner of calculation pursuant to paragraph 1 of this Article, or the result of the conversion mentioned in paragraph 3 of this Article, as the case may be, at the time of signature or when depositing their instruments of ratification, acceptance, approval or accession, or when availing themselves of the option provided for in paragraph 2 of this Article and whenever there is a change in the manner of such calculation or in the result of such conversion.

## PART VII, ARTICLES 27.-34. [OMITTED].

## EEC Convention on Law applicable to contractual Obligations, Rome, 1980

See Schedule I Contracts (Applicable Law) Act 1990 for the text of the Convention

# PROTOCOL AMENDING THE CONVENTION ON THE LIMITATION PERIOD IN THE INTERNATIONAL SALE OF GOODS, VIENNA, 1980

## ARTICLE I

1. Paragraph 1 of Article 3 is replaced by the following provisions:
'1. This Convention shall apply only
(a) if, at the time of the conclusion of the contract, the places of business of the parties to a contract of international sale of goods are in Contracting States; or
(b) if the rules of private international law make the law of a Contracting State applicable to the contract of sale.'
2. paragraph 2 of Article 3 is deleted.
3. paragraph 3 of Article 3 is renumbered as paragraph 2.

## ARTICLE II

1. Subparagraph (a) of Article 4 is deleted and replaced by the following provision:

'(a) of goods bought for personal, family or household use, unless the seller, at any time before or at the conclusion of the contract, neither knew nor ought to have known that the goods were bought for any such use;'

2. Subparagraph (e) of Article 4 is deleted and is replaced by the following provision:

'(e) of ships, vessels, hovercraft or aircraft;'

## ARTICLES III-XIV [OMITTED].

# UNIFORM RULES CONCERNING THE CONTRACT FOR INTERNATIONAL CARRIAGE OF GOODS BY RAIL (CIM), 1980

## TITLE 1

## GENERAL PROVISIONS

### ARTICLE 1 - SCOPE

1. Subject to the exceptions provided for in Article 2, the Uniform rules shall apply to all consignments of goods for carriage under a through consignment note made out for a route over the territories of at least two States and exclusively over lines or services included in the list provided for in Articles 3 and 10 of the convention.

2. In the Uniform rules the expression 'station' covers: railway stations, ports used by shipping services and all other establishments of transport undertakings, open to the public for the execution of the contract of carriage.

### ARTICLE 2 - EXCEPTIONS FROM SCOPE

1. Consignments between sending and destination stations situated in the territory of the same State, which pass through the territory of another State only in transit, shall not be subject to the Uniform Rules:

(a) if the lines or services over which the transit occurs are exclusively operated by a railway of the State of departure; or

(b) if the States or the railways concerned have agreed not to regard such consignments as international.

2. Consignments between stations in two adjacent States and between stations in two states in transit through the territory of a third State shall, if the lines over which the consignments are carried are exclusively operated by a railway of one of those three States, be subject to the internal traffic regulations applicable to that railway if the sender, by using the appropriate consignment note, so elects and where there is nothing to the contrary in the laws and regulation of any of the States concerned.

### ARTICLE 2 - OBLIGATION TO CARRY

1. The railway shall be bound to undertake all carriage of any goods in complete wagon-loads, subject to the terms of the Uniform rules, provided that:

(a) the sender complies with the Uniform rules, the supplementary provisions and the tariffs;

(b) carriage can be undertaken by the normal staff and transport resources which suffice to meet usual traffic requirements;

(c) carriage is not prevented by circumstances which the railway cannot avoid and which it is not in a position to remedy.

2. The railway shall not be obliged to accept goods of which the loading, trans-shipment or unloading requires the use of special facilities unless the stations concerned have such facilities at their disposal.

3. The railway shall only be obliged to accept goods the carriage of which can take place without delay; the provisions in force at the forwarding station shall determine the circumstances in which goods not complying with that condition must be temporarily stored.

4. When the competent authority decides that:
   (a) a service shall be discontinued or suspended totally or partially,
   (b) certain consignments shall be refused or accepted only subject to conditions,

these measures shall, without delay, be brought to the notice of the public and the railways; the latter shall inform the railways of the other States with a view to their publication.

5. The railways may, by joint agreement, concentrate goods traffic between certain places on specified frontier points and transit countries. These measures shall be notified to the Central Office. They shall be entered by the railways in special lists, published in the manner laid down for international tariffs, and shall come into force one month after the date of notification to the Central Office.

6. Any contravention of this Article by the railway may constitute a cause of action for compensation for loss or damage caused.

## ARTICLE 4 - ARTICLES NOT ACCEPTABLE FOR CARRIAGE

The following shall not be accepted for carriage:
   (a) articles the carriage of which is prohibited in any one of the territories in which the articles would be carried;
   (b) articles the carriage of which is a monopoly of the postal authorities in any one of he territories in which the articles would be carried;
   (c) articles which, by reason of their dimensions, their mass, or their packaging, are not suitable for the carriage proposed, having regard to the installations or rolling stock of any one of the railways which would be used;
   (d) substances and articles which are not acceptable for carriage under the Regulations concerning the international carriage of dangerous goods by rail (RID), Annex 1 to the Uniform rules, subject to the exceptions provided for in Articles 5, §2.

## ARTICLE 5 - ARTICLES ACCEPTABLE FOR CARRIAGE SUBJECT TO CONDITIONS

1. The following shall be acceptable for carriage subject to conditions
   (a) substances and articles acceptable for carriage subject to the conditions laid down in the RID or in the agreements and tariff clauses provided for in §2.

(b) funeral consignments, railway rolling stock running on its own wheels, live animals and consignments the carriage of which presents special difficulties by reason of their dimensions, their mass or their packaging: subject to the conditions laid down in the supplementary provision; these may derogate from the Uniform rules.

Live animals must be accompanied by an attendant provided by the consignor. Nevertheless an attendant shall not be required when the international tariffs permit or when the railways participating in the carriage so permit at the consignor's request; in such cases, unless there is an agreement to the contrary, the railway shall not be liable for any loss or damage resulting from any risk which the attendant was intended to avert.

2. Two or more States, by agreement, or two or more railways, by tariff clauses, may jointly determine the conditions with which certain substances or articles not acceptable for carriage under the RID must comply if they are nevertheless to be accepted. States or railways may, in the same manner, make the conditions for acceptance laid down in the RID less rigorous. Such agreements and tariff clauses must be published and notified to the Central Office which will bring them to the notice of the States.

## Article 6 - Tariffs, Private Agreements [Omitted]

## Article 7 - Unit of Account. Rate of Exchange or of Acceptance of Foreign Currency

1. The unit of account referred to in the Uniform rules shall be the Special Drawing Right as defined by the International Monetary Fund.

The value in Special Drawing Right of the national currency of a State which is a Member of the International Monetary fund shall be calculated in accordance with the method of valuation applied by the International Monetary Fund for its own operations and transactions.

2. The value in Special Drawing Right of the national currency of a State which is not a member of the International Monetary Fund shall be calculated by the method determined by that State.

The calculation must express in the national currency a real value approximating as closely to that which would result from the application of §1.

3. In the case of a state which is not a member of the International Monetary Fund and whose legislation does not permit the application of §1 or §2 above, the unit of account referred to in the Uniform Rules shall be deemed to be equal to three gold francs.

The gold franc is defined as 10/31 of a gram of gold of millesimal fineness 900.

The conversion of the gold franc must express in the national currency a real value approximating as closely to that which would result from the application of §1.

4. Within three months after the entry into force of the Convention and each time that a change occurs in their method of calculation or in the value of their

national currency in relation to the unit of account, states shall notify the Central Office of their method of calculation in accordance with §2, or the results of the conversion in accordance with §3.

The Central Office shall notify the States of this information.

5. The railway shall publish the rates at which:
   (a) it converts sums expressed in foreign currencies but payable in domestic currency (rates of conversion);
   (b) It accepts payment in foreign currencies (rates of acceptance).

## ARTICLE 8 - SPECIAL PROVISIONS FOR CERTAIN TYPES OF TRANSPORT

1. In the case of the haulage of privately owned wagons, special provisions are laid down in the Regulations concerning the international haulage of private owners' wagons by rail (RIP), Annex II to the Uniform Rules.

2. In the case of the carriage of containers, special provisions are laid down in the Regulations concerning the international carriage of containers by rail (RICo), Annex III to the Uniform Rules.

3. In the case of express parcels traffic, railways may, by tariff clauses, agree on special provisions in accordance with the Regulations concerning the international carriage of express parcels by rail (RIEx), Annex IV to the Uniform Rules.

4. Two or more States, by special agreement, or two or more railways by supplementary provisions or by tariff clauses, may agree on terms derogating from the Uniform Rules for the following types of consignments:
   (a) consignments under cover of a negotiable document;
   (b) consignments to be delivered only against return of the duplicate of the consignment note;
   (c) consignments of newspapers;
   (d) consignment intended for fairs or exhibitions;
   (e) consignment of loading tackle and of equipment for protection of goods in transit against heat or cold;
   (f) consignments over all or part of the route under cover of consignment notes which are not used for charging and billing;
   (g) consignments sent under cover of an instrument suitable for automatic data transmission.

## ARTICLE 9 - SUPPLEMENTARY PROVISION

1. Two or more States or two or more railways may make supplementary provisions for the execution of the Uniform Rules. They may not derogate from the Uniform Rules unless the latter expressly so provide.

2. The supplementary provisions shall be put into force and published in the manner required by the laws and regulations of each State. The Central Office shall be notified of the supplementary provisions and of their coming into force.

## Article 10 - National Law

1. In the absence of provisions in the Uniform rules, supplementary provisions or international tariffs, national law shall apply.

2. 'National law' means the law of the State in which the person entitled asserts his rights, including the rules relating to conflict of laws.

## Title II

## Making and Execution of the Contract of Carriage.

## Article 11 - Making of the contract of carriage

1. The contract of carriage shall come into existence as soon as the forwarding railway has accepted the goods for carriage together with the consignment note. Acceptance is established by the application to the consignment note and, where appropriate, to each additional sheet, of the stamp of the forwarding station, or accounting machine entry, showing the date of acceptance.

2. The procedure laid done in §1 must be carried out immediately after all the goods to which the consignment note relates have been handed over for carriage and - where the provisions in force at the forwarding station so require - such charges as the consignor has undertaken to pay have been paid or a security deposited in accordance with Article 15, §7. The procedure shall be carried out in the presence of the consignor if he so requests.

3. When the stamp has been affixed or the accounting machine entry has been made, the consignment note shall be evidence of the making and content of the contract.

4. Nevertheless, when the loading of the goods is the duty of the consignor in accordance with tariffs or agreements existing between him and the railway, and provided that such agreements are authorised at the forwarding station, the particulars in the consignment note relating to the mass of the goods or to the number of packages shall only be evidence against the railway when that weight or number of packages has been verified by the railway and certified in the consignment note. If necessary these particulars may be proved by other means.

If it is obvious that there is no actual deficiency corresponding to the discrepancy between the mass or number of packages and the particulars in the consignment note, the latter shall not be evidence against the railway. This shall apply in particular when the wagon is handed over to the consignee with the original seals intact

5. The railway shall certify receipt of the goods and the date of acceptance for carriage by affixing the date stamp to or making the accounting machine entry on the duplicate of the consignment note before returning the duplicate to the consignor. The duplicate shall not have effect as the consignment note accompanying the goods, nor as a bill of lading.

## Article 12 - Consignment note

1. The consignor shall present a consignment note duly completed. A separate consignment note shall be made out for each consignment. One and the same consignment note may not relate to more than a single wagon load. The supplementary provisions may derogate from these rules.

2. The railways shall prescribe, for both *petite vitesse* and *grande vitesse* traffic, a standard form of consignment note, which must include a duplicate for the consignor. The choice of consignment note by the consignor shall indicate whether the goods are to be carried by *petite vitesse* or by *grande vitesse*. A request for *grande vitesse* over one part of the route and *petite vitesse* over the remainder will not be allowed except by agreement between all the railways concerned.

In the case of certain traffic, notably between adjacent countries, the railways may prescribe, in the tariffs, the use of a simplified form of consignment note.

3. The consignment note must be printed in two or where necessary in three languages, at least one of which shall be one of the working languages of the Organisation.

International tariffs may determine the language in which the particulars to be filled in by the consignor in the consignment note shall be entered. In the absence of such provisions, they must be entered in one of the official languages of the State of departure and a translation in one of the working languages of the Organisation must be added unless the particulars have been entered in one of those languages. The particulars entered by the consignor in the consignment note shall be in Roman lettering, save where the supplementary provisions or international tariffs otherwise provide.

## Article 13 - Wording of the Consignment Note

1. The consignment note must contain:

(a) the name of the destination station;
(b) the name and address of the consignee; only one individual or legal person shall be shown as consignee;
(c) the description of the goods;
(d) the mass, or failing that, comparable information in accordance with the provisions in force at the forwarding station;
(e) the number of packages and a description of the packing in the case of consignments in less than wagon loads, and in the case of complete wagon loads comprising one or more packages, forwarded by rail-sea and requiring to be trans-shipped;
(f) the number of the wagon and also, for privately-owned wagons, the tare, in the case of goods where the loading is the duty of the consignor,
(g) a detailed list of the documents which are required by Customs or other administrative authorities and are attached to the consignment note or shown as held at the disposal of the railway at a named station or at an office of the Customs or of any other authority;
(h) the name and address of the consignor; only one individual or legal person shall be shown as the consignor; if the provisions in force at

the forwarding station so require, the consignor shall add to his name and address his written, printed or stamped signature.

The provisions in force at the forwarding station shall determine the meanings of the terms 'wagon load' and 'less than wagon load' for the whole of the route.

2. The consignment note must, where appropriate, contain all the other particulars provided for in the Uniform Rules. It shall not contain other particulars unless they are required or allowed by the laws and regulations of a State, the supplementary provisions or the tariffs, and are not contrary to the Uniform Rules.

3. Nevertheless, the consignor may insert in the consignment note in the space set apart for the purpose, but as information for the consignee, remarks relating to the consignment, without involving the railway in any obligation or liability.

4. The consignment note shall not be replaced by other documents or supplemented by documents other than those prescribed or allowed by the Uniform Rules, the supplementary provisions or the tariffs.

## Article 14 - Route and Tariffs applicable

1. The consignor may stipulate in the consignment note the route to be followed, indicating it by reference to frontier points or frontier stations and where appropriate, to transit stations between railways. He may only stipulate frontier points and frontier stations which are open to traffic between the forwarding and destination places concerned.

2. The following shall be regarded as routing instructions:
   (a) designation of stations where formalities required by customs or other administrative authorities are to be carried out, and of stations where special care is to be given to the goods (attention to animals, re-icing etc,);
   (b) designation of the tariffs to be applied, if this is sufficient to determine the stations between which the tariffs requested are to be applied;
   (c) instructions as to the payment of the whole or a part of the charges up to X (X indicating by name the point at which the tariffs of adjacent countries are applied).

3. Except in the cases specified in Article 3 §§4 and 5, and Article 33 §1, the railway may not carry the goods by a route other than that stipulated by the consignor unless both:
   (a) the formalities required by customs or other administrative authorities, as well as the special care to be given to the goods, will in any event be carried out at the stations indicated by the consignor; and
   (b) the charges and the transit periods will not be greater than the charges and transit periods calculated according to the route stipulated by the consignor.

Sub-paragraph (a) shall not apply to consignments in less than wagon loads if one of the participating railways is unable to adhere to the route chosen by the consignor by virtue of the routing instructions arising from its arrangements for the international carriage of consignments in less than wagon loads.

4. Subject to the provisions of §3, the charges and transit periods shall be calculated according to the route stipulated by the consignor or, in the absence of any such indication, according to the route chosen by the railway.

5. The consignor may stipulate in the consignment note which tariffs are to be applied. The railway must apply such tariffs if the conditions laid down for their application have been fulfilled.

6. If the instructions given by the consignor are not sufficient to indicate the route or tariffs to be applied, or if any of those instructions are inconsistent with one another, the railway shall choose the route or tariffs which appear to it to be the most advantageous to the consignor.

7. The railway shall not be liable for any loss or damage suffered as a result of the choice made in accordance with §6, except in the case of wilful misconduct or gross negligence.

8. If an international tariff exists from the forwarding to the destination station and if, in the absence of adequate instructions from the consignor, the railway has applied that tariff, the railway shall, at the request of the person entitled, refund him the difference between the carriage charges thus applied and those which the application of other tariffs would have produced over the same route, when such difference exceeds four units of account per consignment note.

The same shall apply if, in the absence of adequate instructions from the consignor, the railway has applied consecutive tariffs, even though there is an international tariff offering a more advantageous charge, all other conditions being the same.

## Article 15 - Payment of Charges

1. The charges (carriage charges, supplementary charges, Customs duties and other charges incurred from the time of acceptance for carriage to the time of delivery) shall be paid by the consignor or the consignee in accordance with the following provisions.

In applying these provisions, charges which, according to the applicable tariff, must be added to the standard rates or special rates when calculating the carriage charges, shall be deemed to be carriage charges.

2. A consignor who undertakes to pay a part or all of the charges shall indicate this on the consignment note by using one of the following phrases:

(a)—

(i) 'carriage charges paid', if he undertakes to pay carriage charges only;

(ii) 'carriage charges paid including...', if he undertakes to pay charges additional to those for carriage; he shall give an exact description of those charges; additional indications, which may relate only to the supplementary charges or other charges incurred from the time of acceptance for carriage until the time of delivery as well as to sums collected either by customs or other administrative authorities shall not result in any division of the total amount of any one category of charges (for example, the total amount of Customs duties and of other amounts payable to Customs, value added tax being regarded as a separate category);

(iii) 'carriage charges paid to X' (X indicating by name the point at which the tariffs of adjacent countries are applied), if he undertakes to pay carriage charges to X;

(iv) 'carriage chargers paid to X including...' (X indicating by name the point at which the tariffs of adjacent countries are applied), if he undertakes to pay charges additional to those for carriage to X, but excluding all charges relating to the subsequent country or railway; the provisions of (ii) shall apply analogously:

(b) 'all charges paid', if he undertakes to pay all charges (carriage charges, supplementary charges, customs duties and other charges);

(c) 'charges paid not exceeding...', if he undertakes to pay a fixed sum; save where the tariffs otherwise provide, this sum shall be expressed in the currency of the country of departure.

Supplementary and other charges which, according to the provisions in force at the forwarding station, are to be calculated for the whole of the route concerned, and the charge for interest in delivery laid down in Article 16, §2, shall always be paid in full by the consignor in the case of payment of the charges in accordance with a iv.

3. The international tariffs may, as regards payment of charges, prescribe the exclusive use of certain phrases set out in §2 of this Article or the use of other phrases.

4. The charges which the consignor has not undertaken to pay shall be deemed to be payable by the consignee. Nevertheless, such charges shall be payable by the consignor if the consignee has not taken possession of the consignment note nor asserted his rights under Article 28, §4, nor modified the contract of carriage in accordance with Article 31.

5. Supplementary charges, such as charges for demurrage and standage, warehousing and weighing, which arise from an act attributable to the consignee or from a request which he has made, shall always be paid by him.

6. The forwarding railway may require the consignor to prepay the charges in the case of goods which in its opinion are liable to undergo rapid deterioration or which, by reason of their low value or their nature, do not provide sufficient cover for such charges.

7. If the amount of the charges which the consignor undertakes to pay cannot be ascertained exactly at the time the goods are handed over for carriage, such charges shall be entered in a charges note and a settlement of accounts shall be made with the consignor not later than thirty days after the expiry of the transit period. The railway may require as security a deposit approximating to the amount of such charges, for which a receipt shall be given. A detailed account of charges drawn up from the particulars in the charges note shall be delivered to the consignor in return for the receipt.

8. The forwarding station shall specify, in the consignment note and in the duplicate, the charges which have been prepaid, unless the provisions in force at the forwarding station provide that those charges are only to be specified in the duplicate. In the case provided for in §7 of this Article these charges are not to be specified either in the consignment note or in the duplicate.

## ARTICLE 16 - INTEREST IN DELIVERY

1. Any consignment may be the subject of a declaration of interest in delivery. The amount declared shall be shown in figures in the consignment note in the currency of the country of departure, in another currency determined by the tariffs or in units of account.

2. The charge for interest in delivery shall be calculated for the whole of the route concerned, in accordance with the tariffs of the forwarding railway.

## ARTICLE 17 - CASH ON DELIVERY AND DISBURSEMENTS

1. The consignor may make the goods subject to a cash on delivery payment not exceeding their value at the time of acceptance at the forwarding station. The amount of such cash on delivery payment shall be expressed in the currency of the country of departure; the tariffs may provide for exceptions.

2. The railway shall not be obliged to pay over any amount representing a cash on delivery payment unless the amount in question has been paid by the consignee. That amount shall be placed at the consignor's disposal within thirty days of payment by the consignee; interest at five per cent per annum shall be payable from the date of the expiry of that period.

3. If the goods have been delivered, wholly or in part, to the consignee without prior collection of the amount of the cash on delivery payment, the railway shall pay the consignor the amount of any loss or damage sustained up to the total amount of the cash on delivery payment without prejudice to any right of recovery from the consignee.

4. Cash on delivery consignment shall be subject to a collection fee laid down in the tariffs; such fee shall be payable notwithstanding cancellation or reduction of the amount of the cash on delivery payment by modification of the contract of carriage in accordance with Article 30, §1.

5. Disbursements shall only be allowed if made in accordance with the provisions in force in force at the forwarding station.

6. The amounts of the cash on delivery payment and of disbursements shall be entered in figures on the consignment note.

## ARTICLE 18 - RESPONSIBILITY FOR PARTICULARS FURNISHED IN THE CONSIGNMENT NOTE

The consignor shall be responsible for the correctness of the particulars inserted by, or for, him, in the consignment note. He shall bear all the consequences in the event of those particulars being irregular, incorrect, incomplete, or not entered in the allotted space. If that space is insufficient, the consignor shall indicate therein the place in the consignment note where the rest of the particulars are to be found.

## ARTICLE 19 - CONDITION, PACKING AND MARKING OF GOODS

1. When the railway accepts for carriage goods showing obvious signs of damage, it may require the condition of such goods to be indicated in the consignment note.

2. When the nature of the goods is such as to require packing, the consignor shall pack them in such a way as to protect them from total or partial loss and from damage in transit and to avoid risk of injury or damage to persons, equipment or other goods.

Moreover the packing shall comply with the provisions in force at the forwarding station.

3. If the consignor has not complied with the provisions of §2, the railway may either refuse the goods or require the sender to acknowledge in the consignment note the absence of packing or the defective condition of the packing, with an exact description thereof.

4. The consignor shall be liable for all the consequences of the absence of packing or defective condition of packing and shall in particular make good any loss or damage suffered by the railway from this cause. In the absence of any particulars in the consignment note, the burden of proof of such absence of packing or defective condition of the packing shall rest upon the railway.

5. Save where the tariffs otherwise provide, the consignor of a consignment amounting to less than a wagon load shall indicate on each package or on a label approved by the railway in a clear and indelible manner which will avoid confusion and correspond exactly with the particulars in the consignment note:

(a) the name and address of the consignee;

(b) the destination station.

The details required under a and b above shall also be shown on each article or package comprised in a wagon load forwarded by rail/sea and requiring to be trans-shipped.

Old markings or labels shall be obliterated or removed by the consignor.

6. Save where the supplementary provisions or the tariffs otherwise provide, goods which are fragile or may become scattered in wagons and goods which may taint or damage other goods shall be carried only in complete wagon loads, unless packed or fastened together in such a manner that they cannot become broken or lost, or taint or damage other goods.

## ARTICLE 20 - HANDING OVER OF GOODS FOR CARRIAGE AND LOADING OF GOODS

1. The handing over of goods for carriage shall be governed by the provisions in force at the forwarding station.

2. Loading shall be the duty of the railway or the consignor according to the provisions in force at the forwarding station, unless otherwise provided in the Uniform Rules or unless the consignment note includes a reference to a special agreement between the consignor and the railway.

When the loading is the responsibility of the consignor, he shall comply with the load limit. If different load limits are in force on the lines traversed, the lowest load limit shall be applicable to the whole route. The provisions laying down load limit shall be applicable to the whole route. The provisions laying down load limits shall be published in the same manner as tariffs. If the consignor so requests, the railway shall inform him of the permitted load limit.

3. The consignor shall be liable for all the consequences of defective loading carried out by him and shall, in particular, make good any loss or damage suffered by the railway through this cause. Nevertheless Article 15 shall apply to the payment of costs arising from the reloading of goods in the event of defective loading. The burden of proof of defective loading shall rest upon the railway.

4. Unless otherwise provided in the Uniform Rules, goods shall be carried in covered wagons, open wagons, sheeted open wagons or specially equipped wagons according to the international tariffs. If there are no international tariffs, or if they do not contain any provisions on the subject, the provisions in force at the forwarding station shall apply throughout the whole of the route.

5 The affixing of seals to wagons shall be governed by the provisions in force at the forwarding station.

The consignor shall indicate in the consignment note the number and description of the seals affixed to the wagons by him.

## ARTICLE 21 - VERIFICATION

1. The railway shall always have the right to verify that the consignment corresponds with the particulars furnished in the consignment note by the consignor and that the provisions relating to the carriage of goods accepted subject to conditions have been complied with.

2. If the contents of the consignment are examined for this purpose, the consignor or the consignee, according to whether the verification takes place at the forwarding station or the destination station, shall be invited to be present. Should the interested party not attend, or should the verification take place in transit, it shall be carried out in the presence of two witnesses not connected with the railway, unless the laws or regulations of the State where the verification takes place provide otherwise. The railway may not, however, carry out the verification in transit unless compelled to do so by operational necessities or by the requirements of the Customs or of other administrative authorities.

3. The result of the verification of the particulars in the consignment note shall be entered therein. If verification takes place at the forwarding station, the result shall also be recorded in the duplicate of the consignment note if it is held by the railway.

If the consignment does not correspond with the particulars in the consignment note or if the provisions relating to the carriage of goods accepted subject to conditions have not been complied with, the costs of the verification shall be charged against the goods, unless paid at the time.

## ARTICLE 22 - ASCERTAINMENT OF WEIGHT AND NUMBER OF PACKAGES

1. The provisions in force in each state shall determine the circumstances in which the railway must ascertain the mass of the goods or the number of packages and the actual tare of the wagons.

The railway shall enter in the consignment note the results ascertained.

2. If weighing by the railway, after the contract of carriage has been made, reveals a difference, the mass ascertained by the forwarding station or, failing that, the mass declared by the consignor, shall still be the basis for calculating the carriage charges:

(a) if the difference is manifestly due to the nature of the goods or to atmospheric conditions; or

(b) the weighing takes place on a weighbridge and does not reveal a difference exceeding two per cent of the mass ascertained by the forwarding station or, failing that, of that declared by the consignor.

## ARTICLE 23 - OVERLOADING

1. When overloading of a wagon is established by the forwarding station or by an intermediate station, the excess load may be removed from the wagon even if no surcharge is payable. Where necessary the consignor or, if the contract of carriage has been modified in accordance with Article 31, the consignee shall be asked without delay to give instructions concerning the excess load.

2. Without prejudice to the payment of surcharges under Article 24, the excess load shall be charged for the distance covered in accordance with the carriage charges applicable to the main load. If the excess load is unloaded, the charge for unloading shall be determined by the tariffs of the railway which carries out the unloading

If the person entitled directs that the excess load be forwarded to the same destination station as the main load or to another destination station, or directs that it be returned to the forwarding station, the excess load shall be treated as a separate consignment.

## ARTICLE 24 - SURCHARGES

1. Without prejudice to the railway's entitlement to the difference in carriage charges and to compensation for any possible loss or damage, the railway may impose:

(a) a surcharge equal to one unit of account per kilogram of gross mass of the whole package;
   (i) in the case of irregular, incorrect or incomplete description of substances and articles not acceptable for carriage under the RID;
   (ii) in the case of irregular, incorrect or incomplete description of substances and articles which under the RID are acceptable for carriage subject to conditions, or in the case of failure to observe such conditions;

(b) a surcharge equal to five units of account per 100 kilograms of mass in excess of the load limit, where the wagon has been loaded by the consignor;

(c) a surcharge equal to twice the difference;
   (i) between the carriage charge which should have been payable from the forwarding station to the destination station and that which had been charged, in the case of irregular, incorrect or incomplete description of goods other than those referred to in a, or in general where the description of the consignment would enable it to be carried at a lower tariff than the one that is actually applicable;
   (ii) between the carriage charge for the mass declared and that for the ascertained mass, where the mass declared is less than the real mass.

When a consignment is composed of goods charged at different rates and their mass can be separately determined without difficulty, the surcharge shall be calculated on the basis of the rates respectively applicable to such goods if this method of calculation results in a lower surcharge.

2. Should there be both an under-declaration of mass and overloading in respect of one and the same wagon, the surcharges payable in respect thereof shall be cumulative.

3. The surcharges shall be charged against the goods irrespective of the place where the facts giving rise to the surcharges were established.

4. The amount of the surcharges and the reason for imposing them must be entered in the consignment note.

5. No surcharge shall be due in the case of:

(a) an incorrect declaration of mass, if the railway is bound to weigh the goods under the provisions in force at the forwarding station;
(b) an incorrect declaration of mass, or overloading, if the consignor has requested in the consignment note that the railway should weigh the goods;
(c) overloading arising in the course of carriage from atmospheric conditions if it is proved that the load on the wagon did not exceed the load limit when it was consigned;
(d) an increase in mass during carriage, without overloading, if it is proved that the increase was due to atmospheric conditions;
(e) an incorrect declaration of mass, without overloading, if the difference between the mass indicated in the consignment note and the ascertained mass does not exceed three per cent of the declared mass;
(f) overloading of a wagon when the railway has neither published nor informed the consignor of the load limit in a way which would enable him to observe it.

## Article 25 - Documents for Completion of Administrative Formalities, Custom Seals

1. The consignor must attach to the consignment note the documents necessary for the completion of formalities required by customs or other administrative authorities before delivery of the goods. Such documents shall relate only to goods which are the subject of one and the same consignment note, unless otherwise provided by the requirements of Customs or of other administrative authorities or by the tariffs.

However, when these documents are not attached to the consignment note or if they are to be provided by the consignee, the consignor shall indicate in the consignment note the station, the Customs office or the office of any other authority where the respective documents will be made available to the railway and where the formalities must be completed. If the consignor will himself be present or be represented by an agent when the formalities required by Customs or other administrative authorities are carried out, it will suffice for the documents to be produced at the time when those formalities are carried out.

2. The railway shall not be obliged to check whether the documents furnished are sufficient and correct.

3. The consignor shall be liable to the railway for any loss or damage resulting from the absence or insufficiency of or any irregularity in such documents, save in the case of fault by the railway. The railway shall, where it is at fault, be liable for any consequences arising from the loss, non-use or misuse of the documents referred to in the consignment note and accompanying it or deposited with the railway; nevertheless any compensation shall not exceed that payable in the event of loss of the goods.

4. The consignor must comply with the requirements of Customs or of other administrative authorities with respect to the packing and sheeting of the goods. If the consignor has not packed or sheeted the goods in accordance with those requirements the railway shall be entitled to do so; the resulting costs shall be charged against the goods.

5. The railway may refuse consignments when the seals affixed by Customs or other administrative authorities are damaged or defective.

## Article 26 - Completion of Administrative Formalities

1. In transit, the formalities required by customs or other administrative authorities shall be completed by the railway. The railway may, however, delegate that duty to an agent.

2. In completing such formalities, the railway shall be liable for any fault committed by itself or by its agent; nevertheless, any compensation shall not exceed that payable in the event of loss of the goods.

3. The consignor, by so indicating in the consignment note, or the consignee by giving orders as provided for in Article 31, may ask:

(a) to be present himself or to be represented by an agent when such formalities are carried out, for the purpose of furnishing any information or explanations required;
(b) to complete such formalities himself or to have them completed by an agent, in so far as the laws and regulations of the State in which they are to be carried out so permit;
(c) to pay Customs duties and other charges, when he or his agent is present at or completes such formalities, in so far as the laws and regulations of the state in which they carried out permit such payment.

Neither the consignor, nor the consignee who has the right of disposal, nor the agent of either may take possession of the goods.

4 If, for the completion of the formalities, the consignor designated a station where the provision in force do not permit of their completion, or if he has stipulated for the purpose any other procedure which cannot be followed, the railway shall act in the manner which appears to it to be the most favourable to the interests of the person entitled and shall inform the consignor of the measures taken.

If the consignor, by an entry in the consignment note, has undertaken to pay charges including Customs duty, the railway shall have the choice of completing Customs formalities either in transit or at the destination station.

5. Subject to the exception provided for in the second subparagraph §4, the consignee may complete Customs formalities at the destination station if that station has a Customs office and the consignment note requests Customs clearance on arrival, or, in the absence of such request, if the goods arrive under customs control. The consignee may also complete these formalities at a destination station that has no Customs officer if the national laws and regulations so permit or it the prior authority of the railway and the Customs authorities has been obtained. If the consignee exercises any of these rights, he shall pay in advance the amounts chargeable against the goods.

Nevertheless, the railway may proceed in accordance with §4 if the consignee has not taken possession of the consignment note within the period fixed by the provisions in force at the destination station.

## ARTICLE 27 - TRANSIT PERIODS

1. The transit periods shall be specified either by agreement between the railways participating in the carriage, or by the international tariffs applicable from the forwarding station to the destination station. For certain special types of traffic and on certain routes these periods may also be established on the basis of transport plans applicable between the railways concerned; in that case they must be included in international tariffs or special agreements which, where appropriate, may provide for derogations from §§3 to 9 below.

Such periods shall not in any case exceed those which would result from the application of the following paragraphs.

2. In the absence of any indication in regard to the transit periods as provided for in §1, and subject to the following paras, the transit periods shall be as follows:

(a) for wagon-load consignments:

(i) by *grande vitesse*:

| | |
|---|---|
| period for despatch | 12 hours |
| period for carriage, for each 400 km or fraction thereof | 24 hours |

(ii) by *petite vitesse*:

| | |
|---|---|
| period for despatch | 24 hours |
| period for carriage, for each 300 km or fraction thereof | 24 hours |

(b) for less than wagon-load consignments:

(i) by *grande vitesse*:

| | |
|---|---|
| period for despatch | 12 hours |
| period for carriage, for each 300 km or fraction thereof | 24 hours |

(ii) by *petite vitesse*:

| | |
|---|---|
| period for despatch | 24 hours |
| period for carriage, for each 200 km or fraction thereof | 24 hours |

All these distances shall relate to the kilometric distances contained in the tariffs.

3. The period for carriage shall be calculated on the total distance between the forwarding station and the destination station. the period for despatch shall be counted only one, irrespective of the number of systems traversed.

4. The railway may fix additional transit periods of specified duration in the following cases:

(a) consignments handed in for carriage, or to be delivered, at places other than stations;

(b) consignments to be carried:

(i) by a line or system not equipped to deal rapidly with consignments;

(ii) by a junction line connecting two lines of the same system or of different systems;

(iii) by a second line;

(iv) by lines of different gauge;

(v) by sea or inland navigable waterway;

(vi) by road if there is no rail link;

(c) consignments charged at reduced rates in accordance with special or exceptional internal tariffs;

(d) exceptional circumstances causing an exceptional increase in traffic or exceptional operating difficulties.

5. The additional transit period provided for in §4 (a) to (c) shall be shown in the tariffs or in the provisions duly published in each State.

Those provided for in §4 (d) must be published and may not come into force before their publication.

6. The transit period shall run from midnight next following acceptance of the goods for carriage. In the case, however, of traffic consigned *grande vitesse* the period shall start twenty-four hours later if the day which follows the day of acceptance for carriage is a Sunday or a statutory holiday and if the forwarding station is not open for *grande vitesse* traffic on that Sunday or statutory holiday.

7. Except in the case of any fault by the railway, the transit period shall be extended by the duration of the period necessitated by:

(a) verification or ascertainment in accordance with Article 21 and Article 22, §1, which reveals differences from the particulars shown in the consignment note;

(b) completion of the formalities required by Customs or other administrative authorities;
(c) modification of the contract of carriage under Article 30 or 31;
(d) special care to be given to the goods;
(e) the trans-shipment or reloading of any goods loaded defectively by the consignor;
(f) any interruption of traffic temporarily preventing the commencement or continuation of carriage.

The reason for and the duration of such extensions shall be entered in the consignment note. If necessary proof may be furnished by other means.

8. The transit period shall be suspended for:
(a) *petite vitesse*, on Sundays and statutory holidays;
(b) *grande vitesse*, on Sundays and certain statutory holidays when the provisions in force in any State provide for the suspension of domestic railway transit periods on those days;
(c) *grande vitesse* and *petite vitesse*, on Saturdays when the provisions in force in any State provide for the suspension of domestic railway transit periods on those days.

9. When the transit period ends after the time at which the destination station closes, the period shall be extended until two hours after the time at which the station next opens.

In addition, in the case of *grande vitesse* consignments, if the transit period ends on a Sunday or a holiday as defined in 8 b the period shall be extended until the same time on the next working day.

10. The transit period is observed if , before its expiry:
(a) in cases where consignments are to be delivered at a station and notice of arrival must be given, such notice is given and the goods are held at the disposal of the consignee;
(b) in cases where consignments are to be delivered at a station and notice of arrival need not be given, the goods are held at the disposal of the consignee;
(c) in the case of consignments which are to be delivered at places other than stations, the goods are placed at the disposal of the consignee.

## ARTICLE 28 - DELIVERY

1. The railway shall hand over the consignment note and deliver the goods to the consignee at the destination station against a receipt and payment of the amounts chargeable to the consignee by the railway.

Acceptance of the consignment note obliges the consignee to pay to the railway the amounts chargeable to him.

2. It shall be equivalent to delivery to the consignee if, in accordance with the provisions in force at the destination station:
(a) the goods have been handed over to Customs or *Octroi* authorities at their premises or warehouses, when these are not subject to railway supervision;
(b) the goods have been deposited for storage with the railway, with a forwarding agent or in a public warehouse.

3. The provisions in force at the destination station or the terms of any agreements with the consignee shall determine whether the railway is entitled or obliged to hand over the goods to the consignee elsewhere than at the destination station, whether in a private siding, at his domicile or in a railway depot. If the railway hands over the goods, or arranges for them to be handed over in a private siding, at his domicile or in a depot, delivery shall be deemed to have been effected at the time when they are so handed over. Save where the railway and the user of a private siding have agreed otherwise, operations carried out by the railway on behalf of and under the instructions of that user shall not be covered by the contract of carriage.

4. After the arrival of the goods at the destination station, the consignee may require the railway to hand over the consignment note and deliver the goods to him.

If the loss of the goods is established or if the goods have not arrived on the expiry of the period provided for in Article 39, §1, the consignee may assert, in his own name, any rights against the railway which he may have acquired by reason of the contract of carriage.

5. The person entitled may refuse to accept the goods, even when he has received the consignment note and paid the charges, so long as an examination for which he has asked in order to establish alleged loss or damage has not been made.

6. In all other respects, delivery of goods shall be carried out in accordance with the provisions in force at the destination station.

## Article 29 - Correction of Charges

1. In case of incorrect application of a tariff or of error in the calculation or collection of charges, overcharges shall be repaid by the railway and undercharges paid to the railway only if they exceed four units of account per consignment note. The repayment shall be made as a matter of course.

2. If the consignee has not taken possession of the consignment note the consignor shall be obliged to pay to the railway any amounts undercharged. When the consignment note has been accepted by the consignee or the contract of carriage modified in accordance with Article 31, the consignor shall be obliged to pay any undercharge only to the extent that it relates to the costs which he has undertaken to pay by an entry in the consignment note. Any balance of the undercharge shall be paid by the consignee.

3. Sums due under this Article shall bear interest at five per cent per annum from the day of receipt of the demand for payment or from the day of the claim referred to in Article 53 or, if there has been no such demand or claim, from the day on which legal proceedings are instituted.

If, within a reasonable period allotted to him, the person entitled does not submit to the railway the supporting documents required for the amount of the claim to be finally settled, no interest shall accrue between the expiry of the period laid down and the actual submission of such documents.

## Title III

## Modification of the Contract of Carriage

### Article 30 - Modification by the Consignor

1. The consignor may modify the contract of carriage by giving subsequent orders:

(a) for the goods to be withdrawn at the forwarding station;
(b) for the goods to be stopped in transit;
(c) for delivery of the goods to be delayed;
(d) for the goods to be delivered to a person other than the consignee shown in the consignment note;
(e) for the goods to be delivered at a station other than the destination station shown in the consignment note;
(f) for the goods to be returned to the forwarding station;
(g) for the consignment to be made subject to a cash on delivery payment;
(h) for a cash on delivery payment to be increased, reduced or cancelled;
(i) for charges relating to a consignment which has not been prepaid to be debited to him, or for charges which he has undertaken to pay in accordance with Article 15, §2 to be increased.

The tariffs of the forwarding railway may provide that orders specified in (g) to (i) are not acceptable.

The supplementary provisions or the international tariffs in force between the railways participating in the carriage may provide for the acceptance of orders other than those listed above.

Orders must not in any event have the effect of splitting the consignment.

2. Such orders shall be given to the forwarding station by means of a written declaration in the form laid down and published by the railway. The declaration shall be reproduced and signed by the consignor in the duplicate of the consignment note which shall be presented to the railway at the same time. The forwarding station shall certify that the order has been received by affixing its date stamp on the duplicate note below the declaration made by the consignor and the duplicate shall then be returned to him.

If the consignor asks for a cash on delivery payment to be increased, reduced or cancelled, he shall produce the document which was delivered to him. Where the cash on delivery payment is to be increased or reduced, such document shall be returned to the consignor after correction; in the event of cancellation it shall not be returned. Any order given in a form other than that prescribed shall be null and void.

3. If the railway complies with the consignor's orders without requiring the production of the duplicate, where this has been sent to the consignee, the railway shall be liable to the consignee for any loss or damage caused thereby. Nevertheless, any compensation shall not exceed that payable in the event of loss of the goods.

4. The consignor's right to modify the contract of carriage shall, notwithstanding that he is in possession of the duplicate of the consignment note, be extinguished in cases where the consignee:

(a) has taken possession of the consignment note;
(b) has accepted the goods;
(c) has asserted his rights in accordance with Article 28, §4;
(d) is entitled, in accordance with Article 31, to give orders as soon as the consignment had entered the Customs territory of the country of destination.

From that time onwards, the railway shall comply with the orders and instructions of the consignee.

## ARTICLE 31 - MODIFICATION BY THE CONSIGNEE

1. When the consignor has not undertaken to pay the charges relating to carriage in the country of destination, and has not inserted in the consignment note the words 'Consignee not authorised to give subsequent orders', the consignee may modify the contact of carriage by giving subsequent orders:
(a) for the goods to be stopped in transit;
(b) for delivery of the goods to be delayed;
(c) for the goods to be delivered in the country of destination to a person other than the consignee shown in the consignment note;
(d) for the goods to be delivered in the country of destination at a station other than the destination station shown in the consignment note, subject to contrary provisions in international tariffs;
(e) for formalities required by customs or other administrative authorities to be carried out in accordance with Article 26, §3.

The supplementary provisions or the international tariffs in force between the railways participating in the carriage may provide for the acceptance of orders other than those listed above.

Orders must not in any case have the effect of splitting the consignment. the consignee's orders shall only be effective after the consignment has entered the Customs territory of the country of destination.

2. Such orders shall be given either to the destination station or to the station of entry into the country of destination, by means of a written declaration in the form laid down and published by the railway.

Any order given in a form other than that prescribed shall be null and void.

3. The consignee's right to modify the contract of carriage shall be extinguished in cases where he has:

(a) taken possession of the consignment note;
(b) accepted the goods;
(c) asserted his rights in accordance with Article 28, §4;
(d) designated a person in accordance with §1 (c) and that person has taken possession of the consignment note or asserted his rights in accordance with Article 28, §4.

4. If the consignee has given instructions for delivery of the goods to another person, that person shall not be entitled to modify the contract of carriage.

## Article 32 - Execution of subsequent orders

1. The railway may not refuse to execute orders given under Articles 30 or 31 or delay doing so save where:

(a) it is no longer possible to execute the orders by the time they reach the station responsible for doing so;

(b) compliance with the orders would interfere with normal railway operations;

(c) a change of destination station would contravene the laws and regulations of a State, and in particular the requirements of the Customs or of other administrative authorities;

(d) in the case of a change of destination station, the value of the goods will not, in the railway's view, cover all the charges which would be payable on the goods on arrival at the new destination, unless the amount of such charges is paid or guaranteed immediately.

The person who has given the orders shall be informed as soon as possible of any circumstances which prevent their execution.

If the railway is not in a position to foresee such circumstances, the person who has given the orders shall be liable for all the consequences of starting to execute them.

2. The charges arising from the execution of an order, except those arising from any fault by the railway, shall be paid in accordance with Article 15.

3. Subject to §1, the railway shall, in the case of any fault on its part, be liable for the consequences of failure to execute an order or failure to execute it properly. Nevertheless, any compensation shall not exceed that payable in the event of loss of the goods.

## Article 33 - Circumstances preventing carriage

1. When circumstances prevent the carriage of goods, the railway shall decide whether it is preferable to carry the goods as a matter of course by modifying the route or whether it is advisable in the consignor's interest to ask him for instructions and at the same time give him any relevant information available to the railway.

Save fault on its part, the railway may recover the carriage charges applicable to the route followed and shall be allowed the transit periods applicable to such route.

2. If it is impossible to continue carrying the goods, the railway shall ask the consignor for instructions. It shall not be obliged to do so in the event of carriage being temporarily prevented as a result of measures taken in accordance with Article 3, §4.

3. The consignor may enter in the consignment note instructions to cover the event of circumstances preventing carriage. If the railway considers that such instructions cannot be executed, it shall ask for fresh instructions.

4. The consignor, on being notified of circumstances preventing carriage, may give his instructions either to the forwarding station or to the station where the goods are being held. If those instructions change the consignee or the

destination station or are given to the station where the goods are being held, the consignor must enter them in the duplicate of the consignment note and present this to the railway.

5. If the railway complies with the consignor's instructions without requiring the production of the duplicate, when this has been sent to the consignee, the railway shall be liable to the consignee for any loss or damage caused thereby. Nevertheless, any compensation shall not exceed that payable in the event of loss of the goods.

6. If the consignor, on being notified of a circumstance preventing carriage, fails to give within a reasonable time instructions which can be executed, the railway shall take action in accordance with the provisions relating to circumstances preventing delivery, in force at the place where the goods have been held up. If the goods have been sold, the proceeds of sale, less any amounts chargeable against the goods, shall be held at the disposal of the consignor. If the proceeds are less than those costs, the consignor shall pay the difference.

7. When the circumstances preventing carriage cease to obtain before the arrival of instructions from the consignor, the goods shall be forwarded to their destination without waiting for such instructions; the consignor shall be notified to that effect as soon as possible.

8. When the circumstances preventing carriage arise after the consignee has modified the contract of carriage in accordance with Article 31, the railway shall notify the consignee. §§ 2, 6, 7 and 9 shall apply analogously.

9. Save fault on its part, the railway may raise demurrage or standage charges if circumstances prevent carriage.

10. Article 32 shall apply to carriage undertaken in accordance with Article 33.

## Article 34 - Circumstances preventing delivery

1. When circumstances prevent delivery of the goods, the destination station shall without delay notify the consignor through the forwarding station, and ask for his instructions. The consignor shall be notified direct, either in writing, by telegram or by teleprinter, if he has so requested in the consignment note; the costs of such notification shall be charged against the goods.

2. If the circumstances preventing delivery cease to obtain before the arrival at the destination station of instructions from the consignor the goods shall be delivered to the consignee. The consignor shall be notified without delay be registered letter; the costs of such notification shall be charged against the goods.

3. If the consignee refuses the goods, the consignor shall be entitled to give instructions even if he is unable to produce the duplicate of the consignment note.

4. The consignor may also request, by an entry in the consignment note, that the goods be returned to him as a matter of course in the event of circumstances preventing delivery. Unless such request is made, his express consent is required.

5. Unless the tariffs otherwise provide, the consignor's instructions shall be given through the forwarding station.

6. Except as otherwise provided for above, the railway responsible for delivery shall proceed in accordance with the provisions in force at the place of delivery. If the goods have been sold, the proceeds of sale, less any costs chargeable against the goods, shall be held at the disposal of the consignor. If such proceeds are less than those costs, the consignor shall pay the difference.

7. When the circumstances preventing delivery arise after the consignee has modified the contract of carriage in accordance with Article 31, the railway shall notify the consignee. §§ 1, 2 and 6 shall apply analogously.

8. Article 32 shall apply to carriage undertaken in accordance with Article 34.

## TITLE IV

## LIABILITY

### ARTICLE 35 - COLLECTIVE RESPONSIBILITY OF RAILWAYS

1. The railway which has accepted goods for carriage with the consignment note shall be responsible for the carriage over the entire route up to delivery.

2. Each succeeding railway, by the very act of taking over the goods with the consignment note, shall become a party to the contract of carriage in accordance with the terms of that document and shall assume the obligations arising therefrom, without prejudice to the provisions of Article 55, §3, relating to the railway of destination.

### ARTICLE 36 - EXTENT OF LIABILITY

1. The railway shall be liable for loss or damage resulting from the total or partial loss of, or damage to, the goods between the time of acceptance for carriage and the time of delivery and for the loss or damage resulting from the transit period being exceeded.

2. The railway shall be relieved of such liability if the loss or damage or the exceeding of the transit period was caused by a fault on the part of the person entitled, by an order given by the person entitled other than as a result of a fault on the part of the railway, by inherent vice of the goods (decay, wastage, etc.,) or by circumstances which the railway could not avoid and the consequences of which it was unable to prevent.

3. The railways shall be relieved of such liability when the loss or damage arises from the special risks inherent in one or more of the following circumstances:

(a) carriage in open wagons under the conditions applicable thereto or under an agreement made between the consignor and the railway and referred to in the consignment note;

(b) absence or inadequacy of packing in the case of goods which by their nature are liable to loss or damage when not packed or when not properly packed;

(c) loading operations carried out by the consignor or unloading operations carried out by the consignee under the provisions applicable thereto or under an agreement made between the consignor and the railway and referred to in the consignment note, or under an agreement between the consignee and the railway;

(d) defective loading, when loading has been carried out by the consignor under the provisions applicable thereto or under an agreement made between the consignor and the railway and referred to in the consignment note:

(e) completion by the consignor, the consignee or an agent of either, of the formalities required by Customs or other administrative authorities;

(f) the nature of certain goods which renders them inherently liable to total or partial loss or damage, especially through breakage, rust, interior and spontaneous decay, desiccation or wastage;

(g) irregular, incorrect or incomplete description of articles not acceptable for carriage or acceptable subject to conditions, or failure on the part of the consignor to observe the prescribed precautions in respect of articles acceptable subject to conditions;

(h) carriage of live animals;

(i) carriage which, under the provisions applicable or under an agreement made between the consignor and the railway and referred to in the consignment note, must be accompanied by an attendant, if the loss or damage results from any risk which the attendant was intended to avert.

## ARTICLE 37 - BURDEN OF PROOF

1. The burden of proving that the loss, the damage or the exceeding of the transit period was due to one of the causes specified in Article 36, §2 shall rest upon the railway.

2. When the railway establishes that, having regard to the circumstances of a particular case, the loss or damage could have arisen from one or more of the special risks referred to in Article 36 §3, it shall be presumed that it did so arise. The person entitled shall, however, have the right to prove that the loss or damage was not attributable either wholly or partly to one of those risks.

This presumption shall not apply in the case referred to in Article 36, §3 (a) if an abnormally large quantity has been lost or if a package has been lost.

## ARTICLE 38 - PRESUMPTION IN CASE OF RECONSIGNMENT

1. When a consignment despatched in accordance with the Uniform rules has been reconsigned subject to the same rules and partial loss or damage has been ascertained after the reconsignment, it shall be presumed that it occurred during the latest contract of carriage if the consignment remained in the care of the railway and was reconsigned in the same condition as it arrived at the station from which it was reconsigned.

2. This presumption shall also apply when the contract of carriage prior to the reconsignment was not subject to the Uniform Rules, if the rules would have applied in the case of a through consignment from the original forwarding station to the final destination station.

## ARTICLE 39 - PRESUMPTION OF LOSS OF GOODS

1. The person entitled may, without being required to furnish further proof, consider the goods lost when they have not been delivered to the consignee or are not being held at his disposal within thirty days after the expiry of the transit periods.

2. The person entitled may, on compensation for the lost goods, make a written request to be notified without delay should the goods be recovered within one year after the payment of compensation. The railway shall give a written acknowledgement of such request.

3. Within thirty days after receipt of such notification, the person entitled may require the goods to be delivered to him at any station on the route. In that case he shall pay the charges in respect of carriage from the forwarding station to the station where delivery is effected and shall refund the compensation received, less any costs which may have been included therein. Nevertheless he shall retain his rights to claim compensation for exceeding the transit period provided for in Articles 43 and 46.

4. In the absence of the request mentioned in §2 or of any instructions given within the period specified in §3, or if the goods are recovered more than one year after the payment of compensation, the railway shall dispose of them in accordance with the laws and regulations of the State having jurisdiction over the railway.

## ARTICLE 40 - COMPENSATION FOR LOSS

1. In the event of total or partial loss of the goods the railway must pay, to the exclusion of all other damages, compensation calculated according to the commodity exchange quotation or, if there is no such quotation, according to the current market price, or if there is neither such quotation nor such price, according to the normal value of goods of the same kind and quality at the time and place at which the goods were accepted for carriage.

2. Compensation shall not exceed 17 units of account per kilogram of gross mass short, subject to the limit provided for in Article 45.

3. The railway shall in addition refund carriage charges, Customs duties and other amounts incurred in connection with carriage of the lost goods.

4. When the calculation of compensation requires the conversion of amounts expressed in foreign currencies, conversion shall be at the rate of exchange applicable at the time and place of payment of compensation.

## ARTICLE 41 - LIABILITY FOR WASTAGE IN TRANSIT

1. In respect of goods which, by reason of their nature, are generally subject to wastage in transit by the sole fact of carriage, the railway shall only be liable to the extent that the wastage exceeds the following allowances, whatever the length of the route:

(a) two per cent of the mass for liquid goods or goods consigned in a moist condition, and also for the following goods:

| | |
|---|---|
| Bark | Leather |
| Bones, whole or ground | Liquorice root |
| Coal and coke | Mushrooms, fresh |
| Dye-woods, grated or ground | Peat and turf |
| Fats | Putty or mastic, fresh |
| Fish, dried | Roots |
| Fruit, fresh, dried or cooked | Salt |
| Furs | Sinews, animal |
| Hide cuttings | Soap and solidified oils |
| Hides | Tobacco, cut |
| Hog bristles | Tobacco leaves, fresh |
| Hops | Vegetables, fresh |
| Horns and hooves | Wool; |
| Horsehair | |

(b) one per cent of the weight for all other dry goods.

2. The limitation of liability provided for in §1 may not be invoked if, having regard to the circumstances of a particular case, it is proved that the loss was not due to cause which would justify an allowance.

3. Where several packages are carried under a single consignment note, the wastage in transit shall be calculated separately for each package if its mass on despatch is shown separately in the consignment note or can otherwise be ascertained.

4. In the event of total loss of the goods, no deduction for wastage in transit shall be made in calculating the compensation payable.

5. This Article shall not derogate from Articles 36 and 37.

## ARTICLE 42 - COMPENSATION FOR DAMAGE

1. In case of damage to goods, the railway must pay compensation equivalent to the loss in value of the goods, to the exclusion of all other damages. The amount shall be calculated by applying to the value of the goods

as defined in Article 40 the percentage of loss in value noted at the place of destination.

2. The compensation may not exceed:
   (a) if the whole consignment has lost value through damage, the amount which would have been payable in case of total loss;
   (b) if only part of the consignment has lost value through damage, the amount which would have been payable had that part been lost.

3. The railway shall in addition refund the amounts provided for in Article 40, §3, in the proportion set out in §1.

## ARTICLE 43 - COMPENSATION FOR EXCEEDING THE TRANSIT PERIOD

1. If loss or damage has resulted from the transit period being exceeded, the railway shall pay compensation not exceeding three times the carriage charger.

2. In case of total loss of the goods, the compensation provided for in §1 shall not be payable in addition to that provided for in Article 40.

3. In case of partial loss of the goods, the compensation provided for in §1 shall not exceed three times the carriage charges in respect of that part of the consignment which has not been lost.

4. In case of damage to the goods, not resulting from the transit period being exceeded, the compensation provided for in §1 shall, where appropriate, be payable in addition to that provided for in Article 42.

5. In no case shall the total of compensation payable under §1 together with that payable under Articles 40 and 42 exceed the compensation which would be payable in the event of total loss of the goods.

6. The railway may provide, in international tariffs or in special agreements for other forms of compensation than those provided for in §1 when, in accordance with Article 27, §1, the transit period has been established on the basis of transport plans.

If, in this case, the transit periods provided for in Article 27, §2 are exceeded, the person entitled may demand either the compensation provided for in §1 above or that determined by the international tariff or the special agreement applied.

## ARTICLE 44 - COMPENSATION IN CASE OF WILFUL MISCONDUCT OR GROSS NEGLIGENCE

When the loss, damage or exceeding of the transit period, or the failure to perform or failure to perform properly the railway's additional services provided for in the Uniform Rules, has been caused by wilful misconduct or gross negligence on the part of the railway, full compensation for the loss or damage proved shall be paid to the person entitled by the railway.

In case of gross negligence, liability shall, however, be limited to twice the maxima specified in Articles 25, 26, 30, 32, 33, 40, 42, 43, 45 and 46.

## ARTICLE 45 - LIMITATION OF COMPENSATION UNDER CERTAIN TARIFFS

When the railway agrees to special conditions of carriage through special or exceptional tariffs, involving a reduction in the carriage charge calculated on the basis of the general tariffs, it may limit the amount of compensation payable to the person entitled in the event of loss, damage or exceeding of the transit period, provided that such limit is indicated in the tariff.

When the special conditions of carriage apply only to part of the route, the limit may only be invoked if the event giving rise to the compensation occurred on that part of the route.

## ARTICLE 46 - COMPENSATION IN CASE OF INTEREST IN DELIVERY

In case of a declaration of interest in delivery, further compensation for loss or damage proved may be claimed, in addition to the compensation provided for in Articles 40, 42, 43 and 45, up to the amount declared.

## ARTICLE 47 - INTEREST ON COMPENSATION

1. The person entitled may claim interest on compensation payable, calculated at five per cent per annum, from the date of the claim referred to in Article 53 or, if no such claim has been made, from the day on which legal proceedings are instituted.

2. Interest shall only be payable if the compensation exceeds four units of account per consignment note.

3. If, within a reasonable period allotted to him, the person entitled does not submit to the railway the supporting documents required for the amount of the claim to be finally settled, no interest shall accrue between the expiry of the period laid down and the actual submission of such documents.

## ARTICLE 48 - LIABILITY IN RESPECT OF RAIL-SEA TRAFFIC

1. In rail-sea transport by the services referred to in Article 2, §2 of the Convention each State may, by requesting that a suitable note be included in the list of lines or services to which the Uniform Rules apply, indicate that the following grounds for exemption from liability will apply in their entirety in addition to those provided for in Article 36.

The carrier may only avail himself to these grounds for exemption if he proves that the loss, damage or exceeding of the transit period occurred in the course of the sea journey between the time when the goods were loaded on board the ship and the time when they were discharged from the ship.

The grounds for exemption are as follows:

(a) act, neglect or default on the part of the master, a mariner, pilot or the carrier's servants in the navigation or management of the ship;

(b) unseaworthiness of the ship, if the carrier proves that the unseaworthiness is not attributable to lack of due diligence on his part to make the ship seaworthy, to ensure that it is properly manned, equipped and supplied or to make all parts of the ship in which the goods are loaded fit and safe for their reception, carriage and protection;

(c) fire, if the carrier proves that it was not caused by his act or fault, or that of the master, a mariner, pilot or the carrier's servants;

(d) perils, dangers and accidents of the sea or the navigable waters;

(e) saving or attempting to save life or property at sea;

(f) the loading of goods on the deck of the ship, if they are so loaded with the consent of the consignor given in the consignment note and are not in wagons.

The above grounds for exemption in no way affect the general obligations of the carrier and, in particular, his obligation to exercise due diligence to make the ship seaworthy, to ensure that it is properly manned, equipped and supplied and to make all parts of the ship in which the goods are loaded fit and safe for their reception, carriage and protection.

Even when the carrier can rely on the foregoing grounds for exemption, he shall nevertheless remain liable if the person entitled proves that the loss, damage or exceeding of the transit period is due to a fault of the carrier, the master, a mariner, pilot or the carrier's servants, fault other than provided for under (a).

2. Where one and the same sea route is served by several undertakings included in the list referred to in Articles 3 and 10 of the Convention, the regime of liability applicable to that route shall be the same for all those undertakings.

In addition, where such undertakings have been included in the list at the request of several States, the adoption of this regime shall be the subject of prior agreement between those states.

3. The measures taken under this Article shall be notified to the Central Office. They shall come into force at the earliest at the expiry of a period of thirty days from the date of the letter by which the Central Office notifies them to the other states.

Consignments already in transit shall not be affected by such measures.

## Article 49 - Liability in case of Nuclear Incidents

The railway shall be relieved of liability under the Uniform Rules for less or damage caused by a nuclear incident when the operator of a nuclear installation or another person who is substituted for him is liable for the loss or damage pursuant to a State's laws and regulations governing liability in the field of nuclear energy.

## Article 50 - Liability of the Railway for its Servants

The railway shall be liable for its servants and for any other persons whom it employs to perform the carriage. If, however, such servants and other persons, at the request of an interested party, make out consignment notes, make translations or render other services which the railway itself is under no obligation to render, they shall be deemed to be acting on behalf of the person to whom the services are rendered.

## ARTICLE 51 - OTHER ACTIONS

In all cases to which the Uniform Rules apply, any action in respect of liability on any grounds whatsoever may be brought against the railway only subject to the conditions and limitations laid down in the Rules. The same shall apply to any action brought against those servants and other persons for whom the railway is liable under Article 50.

# TITLE V

# ASSERTION OF RIGHTS

## ARTICLE 52 - ASCERTAINMENT OF PARTIAL LOSS OR DAMAGE

1. When partial loss of, or damage to, goods is discovered or presumed by the railway or alleged by the person entitled, the railway must without delay and if possible in the presence of the person entitled, draw up a report stating, according to the nature of the loss or damage, the condition of the goods, their mass and, as far as possible, the extent of the loss or damage, its cause and the time of its occurrence.

A copy of the report must be supplied free of charge to the person entitled.

2. Should the person entitled not accept the findings in the report, he may request that the condition and mass of the goods and the cause and amount of the loss or damage be ascertained by an expert appointed either by the parties or by a court. The procedure to be followed shall be governed by the laws and regulations in the State in which such ascertainment takes place.

## ARTICLE 53 - CLAIMS

1. Claims relating to the contract of carriage shall be made in writing to the railway specified in Article 55.

2. A claim may be made by persons who have the right to bring an action against the railway under Article 54.

3. To make the claim, the consignor must produce the duplicate of the consignment note. Failing this, he must produce an authorisation from the consignee or furnish proof that the consignee has refused to accept the consignment. To make the claim, the consignee must produce the consignment note if it has been handed over to him.

4. The consignment note, the duplicate and any other documents which the person entitled thinks fit to submit with the claim shall be produced either in the original or as copies, the copies to be duly authenticated if the railway so requires. On settlement of the claim, the railway may require the production, in the original form, of the consignment note, the duplicate or the cash on delivery voucher so that they may be endorsed to the effect that settlement has been made.

## ARTICLE 54 - PERSONS WHO MAY BRING AN ACTION AGAINST THE RAILWAY

1. An action for the recovery of a sum paid under the contract of carriage may only be brought by the person who made the payment.

2. An action in respect of the cash on delivery payments provided for in Article 17 may only be brought by the consignor.

3. Other actions arising from the contract of carriage may be brought:
   (a) by the consignor, until such time as the consignee has:
      (i) taken possession of the consignment note,
      (ii) accepted the goods, or
      (iii) asserted his rights under Article 28, §4 or Article 31;
   (b) by the consignee, from the time when he has:
      (i) taken possession of the consignment note,
      (ii) accepted the goods,
      (iii) asserted his rights under Article 28, §4, or
      (iv) asserted his rights under Article 31 provided that the right of action shall be extinguished from the time when the person designated by the consignee in accordance with Article 31, §1 (c) has taken possession of the consignment note, accepted the goods, or asserted his rights under Article 28, §4.

4. In order to bring an action, the consignor must produce the duplicate of the consignment note. Failing this, in order to bring an action under §3 (a) he must produce an authorisation from the consignee or furnish proof that the consignee has refused to accept the consignment. In order to bring an action, the consignee shall produce the consignment note if it has been handed over to him.

## ARTICLE 55 - RAILWAYS AGAINST WHICH AN ACTION MAY BE BROUGHT

1. An action for the recovery of a sum paid under the contract of carriage may be brought against the railway which has collected that sum or against the railway on whose behalf it was collected.

2. An action in respect of the cash on delivery payments provided for in Article 17 may only be brought against the forwarding railway.

3. Other actions arising from the contact of carriage may be brought against the forwarding railway, the railway of destination or the railway on which the event giving rise to the proceedings occurred. Such actions may be brought against the railway of destination even if it has received neither the goods nor the consignment note.

4. If the plaintiff can choose between several railways, his right to choose shall be extinguished as soon as he brings an action against any one of them.

5. An action may be brought against a railway other than those specified in §§ 1, 2 and 3 when instituted by way of counterclaim or by way of exception to the principal claim based on the same contract of carriage.

## Article 56 - Competence

Actions brought under the Uniform Rules may only be instituted in the competent court of the State having jurisdiction over the defendant railway, unless otherwise provided in agreements between States or in acts of concession. When a railway operates independent railway systems in different States, each system shall be regarded as a separate railway for the purposes of this Article.

## Article 57 - Extinction of Right of Action against the Railway.

1. Acceptance of the goods by the person entitled shall extinguish all rights of action against the railway arising from the contract in case of partial loss, damage or exceeding of the transit period.

2. Nevertheless, the right of action shall not be extinguished:
   (a) in the case of partial loss or of damage, if:
      (i) the loss or damage was ascertained before the acceptance of the goods in accordance with Article 52 by the person entitled;
      (ii) the ascertainment which should have been carried out under Article 52 was omitted solely through the fault of the railway;
   (b) in the case of loss or damage which is not apparent and is not ascertained until after acceptance of the goods by the person entitled, provided that he:
      (i) asks for ascertainment in accordance with Article 52 immediately after discovery of the loss or damage and not later than seven days after the acceptance of the goods;
      (ii) and, in addition, proves that the loss or damage occurred between the time of acceptance for carriage and the time of delivery;
   (c) in cases where the transit period has been exceeded, if the person entitled has, within sixty days, asserted his rights against one of the railways referred to in Article 55, §3;
   (d) if the person entitled furnishes proof that the loss or damage was caused by wilful misconduct or gross negligence on the part of the railway.

3. If the goods have been reconsigned in accordance with Article 38, §1 rights of action in case of partial loss or of damage, arising from one of the previous contracts of carriage, shall be extinguished as if there had been only one contract of carriage.

## Article 58 - Limitation of Action

1. The period of limitation for an action arising from the contract of carriage shall be one year. Nevertheless, the period of limitation shall be two years in the case of an action:
   (a) to recover a cash on delivery payment collected by the railway from the consignee;

(b) to recover the proceeds of a sale affected by the railway;
(c) for loss or damage caused by wilful misconduct;
(d) for fraud;
(e) arising from one of the contracts of carriage prior to the reconsignment in the case provided for in Article 38, §1.

2. The period of limitation shall run:
(a) in actions for compensation for total loss, from the thirtieth day after the expiry of the transit period;
(b) in actions for compensation for partial loss, for damage or for exceeding the transit period, from the day when delivery took place;
(c) in actions for payment or refund of carriage charges, supplementary charges, other charges or surcharges, or for correction of charges in case of a tariff being wrongly applied or of an error in calculation or collection:
(i) if payment has been made, from the day of payment;
(ii) if payment has not been made, from the day when the goods were accepted for carriage if payment is due from the consignor, or from the day when the consignee took possession of the consignment note if payment is due from him;
(iii) in the case of sums to be paid under a charge note, from the day on which the railway submits to the consignor the account of charges provided for in Article 15, §7; if no such account has been submitted, the period in respect of sums due to the railway shall run from the thirtieth day following the expiry of the transit period;
(d) in an action by the railway for recovery of a sum which has been paid by the consignee instead of by the consignor or vice versa and which the railway is required to refund to the person entitled, from the day of the claim for a refund;
(e) in actions relating to cash on delivery as provided for in Article 17, from the thirtieth day following the expiry of the transit period;
(f) in actions to recover the proceeds of a sale, from the day of the sale;
(g) in actions to recover additional duty demanded by Customs or other administrative authorities, from the day of the demand made by such authorities;
(h) in all other cases, from the day when the right of action arises.

The day indicated for the commencement of the period of limitation shall not be included in the period.

3. When a claim is presented to a railway in accordance with Article 53 together with the necessary supporting documents, the period of limitation shall be suspended until the day that the railway rejects the claim by notification in writing and returns the documents. If part of the claim is admitted, the period of limitation shall recommence in respect of that part of the claim still in dispute. The burden of proof of receipt of the claim or of the reply and of the return of the documents shall rest on the party who relies on those facts.

The period of limitation shall not be suspended by further claims having the same object.

4. A right of action which has become time-barred may not be exercised by way of counter claim or relied upon by way of exception.

5. Subject to the foregoing provisions, the suspension and interruption of periods of limitation shall be governed by national law.

## TITLE VI

## RELATIONS BETWEEN RAILWAYS

### ARTICLE 59 - SETTLEMENT OF ACCOUNTS BETWEEN RAILWAYS

1. Any railway which has collected, either at the time of forwarding or on arrival, charges or other sums due under the contract of carriage must pay to the railways concerned their respective shares.

The methods of payment shall be settled by agreements between railways.

2. Subject to its rights of recovery against the consignor, the forwarding railway shall be liable for carriage and other charges which it has failed to collect when the consignor has undertaken to pay them in accordance with Article 15.

3. Should the railway of destination deliver the goods without collecting charges or other sums due under the contract of carriage, it shall be liable for them to the railways which have taken part in the carriage and to the other parties concerned.

4. Should one railway default in payment and such default be confirmed by the Central Office at the request of one of the creditor railways, the consequences thereof shall be borne by all the other railways which have taken part in the carriage in proportion to their shares of the carriage charges.

The right of recovery against the defaulting railway shall not be affected.

### ARTICLE 60 - RECOURSE IN CASE OF LOSS OR DAMAGE

1. A railway which has paid compensation in accordance with the Uniform Rules, for total or partial loss or for damage, has a right of recourse against the other railways which have taken part in the carriage in accordance with the following provision:

(a) the railway which has caused the loss or damage shall be solely liable for it;

(b) when the loss or damage has been caused by more than one railway, each shall be liable for the loss or damage it has caused; if such distinction cannot be made, the compensation shall be apportioned between those railways in accordance with c;

(c) if it cannot be proved that the loss or damage has been caused by one or more railways in particular, the compensation shall be apportioned between all the railways which have taken part in the carriage, except those which can prove that the loss or damage was not caused on their lines; such apportionment shall be in proportion to the kilometric distances contained in the tariffs.

2. In the case of the insolvency of any one of the railways, the unpaid share due from it shall be apportioned among all the other railways which have taken part in the carriage, in proportion to the kilometric distances contained in the tariffs.

## ARTICLE 61 - RECOURSE IN CASE OF EXCEEDING THE TRANSIT PERIOD

1. Article 60 shall apply where compensation is paid for exceeding the transit period. If this has been caused by more than one railway, the compensation shall be apportioned between such railways in proportion to the length of the delay occurring on their respective lines.

2. The transit periods specified in Article 27 shall be apportioned in the following manner:
   (a) where two railways have taken part in the carriage;
      (i) the period for despatch shall be divided equally;
      (ii) the period for transport shall be divided in proportion to the kilometric distances contained in the tariffs;
   (b) where three or more railways have taken part in the carriage;
      (i) the period for despatch shall be divided equally between the forwarding railway and the railway of destination;
      (ii) the period for transport shall be divided between all the railways:
         - one third in equal shares,
         - the remaining two thirds in proportion to the kilometric distances contained in the tariffs.

3. Any additional periods to which a railway may be entitled shall be allocated to that railway.

4. The interval between the time when the goods are handed over to the railway and commencement of the period for despatch shall be allocated exclusively to the forwarding railway.

5. Such apportionment shall only apply if the total transit period has been exceeded.

## ARTICLE 62 - PROCEDURE FOR RECOURSE

1. The validity of the payment made by the railway exercising one of the rights of recourse under Articles 60 and 61 may not be disputed by the railway against which the right of recourse is exercised, when compensation has been determined by a court and when the latter railway duly served with notice, has been afforded an opportunity to intervene in the proceedings. The court seised of the main proceedings shall determine what time shall be allowed for such notification and for intervention in the proceedings.

2. A railway exercising its right of recourse must take proceedings by one and the same action against all the railways concerned with which it has not reached a settlement, failing which it shall lose its right of recourse in the case of those against which it has not taken proceedings.

3. The court shall give its decision in one and the same judgement on all recourse claims brought before it.

4. The railways against which such action has been brought shall have no further right of recourse.

5. Recourse proceedings may not be joined with proceedings for compensation taken by the person entitled on the basis of the contract of carriage.

## Article 63 - Competence for Recourse

1. The courts of the country in which the railway against which the recourse claim has been made, has its headquarters shall have exclusive competence for all recourse claims.

2. When the action is to be brought against several railways, the plaintiff railway shall be entitled to choose the court in which it will bring the proceedings from among those having competence under §1.

## Article 64 - Agreements concerning recourse

By agreement, railways may derogate from the provisions concerning reciprocal rights of recourse set out in Title VI, apart from that contained in Article 62, §5.

## Articles 65-66 [Omitted].

# UNITED NATIONS CONVENTION ON CONTRACTS FOR THE INTERNATIONAL SALE OF GOODS, VIENNA, 1980

## PART I

## SPHERE OF APPLICATION AND GENERAL PROVISIONS

### CHAPTER I

*Sphere of Application*

#### ARTICLE 1

1. This Convention applies to contracts of sale of goods between parties whose places of business are in different states:
   (a) when the States are Contracting States; or
   (b) when the rules of private international law lead to the application of the law of a Contracting State.

2. The fact that the parties have their places of business in different States is to be disregarded whenever this fact does not appear either from the contract or from any dealings between, or from information disclosed by, the parties at any time before or at the conclusion of the contract.

3. Neither the nationality of the parties nor the civil or commercial character of the parties or of the contract is to be taken into consideration in determining the application of this Convention.

#### ARTICLE 2

This Convention does not apply to sales:
   (a) of goods bought for personal, family or household use, unless the seller, at any time before or at the conclusion of the contract, neither knew nor ought to have known that the goods were bought for any such use;
   (b) by auction;
   (c) on execution or otherwise by authority of law;
   (d) of stocks, shares, investment securities, negotiable instruments or money;
   (e) of ships, vessels, hovercraft or aircraft;
   (f) of electricity.

## Article 3

1. Contracts for the supply of goods to be manufactured or produced are to be considered sales unless the party who orders the goods undertakes to supply a substantial part of the materials necessary for such manufacture or production.

2. This convention does not apply to contracts in which the preponderant part of the obligation of the party who furnishes the goods consists in the supply of labour or other services.

## Article 4

This Convention governs only the formation of the contract of sale and the rights and obligations of the seller and the buyer arising from such a contract. In particular, except as otherwise expressly provided in this Convention, it is not concerned with:

(a) the validity of the contract or of any of its provisions or of any usage;
(b) the effect which the contract may have on the property in the goods sold.

## Article 5

This convention does not apply to the liability of the seller for death or personal injury caused by the goods to any person.

## Article 6

The parties may exclude the application of this Convention or, subject to Article 12, derogate from or vary the effect of any of its provisions.

# Chapter II

## General Provisions

## Article 7

1. In the interpretation of this Convention, regard is to be had to its international character and to the need to promote uniformity in its application and the observance of good faith in international trade.

2. Questions concerning matters governed by this Convention which are not expressly settled in it are to be settled in conformity with the general principles on which it is based or, in the absence of such principles, in conformity with the law applicable by virtue of the rules of private international law.

## ARTICLE 8

1. For the purposes of this Convention statements made by and other conduct of a party are to be interpreted according to his intent where the other party knew or could not have been unaware what that intent was.

2. If the preceding paragraph is not applicable, statements made by and other conduct of a party are to be interpreted according to the understanding that a reasonable person of the same kind as the other party would have had in the same circumstances.

3. In determining the intent of a party or the understanding a reasonable person would have had, due consideration is to be given to all relevant circumstances of the case including the negotiations, any practices which the parties have established between themselves, usages and any subsequent conduct of the parties.

## ARTICLE 9

1. The parties are bound by any usage to which they have agreed and by any practices which they have established between themselves.

2. The parties are considered, unless otherwise agreed, to have impliedly made applicable to their contract or its formation a usage of which the parties knew or ought to have known and which in international trade is widely known to, and regularly observed by, parties to contracts of the type involved in the particular trade concerned.

## ARTICLE 10

For the purposes of this Convention:

(a) if a party has more than one place of business, the place of business is that which has the closest relationship to the contract and its performance, having regard to the circumstances known to or contemplated by the parties at any time before or at the conclusion of the contract;

(b) if a party does not have a place of business, reference is to be made to his habitual residence.

## ARTICLE 11

A contract of sale need not be concluded in or evidenced by writing and is not subject to any other requirement as to form. It may be proved by any means, including witnesses.

## Article 12

Any provision of Article 11, Article 29 or Part II of this Convention that allows a contract of sale or its modification or termination by agreement or any offer, acceptance or other indication of intention to be made in any form other than in writing does not apply where any party has his place of business in a Contracting State which has made a declaration under Article 96 of this Convention. The parties may not derogate from or vary the effect of this Article.

## Article 13

For the purposes of this Convention 'writing' includes telegram and telex.

# Part II

## Formation of the Contract

## Article 14

1. A proposal for concluding a contract addressed to one or more specific persons constitutes an offer if it is sufficiently definite and indicates the intention of the offeror to be bound in case of acceptance. A proposal is sufficiently definite if it indicates the goods and expressly or implicitly fixes or makes provision for determining the quantity and the price.

2. A proposal other than one addressed to one or more specific persons is to be considered merely as an invitation to make offers, unless the contrary is clearly indicated by the person making the proposal.

## Article 15

1. An offer becomes effective when it reaches the offeree.

2. An offer, even if it is irrevocable, may be withdrawn if the withdrawal reaches the offeree before or at the same time as the offer.

## Article 16

1. Until a contract is concluded an offer may be revoked if the revocation reaches the offeree before he has dispatched an acceptance.

2. However, an offer cannot be revoked:
   (a) if it indicates, whether by stating a fixed time for acceptance or otherwise, that it is irrevocable; or

(b) if it was reasonable for the offeree to rely on the offer as being irrevocable and the offeree has acted in reliance on the offer.

## ARTICLE 17

An offer, even if it is irrevocable, is terminated when a rejection reaches the offeror.

## ARTICLE 18

1. A statement made by or other conduct of the offeree indicating assent to an offer is an acceptance. Silence or inactivity does not in itself amount to acceptance.

2. An acceptance of an offer becomes effective at the moment the indication of assent reaches the offeror. An acceptance is not effective if the indication of assent does not reach the offeror within the time he has fixed or, if no time is fixed, within a reasonable time, due account being taken of the circumstances of the transaction, including the rapidity of the means of communication employed by the offeror. An oral offer must be accepted immediately unless the circumstances indicate otherwise.

3. However, if, by virtue of the offer or as a result of practices which the parties have established between themselves or of usage, the offeree may indicate assent by performing an act, such as one relating to the dispatch of the goods or payment of the price, without notice to the offeror, the acceptance is effective at the moment the act is performed, provided that the act is performed within the period of time laid down in the preceding paragraph.

## ARTICLE 19

1. A reply to an offer which purports to be an acceptance but contains additions, limitations or other modifications is a rejection of the offer and constitutes a counter-offer.

2. However, a reply to an offer which purports to be an acceptance but contains additional or different terms which do not materially alter the terms of the offer constitutes an acceptance, unless the offeror, without undue delay, objects orally to the discrepancy or dispatches a notice to that effect. If he does not so object, the terms of the contract are the terms of the offer with the modifications contained in the acceptance.

3. Additional or different terms relating, among other things, to the price, payment, quality and quantity of the goods, place and time of delivery, extent of one party's liability to the other or the settlement of disputes are considered to alter the terms of the offer materially.

## Article 20

1. A period of time for acceptance fixed by the offeror in a telegram or a letter begins to run from the moment the telegram is handed in for dispatch or from the date shown on the letter or, if no such date is shown, from the date shown on the envelope. A period of time for acceptance fixed by the offeror by telephone, telex or other means of instantaneous communication, begins to run from the moment that the offer reaches the offeree.

2. Official holidays or non-business days occurring during the period for acceptance are included in calculating the period. However, if a notice of acceptance cannot be delivered at the address of the offeror on the last day of the period because that day falls on an official holiday or a non-business day at the place of business of the offeror, the period is extended until the first business day which follows.

## Article 21

1. A late acceptance is nevertheless effective as an acceptance if without delay the offeror orally so informs the offeree or dispatches a notice to that effect.

2. If a letter or other writing containing a late acceptance shows that it has been sent in such circumstances that if its transmission had been normal it would have reached the offeror in due time, the late acceptance is effective as an acceptance unless, without delay, the offeror orally informs the offeree that he considers his offer as having lapsed or dispatches a notice to that effect.

## Article 22

An acceptance may be withdrawn if the withdrawal reaches the offeror before or at the same time as the acceptance would have become effective.

## Article 23

A contract is concluded at the moment when an acceptance of an offer becomes effective in accordance with the provisions of this Convention.

## Article 24

For the purposes of this Part of the Convention, an offer, declaration of acceptance or any other indication of intention 'reaches' the addressee when it is made orally to him or delivered by any other means to him personally, to his place of business or mailing address or, if he does not have a place of business or mailing address, to his habitual residence.

# PART III

## SALE OF GOODS

## CHAPTER I

### *General Provisions*

### ARTICLE 25

A breach of contract committed by one of the parties is fundamental if it results in such detriment to the other party as substantially to deprive him of what he is entitled to expect under the contract, unless the party in breach did not foresee and a reasonable person of the same kind in the same circumstances would not have foreseen such a result.

### ARTICLE 26

A declaration of avoidance of the contract is effective only if made by notice to the other party.

### ARTICLE 27

Unless otherwise expressly provided in this Part of the Convention, if any notice, request or other communication is given or made by a party in accordance with this Part and by means appropriate in the circumstances, a delay or error in the transmission of the communication or its failure to arrive does not deprive that party of the right to rely on the communication.

### ARTICLE 28

If, in accordance with the provisions of this Convention, one party is entitled to require performance of any obligation by the other party, a court is not bound to enter a judgement for specific performance unless the court would do so under its own law in respect of similar contracts of sale not governed by this Convention.

### ARTICLE 29

1. A contract may be modified or terminated by the mere agreement of the parties.

2. A contract in writing which contains a provision requiring any modification or termination by agreement to be in writing may not be otherwise

modified or terminated by agreement. However, a party may be precluded by his conduct from asserting such a provision to the extent that the other party has relied on that conduct.

## CHAPTER II

## OBLIGATIONS OF THE SELLER

### ARTICLE 30

The seller must deliver the goods, hand over any documents relating to them and transfer the property in the goods, as required by the contract and this Convention.

*Section 1 : Delivery of the goods and handing over of documents.*

### ARTICLE 31

If the seller is not bound to deliver the goods at any other particular place, his obligation to deliver consists:

(a) if the contract of sale involves carriage of the goods - in handing the goods over to the first carrier for transmission to the buyer;
(b) if, in cases not within the preceding subpara, the contract relates to specific goods, or unidentified goods to be drawn from a specific stock or to be manufactured or produced, and at the time of the conclusion of the contract the parties knew that the goods were at, or were to be manufactured or produced at, a particular place — in placing the goods at the buyer's disposal at that place;
(c) in other cases - in placing the goods at the buyer's disposal at the place where the seller had his place of business at the time of the conclusion of the contract.

### ARTICLE 32

1. If the seller, in accordance with the contract or this Convention, hands the goods over to a carrier and if the goods are not clearly identified to the contract by markings on the goods, by shipping documents or otherwise, the seller must give the buyer notice of the consignment specifying the goods.

2. If the seller is bound to arrange for carriage of the goods, he must make such contracts as are necessary for carriage to the place fixed by means of transportation appropriate in the circumstances and according to the usual terms for such transportation.

3. If the seller is not bound to effect insurance in respect of the carriage of the goods, he must, at the buyer's request, provide him with all available information necessary to enable him to effect such insurance.

## Article 33

The seller must deliver the goods:

(a) if a date is fixed by or determinable from the contract, on that date;

(b) if a period of time is fixed by or determinable from the contract, at any time within that period unless circumstances indicate that the buyer is to choose a date; or

(c) in any other case, within a reasonable time after the conclusion of the contract.

## Article 34

If the seller is bound to hand over documents relating to the goods, he must hand them over at the time and place and in the form required by the contract. If the seller has handed over documents before that time, he may, up to that time, cure any lack of conformity in the documents, if the exercise of this right does not cause the buyer unreasonable inconvenience or unreasonable expense. However, the buyer retains any right to claim damages as provided for in this Convention.

### *Section II. Conformity of the goods and third party claims*

## Article 35

1. The seller must deliver goods which are of the quantity, quality and description required by the contract and which are contained or packaged in the manner required by the contract.

2. Except where the parties have agreed otherwise, the goods do not conform with the contract unless they:

(a) are fit for the purposes for which goods of the same description would ordinarily be used;

(b) are fit for any particular purpose expressly or impliedly made known to the seller at the time of the conclusion of the contract, except where the circumstances show that the buyer did not rely, or that it was unreasonable for him to rely, on the seller's skill and judgement;

(c) possess the qualities of goods which the seller has held out to the buyer as a sample or model;

(d) are contained or packaged in the manner usual for such goods or, where there is no such manner, in a manner adequate to preserve and protect the goods.

3. The seller is not liable under subparagraphs a to d of the preceding paragraph for any lack of conformity of the goods if at the time of the conclusion of the contract the buyer knew or could not have been unaware of such lack of conformity.

## ARTICLE 36

1. The seller is liable in accordance with the contract and this Convention for any lack of conformity which exists at the time when the risk passes to the buyer, even though the lack of conformity becomes apparent only after that time.

2. The seller is also liable for any lack of conformity which occurs after the time indicated in the preceding paragraph and which is due to a breach of any of his obligations, including a breach of any guarantee that for a period of time the goods will remain fit for their ordinary purpose or for some particular purpose or will retain specified qualities or characteristics.

## ARTICLE 37

If the seller has delivered goods before the date for delivery, he may, up to that date, deliver any missing part or make up any deficiency in the quantity of the goods delivered, or deliver goods in replacement of any non-conforming goods delivered or remedy any lack of conformity in the goods delivered, provided that the exercise of this right does not cause the buyer unreasonable inconvenience or unreasonable expense. However, the buyer retains any right to claim damages as provided for in this Convention.

## ARTICLE 38

1. The buyer must examine the goods, or cause them to be examined, within a short a period as is practicable in the circumstances.

2. If the contract involves carriage of the goods, examination may be deferred until after the goods have arrived at their destination.

3. If the goods are redirected in transit or redispatched by the buyer without a reasonable opportunity for examination by him and at the time of the conclusion of the contract the seller knew or ought to have known of the possibility of such redirection or redispatch, examination may be deferred until after the goods have arrived at the new destination.

## ARTICLE 39

1. The buyer loses the right to rely on a lack of conformity of the goods if he does not give notice to the seller specifying the nature of the lack of conformity within a reasonable time after he has discovered it or ought to have discovered it.

2. In any event, the buyer loses the right to rely on a lack of conformity of the goods if he does not give the seller notice thereof at the latest within a period of two years from the date on which the goods were actually handed over to the buyer, unless this time-limit is inconsistent with a contractual period of guarantee.

## ARTICLE 40

The seller is not entitled to rely on the provisions of Articles 38 and 39 if the lack of conformity relates to facts of which he knew or could not have been unaware and which he did not disclose to the buyer.

## ARTICLE 41

The seller must deliver goods which are free from any right or claim of a third party, unless the buyer agreed to take the goods subject to that right or claim. However, if such right or claim is based on industrial property or other intellectual property, the seller's obligation is governed by Article 42.

## ARTICLE 42

1. The seller must deliver goods which are free from any right or claim of a third party based on industrial property or other intellectual property, of which at the time of the conclusion of the contract the seller knew or could not have been unaware, provided that the right or claim is based on industrial property or other intellectual property:

(a) under the law of the State where the goods will be resold or otherwise used, if it was contemplated by the parties at the time of the conclusion of the contract that the goods would be resold or otherwise used in that state; or

(b) in any other case, under the law of the State where the buyer has his place of business.

2. The obligation of the seller under the preceding paragraph does not extend to cases where:

(a) at the time of the conclusion of the contract the buyer knew or could not have been unaware of the right or claim; or

(b) the right or claim results from the seller's compliance with technical drawings, designs, formulae or other such specifications furnished by the buyer.

## ARTICLE 43

1. The buyer loses the right to rely on the provisions of Article 41 or Article 42 if he does not give notice to the seller specifying the nature of the right or claim of the third party within a reasonable time after he has become aware or ought to have become aware of the right or claim.

2. The seller is not entitled to rely on the provisions of the preceding paragraph if he knew of the right or claim of the third party and the nature of it.

## ARTICLE 44

Notwithstanding the provisions of paragraph 1 of Article 39 and paragraph 1 of Article 43, the buyer may reduce the price in accordance with Article 50 or claim damages, except for loss of profit, if he has a reasonable excuse for his failure to give the required notice.

### *Section III. Remedies for breach of contract by the seller*

## ARTICLE 45

1. If the seller fails to perform any of his obligations under the contract or this Convention, the buyer may:

(a) exercise the rights provided in Articles 46 to 52;

(b) claim damages as provided in Articles 74 to 77.

2. The buyer is not deprived of any right he may have to claim damages by exercising his right to other remedies.

3. No period of grace may be granted to the seller by a court or arbitral tribunal when the buyer resorts to a remedy for breach of contract.

## ARTICLE 46

1. The buyer may require performance by the seller of his obligations unless the buyer has resorted to a remedy which is inconsistent with this requirement.

2. If the goods do not conform with the contract, the buyer may require delivery of substitute goods only if the lack of conformity constitutes a fundamental breach of contract and a request for substitute goods is made either in conjunction with notice given under Article 39 or within a reasonable time thereafter.

3 If the goods do not conform with the contract, the buyer may require the seller to remedy the lack of conformity by repair, unless this is unreasonable having regard to all the circumstances. A request for repair must be made either in conjunction with notice given under Article 39 or within a reasonable time thereafter.

## ARTICLE 47

1. The buyer may fix an additional period of time of reasonable length for performance by the seller of his obligations.

2. Unless the buyer has received notice from the seller that he will not perform within the period so fixed, the buyer may not, during that period, resort to any remedy for breach of contract. However, the buyer is not deprived thereby of any right he may have to claim damages for delay in performance.

## ARTICLE 48

1. Subject to Article 49, the seller may, even after the date for delivery, remedy at his own expense any failure to perform his obligations, if he can do so without unreasonable delay and without causing the buyer unreasonable inconvenience or uncertainty of reimbursement by the seller of expenses advanced by the buyer. However, the buyer retains any right to claim damages as provided for in this Convention.

2. If the seller requests the buyer to make known whether he will accept performance and the buyer does not comply with the request within a reasonable time, the seller may perform within the time indicated in his request. The buyer may not, during that period of time, resort to any remedy which is inconsistent with performance by the seller.

3. A notice by the seller that he will perform within a specified period of time is assumed to include a request, under the preceding paragraph, that the buyer make known his decision.

4. A request or notice by the seller under paragraph 2 or 3 of this Article is not effective unless received by the buyer.

## ARTICLE 49

1. The buyer may declare the contract avoided:
   (a) if the failure by the seller to perform any of his obligations under the contract or this Convention amounts to a fundamental breach of contract; or
   (b) in case of non-delivery, if the seller does not deliver the goods within the additional period of time fixed by the buyer in accordance with paragraph 1 of Article 47 or declares that he will not deliver within the period so fixed.

2. However, in cases where the seller has delivered the goods, the buyer loses the right to declare the contract avoided unless he does so:
   (a) in respect of late delivery, within a reasonable time after he has become aware that delivery has been made;
   (b) in respect of any breach other than late delivery, within a reasonable time:
      (i) after he knew or ought to have known of the breach;
      (ii) after the expiration of any additional period of time fixed by the buyer in accordance with paragraph 1 of Article 47, or after the seller has declared that he will not perform his obligations within such an additional period; or
      (iii) after the expiration of any additional period of time indicated by the seller in accordance with paragraph 2 of Article 48 or after the buyer has declared that he will not accept performance.

## Article 50

If the goods do not conform with the contract and whether or not the price has already been paid, the buyer may reduce the price in the same proportion as the value that the goods actually delivered had at the time of the delivery bears to the value that conforming goods would have had at that time. However, if the seller remedies any failure to perform his obligations in accordance with Article 37 or Article 48 or if the buyer refuses to accept performance by the seller in accordance with those Articles, the buyer may not reduce the price.

## Article 51

1. If the seller delivers only a part of the goods or if only a part of the goods delivered is in conformity with the contract, Articles 46 to 50 apply in respect of the part which is missing or which does not conform.

2. The buyer may declare the contract avoided in its entirety only if the failure to make delivery completely or in conformity with the contract amounts to a fundamental breach of the contract.

## Article 52

1. If the seller delivers the goods before the date fixed, the buyer may take delivery or refuse to take delivery.

2. If the seller delivers a quantity of goods greater than that provided for in the contract, the buyer may take delivery or refuse to take delivery of the excess quantity. If the buyer takes delivery of all or part of the excess quantity, he must pay for it at the contract rate.

# Chapter III

## Obligations of the Buyer

## Article 53

The buyer must pay the price for the goods and take delivery of them as required by the contract and this Convention.

### *Section I. Payment of the price*

## Article 54

The buyer's obligation to pay the price includes taking such steps and complying with such formalities as may be required under the contract or any laws and regulations to enable payment to be made.

## ARTICLE 55

Where a contract has been validly concluded but does not expressly or implicitly fix or make provision for determining the price, the parties are considered, in the absence of any indication to the contrary, to have impliedly made reference to the price generally charged at the time of the conclusion of the contract for such goods sold under comparable circumstances in the trade concerned.

## ARTICLE 56

If the price is fixed according to the weight of the goods, in case of doubt it is to be determined by the net weight.

## ARTICLE 57

1. If the buyer is not bound to pay the price at any other particular place, he must pay it to the seller:

(a) at the seller's place of business; or

(b) if the payment is to be made against the handing over of the goods or of documents, at the place where the handing over takes place.

2. The seller must bear any increase in the expenses incidental to payment which is caused by a change in his place of business subsequent to the conclusion of the contract.

## ARTICLE 58

1. If the buyer is not bound to pay the price at any other specific time, he must pay it when the seller places either the goods or documents controlling their disposition at the buyer's disposal in accordance with the contract and this Convention. The seller may make such payment a condition for handing over the goods or documents.

2. If the contract involves carriage of the goods, the seller may dispatch the goods on terms whereby the goods, or documents controlling their disposition, will not be handed over to the buyer except against payment of the price.

3. The buyer is not bound to pay the price until he has had an opportunity to examine the goods, unless the procedures for delivery or payment agreed upon by the parties are inconsistent with his having such an opportunity.

## ARTICLE 59

The buyer must pay the price on the date fixed by or determinable from the contract and this convention without the need for any request or compliance with any formality on the part of the seller.

*Section II. Taking delivery*

## ARTICLE 60

The buyer's obligation to take delivery consists:

(a) in doing all the acts which could reasonably be expected of him in order to enable the seller to make delivery; and

(b) in taking over the goods.

*Section III. Remedies for breach of contract by the buyer.*

## ARTICLE 61

1. If the buyer fails to perform any of his obligations under the contract or this Convention, the seller may:

(a) exercise the rights provided in Articles 62 to 65;

(b) claim damages as provided in Articles 74 to 77.

2. The seller is not deprived of any right he may have to claim damages by exercising his right to other remedies.

3. No period of grace may be granted to the buyer by a court or arbitral tribunal when the seller resorts to a remedy for breach of contract.

## ARTICLE 62

The seller may require the buyer to pay the price, take delivery or perform his other obligations, unless the seller has resorted to a remedy which is inconsistent with this requirement.

## ARTICLE 63

1. The seller may fix an additional period of time of reasonable length for performance by the buyer of his obligations.

2. Unless the seller has received notice from the buyer that he will not perform within the period so fixed, the seller may not, during that period, resort to any remedy for breach of contract. However, the seller is not deprived thereby of any right he may have to claim damages for delay in performance.

## ARTICLE 64

1. The seller may declare the contract avoided:

(a) if the failure by the buyer to perform any of his obligations under the contract or this Convention amounts to a fundamental breach of contract; or

(b) if the buyer does not, within the additional period of time fixed by the seller in accordance with paragraph 1 or Article 63, perform his obligation to pay the price or take delivery of the goods, or if he declares that he will not do so within the period so fixed.

2. However, in cases where the buyer has paid the price, the seller loses the right to declare the contract avoided unless he does so:

(a) in respect of late performance by the buyer, before the seller has become aware that performance has been rendered; or

(b) in respect of any breach other than late performance by the buyer, within a reasonable time:

(i) after the seller knew or ought to have known of the breach; or

(ii) after the expiration of any additional period of time fixed by the seller in accordance with paragraph 1 or Article 63, or after the buyer has declared that he will not perform his obligations within such an additional period.

## ARTICLE 65

1. If under the contract the buyer is to specify the form, measurement or other features of the goods and he fails to make such specification either on the date agreed upon within a reasonable time after receipt of a request from the seller, the seller may, without prejudice to any other rights he may have, make the specification himself in accordance with the requirements of the buyer that may be known to him.

2. If the seller makes the specification himself, he must inform the buyer of the details thereof and must fix a reasonable time within which the buyer may make a different specification. If, after receipt of such a communication, the buyer fails to do so within the time so fixed, the specification made by the seller is binding.

## CHAPTER IV

## PASSING OF RISK

## ARTICLE 66

Loss of or damage to the goods after the risk has passed to the buyer does not discharge him from his obligation to pay the price, unless the loss or damage is due to an act or omission of the seller.

## ARTICLE 67

1. If the contract of sale involves carriage of the goods and the seller is not bound to hand them over at a particular place, the risk passes to the buyer when the goods are handed over to the first carrier for transmission to the buyer in accordance with the contract of sale. If the seller is bound to hand the goods

over to a carrier at a particular place, the risk does not pass to the buyer until the goods are handed over to the carrier at that place. The fact that the seller is authorised to retain documents controlling the disposition of the goods does not affect the passage of the risk.

2. Nevertheless, the risk does not pass to the buyer until the goods are clearly identified to the contract, whether by markings on the goods, by shipping documents, by notice given to the buyer or otherwise.

## Article 68

The risk in respect of goods sold in transit passes to the buyer from the time of the conclusion of the contract. However, if the circumstances so indicate, the risk is assumed by the buyer from the time the goods were handed over to the carrier who issued the documents embodying the contract of carriage. Nevertheless, if at the time or the conclusion of the contract of sale the seller knew or ought to have known that the goods had been lost or damaged and did not disclose this to the buyer, the loss or damage is at the risk of the seller.

## Article 69

1. In cases not within Articles 67 and 68, the risk passes to the buyer when he takes over the goods or, if he does not do so in due time, from the time when the goods are placed at his disposal and he commits a breach of contract by failing to take delivery.

2. However, if the buyer is bound to take over the goods at a place other than a place of business of the seller, the risk passes when delivery is due and the buyer is aware of the fact that the goods are placed at his disposal at that place.

3. If the contract relates to goods not then identified, the goods are considered not to be placed at the disposal of the buyer until they are clearly identified to the contract.

## Article 70

If the seller has committed a fundamental breach of contract, Articles 67, 68 and 69 do not impair the remedies available to the buyer on account of the breach.

## Chapter V

## Provisions Common to the Obligations of the Seller and of the Buyer

### *Section I. Anticipatory breach and instalment contracts*

### Article 71

1. A party may suspend the performance of his obligations if, after the conclusion of the contract, it becomes apparent that the other party will not perform a substantial part of his obligations as a result of:
   (a) a serious deficiency in his ability to perform or in his credit worthiness; or
   (b) his conduct in preparing to perform or in performing the contract.

2. If the seller has already dispatched the goods before the grounds described in the preceding paragraph become evident, he may prevent the handing over of the goods to the buyer even though the buyer holds a document which entitles him to obtain them. The present paragraph relates only to the rights in the goods as between the buyer and the seller.

3. A party suspending performance, whether before or after dispatch of the goods, must immediately give notice of the suspension to the other party and must continue with performance if the other party provides adequate assurance of his performance.

### Article 72

1. If prior to the date for performance of the contract it is clear that one of the parties will commit a fundamental breach of contract, the other party may declare the contract avoided.

2. If time allows, the party intending to declare the contract avoided must give reasonable notice to the other party in order to permit him to provide adequate assurance of his performance.

3. The requirements of the preceding paragraph do not apply if the other party has declared that he will not perform his obligations.

### Article 73

1. In the case of a contract for delivery of goods by instalments, if the failure of one party to perform any of his obligations in respect of any instalment constitutes a fundamental breach of contract with respect to that instalment, the other party may declare the contract avoided with respect to that instalment.

2. If one party's failure to perform any of his obligations in respect of any instalment gives the other party good grounds to conclude that a fundamental breach of contract will occur with respect to future instalments, he may declare the contract avoided for the future, provided that he does so within a reasonable time.

3. A buyer who declares the contract avoided in respect of any delivery may, at the same time, declare it avoided in respect of deliveries already made or of future deliveries if, by reason of their interdependence, those deliveries could not be used for the purpose contemplated by the parties at the time of the conclusion of the contract.

### *Section II. Damages*

### Article 74

Damages for breach of contract by one party consist of a sum equal to the loss, including loss of profit, suffered by the other party as a consequence of the breach. Such damages may not exceed the loss which the party in breach foresaw or ought to have foreseen at the time of the conclusion of the contract, in the light of the facts and matters of which he then knew or ought to have known, as a possible consequence of the breach of contract.

### Article 75

If the contract is avoided and if, in a reasonable manner and within a reasonable time after avoidance, the buyer has bought goods in replacement or the seller has resold the goods, the party claiming damages may recover the difference between the contract price and the price in the substitute transaction as well as any further damages recoverable under Article 74.

### Article 76

1. If the contract is avoided and there is a current price for the goods, the party claiming damages may, if he has not made a purchase or resale under Article 75, recover the difference between the price fixed by the contract and the current price at the time of avoidance as well as any further damages recoverable under Article 74. If, however, the party claiming damages has avoided the contract after taking over the goods, the current price at the time of such taking over shall be applied instead of the current price at the time of avoidance.

2. For the purposes of the preceding paragraph, the current price is the price prevailing at the place where delivery of the goods should have been made or, if there is no current price at that place, the price at such other place as serves as a reasonable substitute, making due allowance for differences in the cost of transporting the goods.

## Article 77

A party who relies on a breach of contract must take such measures as are reasonable in the circumstances to mitigate the loss, including loss of profit, resulting from the breach. If he fails to take such measures, the party in breach may claim a reduction in the damages in the amount by which the loss should have been mitigated.

### *Section III. Interest*

## Article 78

If a party fails to pay the price or any other sum that is in arrears, the other party is entitled to interest on it, without prejudice to any claim for damages recoverable under Article 74.

### *Section IV. Exemptions*

## Article 79

1. A party is not liable for a failure to perform any of his obligations if he proves that the failure was due to an impediment beyond his control and that he could not reasonably be expected to have taken the impediment into account at the time of the conclusion of the contract or to have avoided or overcome it or its consequences.

2. If the party's failure is due to the failure by a third person whom he has engaged to perform the whole or a part of the contract, that party is exempt from liability only if:
   (a) he is exempt under the preceding paragraph; and
   (b) the person whom he has so engaged would be so exempt if the provisions of that paragraph were applied to him.

3. The exemption provided by this Article has effect for the period during which the impediment exists.

4. The party who fails to perform must give notice to the other party of the impediment and its effect on his ability to perform. If the notice is not received by the other party within a reasonable time after the party who fails to perform knew or ought to have known of the impediment, he is liable for damages resulting from such non-receipt.

5. Nothing in this Article prevents either party from exercising any right other than to claim damages under this Convention.

## Article 80

A party may not rely on a failure of the other party to perform, to the extent that such failure was caused by the first party's act or omission.

*Section V. Effects of avoidance*

## ARTICLE 81

1. Avoidance of the contract releases both parties from their obligations under it, subject to any damages which may be due. Avoidance does not affect any provision of the contract for the settlement of disputes or any other provision of the contract governing the rights and obligations of the parties consequent upon the avoidance of the contract.

2. A party who has performed the contract either wholly or in part may claim restitution from the other party of whatever the first party has supplied or paid under the contract. If both parties are bound to make restitution, they must do so concurrently.

## ARTICLE 82

1. The buyer loses the right to declare the contract avoided or to require the seller to deliver substitute goods if it is impossible for him to make restitution of the goods substantially in the condition in which he received them.

2. The preceding paragraph does not apply:
   (a) if the impossibility of making restitution of the goods or of making restitution of the goods substantially in the condition in which the buyer received them is not due to his act or omission;
   (b) if the goods or part of the goods have perished or deteriorated as a result of the examination provided for in Article 38; or
   (c) if the goods or part of the goods have been sold in the normal course of business or have been consumed or transformed by the buyer in the course of normal use before he discovered or ought to have discovered the lack of conformity.

## ARTICLE 83

A buyer who has lost the right to declare the contract avoided or to require the seller to deliver substitute goods in accordance with Article 82 retains all other remedies under the contract and this Convention.

## ARTICLE 84

1. If the seller is bound to refund the price, he must also pay interest on it, from the date on which the price was paid.

2. The buyer must account to the seller for all benefits which he has derived from the goods or part of them:
   (a) if he must make restitution of the goods or part of them; or
   (b) if it is impossible for him to make restitution of all or part of the goods or to make restitution of all or part of the goods substantially in

the condition in which he received them, but he has nevertheless declared the contract avoided or required the seller to deliver substitute goods.

### *Section VI. Preservation of the goods*

#### ARTICLE 85

If the buyer is in delay in taking delivery of the goods or, where payment of the price and delivery of the goods are to be made concurrently, if he fails to pay the price, and the seller is either in possession of the goods or otherwise able to control their disposition, the seller must take such steps as are reasonable in the circumstances to preserve them. He is entitled to retain them until he has been reimbursed his reasonable expenses by the buyer.

#### ARTICLE 86

1. If the buyer has received the goods and intends to exercise any right under the contract or this Convention to reject them, he must take such steps to preserve them as are reasonable in the circumstances. He is entitled to retain them until he has been reimbursed his reasonable expenses by the seller.

2. If goods dispatched to the buyer have been placed at his disposal at their destination and he exercises the right to reject them, he must take possession of them on behalf of the seller, provided that this can be done without payment of the price and without unreasonable inconvenience or unreasonable expense. This provision does not apply if the seller or a person authorised to take charge of the goods on his behalf is present at the destination. If the buyer takes possession of the goods under this paragraph, his rights and obligations are governed by the preceding paragraph.

#### ARTICLE 87

A party who is bound to take steps to preserve the goods may deposit them in a warehouse of a third person at the expense of the other party provided that the expense incurred is not unreasonable.

#### ARTICLE 88

1. A party who is bound to preserve the goods in accordance with Article 85 or 86 may sell them by any appropriate means if there has been an unreasonable delay by the other party in taking possession of the goods or in taking them back or in paying the price or the cost of preservation, provided that reasonable notice of the intention to sell has been given to the other party.

2. If the goods are subject to rapid deterioration or their preservation would involve unreasonable expense, a party who is bound to preserve the goods in

accordance with Article 85 or 86 must take reasonable measures to sell them. to the extent possible he must give notice to the other party of his intention to sell.

3. A party selling the goods has the right to retain out of the proceeds of sale an amount equal to the reasonable expenses of preserving the goods and of selling them. He must account to the other party for the balance.

## PART IV. ARTICLES 89-91 [Omitted]

## ARTICLE 92

1. A Contracting State may declare at the time of the signature, ratification, acceptance, approval or accession that it will not be bound by Part II of this Convention or that it will not be bound by Part III of these Convention.

2. A Contracting State which makes a declaration in accordance with the preceding paragraph in respect of Part II or Part III of this Convention is not to be considered a contracting State within paragraph 1 or Article 1 of this Convention in respect of matters governed by the Part to which the declaration applies.

## ARTICLE 93 [Omitted]

## ARTICLE 94

1. Two or more Contracting States which have the same or closely related legal rules on matters governed by this convention may at any time declare that the Convention is not to apply to contracts of sale or to their formation where the parties have their places of business in those States. Such declarations may be made jointly or by reciprocal unilateral declarations.

2. A Contracting State which has the same or closely related legal rules on matters governed by this Convention as one or more non-Contracting States may at any time declare that the Convention is not to apply to contracts of sale or to their formation where the parties have their places of business in those States.

3. [Omitted].

## ARTICLE 95

Any State may declare at the time of the deposit of its instrument of ratification acceptance, approval or accession that it will not be bound by subparagraph 1 b of Article 1 of this Convention.

## Article 96

A Contracting State whose legislation requires contracts of sale to be concluded in or evidenced by writing may at any time make a declaration in accordance with Article 12 that any provision of Article 11, Article 29, or Part II of this Convention, that allows a contract of sale or its modification or termination by agreement or any offer, acceptance, or other indication or intention to be made in any form other than in writing, does not apply where any party has his place of business in that State.

## Articles 97-101 [Omitted]

# UNITED NATIONS CONVENTION ON INTERNATIONAL MULTIMODAL TRANSPORT OF GOODS, GENEVA, 1980

## PART I

## GENERAL PROVISIONS

### ARTICLE 1 - DEFINITIONS

For the purposes of this Convention:

1. 'International multimodal transport' means the carriage of goods by at least two different modes of transport on the basis of a multimodal transport contract from a place in one country at which the goods are taken in charge by the multimodal transport operator to a place designated for delivery situated in a different country. The operation of pick-up and delivery of goods carried out in the performance of a unimodal transport contract, as defined in such contract, shall not be considered as international multimodal transport.

2. 'Multimodal transport operator' means any person who on his own behalf or through another person acting on his behalf concludes a multimodal transport contract and who acts as a principal, not as an agent or on behalf of the consignor or of the carriers participating in the multimodal transport operations, and who assumes responsibility for the performance of the contract.

3. 'Multimodal transport contract' means a contract whereby a multimodal transport operator undertakes, against payment of freight, to perform or to procure the performance of international multimodal transport.

4. 'Multimodal transport document' means a document which evidences a multimodal transport contract, the taking in charge of the goods by the multimodal transport operator, and an undertaking by him to deliver the goods in accordance with the terms of that contract.

5. 'Consignor' means any person by whom or in whose name or on whose behalf a multimodal transport contract has been concluded with the multimodal transport operator, or any person by whom or in whose name or on whose behalf the goods are actually delivered to the multimodal transport operator in relation to the multimodal transport contract.

6. 'Consignee' means the person entitled to take delivery of the goods.

7. 'Goods' includes any container, pallet or similar article of transport or packaging , if supplied by the consignor.

8. 'International convention' means an international agreement concluded among States in written form and governed by international law.

9. 'Mandatory national law' means any statutory law concerning carriage of goods the provision of which cannot be departed from by contractual stipulation to the detriment of the consignor.

10. 'Writing' means, *inter alia*, telegram or telex.

## Article 2 - Scope of application

The provisions of this Convention shall apply to all contracts of multimodal transport between places in two States, if:

(a) The place for the taking in charge of the goods by the multimodal transport operator as provided for in the multimodal transport contract is located in a Contracting State, or

(b) The place for delivery of the goods by the multimodal transport operator as provided for in the multimodal transport contract is located in a Contracting state.

## Article 3 - Mandatory application

1. When a multimodal transport contract has been concluded which according to Article 2 shall be governed by this convention, the provisions of this convention shall be mandatorily applicable to such contract.

2. Nothing in this Convention shall affect the right of the consignor to choose between multimodal transport and segmented transport.

## Article 4 - Regulation and control of multimodal transport

1. This Convention shall not affect, or be incompatible with, the application of any international convention or national law relating to the regulation and control of transport operations.

2. This Convention shall not affect the right of each State to regulate and control at the national level multimodal transport operations and multimodal transport operators, including the right to take measures relating to consultations, especially before the introduction of new technologies and services, between multimodal transport operators, shippers, shippers' organisations and appropriate national authorities on terms and conditions of service; licensing of multimodal transport operators; participation in transport; and all other steps in the national economic and commercial interest.

3. The multimodal transport operator shall comply with the applicable law of the country in which he operates and with the provisions of this Convention.

# Part II

## Documentation

## Article 5 - Issue of multimodal transport document

1. When the goods are taken charge by the multimodal transport operator, he shall issue a multimodal transport document which, at the option of the consignor, shall be in either negotiable or non-negotiable form.

2. The multimodal transport document shall be signed by the multimodal transport operator or by a person having authority from him.

3. The signature on the multimodal transport document may be in handwriting, printed in facsimile, perforated, stamped, in symbols, or made by any other mechanical or electronic means, if not inconsistent with the law of the country where the multimodal transport document is issued.

4. If the consignor so agrees, a non-negotiable multimodal transport document may be issued by making use of any mechanical or other means preserving a record of the particulars stated in Article 8 to be contained in the multimodal transport document. In such a case the multimodal transport operator, after having taken the goods in charge, shall deliver to the consignor a readable document containing all the particulars so recorded, and such document shall for the purposes of the provisions of this Convention be deemed to be a multimodal transport document.

### ARTICLE 6 - NEGOTIABLE MULTIMODAL TRANSPORT DOCUMENT

1. Where a multimodal transport document is issued in negotiable form:

(a) It shall be made out to order or to bearer;
(b) If made out to order it shall be transferable by endorsement;
(c) If made out to bearer it shall be transferable without endorsement;
(d) If issued in a set of more than one original it shall indicate the number of originals in the set;
(e) If any copies are issued each copy shall be marked 'non-negotiable copy'.

2. Delivery of the goods may be demanded from the multimodal transport operator or a person acting on his behalf only against surrender of the negotiable multimodal transport document duly endorsed where necessary.

3. The multimodal transport operator shall be discharged from his obligation to deliver the goods if, where a negotiable multimodal transport document has been issued in a set of more than one original, he or a person acting on his behalf has in good faith delivered the goods against surrender of one of such originals.

### ARTICLE 7 - NON-NEGOTIABLE MULTIMODAL TRANSPORT

1. Where a multimodal transport document is issued in non-negotiable form it shall indicate a named consignee.

2. The multimodal transport operator shall be discharged from his obligation to deliver the goods if he makes delivery thereof to the consignee named in such non-negotiable multimodal transport document or to such other person as he may be duly instructed, as a rule, in writing.

### ARTICLE 8 - CONTENTS OF THE MULTIMODAL TRANSPORT DOCUMENT

1. The multimodal transport document shall contain the following particulars:
   (a) The general nature of the goods, the leading marks necessary for identification of the goods, an express statement, if applicable, as to the dangerous character of the goods, the number of packages or pieces, and the gross weight of the goods or their quantity otherwise expressed, all such particulars as furnished by the consignor;
   (b) The apparent condition of the goods;
   (c) The name and principal place of business of the multimodal transport operator;
   (d) The name of the consignor;
   (e) The consignee, if named by the consignor;
   (f) The place and date of taking in charge of the goods by the multimodal transport operator;
   (g) The place of delivery of the goods;
   (h) The date or the period of delivery of the goods at the place of delivery, if expressly agreed upon between the parties;
   (i) A statement indicating whether the multimodal transport document is negotiable or non-negotiable;
   (j) The place and date of issue of the multimodal transport document;
   (k) The signature of the multimodal transport operator or of a person having authority from him;
   (l) the freight for each mode of transport, if expressly agreed between the parties, or the freight including its currency, to the extent payable by the consignee or other indication that freight is payable by him;
   (m) The intended journey route, modes of transport and places of transhipment, if known at the time of issuance of the multimodal transport document;
   (n) the statement referred to in paragraph 3 of Article 28;
   (o) Any other particulars which the parties may agree to insert in the multimodal transport document, if not inconsistent with the law of the country where the multimodal transport document is issued.

2. The absence from the multimodal transport document of one or more of the particulars referred to in paragraph 1 of this Article shall not affect the legal character of the document as a multimodal transport document provided that it nevertheless meets the requirements set out in paragraph 4 of Article 1.

### ARTICLE 9 - RESERVATIONS IN THE MULTIMODAL TRANSPORT DOCUMENT

1. If the multimodal transport document contains particulars concerning the general nature, leading marks, number of packets or pieces, weight or quantity of the goods which the multimodal transport operator or a person acting on his behalf knows, or has reasonable grounds to suspect, do not accurately represent the goods actually taken in charge, or if he has no reasonable means of checking such particulars, the multimodal transport operator or a person acting on his behalf shall insert in the multimodal transport document a reservation specifying these inaccuracies, grounds of suspicion or the absence of reasonable means of checking.

2. If the multimodal transport operator or a person acting on his behalf fails to note on the multimodal transport document the apparent condition of the

goods, he is deemed to have noted on the multimodal transport document that the goods were in apparent good condition.

### ARTICLE 10 - EVIDENTIARY EFFECT OF THE MULTIMODAL TRANSPORT DOCUMENT

Except for particulars in respect of which and to the extent to which a reservation permitted under Article 9 has been entered:

(a) The multimodal transport document shall be *prima facie* evidence of the taking in charge by the multimodal transport operator of the goods as described therein; and

(b) Proof to the contrary by the multimodal transport operator shall not be admissible if the multimodal transport document is issued in negotiable form and has been transferred to a third party, including a consignee, who has acted in good faith in reliance on the description of the goods therein.

### ARTICLE 11 - LIABILITY FOR INTENTIONAL MISSTATEMENTS OR OMISSIONS

When the multimodal transport operator, with intent to defraud, gives in the multimodal transport document false information concerning the goods or omits any information required to be included under paragraph 1 a or b of Article 8 or under Article 9, he shall be liable, without the benefit of the limitation of liability provided for in this Convention, for any loss, damage or expenses incurred by a third party, including a consignee, who acted in reliance on the description of the goods in the multimodal transport document issued.

### ARTICLE 12 - GUARANTEE BY THE CONSIGNOR

1. The consignor shall be deemed to have guaranteed to the multimodal transport operator the accuracy, at the time the goods were taken in charge by the multimodal transport operator, of particulars relating to the general nature of the goods, their marks, number, weight and quantity and, if applicable, to the dangerous character of the goods, as furnished by him for insertion in the multimodal transport document.

2. The consignor shall indemnify the multimodal transport operator against loss resulting from inaccuracies in or inadequacies of the particulars referred to in paragraph 1 of this Article. The consignor shall remain liable even if the multimodal transport document has been transferred to him. The right of the multimodal transport operator to such indemnity shall in no way limit his liability under the multimodal transport contract to any person other than the consignor.

## ARTICLE 13 - OTHER DOCUMENTS.

The issue of the multimodal transport document does not preclude the issue, if necessary, of other documents relating to transport or other services involved in international multimodal transport, in accordance with applicable international conventions or national law. However, the issue of such other documents shall not affect the legal character of the multimodal transport document.

# PART III

## LIABILITY OF THE MULTIMODAL TRANSPORT OPERATOR

## ARTICLE 14 - PERIOD OF RESPONSIBILITY

1. The responsibility of the multimodal transport operator for the goods under this Convention covers the period from the time he takes the goods in his charge to the time of their delivery.

2. For the purpose of this Article, the multimodal transport operator is deemed to be in charge of the goods:

(a) From the time he has taken over the goods from:

(i) The consignor or a person acting on his behalf; or

(ii) An authority or other third party to whom, pursuant to law or regulations applicable at the place of taking in charge, the goods must be handed over for transport;

(b) Until the time he has delivered the goods:

(i) By handing over the goods to the consignee; or

(ii) In cases where the consignee does not receive the goods from the multimodal transport operator, by placing them at the disposal of the consignee in accordance with the multimodal transport contract or with the law or with the usage of the particular trade applicable at the place of delivery: or

(iii) By handing over the goods to an authority or other third party to whom, pursuant to law or regulations applicable at the place of delivery, the goods must be handed over.

3. In paragraphs 1 and 2 of this Article, reference to the multimodal transport operator shall include his servants or agents or any other person of whose services he makes use for the performance of the multimodal transport contract, and reference to the consignor or consignee shall include their servants or agents.

## ARTICLE 15 - THE LIABILITY OF THE MULTIMODAL TRANSPORT OPERATOR FOR HIS SERVANTS, AGENTS AND OTHER PERSONS

Subject to Article 21, the multimodal transport operator shall be liable for the acts and omissions of his servants or agents, when any such servant or agent is acting within the scope of his employment, or of any other person of whose services he makes use for the performance of the multimodal transport contract, when such person is acting in the performance of the contract, as if such acts and omissions were his own.

## ARTICLE 16 - BASIS OF LIABILITY

1. The multimodal transport operator shall be liable for loss resulting from loss or damage to the goods, as well as from delay in delivery, if the occurrence which caused the loss, damage or delay in delivery took place while the goods were in his charge as defined in Article 14, unless the multimodal transport operator proves that he, his servants or agents or any other person referred to in Article 15 took all measures that could reasonably be required to avoid the occurrence and its consequences.

2. Delay in delivery occurs when the goods have not been delivered within the time expressly agreed upon or, in the absence of such agreement, within the time which it would be reasonable to require of a diligent multimodal transport operator, having regard to the circumstances of the case.

3. If the goods have not been delivered within 90 consecutive days following the date of delivery determined according to paragraph 2 of this Article, the claimant may treat the goods as lost.

## ARTICLE 17 - CONCURRENT CAUSES

Where fault or neglect on the part of the multimodal transport operator, his servants or agents or any other person referred to in Article 15 combines with another cause to produce loss, damage or delay in delivery, the multimodal transport operator shall be liable only to the extent that the loss, damage or delay in delivery is attributable to such fault or neglect, provided that the multimodal transport operator proves the part of the loss, damage or delay in delivery not attributable thereto.

## ARTICLE 18 - LIMITATION OF LIABILITY

1. When the multimodal transport operator is liable for loss resulting from loss of or damage to the goods according to Article 16, his liability shall be limited to an amount not exceeding 920 units of account per package of other shipping unit or 2.75 units of account per kilogram of gross weight of the goods lost or damaged, whichever is the higher.

2. For the purpose of calculating which amount is the higher in accordance with paragraph 1 of this Article, the following rules apply:

(a) Where a container, pallet or similar article of transport is used to consolidate goods, the packages or other shipping units enumerated in the multimodal transport document as packed in such article of transport are deemed packages or shipping units. Except as aforesaid, the goods in such article of transport are deemed one shipping unit.

(b) In cases where the article of transport itself has been lost or damaged, that article of transport, if not owned or otherwise supplied by the multimodal transport operator, is considered one separate shipping unit.

3. Notwithstanding the provisions of paragraphs 1 and 2 of this Article, if the international multimodal transport does not, according to the contract, include carriage of goods by sea or by inland waterways, the liability of the multimodal transport operator shall be limited to an amount not exceeding 8.33 units of account per kilogram of gross weight of the goods lost or damaged.

4. The liability of the multimodal transport operator for loss resulting from delay in delivery according to the provisions of Article 16 shall be limited to an amount equivalent to two and a half times the freight payable for the goods delayed, but not exceeding the total freight payable under the multimodal transport contract.

5. The aggregate liability of the multimodal transport operator, under paragraphs 1 and 4 or paragraphs 3 and 4 of this Article, shall not exceed the limit of liability for total loss of the goods as determined by paragraph 1 or 3 of this Article.

6. By agreement between the multimodal transport operator and the consignor, limits of liability exceeding those provided for in paragraphs 1, 3 and 4 or this Article may be fixed in the multimodal transport document.

7. 'Unit of account' means the unit of account mentioned in Article 31.

### ARTICLE 19 - LOCALISED DAMAGE

When the loss of or damage to the goods occurred during one particular of the multimodal transport, in respect of which an applicable international convention or mandatory national law provides a higher limit of liability than the limit that would follow from application of paragraphs 1 to 3 of Article 18, then the limit of the multimodal transport operator's liability for such loss or damage shall be determined by reference to the provisions of such convention or mandatory national law.

### ARTICLE 20 - NON-CONTRACTUAL LIABILITY

1. The defences and limits of liability provided for in this Convention shall apply in any action against the multimodal transport operator in respect of loss resulting from loss of or damage to the goods, as well as from delay in delivery, whether the action be founded in contract, in tort or otherwise.

2. If an action in respect of loss resulting from loss of or damage to the goods or from delay in delivery is brought against the servant or agent of the multimodal transport operator, if such servant or agent proves that he acted within the scope of his employment, or against any other person of whose services he makes use for the performance of the multimodal transport contract, if such other person proves that he acted within the performance of the contract, the servant or agent of such other person shall be entitled to avail himself of the defences and limits of liability which the multimodal transport operator is entitled to invoke under this Convention.

3. Except as provided in Article 21, the aggregate of the amounts recoverable from the multimodal transport operator and from a servant or agent or any other person of whose services he makes use for the performance of the multimodal transport contract shall not exceed the limits of liability provided for in this Convention.

### ARTICLE 21 - LOSS OF THE RIGHT TO LIMIT LIABILITY

1. The multimodal transport operator is not entitled to the benefit of the limitation of liability provided for in this Convention if it is proved that the loss, damage or delay in delivery resulted from an act or omission of the multimodal transport operator done with the intent to cause such loss, damage or delay or recklessly and with knowledge that such loss, damage or delay would probably result.

2. Notwithstanding paragraph 2 of Article 20, a servant or agent of the multimodal transport operator or other person of whose services he makes use for the performance of the multimodal transport contract is not entitled to the benefit of the limitation of liability provided for in this Convention if it is proved that the loss, damage or delay in delivery resulted from an act or omission of such servant, agent or other person, done with the intent to cause such loss, damage or delay or recklessly and with knowledge that such loss, damage or delay would probably result.

## PART IV

## LIABILITY OF THE CONSIGNOR

### ARTICLE 22 - GENERAL RULE

The consignor shall be liable for loss sustained by the multimodal transport operator if such loss is caused by the fault or neglect of the consignor, or his servants or agents when such servants or agents are acting within the scope of their employment. Any servant or agent of the consignor shall be liable for such loss if the loss is caused by fault or neglect on his part.

### ARTICLE 23 - SPECIAL RULES ON DANGEROUS GOODS

1. The consignor shall mark or label in a suitable manner dangerous goods as dangerous.

2. Where the consignor hands over dangerous goods to the multimodal transport operator or any person acting on his behalf, the consignor shall inform him of the dangerous character of the goods and, if necessary, the precautions to be taken. If the consignor fails to do so and the multimodal transport operator does not otherwise have knowledge of their dangerous character:

(a) The consignor shall be liable to the multimodal transport operator for all loss resulting from the shipment of such goods; and

(b) The goods may at any time be unloaded, destroyed or rendered innocuous, as the circumstances may require, without payment of compensation.

3. The provisions of paragraph 2 of this Article may not be invoked by any person if during the multimodal transport he has taken the goods in his charge with knowledge of their dangerous character.

4. If, in cases where the provisions of paragraph 2 b of this Article do not apply or may not be invoked, dangerous goods become an actual danger to life or property, they may be unloaded, destroyed or rendered innocuous, as the circumstances may require, without payment of compensation except where there is an obligation to contribute in general average or where the multimodal transport operator is liable in accordance with the provisions of Article 16.

## PART V

## CLAIMS AND ACTIONS

### ARTICLE 24 - NOTICE OF LOSS, DAMAGE OR DELAY

1. Unless notice of loss or damage, specifying the general nature of such loss or damage, is given in writing by the consignee to the multimodal transport operator not later than the working day after the day when the goods were handed over to the consignee, such handing over is *prima facie* evidence of the delivery by the multimodal transport operator of the goods as described in the multimodal transport document.

2. Where the loss or damage is not apparent, the provisions of paragraph 1 of this Article apply correspondingly if notice in writing is not given within six consecutive days after the day when the goods were handed over to the consignee.

3. If the state of the goods at the time they were handed over to the consignee has been the subject of a joint survey or inspection by the parties or their authorised representatives at the place of delivery, notice in writing need not be given of loss or damage ascertained during such survey or inspection.

4. In the case of any actual or apprehended loss or damage the multimodal transport operator and the consignee shall give all reasonable facilities to each other for inspecting and tallying the goods.

5. No compensation shall be payable for loss resulting from delay in delivery unless notice has been given in writing to the multimodal transport operator within 60 consecutive days after the day when the goods were delivered by handing over to the consignee or when the consignee has been notified that the goods have been delivered in accordance with paragraph 2 b ii or iii of Article 14.

6. Unless notice of loss or damage, specifying the general nature of the loss or damage, is given in writing by the multimodal transport operator to the

consignor not later than 90 consecutive days after the occurrence of such loss of damage or after the delivery of the goods in accordance with paragraph 2 (b) of Article 14, whichever is later, the failure to give such notice is *prima facie* evidence that the multimodal transport operator has sustained no loss or damage due to the fault or neglect of the consignor, his servants or agents.

7. If any of the notice periods provided for in paragraphs 2, 5 and 6 of this Article terminates on a day which is not a working day at the place of delivery, such period shall be extended until the next working day.

8. For the purpose of this Article, notice given to a person acting on the multimodal transport operator's behalf, including any person of whose services he makes use at the place of delivery, or to a person acting on the consignor's behalf, shall be deemed to have been given to the multimodal transport operator, or to the consignor, respectively.

## ARTICLE 25 - LIMITATION OF ACTIONS

1. Any action relating to international multimodal transport under this convention shall be time-barred if judicial or arbitral proceedings have not been instituted within a period of two years. However, if notification in writing, stating the nature and main particulars of the claim, has not been given within six months after the day when the goods were delivered or, where the goods have not been delivered, after the day on which they should have been delivered, the action shall be time-barred at the expiry of this period.

2. The limitation period commences on the day after the day on which the multimodal transport operator has delivered the goods or part thereof or, where the goods have not been delivered, on the day after the last day on which the goods should have been delivered.

3. The person against whom a claim is made may at any time during the running of the limitation period extend that period by a declaration in writing to the claimant. This period may be further extended by another declaration or declarations.

4. Provided that the provisions of another applicable international convention are not to the contrary, a recourse action for indemnity by a person held liable under this Convention may be instituted even after the expiration of the limitation period provided for in the preceding paragraphs if instituted within the time allowed by the law of the State where proceedings are instituted; however, the time allowed shall not be less than 90 days commencing from the day when the person instituting such action for indemnity has settled the claim or has been served with process in the action against himself.

## ARTICLE 26 - JURISDICTION

1. In judicial proceedings relating to international multimodal transport under this Convention, the plaintiff, at his option, may institute an action in a court which, according to the law of the State where the court is situated, is

competent and within the jurisdiction of which is situated one of the following places:

(a) The principal place of business or, in the absence thereof, the habitual residence of the defendant; or
(b) The place where the multimodal transport contract was made, provided that the defendant has there a place of business, branch or agency through which the contract was made; or
(c) The place of taking the goods in charge for international multimodal transport or the place of delivery; or
(d) Any other place designated for that purpose in the multimodal transport contract and evidenced in the multimodal transport document.

2. No judicial proceedings relating to international multimodal transport under this Convention may be instituted in a place not specified in paragraph 1 of this Article. The provisions of this Article do not constitute an obstacle to the jurisdiction of the Contracting States for provisional or protective measures.

3. Notwithstanding the preceding provisions of this Article, an agreement made by the parties after a claim has arisen, which designates the place where the plaintiff may institute an action, shall be effective.

4.—

(a) Where an action has been instituted in accordance with the provisions of this Article or where judgement in such an action has been delivered, no new action shall be instituted between the same parties on the same grounds unless the judgement in the first action is not enforceable in the country in which the new proceedings are instituted;
(b) For the purposes of this Article neither the institution of measures to obtain enforcement of a judgement nor the removal of an action to a different court within the same country shall be considered as the starting of a new action.

## Article 27 - Arbitration

1. Subject to the provisions of this Article, parties may provide by agreement evidenced in writing that any dispute that may arise relating to international multimodal transport under this Convention shall be referred to arbitration.

2. The arbitration proceedings shall, at the option of the claimant, be instituted at one of the following places:

(a) A place in a State within whose territory is situated:
   (i) The principal place of business of the defendant or, in the absence thereof, the habitual residence of the defendant; or
   (ii) The place where the multimodal transport contract was made, provided that the defendant has there a place of business, branch or agency through which the contract was made; or
   (iii) The place of taking the goods in charge for international multimodal transport or the place of delivery; or
(b) Any other place designated for that purpose in the arbitration clause or agreement.

3. The arbitrator or arbitration tribunal shall apply the provisions of this Convention.

4. The provisions of paragraphs 2 and 3 of this Article shall be deemed to be part of every arbitration clause or agreement and any term of such clause or agreement which is inconsistent therewith shall be null and void.

5. Nothing in this Article shall affect the validity of an agreement on arbitration made by the parties after the claim relating to the international multimodal transport has arisen.

## PART VI

## SUPPLEMENTARY PROVISIONS

### ARTICLE 28 - CONTRACTUAL STIPULATIONS

1. Any stipulation in a multimodal transport contract or multimodal transport document shall be null and void to the extent that it derogates, directly or indirectly, from the provisions of this Convention. The nullity of such a stipulation shall not affect the validity of other provisions of the contract or document of which it forms a part. A clause assigning benefit of insurance of the goods in favour of the multimodal transport operator or any similar clause shall be null and void.

2. Notwithstanding the provisions of paragraph 1 of this Article, the multimodal transport operator may, with the agreement of the consignor, increase his responsibilities and obligations under this Convention.

3. The multimodal transport document shall contain a statement that the international multimodal transport is subject to the provisions of this Convention which nullify any stipulation derogating therefrom to the detriment of the consignor or the consignee.

4. Where the claimant in respect of the goods has incurred loss as a result of a stipulation which is null and void by virtue of the present Article, or as a result of the omission of the statement referred to in paragraph 3 of this Article, the multimodal transport operator must pay compensation to the extent required in order to give the claimant compensation in accordance with the provisions of this Convention for any loss of or damage to the goods as well as for delay in delivery. The multimodal transport operator must, in addition, pay compensation for costs incurred by the claimant for the purpose of exercising his right, provided that costs incurred in the action where the foregoing provision is invoked are to be determined in accordance with the law of the State where proceedings are instituted.

### ARTICLE 29 - GENERAL AVERAGE

1. Nothing in this Convention shall prevent the application of provisions in the multimodal transport contract or national law regarding the adjustment of general average, if and to the extent applicable.

2. With the exception of Article 25, the provisions of this Convention relating to the liability of the multimodal transport operator for loss of or damage to the goods shall also determine whether the consignee may refuse contribution in general average and the liability of the multimodal transport operator to indemnify the consignee in respect of any such contribution made or any salvage paid.

## ARTICLE 30 - OTHER CONVENTIONS

1. This Convention does not modify the rights or duties provided for in the Brussels International Convention for the unification of certain rules relating to the limitation of the liability of owners of sea-going vessels of 25 August 1924; in the Brussels International Convention relating to the limitation of the liability of owners of sea-going ships of 10 October 1957; in the London convention on limitation of liability for maritime claims of 19 November 1976; and in the Geneva Convention relating to the limitation of the liability of owners of inland navigation vessels (CLN) of 1 March 1973, including amendments to these Conventions, or national law relating to the limitation of liability of owners of sea-going ships and inland navigation vessels.

2. The provisions of Articles 26 and 27 of this Convention do not prevent the application of the mandatory provisions of any other international convention relating to matters dealt with in the said Articles, provided that the dispute arises exclusively between parties having their principal place of business in States parties to such other Convention. However, this paragraph does not affect the application of paragraph 3 of Article 27 of this Convention.

3. [Omitted].

4. Carriage of goods such as carriage of goods in accordance with the Geneva Convention of 19 May 1956 on the Contract for the International Carriage of Goods by Road in Article 2, or the Berne Convention of 7 February 1970 concerning the Carriage of Goods by Rail, Article 2, shall not for States Parties to Conventions governing such carriage be considered as international multimodal transport within the meaning of Article 1, paragraph 1, of this Convention, in so far as such States are bound to apply the provisions of such Conventions to such carriage of goods.

## ARTICLE 31 - UNIT OF ACCOUNT OF MONETARY UNIT AND CONVERSION

1. The unit of account referred to in Article 18 of this Convention is the Special Drawing Right as defined by the International Monetary Fund. The amounts referred to in Article 18 shall be converted into the national currency of a State according to the value of such currency on the date of the judgement or award or the date agreed upon by the parties. The value of a national currency, in terms of Special Drawing Right, of a Contracting State which is a member of the International Monetary Fund, shall be calculated in accordance with the method of valuation applied by the International Monetary Fund, in effect on the date in question, for its operations and transactions. The value of a national currency in terms of the Special Drawing Right of a Contracting State which is

not a member of the International Monetary Fund shall be calculated in a manner determined by that State.

2. Nevertheless, a State which is not a member of the International Monetary Fund and whose law does not permit the application of the provisions of paragraph 1 of this Article may, at the time of signature, ratification, acceptance, approval or accession, or at any time thereafter, declare that the limits of liability provided for in this Convention to be applied in its territory shall be fixed as follows: with regard to the limits provided for in paragraph 1 of Article 18, to 13,750 monetary units per package or other shipping unit or 41.25 monetary units per kilogram of gross weight of the goods, and with regard to the limit provided for in paragraph 3 of Article 18, to 124 monetary units.

3. The monetary unit referred to in paragraph 2 of this Article corresponds to sixty-five and a half milligrams of gold of millesimal fineness nine hundred. The conversion of the amount referred to in paragraph 2 of this Article into national currency shall be made according to the law of the State concerned.

4. The calculation mentioned in the last sentence of paragraph 1 of this Article and the conversion referred to in paragraph 3 of this Article shall be made in such a manner as to express in the national currency of the Contracting State as far as possible the same real value for the amounts in Article 18 as is expressed there in units of account.

5. Contracting States shall communicate to the depositary the manner of calculation pursuant to the last sentence of paragraph 1 of this Article, or the result of the conversion pursuant to paragraph 3 of this Article, as the case may be, at the time of signature or when depositing their instruments of ratification, acceptance, approval or accession, or when availing themselves of the option provided for in paragraph 2 of this Article and whenever there is a change in the manner of such calculation or in the result of such conversion.

## PART VII, ARTICLE 32 [OMITTED]

## PART VIII, ARTICLE 33-40 [OMITTED]

## ANNEX : PROVISIONS ON CUSTOMS MATTERS RELATING TO INTERNATIONAL MULTIMODAL TRANSPORT OF GOODS [OMITTED].

# UNIDROIT CONVENTION ON AGENCY IN THE INTERNATIONAL SALE OF GOODS, GENEVA, 1983

## CHAPTER 1 - SPHERE OF APPLICATION AND GENERAL PROVISIONS

### ARTICLE 1

1. This Convention applies where one person, the agent, has authority or purports to have authority on behalf of another person, the principal, to conclude a contract of sale of goods with a third party.

2. It governs not only the conclusion of such a contract by the agent but also any act undertaken by him for the purpose of concluding that contract or in relation to its performance.

3. It is concerned only with relations between the principal or the agent on the one hand, and the third party on the other.

4. It applies irrespective of whether the agent acts in his own name or in that of the principal.

### ARTICLE 2

1. This Convention applies only where the principal and the third party have their places of business in different States and:
   (a) the agent has his place of business in a Contracting State, or
   (b) the rules of private international law lead to the application of the law of a Contracting State.

2. Where, at the time of contracting, the third party neither knew nor ought to have known that the agent was acting as an agent, the Convention only applies if the agent and the third party had their places of business in different States and if the requirements of paragraph 1 are satisfied.

3. Neither the nationality of the parties nor the civil or commercial character of the parties or of the contract of sale is to be taken into consideration in determining the application of this Convention.

### ARTICLE 3

1. This Convention does not apply to:
   (a) the agency of a dealer on a stock, commodity or other exchange;
   (b) the agency of an auctioneer;
   (c) agency by operation of law in family law, in the law of matrimonial property, or in the law of succession;
   (d) agency arising from statutory or judicial authorisation to act for a person without capacity to act;
   (e) agency by virtue of a decision of a judicial or quasi-judicial authority or subject to the direct control of such an authority.

2. Nothing in this Convention affects any rule of law for the protection of consumers.

## ARTICLE 4

For the purposes of this Convention:

(a) an organ, officer, or partner of a corporation, association, partnership or other entity, whether or not possessing legal personality, shall not be regarded as the agent of that entity in so far as, in the exercise of his functions as such, he acts by virtue of an authority conferred by law or by the constitutive documents of that entity;

(b) a trustee shall not be regarded as an agent of the trust, of the person who has created the trust, or of the beneficiaries.

## ARTICLE 5

The principal, or an agent acting in accordance with the express or implied instructions of the principal, may agree with the third party to exclude the application of this Convention or, subject to Article 11, to derogate from or vary the effect of any of its provisions.

## ARTICLE 6

1. In the interpretation of this Convention, regard is to be had to its international character and to the need to promote uniformity in its application and the observance of good faith in international trade.

2. Questions concerning matters governed by this Convention which are not expressly settled in it are to be settled in conformity with the general principles on which it is based or, in the absence of such principles, in conformity with the law applicable by virtue of the rules of private international law.

## ARTICLE 7

1. The principal or the agent on the one hand and the third party on the other are bound by any usage to which they have agreed and by any practices which they have established between themselves.

2. They are considered, unless otherwise agreed, to have impliedly made applicable to their relations any usage of which they knew or ought to have known and which in international trade is widely known to, and regularly observed by, parties to agency relations of the type involved in the particular trade concerned.

### ARTICLE 8

For the purposes of this Convention:

(a) if a party has more than one place of business, the place of business is that which has the closest relationship to the contract of sale, having regard to the circumstances known to or contemplated by the parties at the time of contracting;

(b) if a party does not have a place of business, reference is to be made to his habitual residence.

## CHAPTER II

## ESTABLISHMENT AND SCOPE OF THE AUTHORITY OF THE AGENT

### ARTICLE 9

1. The authorisation of the agent by the principal may be express or implied.

2. The agent has authority to perform all acts necessary in the circumstances to achieve the purposes for which the authorisation was given.

### ARTICLE 10

The authorisation need not be given in or evidenced by writing and is not subject to any other requirement as to form. It may be proved by any means, including witnesses.

### ARTICLE 11

Any provision of Article 10, Article 15 or Chapter IV which allows an authorisation, a ratification or a termination of authority to be made in any form other than in writing does not apply where the principal or the agent has his place of business in a Contracting State which has made a declaration under Article 27. The parties may not derogate from or vary the effect of this paragraph.

## CHAPTER III

## LEGAL EFFECTS OF ACTS CARRIED OUT BY THE AGENT

### ARTICLE 12

Where an agent acts on behalf of a principal within the scope of his authority and the third party knew or ought to have known that the agent was acting as an agent, the acts of the agent shall directly bind the principal and the third party to each other, unless it follows from the circumstances of the case, for example by a reference to a contract of commission, that the agent undertakes to bind himself only.

## ARTICLE 13

1. Where the agent acts on behalf of a principal within the scope of this authority, his acts shall bind only the agent and the third party if:
   (a) the third party neither knew nor ought to have known that the agent was acting as an agent, or
   (b) it follows from the circumstances of the case, for example by a reference to a contract of commission, that the agent undertakes to bind himself only.

2. Nevertheless:
   (a) Where the agent, whether by reason of the third party's failure of performance or for any other reason, fails to fulfil or is not in a position to fulfil his obligations to the principal, the principal may exercise against the third party the rights acquired on the principal's behalf by the agent, subject to any defences which the third party may set up against the agent;
   (b) where the agent fails to fulfil or is not in a position to fulfil his obligations to the third party, the third party may exercise against the principal the rights which the third party has against the agent, subject to any defences which the agent may set up against the third party and which the principal may set up against the agent.

3. The rights under paragraph 2 may be exercised only if notice of intention to exercise them is given to the agent and the third party or principal, as the case may be. As soon as the third party or principal has received such notice, he may no longer free himself from his obligations by dealing with the agent.

4. Where the agent fails to fulfil or is not in a position to fulfil his obligations to the third party because of the principal's failure of performance, the agent shall communicate the name of the principal to the third party.

5. Where the third party fails to fulfil his obligations under the contract to the agent, the agent shall communicate the name of the third party to the principal.

6. The principal may not exercise against the third party the rights acquired on his behalf by the agent if it appears from the circumstances of the case that the third party, had he known the principal's identity, would not have entered into the contract.

7. An agent may, in accordance with the express or implied instructions of the principal, agree with the third party to derogate from or vary the effect of paragraph 2.

## Article 14

1. Where an agent acts without authority or acts outside the scope of his authority, his acts do not bind the principal and the third party to each other.

2. Nevertheless, where the conduct of the principal causes the third party reasonably and in good faith to believe that the agent has authority to act on behalf of the principal and that the agent is acting within the scope of that authority, the principal may not invoke against the third party the lack of authority of the agent.

## Article 15

1. An act by an agent who acts without authority or who acts outside the scope of his authority may be ratified by the principal. On ratification the act produces the same effects as if it had initially been carried out with authority.

2. Where, at the time of the atent's act, the third party neither knew nor ought to have known of the lack of authority, he shall not be liable to the principal, if, at any time before ratification, he gives notice of his refusal to become bound by a ratification. Where the principal ratifies but does not do so within a reasonable time, the third party may refuse to be bound by the ratification if he promptly notifies the principal.

3. Where, however, the third party knew or ought to have known of the lack of authority of the agent, the third party may not refuse to become bound by a ratification before the expiration of any time agreed for ratification, or failing agreement, such reasonable time as the third party may specify.

4. The third party may refuse to accept a partial ratification.

5. Ratification shall take effect when notice of it reaches the third party or the ratification otherwise comes to his attention. Once effective, it may not be revoked.

6. Ratification is effective notwithstanding that the act itself could not have been effectively carried out at the time of ratification.

7. Where the act has been carried out on behalf of a corporation or other legal person before its creation, ratification is effective only if allowed by the law of the State governing its creation.

8. Ratification is subject to no requirements as to form. It may be express or may be inferred from the conduct of the principal.

## Article 16

1. An agent who acts without authority or who acts outside the scope of his authority shall, failing ratification, be liable to pay the third party such compensation as will place the third party in the same position as he would have

been in if the agent had acted with authority and within the scope of his authority.

2. The agent shall not be liable, however, if the third party knew or ought to have known that the agent had no authority or was acting outside the scope of his authority.

## CHAPTER IV

## TERMINATION OF THE AUTHORITY OF THE AGENT

### ARTICLE 17

The authority of the agent is terminated:

(a) when this follows from any agreement between the principal and the agent;

(b) on completion of the transaction or transactions for which the authority was created;

(c) on revocation by the principal or renunciation by the agent, whether or not this is consistent with the terms of the agreement.

### ARTICLE 18

The authority of the agent is also terminated when the applicable law so provides.

### ARTICLE 19

The termination of the authority shall not affect the third party unless he knew or ought to have known of the termination or the facts which caused it.

### ARTICLE 20

Notwithstanding the termination of his authority, the agent remains authorised to perform on behalf of the principal or his successors the acts which are necessary to prevent damage to their interests.

### ARTICLES 21-28 [OMITTED]

### ARTICLE 29

A Contracting State, the whole or specific parts of the foreign trade of which are carried on exclusively by specially authorised organisations, may at any time declare that, in cases where such organisations act either as buyers or sellers in foreign trade, all these organisations or the organisations specified in the declaration shall not be considered for the purposes of Article 13, paragraphs 2(b) and 4, as agents in their relations with other organisations having their place of business in the same State.

## ARTICLE 30

1. A Contracting State may at any time declare that it will apply the provisions of this Convention to specified cases falling outside its sphere of application.

2. Such declaration may, for example, provide that the Convention shall apply to:

(a) contracts other than contracts of sale of goods;

(b) cases where the place of business mentioned in Article 2, paragraph 1, are not situated in Contracting States.

## ARTICLES 31-35 [OMITTED]

# CONVENTION ON THE LAW APPLICABLE TO CONTRACTS FOR THE INTERNATIONAL SALE OF GOODS, THE HAGUE, 1985

## CHAPTER 1 - SCOPE OF THE CONVENTION

### ARTICLE 1

This Convention determines the law applicable to contracts of sale of goods—

(a) between parties having their places of business in different States;

(b) in all other cases involving a choice between the laws of different States, unless such a choice arises solely from a stipulation by the parties as to the applicable law, even if accompanied by a choice of court or arbitration.

### ARTICLE 2

The Convention does not apply to—

(a) sales by way of execution or otherwise by authority of law;

(b) sales of stocks, shares, investment securities, negotiable instruments or money, it does, however, apply to the sale of goods based on documents;

(c) sales of goods bought for personal, family or household use; it does, however, apply if the seller at the time of the conclusion of the contract neither knew nor ought to have known that the goods were bought for any such use.

### ARTICLE 3

For the purposes of the Convention, 'goods' includes—

(a) ships, vessels, boats, hovercraft and aircraft;

(b) electricity.

### ARTICLE 4

1. Contracts for the supply of goods to be manufactured or produced are to be considered contracts of sale unless the party who orders the goods undertakes to supply a substantial part of the materials necessary for such manufacture or production.

2. Contracts in which the preponderant part of the obligations of the party who furnishes goods consists of the supply of labour or other services are not to be considered contracts of sale.

## Article 5

The Convention does not determine the law applicable to—

(a) the capacity of the parties or the consequences of nullity or invalidity of the contract resulting from the incapacity of a party;

(b) the question whether an agent is able to bind a principal, or an organ to bind a company or body corporate or unincorporate;

(c) the transfer of ownership; nevertheless, the issues specifically mentioned in Article 12 are governed by the law applicable to the contract under the Convention;

(d) the effect of the sale in respect of any person other than the parties;

(e) agreements on arbitration or on choice of court, even if such an agreement is embodied in the contract of sale.

## Article 6

The law determined under the Convention applies whether or not it is the law of a Contracting State.

# CHAPTER II - APPLICABLE LAW

### *Section 1 - Determination of the applicable law*

## Article 7

1. A contract of sale is governed by the law chosen by the parties. The parties' agreement on this choice must be express or be clearly demonstrated by the terms of the contract and the conduct of the parties, viewed in their entirety. Such a choice may be limited to a part of the contract.

2. The parties may at any time agree to subject the contract in whole or in part to a law other than that which previously governed it, whether or not the law previously governing the contract was chosen by the parties. Any change by the parties of the applicable law made after the conclusion of the contract does not prejudice its formal validity or the rights of third parties.

## Article 8

1. To the extent that the law applicable to a contract of sale has not been chosen by the parties in accordance with Article 7, the contract is governed by the law of the State where the seller has his place of business at the time of conclusion of the contract.

2 However, the contract is governed by the law of the State where the buyer has his place of business at the time of conclusion of the contract, if -

(a) negotiations were conducted, and the contract concluded by and in the presence of the parties, in that State; or

(b) the contract provides expressly that the seller must perform his obligation to deliver the goods in that State; or
(c) the contract was concluded on terms determined mainly by the buyer and in response to an invitation directed by the buyer to persons invited to bid (a call for tenders).

3. By way of exception, where, in the light of the circumstances as a whole, for instance any business relations between the parties, the contract is manifestly more closely connected with a law which is not the law which would otherwise be applicable to the contract under paragraphs 1 or 2 of this Article, the contract is governed by that other law.

4. Paragraph 3 does not apply if, at the time of the conclusion of the contract, the seller and the buyer have their places of business in States having made the reservation under Article 21 paragraph 1 sub-paragraph b.

5. Paragraph 3 does not apply in respect of issues regulated in the United Nations Convention on Contracts for the International Sale of Goods (Vienna, 11 April 1980) where, at the time for the conclusion of the contract, the seller and the buyer have their places of business in different States both of which are Parties to that Convention.

## ARTICLE 9

A sale by auction or on a commodity or other exchange is governed by the law chosen by the parties in accordance with Article 7 to the extent to which the law of the State where the auction takes place or the exchange is located does not prohibit such choice. Failing a choice by the parties, or to the extent where the auction takes place or the exchange is located shall apply.

## ARTICLE 10

1. Issues concerning the existence and material validity of the consent of the parties as to the choice of the applicable law are determined, where the choice of the applicable law are determined, where the choice satisfies the requirements of Article 7, by the law chosen. If under that law the choice is invalid, the law governing the contract is determined under Article 8

2 The existence and material validity of a contract of sale, or of any term thereof, are determined by the law which under the Convention would govern the contract or term if it were valid.

3 Nevertheless, to establish that he did not consent to the choice of law, to the contract itself, or to any term thereof, a party may rely on the law of the State where he has his place of business, if in the circumstances it is not reasonable to determine that issue under the law specified in the preceding paragraphs.

## ARTICLE 11

1. A contract of sale concluded between persons who are in the same State is formally valid if it satisfies the requirements either of the law which governs it under the Convention or of the law of the State where it is concluded.

2 A contract of sale concluded between persons who are in different States is formally valid if it satisfies the requirements either of the law which governs it under the Convention or of the law of one of those States.

3 Where the contract is concluded by an agent, the State in which the agent acts is the relevant State for the purposes of the preceding paragraphs.

4 An act intended to have legal effect relating to an existing or contemplated contract of sale is formally valid if it satisfies the requirements either of the law which under the Convention governs or would govern the contract, or to the law of the State where the act was done.

5 The Convention does not apply to the formal validity of a contract of sale where one of the parties to the contract has, at the time of its conclusion, his place of business in a State which has made the reservation provided for in Article 1 paragraph 1 sub paragraph c.

*Section 2 - Scope of the applicable law*

## Article 12

The law applicable to a contract of sale by virtue of Articles 7, 8 or 9 governs in particular—

(a) interpretation of the contract;
(b) the rights and obligations of the parties and performance of the contract;
(c) the time at which the buyer becomes entitled to the products, fruits and income deriving from the goods;
(d) the time from which the buyer bears the risk with respect to the goods;
(e) the validity and effect as between the parties of clauses reserving title to the goods;
(f) the consequences of non performance of the contract, including the categories of loss for which compensation may be recovered, but without prejudice to the procedural law of the forum;
(g) the various ways of extinguishing obligations, as well as prescription and limitation of actions;
(h) the consequences of nullity or invalidity of the contract.

## Article 13

In the absence of an express clause to the contrary, the law of the state where inspection of the goods takes place applies to the modalities and procedural requirements for such inspection.

## CHAPTER III - GENERAL PROVISIONS

### ARTICLE 14

1. If a party has more than one place of business, the relevant place of business is that which has the closest relationship to the contract and its performance, having regard to the circumstance known to or contemplated by the parties at any time before or at the conclusion of the contract.

2 If a party does not have a place of business, reference is to be made to his habitual residence.

### ARTICLE 15

In the Convention 'law' means the law in force in a State other than its choice of law rules.

### ARTICLE 16

In the interpretation of the Convention, regard is to be had to its international character and to the need to promote uniformity in its application.

### ARTICLE 17

The Convention does not prevent the application of those provisions of the law of the forum that must be applied irrespective of the law that otherwise governs the contract.

### ARTICLE 18

The application of a law determined by the Convention may be refused only where such application would be manifestly incompatible with public policy (*ordre public*).

### ARTICLES 19-20 [OMITTED]

### ARTICLE 21

1. Any State may, at the time of signature, ratification, acceptance, approval or accession, make any of the following reservations—

(a) that it will not apply the Convention in cases covered by subparagraph (b) of Article 1;

(b) that it will not apply paragraph 3 of Article 8 except where neither party to the contract has his place of business in a State which has made a reservation provided for under this subparagraph;

(c) that for cases where its legislation requires contracts of sale to be concluded in or evidenced by writing, it will not apply the Convention to the formal validity of the contract, where any party has his place of business in its territory at the time of conclusion of the contract.

2. [Omitted].

3. [Omitted].

## ARTICLES 22-31 [OMITTED]

## Convention on Jurisdiction and Enforcement of Judgements in civil and Commercial Matters, Lugano, 1988

See Schedule 3C Civil Jurisdiction and Judgements Act 1982
for text of the Convention

# UNIDROIT CONVENTION ON INTERNATIONAL FACTORING, OTTAWA, 1988

## CHAPTER I - SPHERE OF APPLICATION AND GENERAL PROVISIONS

### ARTICLE 1

1. This Convention governs factoring contracts and assignments of receivables as described in this Chapter.

2. For the purposes of this convention 'factoring contract' means a contract concluded between the party (the supplier) and another party (the factor) pursuant to which:
   (a) the supplier may or will assign to the factor receivables arising from contracts of sale of goods made between the supplier and its customers (debtors) other than those for the sale of goods bought primarily for their personal, family or household use;
   (b) the factor is to perform at least two of the following functions:
   —finance for the supplier, including loans and advance payments;
   —maintenance of accounts (ledgering) relating to the receivables;
   —collection of receivables;
   —protection against default in payment by debtors;
   (c) notice of the assignment of the receivables is to be given to debtors.

3. In this convention references to 'goods' and 'sale of goods' shall include services and the supply of services.

4. For the purposes of this Convention:
   (a) a notice in writing need not be signed but must identify the person by whom or in whose name it is given
   (b) 'notice in writing' includes, but is not limited to, telegrams, telex and any other telecommunication capable of being reproduced in tangible form;
   (c) a notice in writing is given when it is received by the addressee.

### ARTICLE 2

1. This Convention applies whenever the receivables assigned pursuant to a factoring contract arise from a contract of sale of goods between a supplier and a debtor whose places of business are in different States and:
   (a) those States and the State in which the factor has its place of business are Contracting States; or
   (b) both the contract of sale of goods and the factoring contract are governed by the law of a Contracting State.

2. A reference in this Convention to a party's place of business shall, if it has more than one place of business, mean the place of business which has the closest relationship to the relevant contract and its performance, having regard to the circumstances known to or contemplated by the parties at any time before or at the conclusion of that contract.

## Article 3

1. The application of this Convention may be excluded:
   (a) by the parties to the factoring contract; or
   (b) by the parties to the contract of sale of goods, as regards receivables arising at or after the time when the factor has been given notice in writing of such exclusion.

2. Where the application of this Convention is excluded in accordance with the previous paragraph, such exclusion may be made only as regards the Convention as a whole.

## Article 4

1. In the interpretation of this Convention, regard is to be had to its object and purpose as set forth in the preamble, to its international character and to the need to promote uniformity in its application and the observance of good faith in international trade.

2. Questions concerning matters governed by this convention which are not expressly settled in it are to be settled in conformity with the general principles on which it is based or, in the absence of such principles, in conformity with the law applicable by virtue of the rules of private international law.

# Chapter II - Rights and Duties of the Parties

## Article 5

As between the parties to the factoring contract:
   (a) a provision in the factoring contract for the assignment of existing or future receivables shall not be rendered invalid by the fact that contract does not specify them individually, if at the time of conclusion of the contract or when they come into existence they can be identified to the contract;
   (b) a provision in the factoring contract by which future receivables are assigned operates to transfer the receivables to the factor when they come into existence without the need for any new act of transfer.

## Article 6

1. The assignment of a receivable by the supplier to the factor shall be effective notwithstanding any agreement between the supplier and the debtor prohibiting such assignment.

2. However, such assignment shall not be effective against the debtor when, at the time of conclusion of the contract of sale of goods, it has its place of business in a Contracting State which has made a declaration under Article 18 of this Convention

3. Nothing in paragraph 1 shall affect any obligation of good faith owed by the supplier to the debtor or any liability of the supplier to the debtor in respect of an assignment made in breach of the terms of the contract of sale of goods.

## ARTICLE 7

A factoring contract may validly provide as between the parties thereto for the transfer, with or without a new act of transfer, of all or any of the supplier's rights deriving from the contract of sale of goods, including the benefit of any provision in the contract of sale of goods reserving to the supplier title to the goods or creating any security interest.

## ARTICLE 8

1. The debtor is under a duty to pay the factor if, and only if, the debtor does not have knowledge of any other person's superior right to payment and notice in writing of the assignment:

(a) is given to the debtor by the supplier or by the factor with the supplier's authority;
(b) reasonably identifies the receivables which have been assigned and the factor to whom or for whose account the debtor is required to make payment; and
(c) relates to receivables arising under a contract of sale of goods made at or before the time the notice is given.

2. Irrespective of any other ground on which payment by the debtor to the factor discharges the debtor from liability, payment shall be effective for this purpose if made in accordance with the previous paragraph.

## ARTICLE 9

1. In a claim by the factor against the debtor for payment of a receivable arising under a contract of sale of goods the debtor may set up against the factor all defences arising under that contract of which the debtor could have availed itself if such claim had been made by the suppler.

2. The debtor may also assert against the factor any right of set-off in respect of claims existing against the supplier in whose favour the receivable arose and available to the debtor at the time a notice in writing of assignment conforming to Article 8 1 was given to the debtor.

## ARTICLE 10

1. Without prejudice to the debtor's rights under Article 9, non-performance or defective or late performance of the contract of sale of goods shall not by itself entitle the debtor to recover a sum paid by the debtor to the factor if the debtor has a right to recover that sum from the supplier.

2. The debtor who has such a right to recover from the supplier a sum paid to the factor in respect of a receivable shall nevertheless be entitled to recover that sum from the factor to the extent that—:

(a) the factor has not discharged an obligation to make payment to the supplier in respect of that receivable; or
(b) the factor made such payment at a time when it knew of the supplier's non-performance or defective or late performance as regards the goods to which the debtor's payment relates.

## CHAPTER III - SUBSEQUENT ASSIGNMENTS

### ARTICLE 11

1. Where a receivable is assigned by a supplier to a factor pursuant to a factoring contract governed by this Convention:
   (a) the rules set out in Articles 5 to 10 shall, subject to sub-paragraph b of this paragraph, apply to any subsequent assignment of the receivable by the factor or by a subsequent assignee;
   (b) the provisions of Articles 8 to 10 shall apply as if the subsequent assignee were the factor.

2. For the purposes of this Convention, notice to the debtor of the subsequent assignment also constitutes notice of the assignment to the factor.

### ARTICLE 12

This Convention shall not apply to a subsequent assignment which is prohibited by the terms of the factoring contract.

## CHAPTER IV, ARTICLES 3-2 [OMITTED]

# UNITED NATIONS CONVENTION ON INTERNATIONAL BILLS OF EXCHANGE AND INTERNATIONAL PROMISSORY NOTES, 1988

## CHAPTER I. SPHERE OF APPLICATION AND FORM OF THE INSTRUMENT

### ARTICLE 1

1. This Convention applies to an international bill of exchange when it contains the heading 'International bill of exchange (UNCITRAL Convention)' and also contains in its text the words 'International bill of exchange (UNCITRAL Convention)'.

2. This Convention applies to an international promissory note when it contains the heading 'International promissory note (UNCITRAL Convention)' and also contains in its text the words 'International promissory note (UNCITRAL Convention)'.

3. This Convention does not apply to cheques.

### ARTICLE 2

1. An international bill of exchange is a bill of exchange which specifies at least two of the following places and indicates that any two so specified are situated in different States:

(a) The place where the bill is drawn;
(b) The place indicated next to the signature of the drawer;
(c) The place indicated next to the name of the drawee;
(d) The place indicated next to the name of the payee;
(e) The place of payment:

provided that either the place where the bill is drawn or the place of payment is specified on the bill and that such place is situated in a Contracting State.

2. An international promissory note is a promissory note which specifies at least two of the following places and indicates that any two so specified are situated in a different States.

(a) the place where the note is made;
(b) the place indicated next to the signature of the maker;
(c) the place indicated next to the name of the payee;
(d) the place of payment;

provided that the place of payment is specified on the note and that such place is situated in a Contracting State.

3. This Convention does not deal with the question of sanctions that may be imposed under national law in cases where an incorrect or false statement has been made on an instrument in respect of a place referred to in paragraph 1 or 2 of this Article. However, any such sanctions shall not affect the validity of the instrument or the application of this Convention.

## ARTICLE 3

1. A bill of exchange is a written instrument which;
   (a) contains an unconditional order whereby the drawer directs the drawee to pay a definite sum of money to the payee or to his order;
   (b) is payable on demand or at a definite time;
   (c) is dated;
   (d) is signed by the drawer

2 A promissory note is a written instrument which;
   (a) contains an unconditional promise whereby the maker undertakes to pay a definite sum of money to the payee or to his order;
   (b) is payable on demand or at a definite time;
   (c) is dated;
   (d) is signed by the maker

## CHAPTER II. INTERPRETATION

### *Section I. General Provisions*

## ARTICLE 4

In the interpretation of this Convention, regard is to be had to its international character and to the need to promote uniformity in its application and the observance of good faith in international transactions.

## ARTICLE 5

In this Convention:
   (a) 'Bill' means an international bill of exchange governed by this convention;
   (b) 'Note' means an international promissory note governed by this Convention;
   (c) 'Instrument' means a bill or a note;
   (d) 'Drawee' means a person on whom a bill is drawn and who has not accepted it;
   (e) 'Payee' means a person in whose favour the drawer directs payment to be made or to whom the maker promises to pay;
   (f) 'Holder' means a person in possession of an instrument in accordance with Article 15:
   (g) 'Protected Holder' means a holder who meets the requirements of Article 29;
   (h) 'Guarantor' means any person any person who undertakes an obligation of guarantee under Article 46, whether governed by subparagraph b ('guaranteed') or subparagraph c ('*aval*') of paragraph 4 of Article 47;
   (i) 'Party' means a person who has signed an instrument as drawer, maker, acceptor, endorser or guarantor;

(j) 'Maturity' means the time of payment referred to in paragraph 4, 5, 6 and 7 of Article 9;
(k) 'Signature' means a handwritten signature, its facsimile or an equivalent authentication effected by any other means; 'forged signature' includes a signature by the wrongful use of such means;
(l) 'Money' or 'currency' includes a monetary unit of account which is established by an intergovernmental institution or by agreement between two or more states, provided that this Convention shall apply without prejudice to the rules of the intergovernmental institution or to the stipulations of the agreement.

## Article 6

For the purposes of this Convention, a person is considered to have knowledge of a fact if he has actual knowledge of that fact or could not have been unaware of its existence.

### *Section 2. Interpretation of formal requirements*

## Article 7

The sum payable by an instrument is deemed to be a definite sum although the instrument states that it is to be paid;
(a) with interest;
(b) by instalments at successive dates;
(c) by instalments at successive dates with a stipulation in the instrument that upon default in payment of any instalment the unpaid balance becomes due;
(d) according to a rate of exchange indicated in the instrument or to be determined as directed by the instrument; or
(e) in a currency other than the currency in which the sum is expressed in the instrument.

## Article 8

1. If there is a discrepancy between the sum expressed in words and the sum expressed in figures, the sum payable by the instrument is the sum expressed in words.

2. If the sum is expressed more than once in words, and there is a discrepancy, the sum payable is the smaller sum. The same rule applies if the sum is expressed more than once in figures only, and there is a discrepancy.

3. If the sum is expressed in a currency having the same description as that of at least one other state than the State where payment is to be made, as indicated in the instrument, and the specified currency is not identified as the currency of any particular State, the currency is to be considered as the currency of the state where payment is to be made.

4. If an instrument states that the sum is to paid with interest, without specifying the date from which interest is to run, interest runs from the date of the instrument.

5. A stipulation stating that the sum is to be paid with interest is deemed not to have been written on the instrument unless it indicates the rate at which interest is to be paid.

6. A rate at which interest is to be paid may be expressed either as a definite rate or as a variable rate. For a variable rate to qualify for this purpose, it must vary in relation to one or more reference rates of interest in accordance with provisions stipulated in the instrument and each such reference rate must be published or otherwise available to the public and not be subject, directly or indirectly, to unilateral determination by a person who is named in the instrument at the time the bill is drawn or the note is made, unless the person is named only in the reference rate provisions.

7. If the rate at which interest is to be paid is expressed as a variable rate, it may be stipulated expressly in the instrument that such rate shall not be less than or exceed a specified rate of interest, or that the variations are otherwise limited.

8. If a variable rate does not qualify under paragraph 6 of this Article or for any reason it is not possible to determine the numerical value of the variable rate for any period, interest shall be payable for the relevant period at the rate calculated in accordance with paragraph 2 of Article 70.

## Article 9

1. An instrument is deemed to be payable on demand;

(a) If it states that it is payable at sight or on demand or on presentment or if it contains words of similar import; or
(b) If no time of payment is expressed.

2. An instrument payable at a definite time which is accepted or endorsed or guaranteed after maturity is an instrument payable on demand as regards the acceptor, the endorser or the guarantor.

3. An instrument is deemed to be payable at a definite time if it states that it is payable;

(a) On a stated date or at a fixed period after a stated date or at a fixed period after the date of the instrument; or
(b) At a fixed period after sight; or
(c) By instalments at successive dates; or
(d) By instalments at successive dates with the stipulation in the instrument that upon default in payment of any instalment the unpaid balance becomes due.

4. The time of payment of an instrument payable at a fixed period after date is determined by reference to the date of the instrument.

5. The time of payment of a bill payable at a fixed period after sight is determined by the date of acceptance or, if the bill is dishonoured by non-acceptance, by the date of protest or, if protest is dispensed with, by the date of dishonour.

6. The time of payment of an instrument payable on demand is the date on which the instrument is presented for payment.

7. The time of payment of a note payable at a fixed period after sight is determined by the date of the visa signed by the maker on the note or, if his visa is refused, by the date of presentment.

8. If an instrument is drawn, or made, payable one or more months after a stated date or after a date of the instrument or after sight, the instrument is payable on the corresponding date of the month when payment must be made. If there is no corresponding date, the instrument is payable on the last day of that month.

## ARTICLE 10

1. A bill may be drawn;
   (a) By two or more drawers;
   (b) Payable to two or more payees.

2. A note may be made:
   (a) By two or more makers;
   (b) Payable to two or more payees.

3. If an instrument is payable to two or more payees in the alternative, it is payable to any one of them and any one of them in possession of the instrument may exercise the rights of a holder. In any other case the instrument is payable to all of them and the rights of a holder may be exercised only by all of them.

## ARTICLE 11

A bill may be drawn by the drawer:
   (a) On himself;
   (b) Payable to his order.

### *Section 3. Completion of an incomplete instrument*

## ARTICLE 12.

1. An incomplete instrument which satisfies the requirements set out in paragraph 1 of Article 1 and bears the signature of the drawer of the acceptance of the drawee, or which satisfies the requirements set out in paragraph 2 of Article 1 and subparagraph (d) of paragraph 2 of Article 3, but which lacks other elements pertaining to one or more of the requirements set out in Articles 2 and 3, may be completed, and the instrument so completed is effective as a bill or a note.

2. If such an instrument is completed without authority or otherwise than in accordance with the authority given:

(a) a party who signed the instrument before the completion may invoke such lack of authority as a defence against a holder who had knowledge of such lack of authority when he became a holder;

(b) a party who signed the instrument after the completion is liable according to the terms of the instrument so completed.

## CHAPTER III. TRANSFER

### ARTICLE 13

An instrument is transferred:

(a) by endorsement and delivery of the instrument by the endorser to the endorsee; or

(b) by mere delivery of the instrument if the last endorsement is in blank.

### ARTICLE 14

1. An endorsement must be written on the instrument or on a slip affixed thereto ('*allonge*'). It must be signed.

2. An endorsement may be:

(a) In blank, that is, by a signature alone or by a signature accompanied by a statement to the effect that the instrument is payable to a person in possession of it;

(b) Special, that is, by a signature accompanied by an indication of the person to whom the instrument is payable.

3. A signature alone, other than that of the drawee, is an endorsement only if placed on the back of the instrument.

### ARTICLE 15

1. A person is a holder if he is;

(a) The payee in possession of the instrument; or

(b) In possession of an instrument which has been endorsed to him, or on which the last endorsement is in blank, and on which there appears an uninterrupted series of endorsements, even if any endorsement was forged or was signed by an agent without authority.

2. If an endorsement in blank is followed by another endorsement, the person who signed this last endorsement is deemed to be an endorsee by the endorsement in blank.

3. A person is not prevented from being a holder by the fact that the instrument was obtained by him or any previous holder under circumstances, including incapacity or fraud, duress or mistake of any kind, that would give rise to a claim to, or a defence against liability on, the instrument.

## Article 16

The holder of an instrument on which the last endorsement is in blank may:

(a) Further endorse it either by an endorsement in blank or by a special endorsement; or

(b) Convert the blank endorsement into a special endorsement by indicating in the endorsement that the instrument is payable to himself or to some other specified person; or

(c) Transfer the instrument in accordance with subparagraph b of Article 13.

## Article 17

1. If the drawer or the maker has inserted in the instrument such words as 'not acceptable', 'not transferable', 'not to order', 'pay (x) only', or words of similar import, the instrument may not be transferred except for purposes of collection, and any endorsement, even if it does not contain words authorising the endorsee to collect the instrument, is deemed to be an endorsement for collection.

2. If an endorsement contains the words 'not negotiable', 'not transferable', 'not to order', 'pay (x) only', or words of similar import, the instrument may not be transferred further except for purposes of collection, and any subsequent endorsement, even if it does not contain words authorising the endorsee to collect the instrument, is deemed to be an endorsement for collection.

## Article 18

1. An endorsement must be unconditional.

2. A conditional endorsement transfers the instrument whether or not the condition is fulfilled. The condition is ineffective as to those parties and trransferees who are subsequent to the endorsee.

## Article 19

An endorsement in respect of a part of the sum due under the instrument is ineffective as an endorsement.

## Article 20

If there are two or more endorsements, it is presumed, unless the contrary is proved, that each endorsement was made in the order in which it appears on the instrument.

## Article 21

1. If an endorsement contains the words 'for collection', 'for deposit', 'value in collection', 'by procuration', 'pay any bank', or words of similar import

authorising the endorsee to collect the instrument, the endorsee is a holder who:

(a) May exercise all rights arising out of the instrument;
(b) May endorse the instrument only for purposes of collection;
(c) Is subject only to the claims and defences which may be set up against the endorser.

2. The endorser for collection is not liable on the instrument to any subsequent holder.

## ARTICLE 22

1. If an endorsement contains the words 'value in security', 'value in pledge', or any other words indicating a pledge, the endorsee is a holder who:

(a) May exercise all rights arising out of the instrument;
(b) May endorse the instrument only for purposes of collection;
(c) Is subject only to the claims and defences specified in Article 28 or 30.

2. If such an endorsee endorses for collection, he is not liable on the instrument to any subsequent holder.

## ARTICLE 23

The holder of an instrument may transfer it to a prior party or to the drawee in accordance with Article 13; however, if the transferee has previously been a holder of the instrument, no endorsement is required, and any endorsement which would prevent him from qualifying as a holder may be struck out.

## ARTICLE 24

An instrument may be transferred in accordance with Article 13 after maturity, except by the drawee, the acceptor or the maker.

## ARTICLE 25

1. If an endorsement is forged, the person whose endorsement is forged, or a party who signed the instrument before the forgery, has the right to recover compensation for any damage that he may have suffered because of the forgery against:

(a) the forger;
(b) the person to whom the instrument was directly transferred by the forger;
(c) a party or the drawee who paid the instrument to the forger directly or through one or more endorsees for collection.

2. However, an endorsee for collection is not liable under paragraph 1 of this Article if he is without knowledge of the forgery;

(a) at the time he pays the principal or advises him of the receipt of payment, or

(b) at the time he receives payment, if this is later,
unless his lack of knowledge is due to his failure to act in good faith or to exercise reasonable care.

3 Furthermore, a party or the drawee who pays an instrument is not liable under paragraph 1 of this Article if, at the time he pays the instrument, he is without knowledge of the forgery, unless his lack of knowledge is due to his failure to act in good faith or to exercise reasonable care.

4 Except as against the forger, the damages recoverable under paragraph 1 of this Article may not exceed the amount referred to in Article 70 or 71.

## Article 26

1. If an endorsement is made by an agent without authority or power to bind his principal in the matter, the principal, or a party who signed the instrument before such endorsement, has the right to recover compensation for any damage that he may have suffered because of such endorsement against;

(a) The agent;
(b) The person to whom the instrument was directly transferred by the agent;
(c) A party or the drawee who paid the instrument to the agent directly or through one or more endorsees for collection.

2. However, an endorsee for collection is not liable under paragraph 1 of this Article if he is without knowledge that the endorsement does not bind the principal;

(a) At the time he pays the principal or advises him of the receipt of payment, or
(b) At the time he receives payment, if this is later,

unless his lack of knowledge is due to his failure to act in good faith or to exercise reasonable care.

3. Furthermore, a party or the drawee who pays an instrument is not liable under paragraph 1 of this Article if, at the time he pays the instrument, he is without knowledge that the endorsement does not bind the principal, unless his lack of knowledge is due to his failure to act in good faith or to exercise reasonable care.

4. Except as against the agent, the damages recoverable under paragraph 1 of this Article may not exceed the amount referred to in Article 70 or 71.

## Chapter IV. Rights and Liabilities

### *Section 1. The rights of a holder and a protected holder*

## Article 27

1. The holder of an instrument has all the rights conferred on him by this Convention against the parties to the instrument.

2. The holder may transfer the instrument in accordance with Article 13.

## ARTICLE 28

1. A party may set up against a holder who is not a protected holder;
   (a) Any defence that may be set up against a protected holder in accordance with paragraph 1 of Article 30;
   (b) Any defence based on the underlying transaction between himself and the drawer or between himself and his transferee, but only if the holder took the instrument with knowledge of such defence or if he obtained the instrument by fraud or theft or participated at any time in a fraud or theft concerning it;
   (c) Any defence arising from the circumstances as a result of which he became a party, but only if the holder took the instrument with knowledge of such defence or if he obtained the instrument by fraud or theft or participated at any time in a fraud or theft concerning it;
   (d) Any defence which may be raised against an action in contract between himself and the holder;
   (e) Any other defence available under this Convention.

2. The rights to an instrument of a holder who is not a protected holder are subject to any valid claim to the instrument on the part of any person, but only if he took the instrument with knowledge of such claim or if he obtained the instrument by fraud or theft or participated at any time in a fraud or theft concerning it.

3. A holder who takes an instrument after the expiration of the time-limit for presentment for payment is subject to any claim to, or defence against liability on, the instrument to which his transferor is subject.

4. A party may not raise as a defence against a holder who is not a protected holder the fact that a third person has a claim to the instrument unless;
   (a) The third person asserted a valid claim to the instrument; or
   (b) The holder acquired the instrument by theft or forged the signature of the payee or an endorsee, or participated in the theft or the forgery.

## ARTICLE 29

'Protected holder' means the holder of an instrument which was complete when he took it or which was incomplete within the meaning of paragraph 1 of Article 12 and was completed in accordance with authority given, provided that when he became a holder;
   (a) He was without knowledge of a defence against liability on the instrument referred to in subparagraphs (a), (b), (c) and (e) of paragraph 1 of Article 28;
   (b) He was without knowledge of a valid claim to the instrument of any person;
   (c) He was without knowledge of the fact that it had been dishonoured by non-acceptance or by non-payment;
   (d) The time-limit provided by Article 55 for presentment of that instrument for payment had not expired; and

(e) He did not obtain the instrument by fraud or theft or participate in a fraud or theft concerning it.

### Article 30

1. A party may not set up against a protected holder any defence except:

(a) Defences under Articles 33 §1, 34, 35 §1, 36 §3, 53 §1, 57 §1, 63 §1 and 84 of this Convention;

(b) Defences based on the underlying transaction between himself and such holder or arising from any fraudulent act on the part of such holder in obtaining the signature on the instrument of that party;

(c) Defences based on his incapacity to incur liability on the instrument or on the fact that he signed without knowledge that his signature made him a party to the instrument, provided that his lack of knowledge was not due to his negligence and provided that he was fraudulently induced so to sign.

2. The rights to an instrument of a protected holder are not subject to any claim to the instrument on the part of any person, except a valid claim arising from the underlying transaction between himself and the person by whom the claim is raised.

### Article 31

1. The transfer of an instrument by a protected holder vests in any subsequent holder the rights to and on the instrument which the protected holder had.

2. Those rights are not vested in a subsequent holder if;

(a) He participated in a transaction which gives rise to a claim to, or a defence against liability on, the instrument;

(b) He has previously been a holder, but not a protected holder.

### Article 32

Every holder is presumed to be a protected holder unless the contrary is proved.

## *Section 2. Liabilities of the parties*

### A. General Provisions

### Article 33

1. Subject to the provisions of Articles 34 and 36, a person is not liable on an instrument unless he signs it.

2. A person who signs an instrument in a name which is not his own is liable as if he had signed it in his own name.

## ARTICLE 34

A forged signature on an instrument does not impose any liability on the person whose signature was forged. However, if he consents to be bound by the forged signature or represents that it is his own, he is liable as if he had signed the instrument himself.

## ARTICLE 35

1. If an instrument is materially altered:
   (a) A party who signs it after the material alteration is liable according to the terms of the altered text;
   (b) A party who signs it before the material alteration is liable according to the terms of the original text. However, if a party makes, authorises or assents to a material alteration, he is liable according to the terms of the altered text.

2. A signature is presumed to have been placed on the instrument after the material alteration unless the contrary is proved.

3. Any alteration is material which modifies the written undertaking on the instrument of any party in any respect.

## ARTICLE 36

1. An instrument may be signed by an agent.

2. The signature of an agent placed by him on an instrument with the authority of his principal and showing on the instrument that he is signing in a representative capacity for that named principal, or the signature of a principal placed on the instrument by an agent with his authority, imposes liability on the principal and not on the agent.

3. A signature placed on an instrument by a person as agent but who lacks authority to sign or exceeds his authority, or by an agent who has authority to sign but who does not show on the instrument that he is signing in a representative capacity for a named person, or who shows on the instrument that he is signing in a representative capacity but does not name the person whom he represents, imposes liability on the person signing and not on the person whom he purports to represent.

4. The question whether a signature was placed on the instrument in a representative capacity may be determined only be reference to what appears on the instrument.

5. A person who is liable pursuant to paragraph 3 of this Article and who pays the instrument has the same rights as the person for whom he purported to act would have had if that person had paid the instrument.

### ARTICLE 37

The order to pay contained in a bill does not of itself operate as an assignment to the payee of funds made available for payment by the drawer with the drawee.

## B. THE DRAWER

### ARTICLE 38

1. The drawee engages that upon dishonour of the bill by non-acceptance or by non-payment, and upon any necessary protest, he will pay the bill to the holder, or to any endorser or any endorser's guarantor who takes up and pays the bill.

2. The drawer may exclude or limit his own liability for acceptance or for payment by an express stipulation in the bill. Such a stipulation is effective only with respect to the drawer. A stipulation excluding or limiting liability for payment is effective only if another party is or becomes liable on the bill.

## C . THE MAKER

### ARTICLE 39

1. The maker engages that he will pay the note in accordance with its terms to the holder, or to any party who takes up and pays the note.

2. The maker may not exclude or limit his own liability by a stipulation in the note. Any such stipulation is ineffective.

## D. THE DRAWEE AND THE ACCEPTOR

### ARTICLE 40

1. The drawee is not liable on a bill until he accepts it.

2. The acceptor engages that he will pay the bill in accordance with the terms of his acceptance to the holder, or to any party who takes up and pays the bill.

### ARTICLE 41

1. An acceptance must be written on the bill and may be affected;

(a) By the signature of the drawee accompanied by the word 'accepted' or by words of similar import; or
(b) By the signature alone of the drawee.

2. An acceptance may be written on the front or on the back of the bill.

## Article 42

1. An incomplete bill which satisfies the requirements set out in paragraph 1 of Article 1 may be accepted by the drawee before it has been signed by the drawer, or while otherwise incomplete.

2. A bill may be accepted before, at or after maturity, or after it has been dishonoured by non-acceptance or by non-payment.

3. If a bill drawn payable at a fixed period after sight, or a bill which must be presented for acceptance before a specified date, is accepted, the acceptor must indicate the date of his acceptance; failing such indication by the acceptor, the drawer or the holder may insert the date of acceptance.

4. If a bill drawn payable at a fixed period after sight is dishonoured by non-acceptance and the drawee subsequently accepts it, the holder is entitled to have the acceptance dated as of the date on which the bill was dishonoured.

## Article 43

1. An acceptance must be unqualified. An acceptance is qualified if it is conditional or varies the terms of the bill.

2. If the drawee stipulates in the bill that his acceptance is subject to qualification:
(a) He is nevertheless bound according to the terms of his qualified acceptance;
(b) The bill is dishonoured by non-acceptance.

3. An acceptance relating to only a part of the sum payable is a qualified acceptance. If the holder takes such an acceptance, the bill is dishonoured by non-acceptance only as to the remaining part.

4. An acceptance indicating that payment will be made at a particular address or by a particular address or by a particular agent is not a qualified acceptance, provided that:
(a) The place in which payment is to be made is not changed;
(b) The bill is not drawn payable by another agent.

## E. The Endorser

### Article 44

1. The endorser engages that upon dishonour of the instrument by non-acceptance or by non-payment, and upon any necessary protest, he will pay the instrument to the holder, or to any subsequent endorser or any endorser's guarantor who takes up and pays the instrument.

2. An endorser may exclude or limit his own liability by an express stipulation in the instrument. Such a stipulation is effective only with respect to that endorser.

## F. The Transferor by Endorsement or by mere Delivery

### Article 45

1. Unless otherwise agreed, a person who transfers an instrument, by endorsement and delivery or by mere delivery, represents to the holder to whom he transfers the instrument that:

(a) The instrument does not bear any forged or unauthorised signature;

(b) the instrument has not been materially altered;

(c) At the time of transfer, he has no knowledge of any fact which would impair the right of the transferee to payment of the instrument against the acceptor of a bill or, in the case of an unaccepted bill, the drawer, or against the maker of a note.

2. Liability of the transferor under paragraph 1 of this Article is incurred only if the transferee took the instrument without knowledge of the matter giving rise to such liability.

3. If the transferor is liable under paragraph 1 of this Article, the transferee may recover, even before maturity, the amount paid by him to the transferor, with interest calculated in accordance with Article 70 against return on the instrument.

## G. The Guarantor

### Article 46

1. Payment of an instrument, whether or not it has been accepted, may be guaranteed, as to the whole or part of its amount, for the account of a party or the drawee. A guarantee may be given by any person, who may or may not already be a party.

2. A guarantee must be written on the instrument or on a slip affixed thereto ('*allonge*').

3. A guarantee is expressed by the words 'guaranteed', '*aval*', 'good as *aval*' or words of similar import, accompanied by the signature of the guarantor.

For the purposes of this Convention, the words 'prior endorsements guaranteed' or words of similar import do not constitute a guarantee.

4. A guarantee may be effected by a signature alone on the front of the instrument. A signature alone on the front of the instrument, other than that of the maker, the drawer or the drawee, is a guarantee.

5 A guarantor may specify the person for whom he has become guarantor. In the absence of such specification, the person for whom he has become guarantor is the acceptor or the drawee in the case of a bill, and the maker in the case of a note.

6 A guarantor may not raise as a defence to his liability the fact that he signed the instrument before it was signed by the person for whom he is a guarantor, or while the instrument was incomplete.

## ARTICLE 47

1. The liability of a guarantor on the instrument is of the same nature as that of the party for whom he has become guarantor.

2. If the person for whom he has become guarantor is the drawee, the guarantor engages:
   (a) To pay the bill at maturity to the holder, or to any party who takes up and pays the bill;
   (b) If the bill is payable at a definite time, upon dishonour by non-acceptance and upon any necessary protest, to pay it to the holder, or to any party who takes up and pays the bill.

3. In respect of defences that are personal to himself, a guarantor may set up:
   (a) Against a holder who is not a protected holder only those defences which he may set up under paragraphs 1, 3 and 4 of Article 28;
   (b) Against a protected holder only those defences which he may set up under paragraph 1 of Article 30.

4. In respect of defences that may be raised by the person for whom he has become a guarantor:
   (a) A guarantor may set up against a holder who is not a protected holder only those defences which the person for whom he has become a guarantor may set up against such holder under paragraphs 1, 3 and 4 of Article 28;
   (b) A guarantor who expresses his guarantee by the words 'guaranteed', 'payment guaranteed' or collection guaranteed', or words of similar import, may set up against a protected holder only those defences which the person for whom he has become a guarantor may set up against a protected holder under paragraph 1 of Article 30;
   (c) A guarantor who expresses his guarantee by the words '*aval*' or 'good as *aval*' may set up against a protected holder only;
   (i) The defence, under subparagraph (b) of paragraph 1 of Article 30, that the protected holder obtained the signature on the instrument of the person for whom he has become a guarantor by a fraudulent act;

(ii) The defence, under Article 53 or 57, that the instrument was not presented for acceptance or for payment;
(iii) The defence, under Article 63, that the instrument was not duly protested for non-acceptance or for non-payment;
(iv) The defence, under Article 84, that a right of action may no longer be exercised against the person for whom he has become guarantor;

(d) A guarantor who is not a bank or other financial institution and who expresses his guarantee by a signature alone may set up against a protected holder only the defences referred to in subparagraph b of this paragraph;
(e) A guarantor which is a bank or other financial institution and which expresses its guarantee by a signature alone may set up against a protected holder only the defences referred to in subparagraph c of this paragraph.

## Article 48

1. Payment of an instrument by the guarantor in accordance with Article 72 discharges the party for whom he became guarantor of his liability on the instrument to the extent of the amount paid.

2. The guarantor who pays the instrument may recover from the party for whom he has become guarantor and from the parties who are liable on it to that party the amount paid and any interest.

# Chapter V. Presentiment, Dishonour by Non-Acceptance or Non-Payment, and Recourse

### *Section 1. Presentment for acceptance and dishonour by non-acceptance*

## Article 49

1. A bill may be presented for acceptance.

2. A bill must be presented for acceptance:
(a) If the drawer has stipulated in the bill that it must be presented for acceptance;
(b) If the bill is payable at a fixed period after sight; or
(c) If the bill is payable elsewhere than at the residency or place of business of the drawee, unless it is payable on demand.

## Article 50

1. The drawer may stipulate in the bill that it must not be presented for acceptance before a specified date or before the occurrence of a specified event. Except where a bill must be presented for acceptance under subparagraph b or c of paragraph 2 of Article 49, the drawer may stipulate that it must not be presented for acceptance.

2. If a bill is presented for acceptance notwithstanding a stipulation permitted under paragraph 1 of this Article and acceptance is refused, the bill is not thereby dishonoured.

3. If the drawee accepts a bill notwithstanding a stipulation that it must not be presented for acceptance, the acceptance is effective.

## ARTICLE 51

A bill is duly presented for acceptance if it is presented in accordance with the following rules:

(a) The holder must present the bill to the drawee on a business day at a reasonable hour;

(b) Presentment for acceptance may be made to a person or authority other than the drawee if that person or authority is entitled under the applicable law to accept the bill;

(c) If a bill is payable on a fixed date, presentment for acceptance must be made before or on that date;

(d) A bill payable on demand or at a fixed period after sight must be presented for acceptance within one year of its date;

(e) A bill in which the drawer has stated a date or time limit for presentment for acceptance must be presented on the stated date or within the stated time-limit.

## ARTICLE 52

1. A necessary or optional presentment for acceptance is dispensed with if;

(a) The drawee is dead, or no longer has the power freely to deal with his assets by reason of his insolvency, or is a fictitious person, or is a person not having capacity to incur liability on the instrument as an acceptor; or

(b) The drawee is a corporation, partnership, association or other legal entity which has ceased to exist.

2.. A necessary presentment for acceptance is dispensed with if;

(a) A bill is payable on a fixed date, and presentment for acceptance cannot be effected before or on that date due to circumstances which are beyond the control of the holder and which he could neither avoid nor overcome; or

(b) A bill is payable at a fixed period after sight, and presentment for acceptance cannot be effected within one year of its date due to circumstances which are beyond the control of the holder and which he could neither avoid nor overcome.

3. Subject to paragraphs 1 and 2 of this Article, delay in a necessary presentment for acceptance is excused, but presentment for acceptance is not dispensed with, if the bill is drawn with a stipulation that it must be presented for acceptance within a stated time-limit, and the delay in presentment for acceptance is caused by circumstances which are beyond the control of the holder and which he could neither avoid nor overcome. When the cause of the delay ceases to operate, presentment must be made with reasonable diligence.

## Article 53

1. If a bill which must be presented for acceptance is not so presented, the drawer, the endorsers and their guarantors are not liable on the bill.

2. Failure to present a bill for acceptance does not discharge the guarantor of the drawee of liability on the bill.

## Article 54

1. A bill is considered to be dishonoured by non-acceptance:
   - (a) If the drawee, upon due presentment, expressly refuses to accept the bill or acceptance cannot be obtained with reasonable diligence or if the holder cannot obtain the acceptance to which he is entitled under this Convention;
   - (b) If presentment for acceptance is dispensed with pursuant to Article 52, unless the bill is in fact accepted.

2.—
   - (a) If a bill is dishonoured by non acceptance in accordance with subparagraph a of paragraph 1 of this Article, the holder may exercise an immediate right of recourse against the drawer, the endorsers and their guarantors, subject to the provisions of Article 59.
   - (b) If a bill is dishonoured by non-acceptance in accordance with subparagraph b of paragraph 1 of this Article, the holder may exercise an immediate right of recourse against the drawer, the endorsers and their guarantors.
   - (c) If a bill is dishonoured by non-acceptance in accordance with paragraph 1 of this Article, the holder may claim payment from the guarantor of the drawee upon any necessary protest.

3. If a bill payable on demand is presented for acceptance, but acceptance is refused, it is not considered to be dishonoured by non-acceptance.

### *Section 2. Presentment for payment and dishonour by non payment*

## Article 55

An instrument is duly presented for payment if it is presented in accordance with the following rules:
   - (a) The holder must present the instrument to the drawee or to the acceptor or to the maker on a business day at a reasonable hour;
   - (b) A note signed by two or more makers may be presented to any one of them, unless the note clearly indicates otherwise;
   - (c) If the drawee or the acceptor or the maker is dead, presentment must be made to the persons who under the applicable law are his heirs or the persons entitled to administer his estate;

(d) Presentment for payment may be made to a person or authority other than the drawee, the acceptor or the maker if that person or authority is entitled under the applicable law to pay the instrument;
(e) An instrument which is not payable on demand must be presented for payment on the date of maturity or on one of the two business days which follow;
(f) An instrument which is payable on demand must be presented for payment within one year of its date;
(g) An instrument must be presented for payment:
  (i) At the place of payment specified on the instrument; or
  (ii) If no place of payment is specified, at the address of the drawee or the acceptor or the maker indicated in the instrument; or
  (iii) If no place of payment is specified and the address of the drawee or the acceptor or the maker is not indicated, at the principal place of business or habitual residence of the drawee or the acceptor or the maker;
(h) An instrument which is presented at a clearing-house is duly presented for payment if the law of the place where the clearing-house is located or the rules or customs of that clearing-house so provide.

## ARTICLE 56

1. Delay in making presentment for payment is excused if the delay is caused by circumstances which are beyond the control of the holder and which he could neither avoid nor overcome. When the cause of the delay ceases to operate, presentment must be made with reasonable diligence.

2. Presentment for payment is dispensed with:
(a) If the drawer, an endorser or a guarantor has expressly waived presentment; such waiver:
  (i) If made on the instrument by the drawer. binds any subsequent party and benefits any holder;
  (ii) If made on the instrument by a party other than the drawer, binds only that party but benefits any holder;
  (iii) If made outside the instrument, binds only the party making it and benefits only a holder in whose favour it was made;

(b) If an instrument is not payable on demand, and the cause of delay in making presentment referred to in paragraph 1 of this Article continues to operate beyond 30 days after maturity;
(c) If an instrument is payable on demand, and the cause of delay in making presentment referred to in paragraph 1 of this Article continues to operate beyond 30 days after the expiration of the time-limit for presentment for payment;
(d) If the drawee, the maker or the acceptor has no longer the power freely to deal with his assets by reason of his insolvency, or is a fictitious person or a person not having capacity to make payment, or if the drawee, the maker or the acceptor is a corporation, partnership, association or other legal entity which has ceased to exist;
(e) If there is no place at which the instrument must be presented in accordance with subparagraph g of Article 55.

3. Presentment for payment is also dispensed with as regards a bill, if the bill has been protested for dishonour by non-acceptance.

## Article 57

1. If an instrument is not duly presented for payment, the drawer, the endorsers and their guarantors are not liable on it.

2. Failure to present an instrument for payment does not discharge the acceptor, the maker and their guarantors or the guarantor of the drawee of liability on it.

## Article 58

1. An instrument is considered to be dishonoured by non-payment:
   (a) If payment is refused upon due presentment or if the holder cannot obtain the payment to which he is entitled under this Convention;
   (b) If presentment for payment is dispensed with pursuant to paragraph 2 of Article 56 and the instrument is unpaid at maturity.

2. If a bill is dishonoured by non-payment, the holder may, subject to the provisions of Article 59, exercise a right of recourse against the drawer, the endorsers and their guarantors.

3. If a note is dishonoured by non-payment, the holder may, subject to the provisions of Article 59, exercise a right of recourse against the endorsers and their guarantors.

*Section 3. Recourse*

## Article 59

If an instrument is dishonoured by non-acceptance or by non-payment, the holder may exercise a right of recourse only after the instrument has been duly protested for dishonour in accordance with the provisions of Articles 60 to 62.

## A. Protest

## Article 60

1. A protest is a statement of dishonour drawn up at the place where the instrument has been dishonoured and signed and dated by a person authorised in that respect by the law of that place. The statement must specify:
   (a) The person at whose request the instrument is protested;
   (b) The place of protest; and
   (c) The demand made and the answer given, if any, or the fact that the drawee or the acceptor or the maker could not be found.

2. A protest may be made;
   (a) On the instrument or on a slip affixed thereto ('*allonge*'); or
   (b) As a separate document, in which case it must clearly identify the instrument that has been dishonoured.

3. Unless the instrument stipulates that protest must be made, a protest may be replaced by a declaration written on the instrument and signed and dated by the drawee or the acceptor or the maker, or, in the case of an instrument domiciled with a named person for payment, by that named person; the declaration must be to the effect that acceptance or payment is refused.

4. A declaration made in accordance with paragraph 3 of this Article is a protest for the purpose of this Convention.

## ARTICLE 61

Protest for dishonour of an instrument by non-acceptance or by non payment must be made on the day on which the instrument is dishonoured or on one of the four business days which follow.

## ARTICLE 62

1. Delay in protesting an instrument for dishonour is excused if the delay is caused by circumstances which are beyond the control of the holder and which he could neither avoid nor overcome. When the cause of the delay ceases to operate, protest must be made with reasonable diligence.

2. Protest for dishonour by non-acceptance or by non-payment is dispensed with:
   (a) If the drawer, an endorser or a guarantor has expressly waived protest; such waiver:
      (i) If made on the instrument by the drawer, binds any subsequent party and benefits any holder;
      (ii) If made on the instrument by a party other than the drawer, binds only that party but benefits any holder;
      (iii) If made outside the instrument, binds only the party making it an benefits only a holder in whose favour it was made;
   (b) If the cause of the delay in making protest referred to in paragraph 1 of this Article continues to operate beyond 30 days after the date of dishonour;
   (c) As regards the drawer of a bill, if the drawer and the drawee or the acceptor are the same person;
   (d) If presentment for acceptance or for payment is dispensed with in accordance with Article 52 or paragraph 2 of Article 56.

## ARTICLE 63

1. If an instrument which must be protested for non-acceptance or for non payment is not duly protested, the drawer, the endorsers and their guarantors are not liable on it.

2 Failure to protest an instrument does not discharge the acceptor, the maker and their guarantors or the guarantor of the drawee of liability on it.

## B Notice of Dishonour

### Article 64

1. The holder, upon dishonour of an instrument by non-acceptance or by non-payment, must give notice of such dishonour;
   (a) To the drawer and the last endorser, and
   (b) To all other endorsers and guarantors whose addresses the holder can ascertain on the basis of information contained in the instrument.

2. An endorser or a guarantor who receives notice must give notice of dishonour to the last party preceding him and liable on the instrument.

3. Notice of dishonour operates for the benefit of any party who has a right of recourse on the instrument against the party notified.

### Article 65

1. Notice of dishonour may be given in any form whatever and in any terms which identify the instrument and state that it has been dishonoured. The return of the dishonoured instrument is sufficient notice, provided it is accompanied by a statement indicating that it has been dishonoured.

2. Notice of dishonour is duly given if it is communicated or sent to the party to be notified by means appropriate in the circumstances, whether or not it is received by that party.

3. The burden of proving that notice has been duly given rests upon the person who is required to give such notice.

### Article 66

Notice of dishonour must be given within the two business days which follow:

(a) The day of protest or, if protest is dispensed with, the day of dishonour; or
(b) The day of receipt of notice of dishonour.

### Article 67

1. Delay in giving notice of dishonour is excused if the delay is caused by circumstances which are beyond the control of the person required to give notice, and which he could neither avoid nor overcome. When the cause of the delay ceases to operate, notice must be given with reasonable diligence.

2. Notice of dishonour is dispensed with:
   (a) If, after the exercise of reasonable diligence, notice cannot be given;
   (b) If the drawer, an endorser or a guarantor has expressly waived notice of dishonour; such waiver;
      (i) If made on the instrument by the drawer, binds any subsequent party and benefits any holder;
      (ii) If made on the instrument by a party other than the drawer, binds only that party but benefits any holder;
      (iii) If made outside the instrument, binds only the party making it and benefits only a holder in whose favour it was made;
   (c) As regards the drawer of the bill, if the drawer and the drawee or the acceptor are the same person.

## ARTICLE 68

If a person who is required to give notice of dishonour fails to give it to a party who is entitled to receive it, he is liable for any damages which that party may suffer from such failure, provided that such damages do not exceed the amount referred to in Article 70 or 71.

### *Section 4. Amount payable*

## ARTICLE 69

1. The holder may exercise his rights on the instrument against any one party, or several or all parties, liable on it and is not obliged to observe the order in which the parties have become bound. Any party who takes up and pays the instrument may exercise his rights in the same manner against parties liable to him.

2. Proceedings against a party do not preclude proceedings against any other party, whether or not subsequent to the party originally proceeded against.

## ARTICLE 70

1. The holder may recover from any party liable;
   (a) At maturity: the amount of the instrument with interest, if interest has been stipulated for;
   (b) After maturity:
      (i) The amount of the instrument with interest, if interest has been stipulated for, to the date of maturity;
      (ii) If interest has been stipulated to be paid after maturity, interest at the rate stipulated, or, in the absence of such stipulation, interest at the rate specified in paragraph 2 of this Article, calculated from the date of presentment on the sum specified in subparagraph b i of this paragraph;
      (iii) Any expenses of protest and of the notices given by him;
   (c) Before maturity:
      (i) The amount of the instrument with interest, if interest has been stipulated for, to the date of payment; or, if no interest has been

stipulated for, subject to a discount from the date of payment to the date of maturity, calculated in accordance with paragraph 4 of this Article;

(ii) Any expenses of protest and of the notices given by him.

2. The rate of interest shall be the rate that would be recoverable in legal proceedings taken in the jurisdiction where the instrument is payable.

3. Nothing in paragraph 2 of this Article prevents a court from awarding damages or compensation for additional loss caused to the holder by reason of delay in payment.

4. The discount shall be at the official rate (discount rate) or other similar appropriate rate effective on the date when recourse is exercised at the place where the holder has his principal place of business, or, if he does not have a place of business his habitual residence, or, if there is no such rate, then at such rate as is reasonable in the circumstances.

### ARTICLE 71

A party who pays an instrument and is thereby discharged in whole or in part of his liability on the instrument may recover from the parties liable to him:

(a) The entire sum which he has paid;

(b) Interest on that sum at the rate specified in paragraph 2 of Article 70, from the date on which he made payment;

(c) Any expenses of the notices given by him.

## CHAPTER VI. DISCHARGE

### *Section 1. Discharge by payment*

### ARTICLE 72

1. A party is discharged of liability on the instrument when he pays the holder, or a party subsequent to himself who has paid the instrument and is in possession of it, the amount due pursuant to Article 70 or 71:

(a) At or after maturity; or

(b) Before maturity, upon dishonour by non-acceptance.

2. Payment before maturity other than under subparagraph (b) of paragraph 1 of this Article does not discharge the party making the payment of his liability on the instrument except in respect of the person to whom payment was made.

3. A party is not discharged of liability if he pays a holder who is not a protected holder, or a party who has taken up and paid the instrument, and knows at the time of payment that the holder or that party acquired the instrument by theft or forged the signature of the payee or an endorsee, or participated in the theft or the forgery.

4.—

(a) A person receiving payment of an instrument must, unless agreed otherwise, deliver:

(i) To the drawee making such payment, the instrument;

(ii) To any other person making such payment, the instrument, a receipted account, and any protest.

(b) In the case of an instrument payable by instalments at successive dates, the drawee or a party making a payment of the last instalment, may require that mention of such payment be made on the instrument or on a slip affixed thereto ('*allonge*') and that a receipt therefore be given to him.

(c) If an instrument payable by instalments at successive dates is dishonoured by non-acceptance or by non-payment as to any of its instalments and a party, upon dishonour, pays the instalment, the holder who receives such payment must give the party a certified copy of the instrument and any necessary authenticated protest in order to enable such party to exercise a right on the instrument.

(d) The person from whom payment is demanded may withhold payment if the person demanding payment does not deliver the instrument to him. Withholding payment in these circumstances does not constitute dishonour by non-payment under Article 58.

(e) If payment is made but the person paying, other than the drawee, fails to obtain the instrument, such person is discharged but the discharge cannot be set up as a defence against a protected holder to whom the instrument has been subsequently transferred.

## Article 73

1. The holder is not obliged to take partial payment.

2. If the holder who is offered partial payment does not take it, the instrument is dishonoured by non-payment.

3. If the holder takes partial payment from the drawee, the guarantor of the drawee, or the acceptor or the maker:

(a) The guarantor of the drawee, or the acceptor or the maker is discharged of his liability on the instrument to the extent of the amount paid; and

(b) The instrument is to be considered as dishonoured by non-payment as to the amount unpaid.

4. If the holder takes partial payment from a party to the instrument other than the acceptor, the maker or the guarantor of the drawee:

(a) The party making payment is discharged of his liability on the instrument to the extent of the amount paid; and

(b) The holder must give such party a certified copy of the instrument and any necessary authenticated protest in order to enable such party to exercise a right on the instrument.

5. The drawee or a party making partial payment may require that mention of such payment be made on the instrument and that a receipt therefor be given to him.

6. If the balance is paid, the person who receives it and who is in possession of the instrument must deliver to the payor the receipted instrument and any authenticated protest.

## ARTICLE 74

1. The holder may refuse to take payment at a place other than the place where the instrument was presented for payment in accordance with Article 55.

2. In such case if payment is not made at the place where the instrument was presented for payment in accordance with Article 55, the instrument is considered to be dishonoured by non-payment.

## ARTICLE 75

1. An instrument must be paid in the currency in which the sum payable is expressed.

2. If the sum payable is expressed in a monetary unit of account within the meaning of subparagraph 1 of Article 5 and the monetary unit of account is transferable between the person making payment and the person receiving it, then, unless the instrument specifies a currency of payment, payment shall be made by transfer of monetary units of account. If the monetary unit of account is not transferable between those persons, payment shall be made in the currency specified in the instrument or, if no such currency is specified, in the currency of the place of payment.

3. The drawer or the maker may indicate in the instrument that it must be paid in a specified currency other than the currency in which the sum payable is expressed. In that case:

(a) The instrument must be paid in the currency so specified;

(b) The amount payable is to be calculated according to the rate of exchange indicated in the instrument. Failing such indication, the amount payable is to be calculated according to the rate of exchange for sight drafts (or, if there is no such rate, according to the appropriate established rate of exchange) on the date of maturity:

(i) Ruling at the place where the instrument must be presented for payment in accordance with subparagraph (g) of Article 55, if the specified currency is that of that place (local currency); or

(ii) If the specified currency is not that of that place, according to the usages of the place where the instrument must be presented for payment in accordance with subparagraph (g) of Article 55;

(c) If such an instrument is dishonoured by non-acceptance, the amount payable is to be calculated:

(i) If the rate of exchange is indicated in the instrument, according to that rate;

(ii) If no rate of exchange is indicated in the instrument, at the option of the holder, according to the rate of exchange ruling on the date of dishonour or on the date of actual payment;

(d) If such an instrument is dishonoured by non-payment, the amount payable is to be calculated:

(i) If the rate of exchange is indicated in the instrument, according to that rate;

(ii) If no rate of exchange is indicated in the instrument, at the option of the holder, according to the rate of exchange ruling on the date of maturity or on the date of actual payment.

4. Nothing in this Article prevents a court from awarding damages for loss caused to the holder by reason of fluctuations in rates of exchange if such loss is caused by dishonour for non-acceptance or by non-payment.

5. The rate of exchange ruling at a certain date is the rate of exchange ruling, at the option of the holder, at the place where the instrument must be presented for payment in accordance with subparagraph (g) of Article 55 or at the place of actual payment.

## Article 76

1. Nothing in this Convention prevents a Contracting State from enforcing exchange control regulations applicable in its territory and its provisions relating to the protection of its currency, including regulations which it is bound to apply virtue of international agreements to which it is a party.

2.—

(a) If, by virtue of the application of paragraph 1 of this Article, an instrument drawn in a currency which is not that of the place of payment must be paid in local currency, the amount payable is to be calculated according to the rate of exchange for sight drafts (or, if there is no such rate, according to the appropriate established rate of exchange) on the date of presentment ruling at the place where the instrument must be presented for payment in accordance with subparagraph (g) of Article 55.

(b)—

(i) If such an instrument is dishonoured by non-acceptance, the amount payable is to be calculated, at the option of the holder, at the rate of exchange ruling on the date of dishonour or on the date of actual payment.

(ii) If such an instrument is dishonest by non-payment, the amount is to be calculated, at the option of the holder, according to the rate of exchange ruling on the date of presentment or on the date of actual payment.

(iii) Paragraphs 4 and 5 of Article 75 are applicable where appropriate.

### *Section 2. Discharge of other parties*

## Article 77

1. If a party is discharged in whole or in part of his liability on the instrument, any party who has a right on the instrument against him is discharged to the same extent.

2. Payment by the drawee of the whole or a part of the amount of a bill to the holder, or to any party who takes up and pays the bill, discharges all parties of their liability to the same extent, except where the drawee pays a holder who is not a protected holder, or a party who has taken up and paid the bill, and knows at the time of payment that the holder or that party acquired the bill by theft or forged the signature of the payee or an endorsee, or participated in the theft or the forgery.

## Chapter VII. Lost Instruments

### Article 78

1. If an instrument is lost, whether by destruction, theft or otherwise, the person who lost the instrument has, subject to the provisions of paragraph 2 of this Article, the same right to payment which he would have had if he had been in possession of the instrument. The party from whom payment is claimed cannot set up as a defence against liability on the instrument the fact that the person claiming payment is not in possession of the instrument.

2.—

(a) The person claiming payment of a lost instrument must state in writing to the party from whom he claims payment;

(i) The elements of the lost instrument pertaining to the requirements set forth in paragraph 1 or 2 of Articles 1, 2 and 3; for this purpose the person claiming payment of the lost instrument may present to that party a copy of that instrument;

(ii) The facts showing that, if he had been in possession of the instrument, he would have had a right to payment from the party from whom payment is claimed;

(iii) The facts which prevent production of the instrument.

(b) The party from whom payment of a lost instrument is claimed may require the person claiming payment to give security in order to indemnify him for any loss which he may suffer by reason of the subsequent payment of the lost instrument.

(c) The nature of the security and its terms are to be determined by agreement between the person claiming payment and the party from whom payment is claimed. Failing such an agreement, the court may determine whether security is called for and, if so, the nature of the security and its terms.

(d) If the security cannot be given, the court may order the party from whom payment is claimed to deposit the sum of the lost instrument, and any interest and expenses which may be claimed under Article 70 or 71, with the court or any other competent authority or institution, and may determine the duration of such deposit. Such deposit is to be considered as payment to the person claiming payment.

## ARTICLE 79

1. A party who has paid a lost instrument and to whom the instrument is subsequently presented for payment by another person must give notice of such presentment to the person whom he paid.

2. Such notice must be given on the day the instrument is presented or on one of the two business days which follow and must state the name of the person presenting the instrument and the date and place of presentment.

3. Failure to give notice renders the party who has paid the lost instrument liable for any damages which the person whom he paid may suffer from such failure, provided that the damages do not exceed the amount referred to in Article 70 or 71.

4. Delay in giving notice is excused when the delay is caused by circumstances which are beyond the control of the person who has paid the lost instrument and which he could neither avoid nor overcome. When the cause of the delay ceases to operate, notice must be given with reasonable diligence.

5. Notice is dispensed with when the cause of delay in giving notice continues to operate beyond 30 days after the last day on which it should have been given.

## ARTICLE 80

1. A party who has paid a lost instrument in accordance with the provisions of Article 78 and who is subsequently required to, and does, pay the instrument, or who, by reason of the loss of the instrument, then loses his right to recover from any party liable to him, has the right:

(a) If security was given, to realise the security; or

(b) If an amount was deposited with the court or other competent authority or institution, to reclaim the amount so deposited.

2. The person who has given security in accordance with the provisions of subparagraph b of paragraph 2 of Article 78 is entitled to obtain release of the security when the party for whose benefit the security was given is no longer at risk to suffer loss because of the fact that the instrument is lost.

## ARTICLE 81

For the purpose of making protest for dishonour by non-payment, a person claiming payment of a lost instrument may use a written statement that satisfies the requirements of subparagraph (a) of paragraph 2 of Article 78.

## ARTICLE 82

A person receiving payment of a lost instrument in accordance with Article 78 must deliver to the party paying the written statement required under subparagraph a of paragraph 2 of Article 78, receipted by him, and any protest and a receipted account.

## ARTICLE 83

1. A party who pays a lost instrument in accordance with Article 78 has the same rights which he would have had if he had been in possession of the instrument.

2 Such party may exercise his rights only if he is in possession of the receipted written statement referred to in Article 82.

## CHAPTER VIII. LIMITATION (PRESCRIPTION)

## ARTICLE 84

1. A right of action arising on an instrument may no longer be exercised after four years have elapsed;

(a) Against the maker, or his guarantor, of a note payable on demand, from the date of the note;

(b) Against the acceptor or the maker or their guarantor of an instrument payable at a definite time, from the date of maturity;

(c) Against the guarantor of the drawee of a bill payable at a definite time, from the date of maturity or, if the bill is dishonoured by non-acceptance, from the date of protest for dishonour or, where protest is dispensed with, from the date of dishonour;

(d) Against the acceptor of a bill payable on demand or his guarantor, from the date on which it was accepted or, if no such date is shown, from the date of the bill;

(e) Against the guarantor of the drawee of a bill payable on demand, from the date on which he signed the bill or, if no such date is shown, from the date of the bill;

(f) Against the drawer or an endorser or their guarantor, from the date of protest for dishonour by non-acceptance or by non-payment or, where protest is dispensed with, from the date of dishonour.

2. A party who pays the instrument in accordance with Article 70 or 71 may exercise his right of action against a party liable to him within one year from the date on which he paid the instrument.

## CHAPTER IX, ARTICLES 85-90 [OMITTED]

ISBN 1-874241-11-2

9 781874 241119 >